Indra's Net

Indra's Net

DEFENDING HINDUISM'S
PHILOSOPHICAL UNITY

Rajiv Malhotra

HarperCollins *Publishers* India

First published in hardback in India in 2014 by
HarperCollins *Publishers* India

Copyright © Infinity Foundation 2014

ISBN: 978-93-5136-244-9

2 4 6 8 10 9 7 5 3 1

HarperCollins *Publishers*
A-53, Sector 57, Noida, Uttar Pradesh 201301, India
77-85 Fulham Palace Road, London W6 8JB, United Kingdom
Hazelton Lanes, 55 Avenue Road, Suite 2900, Toronto, Ontario M5R 3L2
and 1995 Markham Road, Scarborough, Ontario M1B 5M8, Canada
25 Ryde Road, Pymble, Sydney, NSW 2073, Australia
31 View Road, Glenfield, Auckland 10, New Zealand
10 East 53rd Street, New York NY 10022, USA

Typeset in 11/14 Dante MT Std
By Saanvi Graphics Noida

Printed and bound at
Thomson Press (India) Ltd.

To my mother,
who raised me with the experience of Hinduism

Contents

Preface:
Why this book

Each of my books tries to provoke a new kind of conversation, the goal of which is to confront some specific prejudice against Indian civilization. Established biases covering a wide range of issues need to be exposed, especially when they are unsubstantiated. The objective of every book of mine is to pick a particular dominant narrative which is sustained by a nexus of scholars specializing in that theme, and then target it to effectively subvert it. The success of any such book may be measured in terms of how much challenge it generates against the incumbent positions. If my counter-discourse can become established in the minds of a sufficient number of serious thinkers, then it will assume a life of its own and its effects will continue to snowball without my direct involvement. This is the end result I seek. To be effective, a book must resist straying from its strategic priorities and must avoid arguing too broadly.

For example, I developed the strategy, overall thesis, and much of the content of *Invading the Sacred* so as to take aim at the Freudian psychoanalytical critiques of Hinduism. This hegemonic discourse was being propagated by a powerful nexus in the heart of the Western academia, and had spread as a fad among Indian intellectuals. *Invading the Sacred* gave birth to, and incubated, a solid opposition which cannot be ignored today. It spurred the Indian diaspora to recognize the syndrome and audaciously 'talk back' to the establishment of scholars.[1]

My subsequent book, *Breaking India*, focused on demonstrating how external forces are trying to destabilize India by deliberately undermining its civilization. Such efforts are targeted at confusing and ultimately aborting any collective positive identity based on Indian civilization. The book exposed the foreign interests and their Indian sepoys who see Hinduism as a random juxtaposition of incoherent and fragmented traditions. Many watchdog movements have sprung into action because of that book. It has triggered a domino effect with other researchers now exposing more instances of the same syndrome.

My most recent book, *Being Different*, presents a coherent and original view of *dharma* as a family of traditions that challenges the West's claim of universalism. Because Western universalism is unfortunately being used as the template for mapping and defining all cultures, it is important to become conscious of its distorted interpretation of Indian traditions. *Being Different* is prompting many Indians to question various simplistic views concerning their traditions, including some that are commonly espoused by their own gurus and political leaders. It is a handbook for serious intellectuals on how to 'take back' Hinduism by understanding it on its own terms.

The present book exposes the influential narrative that Hinduism was fabricated during British rule and became a dangerous *new* religion. The central thesis which I seek to topple asserts that Swami Vivekananda plagiarized Western secular and Christian ideas and then recast them in Sanskrit terminology to claim Indian origins for them. Besides critiquing this nexus and defending Vivekananda's vision, this book also presents my own vision for the future of Hinduism and its place in the world.

Hence, the book has two purposes: to defend the unity of Hinduism as we practise it today, and to offer my own ideas about how to advance Vivekananda's 'revolution' to the next stage.

This volume introduces some new vocabulary. Readers will learn the metaphor of 'Indra's Net' as a poetic expression of deep Hindu insights which subsequently became incorporated as the most central principle of Buddhism. They will understand Vivekananda's system of '*tat tvam asi* ethics' as an innovative social theory premised on *seva* (service to others), but firmly grounded in Vedic thought. They will also become familiar with the 'neo-Hinduism camp', which is my name for the group of scholars who have developed the thesis aimed at undermining Vivekananda's innovations and de-legitimizing contemporary Hinduism.

The book introduces and explains such ideas as 'open architecture' and 'toolbox', which are critical to my insights on Hinduism. While openness has always been characteristic of Hindus, too much of a good thing can be dangerous. I argue that this very quality of openness has made Hinduism susceptible to becoming 'digested'. Digestion, a concept introduced in my earlier books, is further elaborated in these pages.

In the Conclusion, I stick my neck out and introduce a set of defensive strategies for safeguarding against digestion. I call these strategies the 'poison pill' (borrowing from corporate jargon) and the 'porcupine defence'. I hope this provocative proposition will trigger debate and controversy.

Some of the new vocabulary that was introduced in *Being Different*—such as 'history centrism', 'integral unity' and 'embodied knowing'—will be further sharpened in these pages. I will also ascribe new meanings to the old Sanskrit terms *astika* and *nastika*, and utilize them differently than in the tradition.

As an author, I am often asked who my target audience is. This is not an easy question to answer. Clearly, I wish to influence mainstream Hindus who are often seriously misinformed about their own traditions. But if I were simply dishing out what they want to hear, appealing to their 'feel-good' sensibility, I would be doing them a disservice; I would also be failing in my goal to radically change the discourse. Bombastic books that present Hinduism in a chauvinistic manner are counter-productive and a recipe for disaster. My hope is to spur the genesis of what I call a 'home team' of intellectual leaders who would research, reposition and articulate Hinduism in a responsible way on important issues today. Therefore, my writings must be rigorous to withstand the scrutiny of harsh critics.

This means I must also write for the secular establishment and the old guard of Hindu leaders, both of whom will be provoked by this book for different reasons. The secularists will attack it as a defence of Hinduism which to them is synonymous with 'communalism'. The Hindus with tunnel vision will complain that it deviates from their narrow, fossilized lineage boundaries. While trying to educate the mainstream readers in the middle, I also wish to debate both these extremes.

Let me confess up-front that I have made some compromises for practical reasons. For instance, I use the term 'philosophy' to refer not only to Western philosophy but also, at times, to Indian thought, even though the latter would more accurately be called *darshana*. In every book I like to introduce a small number of non-translatable Sanskrit terms which I attempt to explain deeper than merely providing a reductive English equivalent. This book contains several such non-translatables, but 'darshana' is not one of them. I use the word 'philosophy' even where 'darshana' would perhaps be more appropriate. I apologize for this pragmatic simplification because I do not wish to overload my reader.

The difference between philosophy and darshana is significant. Philosophy resides in the analytic realm, is entirely *dis*-embodied, and is an intellectual tool driven by the ego. Darshana includes philosophy but goes much further because it also includes embodied experience. Traditionally, Indian thought has been characterized by the interplay of intellectual analysis and *sadhana* (spiritual practice), with no barriers between the two. Hindu practices cultivate certain states of mind as preparation for receiving advanced knowledge. In other words, darshana includes *anubhava* (embodied experience) in addition to the study of texts and reasoning. The ordinary mind is an instrument of knowing, and its enhancement through meditation and other sadhana is seen as essential to achieving levels of knowledge higher than reasoning alone can provide. Western philosophy emphasizes reason to the exclusion of anubhava and thus consists essentially of the *dis*-embodied analysis of 'mental objects'. Such a philosophy can never cross the boundary of dualism.

Another discomforting choice I make is to use the term 'contemporary Hinduism' to refer to Hinduism as we know it today. Hinduism is an ancient tradition that has been adapted many times, most recently for the present era. In the context of this book, the term simply denotes a new variation of something that is not exactly the same as it was previously. The very existence of *smritis*—texts that are written and rewritten to fit the context of each specific period and place—indicates that our tradition has never been frozen in time. It has evolved in step with the needs and challenges of each era.

My choice of this term, then, is intended to make the mainstream 'contemporary Hindu' readers comfortable. By the end of the book, I hope to have convinced readers that Hinduism cannot be pigeon-holed into tradition, modern and post-modern straitjackets in the way the West sees itself, because Hinduism has always been all three of these simultaneously and without contradiction.

The book focuses on toppling a specific, well-entrenched line of discourse that tries to isolate tradition in order to create conflicts and contradictions. My challenge is to help general readers undergo some serious mental shifts. Accordingly, I prefer not to overburden them by introducing too many unfamiliar terms. My hope is that most of my readers will be comfortable with such terms as 'philosophy' and 'contemporary Hinduism', and not be bothered that some theoreticians might find them problematic.

Additionally, in the interest of reader friendliness, an editorial decision was made to avoid using diacritic marks for Sanskrit pronunciation. Most Sanskrit terms are being italicized when they appear for the first time, and this may be repeated in some situations. A Sanskrit term will often be accompanied by a brief phrase in parentheses, giving its *approximate* meaning in English. Many Sanskrit terms are spelled in more than one way depending on the source—for instance, 'Shankara' is also spelled as 'Sankara'. Vivekananda is frequently mentioned without the 'Swami' title. I anticipate purists in Indian scholarship to raise issues with some of these compromises. But, as explained at the very beginning, I must pick my battles carefully and in a focused way, and this means making practical accommodations.

Summary of the major propositions and arguments in the book:

The following is a list of major propositions being explained and argued in this book. I furnish this list so the reader knows what to expect and can target his or her reading better:

1. **The openness of Hinduism:** The metaphors of 'Indra's Net', 'open architecture', and 'toolbox' are among the devices I use to explain that Hinduism is inherently an open system and that its unity and continuity are different from that which is found in the Abrahamic religions. The Introduction, Chapter 11 and Conclusion explain the concepts behind these metaphors. I also explain how the Vedic metaphor of Indra's Net has travelled into the very heart of Buddhist philosophy, and from there into contemporary Western thought and culture. Hindu and Buddhist dharma is the art of surfing Indra's Net.

2. **The 'neo-Hinduism' allegation against contemporary Hinduism:** I strongly oppose the work of a prominent school of thought which claims that contemporary Hinduism, as we know it, is artificial and Western-generated, and that it was constructed and perpetrated by Swami Vivekananda for political motives. Chapters 1 through 7 explain the details of this subversive thesis (called the 'neo-Hinduism' thesis), the backgrounds of its main proponents, and the history of how it came about. All of this lays the groundwork for my rejoinder that follows.

3. **My defence of contemporary Hinduism:** Not only are the charges against contemporary Hinduism refuted, point by point, in chapters 6, 8, 9, 10 and 11, but a countervailing view crystallizes, seeing contemporary Hinduism as unified, coherent and rooted in tradition. Chapter 6 explains the serious consequences of the 'neo-Hinduism' thesis in the form of popular literature and media biases in India.

4. **Digestion and fake liberalism:** Many of the precious ideas and concepts in Hinduism have been systematically removed and placed in Western garb. Meanwhile, the original Hindu sources are allowed to atrophy and made to appear obsolete. Chapter 12 and the Conclusion articulate this syndrome with examples and discuss the existential danger this poses to Hinduism.

5. **The 'porcupine defense' and 'poison pills':** With these I present my own strategy for safeguarding Hinduism from getting digested and thereby made to disappear. This defence entails the use of certain Hindu philosophical elements and practices which the predator cannot swallow without ceasing to exist in its current form. Such protective devices can help gurus free their Western followers from bondage to their religion of birth, such as claims to unique historical revelations, hyper-masculinized ideas of the divine, and institutionalized dogmatic beliefs. This is explained in the Conclusion.

6. **The future of astika and nastika:** Using these age-old Sanskrit terms in a novel way, I propose how persons of different faiths can demonstrate mutual respect for one another. This will result in an open space in which adherents of all faiths can examine their tenets, and make whatever adjustments are needed to comply with the multi-civilizational ecosystem in which we live. Redefined for this new purpose, the astika-nastika categorisation can become a powerful weapon to defend Hinduism and reposition it as an important resource for humanity. This, too, is explained in the Conclusion.

Introduction:
Debating Hinduism

Overview

This book is about the ongoing battle over Hinduism's positioning on par with the world's major religions. It rebuts an increasingly powerful school of thought amongst the academia, which posits that Hinduism, as such, has never existed. What is popularly considered to be Hinduism today is dismissed as a potent myth concocted by Swami Vivekananda, who supposedly appropriated and repackaged Western concepts and practices as part of a nationalist project. Moreover, it is alleged that this project has produced many of the social ills found in India today.

This battle is not merely a philosophical debate. The ramifications of a discourse that pits *contemporary* Hinduism against its hoary past are profound and terrifying. The claim made by my opponents that there is no such thing as Hinduism—regardless of the name we might choose to

1

assign it—simply denies the existence of an integrated unified spiritual substratum in ancient India. This battle, therefore, is also an intellectual one, with implications for the very survival of Hinduism as a tradition with a rich past, to be understood on its own terms.

The school of thought I debunk here represents an insidious, subtle, but nevertheless powerful, form of colonialism and conversion. Indeed, no explicit act of 'conversion' is even necessary; one is systemically re-programmed to believe that one was never a Hindu in the first place, and that the things one cherished about Hinduism all along were simply a repackaged collection of Christian and Western secular beliefs and values. Thus, one is made to feel that one loses nothing by abandoning Hinduism other than the term itself.

This pernicious ploy is used to create fissures in Hindu society by pitting the spiritual giants of Hinduism against one other, and to distort their subtle and deeply intricate viewpoints. The book not only disproves this dangerous line of thought; it offers a new framework in which to understand and interpret Hindu identity that is broad and yet well-defined, authentic and yet accessible, embracing both the traditional and the contemporary.

Two opposing camps: continuity vs. discontinuity; unity vs. disunity

There are two opposing views of Hinduism that are widely held today. Most Hindu practitioners see it as unified and coherent, marked by a continuity that extends from ancient times to the present. Such people share my conception of it as an open system that accommodates and adapts.

However, an opposing view originating from some Western academics in the 1950s has spread widely among Indian intellectuals, even to the extent of influencing many gurus. In this view, Hinduism as practised today is a product of Vivekananda's fertile imagination, an artificial unity he constructed for political purposes. It is alleged that Vivekananda fabricated present-day Hinduism by appropriating Western religious and secular ideas and restating them in Sanskrit. The proponents of this view hold that Vivekananda had two motives for fabricating Hinduism. In the first place, they say, he was reacting to the inferiority complex of most Indians vis-à-vis Western social ethics and Western science. Hence, he invented *karma yoga* to match Western social ethics, and claimed Vedic traditions to contain scientific merit. Secondly, he was serving a nationalistic agenda by proposing Hinduism as a tool to unify Indians against the British.

Since Vivekananda is supposed to have assembled Hinduism out of a hodgepodge of unrelated ideas and practices, its present-day existence as a coherent entity is believed to mask a mess of underlying contradictions. Moreover, the entity known as contemporary Hinduism is accused of having had a negative effect on India's minorities, and of driving politics towards a totalitarian state. So the story goes, according to these critics.

This camp refers to Hinduism as 'neo-Hinduism'. Anyone who rebuts their views with findings of coherence and unity in Hinduism is suspected of harboring 'identity politics' and causing communal disharmony. The first half of this book explains the neo-Hinduism thesis in detail, recounting its origins, arguments and implications. The second half articulates my response. I defend the unity of Hinduism not on the basis of identity politics or some imagined 'ancient perfection' but with evidence of its philosophical unity and its significance as a living, evolving, and progressive force in the world.

The claim that contemporary Hindu leaders were influenced by Western thought, and sought to revise their traditions in light of new circumstances, is true enough. However, a serious misunderstanding arises when this alien influence is exaggerated; what gets downplayed is the organic movement for revision and development based firmly within dharma itself—i.e., the in-built evolutionary mechanism that has engendered many precedents throughout its history. When a scholar such as Ursula King describes pre-modern Hindu practices as entirely 'local, regional, sectarian and exclusive', she exemplifies the approach of the neo-Hinduism camp.

The perception that a unified idea of Hinduism lacks legitimacy has rapidly spread into mainstream intellectual circles. At first it might seem that this only targets contemporary Hinduism, but it is used as a prelude to questioning the legitimacy of all Hinduism, ancient and contemporary. This implication is seldom realized by many who echo this position without weighing the considerable evidence against it or recognizing its consequences.

This book sides with the majority of practising Hindus against what is now the majority of academic scholars. This engagement is a kind of inter-civilizational *kurukshetra*, or field of encounter. I am amazed that no serious thinker in the past has written a systematic critique of the neo-Hinduism camp. Thus far, Hindu thinkers have reacted tactically to each particular episode in this conflict as an isolated event; they have failed to connect the dots and recognize the big picture of whence such seemingly sporadic allegations originate.

Worse still, many of the biased perspectives of colonial Indology have now become internalized by large numbers of Indians who frequently serve as influential voices within the Hindu community. In the intellectual kurukshetra of globalization, civilizations compete to gain 'mindshare'. It is essential that we resist the fresh colonization being imposed on our minds.

But to set the stage, I will first establish the foundation of Hinduism as I see it, using the Vedic metaphor of Indra's Net.

We are all jewels in Indra's Net

The title of this book is a metaphor for the profound cosmology and outlook that permeates Hinduism. Indra's Net symbolizes the universe as a web of connections and interdependencies among all its members, wherein every member is both a manifestation of the whole and inseparable from the whole. In these pages, I seek to revive it as the foundation for Vedic cosmology and show how it went on to become the central principle of Buddhism, and from there spread into mainstream Western discourse across several disciplines.

The metaphor of Indra's Net originates from the *Atharva Veda* (one of the four Vedas), which likens the world to a net woven by the great deity Shakra or Indra. The net is said to be infinite, and to spread in all directions with no beginning or end. At each node of the net is a jewel, so arranged that every jewel reflects all the other jewels. No jewel exists by itself independently of the rest. Everything is related to everything else; nothing is isolated.[1]

Indeed, the fundamental idea of unity-in-diversity underpins all dharmic traditions; even though there are many perspectives from which Indra's Net may be viewed and appreciated, it is ultimately recognized as one indivisible and infinite unity. From the Hindu viewpoint, the One that manifests as many is named *Brahman*; even seemingly disparate elements are in fact nothing other than reflections of Brahman, and hence of one another. This notion of an organic unity is a signature of Hinduism, and distinguishes it from all major Western religions, philosophies and cultures.

Each jewel of Indra's Net includes the reflections of all the other jewels; the significance of this symbolism is that each entity in the universe contains within itself the entire universe. This idea, rather than positing interdependence among separately existing entities, asserts that the whole does not owe its existence to the coming together of individual parts that have independent existence. Indeed, the existence of each individual part is contingent upon, and relative to, the existence of the whole and of all the other parts. Yet, paradoxically, each individual part also 'contains' the whole within itself. Put simply, the whole and the parts are inseparable.

Every jewel in Indra's Net is a microcosm of the whole net; every component is the cause of the whole and also the effect of the whole. Nothing exists outside the net.[2] In the Hindu worldview, the only essence that ultimately exists is Brahman; Brahman is the foundation for Indra's Net, and no jewel exists apart from Brahman.

The jewels of Indra's Net are *not* meant to symbolize static substances. Each jewel is merely a reflection of other jewels, and individual jewels always remain in flux. Each jewel exists only momentarily, to be continuously replaced by its successor, in mutual causation with other jewels. Just as the interdependent cells of the human body are perpetually changing, so also everything in Indra's Net is perpetually in flux. Reality is always in the flux of becoming.

This concept is different from the notion of real, independently existing entities undergoing modification, or static entities that happen to be woven together.

Swami Vivekananda applied the great Upanishadic saying, 'tat tvam asi' ('that thou art') as the basis for Hindu ethics. He said, in essence, that we are all jewels in Indra's Net (even though he did not use this metaphor to say it). Thus, Vivekananda defined a Hindu platform for determining ethical conduct, not only towards all humans but towards animals and all entities in general—because everyone and everything is a jewel in Indra's Net. Since the attack on Vivekananda has been heavily predicated on what are called his 'tat tvam asi ethics', I shall return to this point several times in later chapters.

The Sanskrit word *bandhu* is frequently used to describe the interrelationship between the jewels of Indra's Net. 'Bandhu' defines a corresponding entity; for example, a relationship between x and y can be stated as 'x is a bandhu of y'. In traditional Indian discourse, this term is often used to explain the unity between the whole and its seemingly diverse parts. For example, ancient thinkers have described specific bandhus which express the paradoxical relationship of the microcosm to the macrocosm. While the microcosm is generally perceived as a map of the macrocosm, it is also the case that both microcosm and macrocosm continuously mirror one another.

Bandhu can also refer to the connections among various facets of our overall unified reality, linking sounds, numbers, colors and ideas together. No object—whether physical, mental, emotional, or conceptual—has any existence by itself and is merely another facet of this unified whole. In addition, bandhu describes how the transcendental worlds correspond with the perceptible world, implying that whatever we perceive through our senses is but a pointer to something beyond.

Kapila Vatsyayan, a scholar of classical Indian art, has cited many examples of bandhu in the form of common metaphors. Significant symbols may be found in the *Rig Veda*, the *Natya-shastra* (a seminal text on aesthetics and performing arts) and the *Tantrasamuccya* (a text on temple architecture). The seed (*bija*) is often used to symbolize the beginnings. The tree (*vriksha*) rises from the bija and represents the vertical pole uniting the realms. The *nabhi* (navel) or the *garbha* (womb) brings together the concepts of the un-manifest (*avyakta*) and the manifest (*vyakta*). The *bindu* (point or dot) is the reference point or metaphorical centre around which are drawn geometrical shapes, which in turn facilitate the comprehension of notions of time and space. The *sunya* (void) is a symbol of fullness and emptiness. From its *arupa* nature (formless) arises the *rupa* nature (form) and the *parirupa* (beyond form). There is equivalence in the relationship between sunya (emptiness) and *purna* (completeness or wholeness), the paradox being that the void has within it the whole.[3]

In Hinduism, the concept of unity-in-diversity can also be understood as a manifestation of Brahman, an agency that penetrates, pervades and harmonizes the entire universe. Brahman enters and shapes the mould of every entity giving it form, substance and individuality. It is only human pre-conditioning that causes us to visualize the multiplicity of forms as separate entities, and hence the world appears to be full of contradictions. The *Brhadaranyaka Upanishad* says:

> Brahman is responsible for the interconnectedness of things and has become the living and the non-living; the visible and the invisible; the creatures which are two-footed and those that are four-footed. He became the subtle body and then the gross body by means of a subtle instrument known as the subtle body. This very Being became the vital consciousness of all. This is known as the Madhu-Vidya, the sense of the 'honey' of all beings, the knowledge of the inter-dependence of things and the vital connection of everything, under every condition, at every time, everywhere.[4]

Another apt metaphor to describe the Hindu worldview is that of a forest. Forests have always been a symbol of beneficence in India, and embody many of the same qualities as Indra's Net. In the forest, thousands of species of animals, plants and microorganisms exist in a state of mutual interdependence. At any given level of the forest, the microcosm is always connected with its enveloping macrocosm; there exist many worlds-within-worlds, which are never separate or isolated from one another. All the elements of a forest are immensely adaptive to one another, and easily mutate or fuse into new forms over time. In India, a forest suggests fertility, plurality, adaptation, interdependence and evolution. The forest loves to play host, and is never closed to outsiders; newer life forms that migrate into it are welcomed and rehabilitated as natives. The growth of a forest is organic; new forms of life co-exist without requiring the destruction of prior ones. The forest has no predefined final end-state. Its dance is ever-evolving. Indian thought, analogously, is largely based on this kind of openness and blending.

The forest's diversity is an expression of God's immanence—God is manifested as bird, mammal, plant, and many other creatures. Just as infinite processes are constantly under way in the forest, so there are infinite ways of communicating with God. Indeed, Hinduism's spiritual outlook rests on this very principle: that the divine is immanent and inseparable from life and nature in all its forms.

The forest, like the human body, provides a context for describing complex relationships. In the forest of dharma traditions, multiple texts and rituals flow into each other in complex ways, defying any attempt to classify them with rigidly linear chronologies. Dharma traditions took root on the banks of rivers with sacred waters flowing, their currents being symbolic of constant change and evolution. The experience of endless organic evolution characterizes all our texts, deities, rituals, spiritual practices and festivals. The idea of an ultimate harmony underpinning this vast mélange of elements arose from the forest and its interwoven nature. As a people, the descendants of forest dwellers can be expected to have inherited a profound respect for nature, as well as an ingrained regard for all its creatures. This stands in stark contrast to the desert-originated Judeo-Christian idea that God made the world for humanity's dominion.

Some of the earliest Indian classics are called *aranyakas*, or 'forest discourses'. *Rishis*, the exemplars of Indian thought, are also known as 'forest dwellers'. Among the stages of life advocated for individuals, the penultimate one, in which the individual severs the bonds of family to pursue spiritual goals, is termed *vanaprastha*, which literally means 'the forest stage of life'. Sri Aurobindo uses a forest analogy to show some essential differences between Indian and Western traditions:

> The endless variety of Indian philosophy and religion seems to the European mind interminable, bewildering, wearisome, and useless; it is unable to see the forest because of the richness and luxuriance of its vegetation; it misses the common spiritual life in the multitude of its forms. But this infinite variety is itself, as Vivekananda pertinently pointed out, a sign of a superior religious culture. The Indian mind has realized that the Supreme is the Infinite; it has perceived, right from its Vedic beginnings, that to the soul in Nature the Infinite must always present itself in an endless variety of aspects. The mentality of the West has long cherished the aggressive and quite illogical idea of a single religion for all mankind, a religion universal by the very force of its narrowness, one set of dogmas, one cult, one system of ceremonies, one array of prohibitions and injunctions, one ecclesiastical ordinance.[5]

A related metaphor is that of the banyan tree, beloved in myths and stories across Asia. The banyan is unique among trees in that the branches sprout and bow down to the ground, becoming additional roots of the same tree; each root contributes nourishment and stability to the entire tree, forming eventually into a trunk in its own right. The tree is a single structure but functions like a complex, self-organizing network, providing shelter and nourishment to birds, beasts and humans. Its multiple roots, trunks and branches represent multiple origins and sources. They are all part of the same living organism, even if the complexity of the whole cannot be comprehended at a single glance. Each of the separate roots feeds every trunk, and hence every leaf is connected to the entire root system. The tree has no well-defined center, because its multiple roots, trunks and branches are all interlocked and inseparable. It is, in effect, polycentric.

The forest and the banyan tree may be seen as metaphors for context-based cultures, and they help explain why people living in such cultures are comfortable with pluralism and complexity. Such metaphors are commonly found in Indian narratives.

In the Mahabharata, the ceremony for the oath of a new king includes the admonition: 'Be like a garland-maker, O king, and not like a charcoal burner.'[6] The garland symbolizes social coherence; it is a metaphor for dharmic diversity in which flowers of many colors and forms are strung harmoniously for the most pleasing effect. In contrast, the charcoal burner is a metaphor for the brute-force reduction of diversity into homogeneity, where diverse living substances are transformed into uniformly lifeless ashes.

In taking this oath, the king is promising to support a coherent diversity in which a profoundly variegated culture may thrive as a unity (garland) of distinct elements (flowers). This schema avoids the two extremes that would prove deleterious to a society: incoherence, comparable to a chaotic scattering of flowers, and the reductionist, homogenous lifelessness of charcoal. The king's oath, then, is essentially a pledge to respect the spirit of Indra's Net.

Hinduism devotes much thought to exploring the relationships between the jewels of Indra's Net, and how they are manifestations and reflections of each other. Hindu thought is distinct from Abrahamic religions, which are premised on the existence of one *separate* God, one absolute event in history, and one inviolable set of injunctions. Hindus, for better or for worse, tend to be natural de-centralists. This is why it is hard to understand Hinduism, and difficult to organize and mobilize Hindus under an overarching corporate institution. It is also why Hinduism has proved, thus far, difficult to destroy.

I have referred to this idea as 'integral unity' in my previous writings, and Chapter 11 will explain it further. The integral unity of the whole manifests itself in the parts, and they in turn aspire to unite with the whole; this principle is reflected in every domain of dharmic knowledge, including philosophy, science, religion, ethics, spirituality, art, music, dance, education, literature, oral narratives, politics, marriage rituals, economics, and social structures. Each domain of dharmic knowledge is itself a jewel in Indra's Net, and reflects all the others. In other words, the same underlying principles are represented in these specialties in different ways.

For example, Hindu dance is not merely an isolated form of cultural expression but a complete and rigorous discipline through which one may learn and experience philosophy. This quality of correspondences across many domains of knowledge is striking. Music and sacred dance have a formal grammar based on Hindu cosmology. The Sanskrit *Natya-shastra*, a seminal text on performing arts and aesthetics, treats *natya* as a total art form; its scope includes: representation, poetry, dance, music, make-up, indeed every aspect of life. The Natya-shastra presents an integral view encompassing the Vedic rituals, Shaivite dance and music, and the epics. The eight traditional *rasas* it describes (love, humour, heroism, wonder, anger, sorrow, disgust, and fear) mirror a complete experience of the real world like the jewels of Indra's Net, and together facilitate a practitioner's pursuit of the *purusharthas* (human goals).[7]

Some other examples across various domains are as follows:

- The Vedic ritual altar is a representation of the entire cosmos.
- The architecture of Hindu temples is based on physical dimensions which correspond to various astronomical metrics.
- The *yantra*, an important device of sacred geometry, represents the whole universe.
- Any deity can be conceived of in multiple ways: as a personal manifestation of the divine, as a metaphor for certain cosmic qualities and powers, and as an amalgamation of qualities and energies to be invoked and established in a person through ritual, meditation and yoga. Based on individual preferences, a deity can be approached as another entity in the mode of devotion, or as an object of meditation, or as a means for self-realization within oneself.
- In Ayurvedic diagnosis, a correspondence is posited between specific points on the tongue and all parts of the entire body; thus, an expert in this field examines the tongue as a means of analysing the patient's overall condition. The tongue is thus a jewel in which the entire physical and psychic body is reflected.

The core principle of integral unity is encoded in the symbolism of Indian art, architecture, literature, ritual, mythology, festivals, and customs, all of which are intended to facilitate access to higher knowledge that goes beyond the conventional scope of any specific domain. Integration between disciplines is built-in and no effort is needed to create unity by bringing separate parts together. Even when certain disciplines and practices were destroyed, other disciplines encoding the same principles survived and helped preserve and re-ignite the overall tradition.

Dharmic cosmology is governed by bandhu interconnections among the astronomical, terrestrial, physiological, and spiritual realms; and each of these realms is itself connected, in the broadest sense, with the arts, healing systems, and culture. As discussed previously, bandhu describes a correspondence between the whole universe and the individual consciousness, which can be explored and developed from many alternative starting points. Thus, dharmic traditions have a common current that impels the individual along a natural quest to discover the reality beneath the appearances and to appreciate relationships among seemingly unrelated phenomena.

By contrast, Western disciplines and arts emerged separately and independently from each other; as a result, their theories and assumptions are disjointed. This is why, despite many efforts to foster 'inter-disciplinary' work, it has proved so difficult in the West to harmonize disparate disciplines. I have referred to this as a synthetic (and not integral) type of unity.

Dharmic traditions consider the common experience of reality as merely the transient reflection of a system in flux, interconnected with other realities across the past, present and future. In this flux, which affects all phenomena, repeating patterns may appear as static and independent 'objects', but this perception is just an illusory artifact of the limited mind. The individual person, of course, is himself a part of this flux. With the aid of meditation, he is able to witness reality as a detached observer—to see the personal ego, and indeed all fixed objects, as mere reflections of a moment in the flux.

In contrast, the Western view (at least until relatively recently) has generally assumed that space-time is finite, with a defined beginning and end contained within a deterministic Cartesian grid. This type of world can be controlled, intellectually and conceptually, at the level of the ego. Accordingly, the West seeks a reality consisting of stable atomistic parts which are amenable to control and manipulation. Westerners have difficulty with dharma because the static, isolated categories of Western essentialism are inadequate for 'capturing' the dynamic, intertwined character of Indian thought. The Western mind prefers everything to be fixed, separated and in its 'proper place'. Such ideas as dissolution of conventional boundaries, or intermingling across partitions, are considered chaotic and threatening, even evil.

Indra's Net and Buddhism

Important Buddhist texts use Indra's Net to describe an infinite universe with no beginning or end, in which every element is mutually related to every other element. Indra's Net is a quintessential metaphor for Buddhist philosophy, describing how everything exists only in mutual causation with everything else, and nothing can be isolated.

The *Avatamsaka Sutra* (which means 'Flower Garland') of Mahayana Buddhism uses the metaphor of Indra's Net to explain cosmic interpenetration. This sutra explains everything as both a mirror reflecting all and an image reflected by all. Everything is simultaneously cause and effect, support and supported. This important sutra was translated from Sanskrit, and its logic further developed in China under the name of Hua-yen Buddhism.

The Hua-yen tradition was developed by a series of thinkers, most notably Fa-tsang (CE 643-712). Through him, it passed on to Korea and other East Asian countries, becoming known as 'Kegon' in Japan. Hua-yen is praised as the highest development of Chinese Buddhist thought. D.T. Suzuki called Hua-yen the philosophy of Zen, and Zen the meditation practice of Hua-yen. Francis Cook explains the core philosophy of Hua-yen as follows:

Far away in the heavenly abode of the great god Indra, there is a wonderful net that has been hung by some cunning artificer in such a manner that it stretches out infinitely in all directions. In accordance with the extravagant tastes of deities, the artificer has hung a single glittering jewel in each 'eye' of the net, and since the net itself is infinite in all dimensions, the jewels are infinite in number. There hang the jewels, glittering like stars of the first magnitude, a wonderful sight to behold. If we now arbitrarily select one of these jewels for inspection and look closely at it, we will discover that in its polished surface there are reflected all the other jewels in the net, infinite in number. Not only that, but each of the jewels reflected in this one jewel is also reflecting all the other jewels, so that there is an infinite reflecting process occurring.[8]

Cook goes on to explain that Indra's Net 'symbolizes a cosmos in which there is an infinitely repeated interrelationship among all the members of the cosmos'. He adds that 'the cosmos is, in short, a self-creating, self-maintaining, and self-defining organism'. Furthermore, there is no theory of a beginning time, and such a universe has no hierarchy. 'There is no center, or, perhaps if there is one, it is everywhere.'

Hua-yen is built on the primary concern of Indian thought which is about the nature of causation. This is evident in the Sanskrit name for Hua-yen, *'dharmadhatu pratitya-samutpada'* (the interdependent co-arising which is the universe). Key principles of Madhyamika Buddhism, regarding non-substantiality and non-origination, have exact equivalents in Hua-yen. The Avatamsaka philosophy emphasizes the illusory nature of things when they are seen separately.[9]

David Loy, a Buddhist practitioner and scholar who has spent most of his life in Kyoto, uses the analog of *lila* (play) to refer to the Buddhist ideal of life. While the ordinary ego is a player struggling, out of anxiety, to ground itself in the net, the liberated player has realized that he *is* the net. There is no separate 'me' to possess anything, nor any separate thing to be possessed. He explains:

Life becomes play; ... the issue is whether we suffer our games because they are the means whereby we hope to ground ourselves somewhere in Indra's Net, or whether we dance freely within the Net because we are it. The dangers of relativism in ethics are vitiated to the extent I realize my interdependence with other beings: I shall indeed love my neighbour as myself when I experience that I am my neighbour.[10]

It is interesting to note that over a period of many centuries Buddhist thinkers across East Asia have meticulously preserved the Sanskrit terms originally used to define Buddhist ideas, and fully credited Indian sources. Recently, however, as Buddhist ideas have travelled to the West and spread across many disciplines, the tendency has been to disconnect Hinduism from these ideas. Thankfully, the term 'Indra's Net' has been preserved, and this allows scholars like myself to retrace the Vedic origins of these widely popular ideas.

Influences on modern society

Indra's Net has inspired thinkers and movements in the West ranging from philosophy to ecology. David Loy has described how the major milestones of Western post-modernist thought resemble the ideas inherent in Indra's Net. He cites Sigmund Freud's approach in psychology, Ferdinand Saussure's work in linguistics, Roland Barthes's ideas in literary theory, and Jacques Derrida's approaches to deconstruction as examples of twentieth-century pioneers who have utilized the ideas of Indra's Net (mostly without explicit acknowledgement). The result of this has been nothing short of a revolution in Western philosophy, shaking the age-old Western premise that entities have separate, absolute, independent existences. Deconstructing the self-existence of things is the very signature principle of post-modern thought, and is a subset of the philosophical ideas contained in Indra's Net.[11]

Post-modern deconstruction, however, promises only textual liberation; since it does not help one go beyond text, one becomes trapped indefinitely in the labyrinth of logo-centrism. The post-modernist remains inscribed within an endless web of concepts because he still identifies with language; consequently, his anxiety impels him to try to retain the ego's ground. This is why one finds post-modernists so proudly fixated on their 'theories'. To objectify oneself and one's texts and to conceive of things as having separate existences binds one ever more firmly to the service of the ego's project—a pitfall that Hindu and Buddhist philosophies address comprehensively. A great Vedanta masterpiece, *Vivekachudamani*, cautions: '*shabdajaalam maharanyam chitta bhramana kaaranam*' (the net of words is a great forest that causes confusion). *Shastras* (spiritual texts) provide useful pointers to the spiritual seeker, but must eventually be transcended lest they become a trap in their own way.

It is for this reason that meditation is important. As a technique, meditation enables the seeker to attain a 'non-site' from which to know the intellect and its limitations. One method of meditation employs *mantra* as a means to let go of all thought and language. In the process, one's own body, at each layer and every level, becomes a 'text' for systematic deconstruction. This idea will be addressed more deeply in the Conclusion, where I discuss the notion of embodied knowing. Post-modernism is ultimately rendered bankrupt by its inability to deconstruct one's own *self as text*.

Steve Odin has noted how Alfred North Whitehead used similar ideas as part of his process philosophy.[12] Whitehead was influenced most particularly by Abhidharma Buddhism. Therefore, what is widely credited by Western thinkers as 'Whiteheadean' thought should more appropriately be termed the 'process philosophy of Indra's Net' (or even more specifically, Abhidharma Buddhism).

Gregory Fahy has examined John Dewey's idea of local, contextual and relational metaphysics as a subset of the Hua-yen thinking of Indra's Net.[13] Mathematicians studying chaos theory and fractals have described the beauty of structures as 'Indra's net', 'Indra's necklace' and 'Indra's pearls'.[14] In physics, the notion of quantum entanglement is a special case of the kind of interconnectivity we are describing. It is not at all surprising that Indra's Net has been used as a metaphor to explain holograms, wherein, by definition, each part also includes the whole within itself. Indra's Net has also been cited as the metaphor for the internet.

In the field of environmentalism, Leslie Paul Thiele has explained that Indra's Net represents the Sanskrit concept of *prajna* (the wisdom of the interdependency of things), with the key implication that causes and effects are inseparable. He mentions that the word 'ecology' was coined in 1873 to mean the interactive relations between plants and animals, and that its meaning has recently expanded to include all of nature's interrelationships in a wider sense. Sustainability is inherently a matter of interdependence, so the applicability of these ideas to the modern ecology movement is obvious.[15] Indra's Net, of course, embodies a far wider scope than just the material aspects of nature.

The basic principle is that each individual is both the cause for the whole and is caused *by* the whole. Ecological interdependence implies that if any one part of a system is disturbed, the whole system is affected. In this regard, Francis Cook has described Indra's Net as a kind of 'cosmic ecology'.[16] Unlike in Western (disembodied) philosophy, nature is not seen as a backdrop for human existence; rather, humans are seen as inseparable from nature. A special issue of the journal *Philosophy East and West* was devoted to the applications of Indra's Net to the field of environmental ethics.[17]

Another example of contemporary applications is an NGO called Indra's Net Community, a South Korean movement that addresses concerns in the daily lives of lay people. Inspired by the interdependency principle of Indra's Net, it was started by a group of visionary monks. They established grassroots communities to promote an alternative lifestyle in response to contemporary society's emphasis on mass consumption, commercialism, competition, and the exploitation of natural resources.[18]

Clearly, Indra's Net, with its profound beginnings in the Vedas, has spread far and wide.

Who is a Hindu?

Despite the fact that most Hindus lack the theoretical and historical background to articulate the symbolism of Indra's Net, the awe-inspiring understanding of the reality it encodes has always been implicit in the average Hindu's outlook. Given this outlook, most Hindus are bewildered when asked to define who they are. It seems like a silly question. They have grown up experiencing life as a rich diversity of ideas and practices passed down from their ancestors. So vast is their sense of openness that they feel no natural urge to draw boundaries between themselves and others. Indeed, many Hindus are surprised as to why someone would ask such a strange question.

When Hindus are pressed for an answer to the question of their identity, they often experience discomfort or else offer a flippant response such as, 'Hinduism is a way of life'. This, of course, is a nonsensical statement. Bin Laden's lifestyle was also 'a way of life', as were those of Hitler and Ravana; could their ways of life, and indeed *every* possible way of life be considered to characterize Hinduism? No human can exist without espousing some 'way of life', and for that matter, every dog, cat and other animal also has some kind of a 'way of life'. How does saying 'Hinduism is a way of life' describe usefully what *particular* way is meant? Is it not as silly and meaningless as trying to define a car as 'a collection of atoms'? Clearly, if no 'way of life' is outside Hinduism, then the term is meaningless. Yet, this absurd answer is very often repeated by many 'experts' of the tradition.

Some of the confusion Hindus experience about their identity also stems from the fact that 'Hindu' and 'Hinduism' are not words that derive from an Indian language. The '-isms' associated with Indian civilization—Hinduism, Buddhism, Jainism, Sikhism—are all Anglicized markers. Yet what is represented by each of these markers has indeed come from our tradition. The fact that a particular name is not necessarily Indian does not empty it of reference and usefulness. Making a fetish of avoiding the terms 'Hindu' or 'Hinduism' is ultimately pointless and counter-productive. Many Hindus today feel the need for an indigenous word that jettisons the baggage of Western terminology and prefer the term '*Sanatana Dharma*'. This book, nevertheless, is concerned with the substance itself; the origins of the word used to designate the substance are immaterial. I will continue to use the term 'Hinduism' for convenience.

Another reason the term Hinduism is often questioned is that it does not refer to a rigid entity with dogmas enforced by some centralized authority equivalent to the church. As Indra's Net captures very poetically, Hinduism is a diverse, thriving ecosystem that has adapted and evolved over a long history. It exemplifies an age-old spirit of open inquiry and challenge. Indeed, such independent thinking has been a critical aspect of keeping it vibrant.

While the central authority of the church plays the role of reifying and guarding Christian identity, Hindus have historically relied on a living web of scholastic lineages to reflect their thoughts, debates, practices and experiences. Even though the colonial onslaught disrupted this ecosystem, Hinduism has continued to produce great thinkers who reinvigorate it with fresh ideas. The absence of a central authority that adjudicates the 'one truth' also makes it hard to explain what exactly Hinduism is. This flexible, hard to define quality is what I call the 'open architecture' of Hinduism and I will explain it throughout this book.

Unfortunately, this same flexibility is being cited by critics as proof for why Hinduism cannot be considered a legitimate 'world religion', i.e., because it has no single founder, no linear history (as such), and no canon on which authorities can agree. Dharma certainly has coherence and unity; the fact that it is contextual, rather than dogmatic, does not detract from its integrity in any way. A major reason for my writing *Being Different* was to offer an alternative appreciation for coherence and unity in Hinduism. This approach does not depend on an appeal to history, to a particular founder, or to a canon of texts.

The quality of openness leads to the question: How elastic is Hinduism? To answer this, I start by rejecting two extreme kinds of responses. Those in the ultra-orthodox camp see Hinduism as inelastic, rigid and unchangeable; they dismiss Hindu revolutionary thinkers like

Vivekananda as inauthentic for having violated its sanctity. Such a view fossilizes Hinduism and stunts its natural tendency to evolve.

Those on the opposite extreme, such as the purveyors and followers of fashionable 'pop' Hinduism or 'new age spirituality' movements, see Hinduism as infinitely elastic—a kind of 'perennial philosophy' which can be interpreted as vaguely as one pleases, giving rise to an attitude of 'anything goes'. This approach heralds the slippery slope into sameness and relativism that turns Hinduism into a joke. It spawns such silly, evasive non-sequiturs as the definition of Hinduism as 'a way of life'. Neither extreme is useful.

Hinduism: Surfing Indra's Net

I see Hinduism neither as a 'fixed' religion akin to Christianity or Islam, nor as the modern-day remnant of some vaguely-defined 'perennial philosophy'. I prefer to see it as an open architecture framework that can be populated by a range of ideas, practices, symbols, rituals, and so on. The term 'open architecture' is, of course, taken from the domain of information technology. It is important to note that the internet is not infinitely open but only relatively so: its boundaries are defined by what it rejects—for example, viruses or abusive elements. Despite these rejections, the internet has abundant flexibility for the future.

Similarly, Hinduism does not comprise all conceivable kinds of spirituality and religious claims, because it must exclude those that would destroy its underlying principles of integral unity, openness and flexibility. Exclusivist religious claims, for example, run counter to the openness of Hinduism because they are incapable of offering mutual respect; the open architecture of Hinduism must reject such claims, just as the internet rejects viruses. Chapter 11 explains open architecture in this context further, and the importance of seeing Hinduism from this perspective for the future.

The two terms 'unity' and 'open architecture' are used extensively in this book, and must be understood as qualities that balance and complement one other. Unity by itself can be autocratic; indeed, most militant groups and dictatorial regimes demonstrate a high degree of unity, but such entities lack the openness to bring about flexibility and change. Religions based on absolute narratives of history tend to have centralized governance and power structures, giving them unity but at the cost of openness.

The opposite extreme of too much openness is also counter-productive, because the survival of the entire system would be compromised if it were to embrace everything unconditionally. A system that is too open lacks stability and can be harmed by infiltration. I shall attempt to present a healthy balance of both unity and openness.

In *Being Different* I have gone into great detail to explain the difference between dharma and religion. I have argued that Hindu dharma is not accurately represented as a 'religion' in the same sense as the Abrahamic religions. (For a short summary, please see my blogs on this.[19]) The following statement encapsulates my overall approach: Hindu dharma may be seen as a dynamic portfolio of ideas, practices and traditions that come with a toolbox for customizing creative expression, personalization and sub-group formation. Because of its openness, and the variety of ways in which it can be actualized, this portfolio provides great flexibility as well as enormous freedom to adapt and evolve. At the same time, the portfolio has a boundary and excludes hostile elements that do not wish to reflect other jewels or an underlying unity. This boundary protects the portfolio from becoming infinitely elastic and subsiding into fragmentation and relativism, i.e., falling prey to the attitude of 'anything goes' or 'sameness'.

Hinduism also has many of the same characteristics as scientific methodology. Scientific observations are often made and developed into theories by experts who are not in complete agreement with one another. Many theories and concepts arising from scientific research have no single history of a linear development; at any given moment during the process of discovery, things are in flux. Challenges arise constantly as new theories are developed and tested in open competition with one another. Yet nobody dismisses the legitimacy of science as a unified enterprise with its own guiding principles and corrective processes.[20]

Being Different explains that Hinduism cannot be accurately understood by mapping it onto the framework of Abrahamic 'religion', or by gazing at it through a Western secular lens. To dismiss the unity, coherence, and continuity of Hinduism by adopting Western criteria, is simply unfair. Contrary to Western depictions, Hinduism is not an amorphous conglomerate and India is not a creation of the British. Both Hinduism and India must be understood on their own terms. Indeed, the term *'Bharat'* has been commonly used to refer to the traditional idea of nation; hence the relatively recent origin of the term 'India' should not have any bearing on understanding its antiquity regardless of how we name it.

The Conclusion chapter introduces my criteria for defining systems I regard as dharmic. For this purpose, I will adapt the old terms *'astika'* (those who affirm) and *'nastika'* (those who deny) in a manner that is consistent with the principles of unity and open architecture. My strategy in that chapter is to pinpoint what is to be rejected, i.e., nastika. What remains after this process is a large space in which the ecosystem of Hinduism may thrive. This approach avoids the kind of reductionism that would pigeon-hole the dharma into a narrow space. Dharma defined this way has immense freedom and flexibility.

Framing the debate in three disciplines

Having presented an overview of how I see Hinduism, I shall now give a brief snapshot of the debate between my opponents' camp and my arguments to counter their erroneous positions in the remaining chapters. The key areas of difference between both sides may be summarized in terms of three distinct disciplines shown below.

Philosophy	The neo-Hinduism thesis (which I oppose) claims that Hinduism is philosophically incoherent and ridden with contradictions. It is a mishmash of incompatible ideas, rituals, practices and groups. In particular, Vedanta cannot be reconciled with yoga, whether it takes the form of meditation, *bhakti* yoga, karma yoga, or other forms. According to them 'unified Hinduism' is an oxymoron.
	This book will establish that, despite the appearance of diversities, tensions and complexities, there has always existed an underlying core of shared values and attitudes that define Hinduism. Most Hindus feel comfortable despite the differences, and do not feel anxious to resolve them.
History	The neo-Hinduism thesis claims that prior to colonial influence the diverse elements that constitute Hinduism lacked any shared sense of identity, purpose or principle. It was the colonizers who fabricated a unified Hinduism, partly out of romantic ignorance, and partly in order to govern using common laws and frameworks that could be applied to all Indians. Indian nationalists suffered an inferiority complex and hence copied the Westerners' formulation of Hinduism in order to build national unity and pride. Hinduism is a byproduct of the Indian nationalist movement with Vivekananda as its chief architect.
	The Western influence need not be denied; its incorporation is not a problem given the open architecture of Hinduism. This book will demonstrate how, even prior to colonialism, there existed unification movements similar to the one led by Vivekananda. Vijnanabhikshu is one example of such a thinker in the pre-colonial era. The key elements that Vivekananda brought together can be found in numerous aspects of Hinduism from earlier times.

Politics	The neo-Hinduism thesis claims Vivekananda was politically motivated to manufacture Hinduism in order to unite the Indians against the British. This was an elitist enterprise, undertaken at the expense of suppressing the traditions of the Indian masses. The Hindutva forces have now taken over Vivekananda's project by making Hinduism even more oppressive against Dalits, tribal communities, minority religions and women.
	This book takes the stand that contemporary Hinduism's open architecture is quite the reverse of the oppressive entity alleged by its detractors. In fact, Hinduism accommodates the diversity of faiths, and the solutions it offers to pluralism are far superior to those that originate in the Abrahamic religions.

This book will juxtapose all three disciplines and show how they are interrelated. The scholars I critique often begin their attacks from a standpoint of modern politics, and use it to attribute a multitude of ills in present-day India to Hinduism. Working backwards from this position, they proceed to fabricate a historical account in which Hindu society is held responsible for all of India's problems. Reaching even further, they identify philosophical principles in Hinduism which they claim are its fatal flaws.

The resulting discourse has become a fashionable lens through which to analyse present-day Indian society and politics. The prevailing Hindutva ideology is immediately declared a direct result of the neo-Hinduism that was allegedly constructed to bolster the independence movement—the claim being that an oppressive, artificial religion invented by Vivekananda has somehow morphed into Hindu nationalism. This thesis has become a convenient weapon in the hands of Marxists, pseudo-secularists, subalternists, Christian apologists, and Islamist apologists seeking to attack Hinduism. Consequently, any discussion of a unified Hindu identity is often viewed with suspicion in intellectual circles, and its proponents regularly attacked as fundamentalists, radicals, or even fascists.

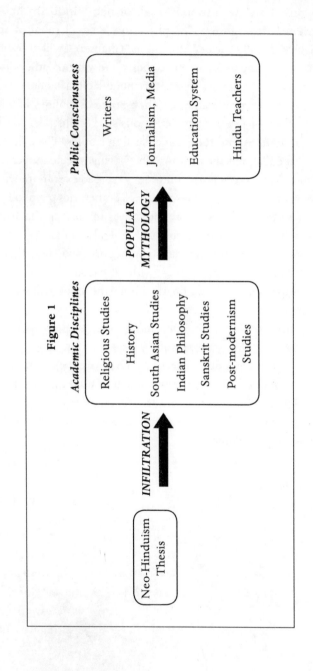

Figure 1

Figure 1 shows how the myth of neo-Hinduism has spread. Chapters 1 through 6 will explain how a small cabal of academic specialists initially formed this thesis. Chapter 7 will show how the myth then spread as an accepted thesis into various other disciplines, often because academics in one discipline have a tendency to utilize the consensus formulated in another. Some disciplines in which this thesis is firmly rooted include: religious studies, history, post-modern thought, South Asian studies, and Sanskrit studies. The column to the right of the diagram shows how, after having infected several spheres of academia, this contagion continues to spread ever more widely into the mainstream of public consciousness. Sometimes the neo-Hinduism myth is stated explicitly; more often, it is implicit in the attitudes of people who are uninformed about it.

Ironically, there are also many Hindu gurus who brag that no such thing as Hinduism ever existed—without pausing to reflect seriously on the implications of their boasts. I hope this book will serve as their wake-up call.

The position I am critiquing has gone unchallenged for so long that it has become unconsciously accepted by large numbers of intellectuals and pseudo-intellectuals. These are the people who spout such platitudes as: 'We were never a nation until the British invented India.' Those who disagree with this ideology face a huge burden in presenting their case and are even attacked personally for daring to challenge or question it.

PART 1

PURVA PAKSHA
(Examination of My Opponents' Positions)

1

Eight Myths to be Challenged

For most Hindus today, the legacy of Swami Vivekananda is assured. It is an article of faith that he was a great leader who influenced many others and inspired the practice of Hinduism over the past century. He is remembered as a visionary who expanded our understanding of the Hindu tradition by putting it on the world stage and making it relevant to his time.

It would surprise many of us, then, to know that an opposite view of this legacy is entrenched in academic circles, and that it is fast becoming the default interpretation among public intellectuals. As mentioned in the Introduction, this thesis brands Vivekananda's movement as 'neo-Hinduism' where 'neo' implies something phoney. It is troubling to see the acceptance, in many important circles, of the specious theory that his formulation of Hinduism was utterly decoupled from 'traditional' Hinduism. In fact, even many naïve and unsuspecting followers of Vivekananda believe a version of it. This is an epidemic of which most Hindus are unaware.

The thesis blames the prominent leaders of contemporary Hinduism for duping the Indian public. The accused conspirators include: Ram

Mohan Roy (1772-1833); Swami Vivekananda (1863-1902); Balgangadhar
Tilak (1856-1920); Mohandas Gandhi (1869-1948); Rabindranath Tagore
(1861-1941); Vinoba Bhave (1895-1982); Sri Aurobindo (1872-1950); and
Sarvepalli Radhakrishnan (1888-1975).

This book will show that the branding of contemporary Hinduism as
a faux 'neo-Hinduism' is a gross mischaracterization of both traditional
and contemporary Hinduism. I will use the term 'contemporary
Hinduism' in a positive sense, and distinct from the dismissive 'neo-
Hinduism', and show that contemporary Hinduism is a continuation
of a dynamic tradition. It is not in any way less authentic or less 'Hindu'
than what may be dubbed traditional Hinduism. There are negative
connotations to the term 'neo' which imply something artificial, untrue,
or unfaithful to the original. Other world religions have undergone
similar adaptations in modern times, though there are no such
references to 'neo-Christianity', for instance. I resist the wide currency
being gained for the term 'neo-Hinduism', because this fictional divide
between 'neo' and 'original' Hinduism subverts Hinduism.

Chapter 8 will draw on ancient Sanskrit sources and historical
documents to show a continuing tradition that was alive and well
during the twelfth to seventeenth centuries CE. This shows that there
are historic precedents within the framework of the tradition for the
kind of change that contemporary Hinduism is bringing about.

I will now summarize the basic assumptions or myths underlying
the theory of 'neo-Hinduism', with a brief response to each. These
responses are elaborated in later chapters.

Myth 1: India's optimum state is Balkanization

One of the most dangerous assertions being made is that India's natural
state is one of balkanization. In other words, before colonialism, it
was never unified. Those who hold this view believe India should
be returned to that pre-colonial state by disempowering Hinduism
(because it is considered to be a unifying force that benefits only the
elites), and by empowering the forces of fragmentation. Richard King

illustrates this view, insisting explicitly that 'it makes no sense to talk of an Indian nation'.

Such a discourse on the fragmentation of India has been used to stir up internal divisiveness and conflict—ironically, in the name of human rights. (*Breaking India* shows how this has come about, along with its political ramifications.)

Theories of the coherence of India and its civilization are dismissed by alleging that such claims necessarily imply an imposition of homogeneity and hegemony. As a corollary, there is the conclusion that Indians ought to simply deny any unified positive identity based on their own past, and instead seek a common identity based on the further importation of modern Western principles of society and politics. Those few individuals who dare articulate Indian coherence are therefore characterized as dangerous and accused of fascism, identity politics, fundamentalism, and links to atrocities.

This myth will be discussed in detail in Chapter 7, where we will see that it is based on a misconception about the nature of pre-colonial India. This misconception denies India's cultural unity based on the dharmic traditions.

Myth 2: Colonial Indology's biases were turned into Hinduism

It is generally true that prejudiced colonial Indologists constructed Hinduism in a way that fit their own agendas. These agendas included Christian missionary attempts to depict the heathens as so lowly and uncivilized that they required evangelization. There was also the imposition, by colonial governments, of a uniform method of rule that would make the population easy to control. I also accept that many Europeans laboured hard to recover Sanskrit texts, did important philological work, and struggled to understand Hindu traditions, even if only through their own lenses.

However, I disagree with the charge that Indian leaders took their cues exclusively from the West in reclaiming their textual traditions, and that they reinterpreted these texts in line with Western ideas.

To assume Indians passively read their own texts under the tutelage of Europeans, without any sense of their traditional meanings, is tendentious and untrue.

Being open to influence from others does not render a culture 'inauthentic'. Hinduism has always insisted that the way its traditions are interpreted and practised are a product of place, time and custom. If the truths are expressed in a way that is Western in form for the sake of wider communication, it does not make the substance of it any less Hindu.

Myth 3: Hinduism was manufactured and did not grow organically

The overarching charge made by proponents of the neo-Hinduism thesis is that contemporary Hindu leaders, particularly Vivekananda, Gandhi and Aurobindo, invented wholesale a new religion which we call Hinduism, using purely Western ingredients in order to promote a particular political agenda and a 'macho' national identity. Since Vivekananda heralds the modern revival of India's spirituality, many intellectuals target him as the creator of a synthetic and artificial new religion called Hinduism.

This characterization reveals a serious misunderstanding of Indian culture. Since the earliest times, prominent Hindus have disagreed among themselves, and their ideas were not static or frozen; new ideas were constantly introduced to challenge old ones. This process of change and adaptation has not stopped, nor should it. Hence, Vivekananda ought to be seen as a new thinker updating the tradition for modern times, not as someone fabricating something insidious or inauthentic. He was continuing the ancient tradition of innovation, while profoundly immersed in his own tradition. Yet he was receptive to Western influence, demonstrating a broadmindedness that is intrinsic to Hinduism.

Vivekananda and his heirs *did* articulate Hinduism in a new way, using the English language in a European idiom. They also emphasized (perhaps more than previously) action and social responsibility, and engaged explicitly with science. But these ideas were deeply rooted even in pre-colonial Hinduism. They were part of a natural and organic development through which Hinduism has stayed relevant, not unlike the changes that the traditional religions of Europe underwent on multiple occasions. Indeed, the modernization of Hinduism has occurred with less violence and distortion than similar movements in modern Christianity in Europe, as discussed in *Being Different*.

Vivekananda's understanding of Vedanta amalgamated teachings from various Hindu traditions. His reinterpretation of four intertwined pathways of yoga to attain *moksha*—*jnana* yoga (knowledge), *raja* yoga (meditation), karma yoga (selfless service) and bhakti yoga (devotion) —has an antecedent in Vijnanabhikshu, a prominent Indian thinker who lived long before the colonial period.[1] This contradicts the myth that he copied Western ideas and that these ideas were absent in pre-colonial Hinduism.

Since many Indian trains of thought have always co-existed, there is no reason for tradition and modernity to fight each other. The very notion that there are mutually conflicting *stages* of tradition, modern and post-modern, is a Eurocentric one. These 'stages' refer to the way things progressed in Western history, but this cannot be extrapolated as universal. Indeed, dharma includes within it the attitudes that are considered to belong to tradition, modern and post-modern, all in parallel, and not necessarily in mutual contradiction.

Myth 4: Yogic experience is not a valid path to enlightenment and tries to copy Western science

One of the controversies at the heart of the debate has to do with the status of yogic *anubhava*, the direct experience of higher states of consciousness attained in meditation. Such meditation practices are part of what is referred to as *adhyatma-vidya*, or 'inner science'. Exalted experiences are at the foundation of classical Indian texts and are emphasized anew in contemporary Hinduism.

Many cutting-edge Western cognitive scientific research programmes today have evolved under the profound influence of dharmic traditions, and such practices are referred to as first-person empiricism by neuroscientists. To call into question the authenticity of such practices, or to set them aside as inferior to the authority of scripture, would deprive Hindus of one of their most valuable assets and eliminate a unique aspect of their tradition, i.e., its profound investment in adhyatma-vidya. Chapter 11 elaborates on this correlation between cognitive science and dharmic traditions.

Unfortunately, the importance of direct experience in Hinduism is vigorously contested by members of the neo-Hinduism camp. They claim that authentic tradition, especially *Advaita Vedanta*, considers only the *sruti* (Vedic text) as the path to moksha (enlightenment); therefore, anubhava, or direct experience, cannot lead to moksha. They cite Shankara's works (of the eighth century CE) to support their position. Since Vivekananda emphasized anubhava, he is accused of having violated this core tenet of classical Hinduism.

The dangerous implication of this position is that it makes Vedanta and yoga appear mutually incompatible, thereby undermining Hinduism's unity. This is the main philosophical attack denying the existence of Hinduism as a coherent, unified and continuous system.

Vivekananda and other proponents of contemporary Hinduism say that although the sruti text is important, the goal is to attain the higher states of consciousness to which they point, not to reify the text into dogma. Whether one is more suited to textual study or to yogic practice depends on one's temperament. Furthermore, there are deep linkages between textual study and yogic practice; they are to be practised in combination, not in isolation. Hinduism has room both for textual authority and direct experience. This openness is also present in Shankara, who is often wrongly depicted as a sort of bookworm fixated on texts.

Vivekananda's approach revolved around a unified Vedanta-Yoga as spiritual praxis (anubhava) that is informed by Vedic precepts, insights, and authority (sruti). This is consistent with many earlier thinkers (such as Vijnanabhikshu, to be discussed in Chapter 8) who insist that one must not rely solely on sruti but also attain a direct experience of the truth which the practice of yoga can bring. A classical concept in Hinduism has been that a true proposition has to be consistent with sruti, *yukti* (reason/logic) and anubhava.

There are, indeed, well-known philosophical differences between Shankara and Vivekananda, but one should not read their works too narrowly. Such differences are the products of different ages with different needs for the revival of dharma. Vivekananda operated in the context of distinguishing Hinduism vis-à-vis the West whereas Shankara was operating in an environment dominated by Buddhism. These differences become acute only when seen through the singular goal of attaining moksha, whereas the discourse on Hinduism should not be limited merely to any approach for moksha.

Neo-Hinduism claims that the emphasis on yogic direct experience originated only as a result of appropriating Western science so as to make Hinduism seem scientific. Since science emphasizes empirical evidence, the closest thing to it which Hindus could claim was that mysticism was a form of empiricism. This incorrect interpretation of yoga's long history of experiential exploration will be challenged in Chapter 11.

Myth 5: Western social ethics was incorporated as seva and karma yoga

The neo-Hinduism camp also insists that the emphasis on social responsibility and social action in the thought of Vivekananda, Gandhi and Aurobindo was imported from Christianity. While there has definitely been Western influence, this charge is overstated. Concepts such as *seva* and karma yoga were not absent from the prior tradition, even in the works of Shankara. Secondly, contemporary Hindus should not be discredited for rising to the challenge posed by social degradation under colonial rule.

Chapter 9 will show that, counter to the neo-Hinduism thesis, *lokasangraha* (service to others) and bhakti (devotional surrender) derive from ancient Hinduism, with roots going back to the Bhagavad-Gita and even earlier. Vivekananda translated 'lokasangraha' as 'working for the good of others' and called this 'a very powerful idea' in the modern context. The individual is encouraged to move away from selfish desires by using the notions of karma (action), bhakti (devotion) and jnana (knowledge). The application of these old ideas to new contexts does not amount to a discontinuity or contradiction.

There have been numerous examples of warrior ascetics in traditional India long before the arrival of the British, which goes to show that social activism is not a recent response to colonialism.[2] The kind of Indian rule Vivekananda envisaged was in line with an unbroken chain that goes back to the classical texts of *Arthashastra* and *Panchatantra*.[3] Chapter 9 will also show how Sahajanand Swami, free from any colonial influence, had created a large, vibrant community of sadhus who devoted their lives serving the public rather than withdrawing from society and living as recluses.

Myth 6: Hinduism had no prior self-definition, unity or coherence

Another common charge in the campaign to de-legitimize Hinduism is that it had no self-defined and conscious understanding of its own distinctiveness from other religions. The foundation of neo-Hinduism is said to have been built by distorting prior traditions, which themselves had no unity and were a mishmash of irreconcilable texts and local customs.

Since there is no central authority or ecclesiastical structure in Hinduism, no closed canon or 'Bible' of sacred texts, and since there are no 'creeds' to which members of the faith must subscribe, Westerners tend to denigrate it as random, fragmented, chaotic and without unity. Sociologists and anthropologists often focus on conflicts and oppression in modern Indian society, and project their findings onto ancient Hindu texts to show that incoherence has always been characteristic of India.

This view ignores the fact that besides top-down structures and reified codes of orthodoxy, there can be other modes of unity that are decentralized. The phenomenon known as *Kumbha Mela* illustrates this decentralization beautifully. No one organizes this mass pilgrimage; there is no governing body or official charter by any founder; there is no 'event manager' who sends out a programme; and there are no official creeds. Yet it is both perceptually and philosophically a 'Hindu event'.

In *Being Different*, I argue that the Western notion of unity and coherence is based on an obsession for control, expansion and hegemony. Generally, the Western style of working is exemplified in the way a large multi-national corporation functions. Various institutional mechanisms are in place to standardize labour policies, internal procedures, products, sales channels, and so on. It's no surprise the Roman Catholic Church was the world's first major corporate multinational (and is still arguably the largest). It developed the first commercial multinationals, such as the Knights Templar.[4] The East India Company borrowed the structures for systematic control and order from these Christian sources, and modern historians of corporations regard that company as the template for modern multinational governance.

But this central control represents only one kind of coherence. It is not the model on which Indian coherence is built. *Being Different* summarizes various Western imaginings of a 'chaotic India', and offers an Indian response by reversing the gaze, as it were, so that it is directed at the West's fixation on normative 'order'.

There are several aspects to Hinduism that are distorted when seen through the Western lens. For example, through the assumption of Hinduism's lack of internal consistency and unity, such scholars, in effect, undermine any claim made on its behalf. Any attempt to speak of such an entity in positive terms is frequently debunked by asking, 'To which "Hinduism" are you referring?' Often this charge of incoherence goes beyond Hinduism, and serves as the basis for Myth 1, i.e., that India itself lacks any unity in the positive sense.

The characterization of Hinduism as incoherent serves to protect Western hegemony. The intellectual sophistication of Hinduism offers a vantage point from which the West's assumed universalism can be strongly challenged. Since acknowledging such a stance would pose a grave threat to Western universalism and its place on a pedestal, it becomes important to undermine the legitimacy of Hinduism as a coherent position from which to gaze.

Brian Smith understands the dangers of the 'chaotic Hinduism' thesis and has analysed this kind of scholarship in detail. He notes that Hinduism is considered too disorganized and 'exotically other' or else too complex and 'recondite'; this makes it hard to apply standard methods of analysis used in Western religious studies. He says this view has become 'standard received wisdom' today. As a result, the term 'Hinduism' ends up meaning nothing at all. Smith recognizes the absurdity here, though he does not speak of the full ramifications.[5]

It is even fashionable now to put Hinduism within scare quotes. Scholars who might otherwise appreciate it often portray it as an exotic and unintelligible collection of peculiar practices and strange problems, reminiscent of primitive societies that were superseded by the West.

Many architects of the myth of neo-Hinduism also dismiss the unity of any earlier dharma. Richard King, for instance, outright rejects the fluid concept of dharma as a basis for future development. These scholars seem determined to resurrect some state of pre-modern tribalism or balkanization.

Myth 7: Hinduism is founded on oppression and sustained by it

It is fashionable to vilify Hinduism openly as a construct invented to serve regressive nationalistic and proto-fascist identity politics; it is accused of violating the rights of minorities, women and others. This attack is often mounted in the name of defending human rights.

Contemporary Hinduism shapes India just as the Western religious traditions shape America. And just as civilizations shaped by the Western religions can support and sustain a responsible and pluralistic society, so too can Hinduism (in several respects, even more naturally).

As per the description of open architecture given in Chapter 11, dharmic culture has a strong foundation for absorbing multiple communities, metaphysical points of view, and new scientific developments than do the Abrahamic religions. This is so because dharma is not burdened by the imperative to reconcile itself with an absolute history; nor was dharma formulated under any centralized governance or adjudicating authority.

The neo-Hinduism thesis also demonizes Sanskrit as oppressive and fossilized, thus discarding centuries of cultural and philosophical development. The equivalent idea applied to the West would be to dismiss the entire corpus of Greek and Latin literature and philosophy for being corrupted by its elitism. Not only does the dismissal of Sanskrit rob India of a crucial resource; it deprives it of a sense of unity that pre-dates colonialism.

Myth 8: Hinduism presumes the sameness of all religions

While defending contemporary Hinduism, I do not treat every one of its tenets as sacrosanct. One of the aspects of which I am especially critical (and where I actually agree with my opponents in the neo-Hinduism camp) is the assertion attributed to Vivekananda and many of his heirs that all religions are paths to the same goal. I am troubled by the tendency to see all religions as offering equivalent things in the hope of reconciling them in a kind of perennial philosophy. *Being Different* was written precisely for the purpose of arguing against this position. The Conclusion has a section specifically to give my rejoinder to the 'sameness' thesis.

Summary of both sides of the debate

The neo-Hinduism thesis is well-defined and consistently applied amongst the academics. Other, competing views are often not articulated, or are not articulated as effectively. Thus, in order to highlight the key tenets of neo-Hinduism and my responses, I shall focus on these two opposing poles in debate. My goal is not to force readers into an 'either/or' position, but to encourage more participants to enter the debate.

The table below summarizes, as sharply as possible, the differences between the neo-Hinduism thesis and my own understanding of contemporary Hinduism.

Neo-Hinduism—Opposing Thesis	Contemporary Hinduism—My Thesis
Swami Vivekananda manufactured a new religion popularly called Hinduism, and other Indian nationalists such as Gandhi, Radhakrishnan, Rabindranath Tagore and Sri Aurobindo subsequently crystallized it.	These thinkers evolved contemporary Hinduism using traditions as the base into which they assimilated new ideas, including Western ones. Similar changes occur in every religion.
Hinduism is discontinuous with past traditions, and hence is something 'neo' or inauthentic.	Hinduism is continuous with past traditions, even though it changes and evolves just as it has done many times before.
The 'inventors' of this new religion of Hinduism allegedly suffered from a serious inferiority complex under British colonial rule. The neo-Hindus were concerned about the internal decay of Indian society and about the Christian missionary attacks against traditional Hinduism as otherworldly and elitist.	This was true to some extent but the authenticity of Hinduism is not undermined regardless of the factors that modernized it.

Prior to colonialism, Indian traditions had no sense of unity. Intense conflict and mutual contradiction characterized the relationship between them. Indian nationalists, seeing the need for a united India to rise up against the British, fabricated the idea of unity.	Despite the immense diversity across various Hindu groups, philosophies, paths, etc., there was already an overarching unity underneath. The terms 'astika' (insiders) and 'nastika' (outsiders) are old and dynamic, showing that notions of unity existed previously and were contested vibrantly.
Neo-Hinduism's major ideas are imported from the West, and this influence is camouflaged by using Sanskrit words to express them.	The major resources used for bringing about change come from within the tradition itself.
Shankara says the Vedas are required as *pramana* (means of knowing) because one cannot know Brahman like an object, making anubhava (personal experience) incapable of facilitating enlightenment. Direct experience can also be unreliable. Vivekananda's jealousy of Western science led him to re-imagine yoga as a science. The new emphasis on anubhava also created an artificial harmony between Vedanta and yoga to overcome what had earlier been a conflict between them.	Adhyatma-vidya has been an ancient science that utilizes each person's own human potential beyond ordinary mental states. Hence Vivekananda's emphasis on anubhava continues the tradition of the rishis' direct experiences as empirical evidence. Vedas as pramanas are not sidelined but supplemented by direct experience.
Christian ideals of helping society and Western secular theories of social ethics inspired Indian nationalists to appropriate them; karma yoga was used merely as a garb to make this plagiarized idea look Hindu.	Social activism and ethics have been enshrined in the tradition of karma yoga, and this has been modernized to keep up with the times. The Vedas offer a basis for ethical principles that transforms the psychology of the individual.

The Bhagavad-Gita was not a central text until Western Indologists made it important, leading neo-Hindus to adopt it as their focal text.	The Bhagavad-Gita was a primary text long before European colonialism. Every major Hindu thinker (including Shankara, Ramanuja, and Madhava) wrote extensive commentaries on it.
Hinduism is inherently oppressive of minorities such as Muslims, Christians, Dalits and women. It forces others into its own homogeneity for gaining political control. Hindutva is its latest incarnation and its goal has been to impose homogeneity.	Contemporary Hinduism renews the coherence and unity of diverse Indian traditions. It does not harm their diversity, and has, in fact, the most open architecture among the main faiths of the world. Its lack of historical absolutes (in the sense of the Abrahamic religions) accounts for these extraordinary qualities.
Hinduism is a dangerous conspiracy that is being spread worldwide by duping naïve Westerners into thinking that it is a genuine tradition of peace and equality, which it is not.	Contemporary Hinduism can be a great gift to humanity because of its practical and theoretical resources and its promotion of harmony among diverse views and practices.

It is clear from the above table that the two views of Hinduism are diametrically opposed. The clash is not trivial. The assumptions of neo-Hinduism dominate the academia and in large sections of Indian education, media, public policymaking, and popular discourse. Ironically, many Hindu gurus, in embracing a global audience, have adopted this posture as well. This book will show how the definition of neo-Hinduism has been contrived and how it has gained authenticity, in part because it suits certain academic and political agendas, and in part because it has been reiterated extensively without adequate critical response.

I do not wish to discourage criticisms of Hinduism or of any of its leaders. But I do object to the way Vivekananda has been made to look captive to Western models and to the denial of the internal coherence and agency in Hinduism. The attempt to discredit and delegitimize Hinduism and do away with any notion of unity pre-dating colonialism is mischievous. There is a deplorable tone of disparagement, denigration, and sometimes outright contempt toward the spiritual leadership of such figures as Vivekananda, Tagore, Aurobindo and Gandhi.

What, may I ask, is wrong with trying to modernize a traditional faith in light of contemporary and emerging understandings of the world? Why is such a project okay when undertaken in other parts of the world, for example by the Catholic Church in Vatican II, and not okay when undertaken by proponents of Hinduism? And why is it wrong to strive to establish and foster a spiritual basis for the Indian polity now? Why is it assumed that fragmentation of this polity is both an established fact and a good thing?

Far from starting any regressive discourse, Vivekananda was engaged in a natural process of renewal and expansion. He revised an existing tradition by fusing yogic practice, Vedanta, and the best of Western science and humanism. Historically such changes have been achieved organically from within Hinduism and its enduring repertoire of principles and practices.

The next few chapters will detail the individual arguments of the important academics—Paul Hacker, Agehananda Bharati, Ursula King and Anantanand Rambachan—and then discuss their influence on the discourse today.

2

The Mythmakers: A Brief History

My wake-up call: How I discovered the myth

Until November 2012, I had no plans to write a book like this. I knew of several separate instances of bias where the great Hindu visionaries of the modern era were being charged with proto-fascism, which struck me as bizarre. But I had not connected the dots or realized how insidious and widespread such a theory had become. Once I started to unravel the myth-making of neo-Hinduism and the ideological motivations behind it, I saw the dire need to contest its widespread acceptance among academic scholars and so-called experts on Hinduism. I decided that the battle must be taken to the academic fortress where the nexus is headquartered and from where it spreads its narratives. Let me explain how I first encountered the monster that I call the *myth of neo-Hinduism* and what prompted me to confront it.

I was on a panel at the annual conference of the American Academy of Religion in November 2012 in Chicago. The purpose of the panel was to discuss my latest book, *Being Different: An Indian Challenge to Western Universalism*. I had gone prepared for a healthy debate with academic scholars. Lively and sometimes contentious public discussions are normal for important books that challenge people's comfort zones, and I quite thrive on them. However, this particular event proved surprising because the critics present barely engaged with the ideas contained in my book; rather, they were shadow-boxing against an imaginary straw man. They were fixated on arguing against the very existence of any unified Hindu tradition. What I knew as Hinduism was now being rebranded as 'neo-Hinduism', a false ideology. Having spent my entire life as a Hindu, I was shocked by the allegation that my reference to the notion of Hinduism marked me as a dangerous person. I wondered: What could be the basis of such an attack? Why was it being represented thus by respected scholars?

Anantanand Rambachan and Brian Pennington (both senior and politically influential amongst Western academics) were the two panelists who led this attack. Between the two, Pennington understood my work the least, overlooking my most important arguments and dismissing my work in a condescending way. But Rambachan was a well-informed, serious scholar making logical objections, though even he failed to engage with my most important points. Also, he seemed to function in a very narrow context, disconnected with Hinduism's overall position that was the topic at hand.

Both based their objections against *Being Different* on the single premise that that there is no such thing as a unified Hindu tradition.[1] I realized, even at the time, that the tendentious reactions to *Being Different* emerged from their premise that my work was following nineteenth-century Hindu thinkers, most notably Swami Vivekananda. (But in fact, *Being Different* is my original conception of the key differences between dharma and the Abrahamic religions.) These scholars regarded any notion of Hindu unity as a dangerous fabrication and saw me as guilty of propagating it. The attack on *Being Different* emerged as an indictment not only of Vivekananda but of many spiritual leaders who had followed after him, as well as the Ramakrishna Math (which he started) and virtually every mainstream Hinduism movement today.

Pennington's commitment to debunking contemporary Hinduism is the subject of his most famous book, *Was Hinduism Invented?* He was especially upset by what he saw as my book's attempt to 'construct an authentic Hinduism'.[2] Only after further reflection and research did it dawn on me that Rambachan's and Pennington's attacks were based on a superimposition of their own entrenched thesis about a pernicious neo-Hinduism. It also became clear that they were speaking for a large number of scholars with views that are entrenched and influential beyond the religious studies academy. These scholars saw me continuing a sinister conspiracy started by Vivekananda.

An important academic journal invited me to write my response for a special issue that would be dedicated to my book. In my research for this, I soon unearthed the nexus of Western and Indian scholars who had originated this thesis in the past half-century, after which it had rapidly gained currency in the humanities. I began asking the following questions about these scholars: What is their main thesis in regard to this 'invented' nature of contemporary Hinduism? What is their basis for such claims? What are their affiliations—social, political, religious and ideological? Who is funding such research and to what aim? What kinds of institutions are involved? What are the politics of power behind this kind of knowledge production? What are the consequences for India in general, and for Hinduism in particular? Questions such as these are necessary because this myth-making now informs the general discourse on contemporary Hinduism.

Missionary origins

The thesis (or myth) of neo-Hinduism is not the brainchild of a single scholar but was developed by several individuals over a long period. Its roots lie in the Christian missionaries' characterization of India's past as being chaotic, incoherent and without clear ethical and philosophical foundations. Even in the 1800s and early 1900s, many Western missionaries were writing that Hinduism was merely an eclectic, amorphous collection of disparate elements.

For example, in 1902, one T.E. Slater of the London Missionary Society was invited to write a 'Missionary Prize Essay' that would 'instruct educated friends of missions at home in the true genius of the Hindu religion and its fundamental distinction from Christianity, as well as to aid the missionary abroad in his conflict with Hinduism'.[3] It is worth quoting Slater below to show how deep-seated this view of Hinduism was among missionaries:

> The Hindu writings are the product of a national genius, but there is no orderly development, no progressive manifestation of truth; they lead up to no commanding eminence from which all becomes clear. They constitute an anthology, not one organic whole … What is styled 'Hinduism', however, is a vague eclecticism. … We cannot properly speak of the religion of India any more than we can speak of India as a country.[4]

He argued that what characterizes Hinduism is a vague eclecticism, an amalgam of past religious ideas, riddled with caste and custom. The caste system was in his view the defining characteristic of Hinduism: 'Wherever caste is, Hinduism exists', he said. The non-existence of Hinduism as a unified entity was clearly linked, in his mind, to the lack of national integrity of India. He called India no more than a 'geographical expression', concluding:

> No assumption of its [Hinduism's] being a universal religion is therefore possible; it is rather a congeries of divergent systems of thought, of various types and characters of the outward life, each of which at one time or another calls itself Hinduism, but forms no part of a consistent whole.[5]

Western scholars subsequently began to amplify such views in their own voices and crystallized the notion that contemporary Hinduism was an attempt to fabricate a common identity that had never before existed.

Founders of the Myth of Neo-Hinduism

Figure 2 depicts the main players and flow of events in the construction of the myth of neo-Hinduism as understood in the humanities and social sciences. The box at the top shows the pioneers who established this thesis. The box on the left lists some of the prominent Westerners who elaborated and spread this thesis, while the box on the right lists some of the scholars working in India who have written influential works along similar lines. The box at the bottom shows that many Hindus have adopted this thesis, sometimes with naïve intentions. I shall elaborate on these boxes in the chapters that follow.

The top of the diagram shows the importance of Paul Hacker, who was the first academic scholar to develop this set of ideas in the 1950s. Hacker was a prominent Sanskrit philologist of considerable competence. He spent his career in the intense study of Sanskrit and its texts, as did many other Europeans during the past two centuries. He published a series of academic works over several years to put forth this thesis as a serious proposition. In these writings, he popularized the use of the term 'neo-Hinduism' to refer to the modernization of Hinduism that had been brought about by many Indian thinkers, the most prominent being Swami Vivekananda. Hacker charged that 'neo-Hindus' had disingenuously adopted Western ideas and expressed them using Sanskrit.

What is less known about Hacker is that he was also an unabashed Christian apologist, who freely used his academic standing to further the cause of his Christian agenda. He led a parallel life passionately advocating Christianity while presenting the academic face of being neutral and objective.

Hacker saw Advaita Vedanta as a world-negating and impractical worldview. He writes: 'The traditionalistic Advaitists hold that the world, in fact, all matter, all difference and diversity, all action, and all psychic phenomena are ultimately unreal. Phenomenal reality is a

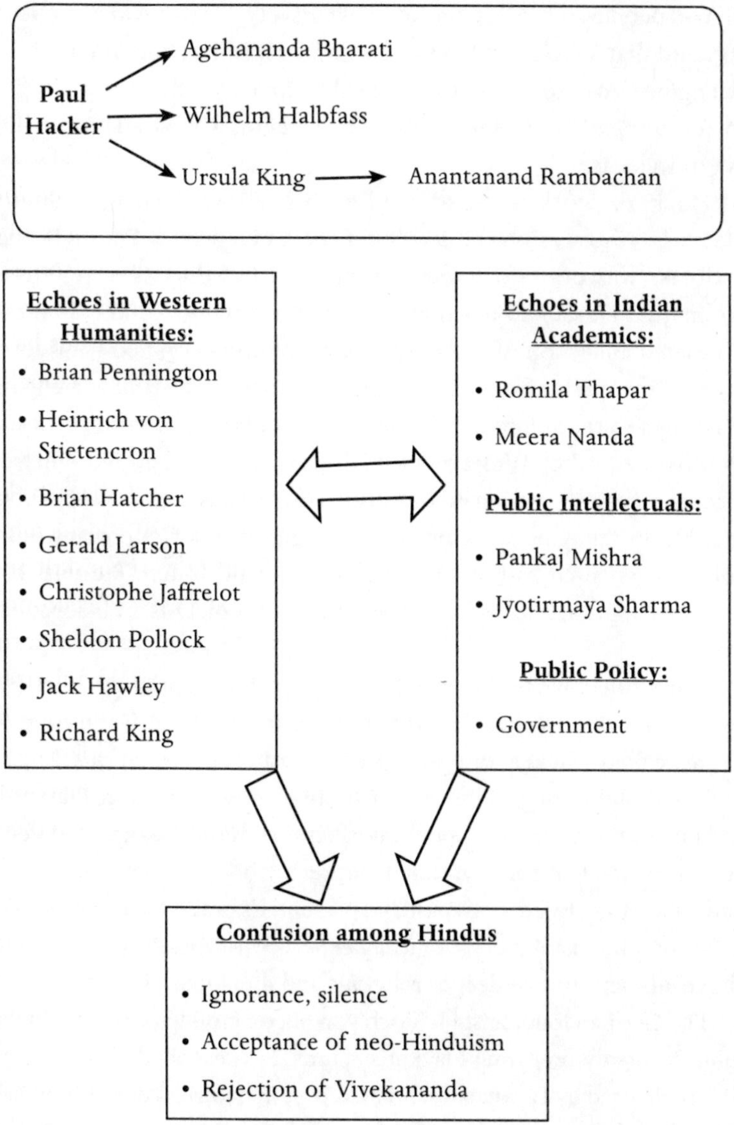

Figure 2: Founders of the Myth of Neo-Hinduism

Paul Hacker → Agehananda Bharati

→ Wilhelm Halbfass

↘ Ursula King → Anantanand Rambachan

Echoes in Western Humanities:

- Brian Pennington
- Heinrich von Stietencron
- Brian Hatcher
- Gerald Larson
- Christophe Jaffrelot
- Sheldon Pollock
- Jack Hawley
- Richard King

Echoes in Indian Academics:

- Romila Thapar
- Meera Nanda

Public Intellectuals:

- Pankaj Mishra
- Jyotirmaya Sharma

Public Policy:

- Government

Confusion among Hindus

- Ignorance, silence
- Acceptance of neo-Hinduism
- Rejection of Vivekananda

mere appearance.'[6] Such a world-negating philosophy was incapable, in his view, of inducing Indians to act in the mundane world as a unified people and to face the West assertively. Hacker and his cohorts contend that Vivekananda saw this flaw in Vedanta and intentionally re-engineered it to make it look world-*affirming* and hence attractive to Westerners. But this fabrication, they claim, was based on copying Western ideas.

Hacker's work was endorsed by his fellow-German Wilhelm Halbfass, who was on the faculty at the University of Pennsylvania. Halbfass was one of the most influential Indologists of his time. He invited Hacker to teach at his university in 1971 and edited the translated collection of Hacker's numerous works on neo-Hinduism. Most of my quotes from Hacker and references to his works are from Halbfass's edited volume. This compilation of Hacker's writings started to influence other Westerners. Halbfass boosted the credibility of Hacker's thesis by writing in the introduction to this edited compilation, that Hacker may be seen in the same light as other important post-colonialists, such as Edward Said and Ronald Inden. He felt that Hacker's approach to India 'is perhaps less obsolete than it seems at first'.[7]

Many other well-established scholars joined in praising Hacker's work. Patrick Olivelle, an eminent Sanskritist at the University of Texas, called Hacker 'one of the most important modern scholars of Indian philosophy'. Francis X. Clooney, a Jesuit, now at Harvard, and one of the most prominent interlocutors in the dialogue between Hinduism and Christianity, called Hacker's work 'indispensable' for its understanding of Vedanta's past and present; he praised Hacker's essays as 'ground-breaking', 'philologically expert', 'historically attuned', and above all, 'sensitive to deeper religious and theological issues'.[8]

The German Indologist Heinrich von Stietencron wrote on the same subject, mostly repeating Hacker's claims. He described Hinduism as 'an orchid bred by European scholarship ... In nature, it does not exist'. He depicted the unity of Hinduism as a nineteenth-century invention which conceals a collection of irreconcilable sects in India. Before the nineteenth century, Stietencron claims, there was no Hindu religious identity that transcended narrow sectarian boundaries, and the idea of a unified Hindu religion is counter both to religious practice and to the theological doctrines of Indians.

It is noteworthy that the early Indologists who championed this neo-Hinduism thesis and gave it academic credibility were all Germans and/or Austrians who had lived through the Nazi era: Paul Hacker, Leopold Fischer (who adopted the name Agehananda Bharati), Wilhelm Halbfass and Heinrich von Stietencron. They were clearly influenced by the Nazis in complex ways, including the ways in which they reacted against the Nazis, perhaps out of a sense of associative guilt.

Bharati (Fischer), for example, had a romantic fantasy about Indian culture and languages since childhood. He studied about India in Vienna and later joined the German army. His job was to use his knowledge of Indian languages and culture as a means of influencing Indians living in Germany at that time. Following the war, he went to India to get initiated as a Hindu monk, and then taught in Banaras Hindu University and the Nalanda Institute for Buddhist Research and Pali. However, his experiment in becoming a Hindu was not sustainable for various reasons, so he switched from being a devout practitioner of Hinduism who had been impressed with its ancient traditions to being an outspoken critic of contemporary Hinduism. His career then changed to teaching the anthropology of Hinduism in the West.

But he did not return to Europe. His experience as a Hindu sannyasin in India changed him and he went to North America instead. It was in this phase of his career—i.e., after leaving Hinduism as a practitioner and teaching 'about' it as an outsider in the West—when he wrote his scathing attacks on Hinduism. He is known mainly under his Hindu adopted name, Agehananda Bharati. He coined the phrase 'Pizza Effect', to explain his theory that contemporary Hinduism was largely a romantic projection of Europeans, re-imported into India by Indians themselves to bolster a faltering sense of self-worth.

It is important to point out that the German romanticizing of India since the eighteenth century had culminated in the Aryan theory, and this subsequently served as the mythology on which Nazism was based. During Hacker's and Bharati's formative years, their German

Indologist predecessors had romanticized the Vedic texts to the extent of suggesting they were authored by German Aryans.[9] Hacker, Bharati and other German Indologists like them later witnessed the horrific sights of Nazism, which in turn led to the need to reject the glorified Aryan identity. The Lutheran Church had been close to the Nazis, and it is not surprising that Hacker later rejected Lutheranism and converted to a different denomination. Similarly, Bharati's experiences serving in the German army caused him to revolt against it as well.

In both cases, a part of the purge to remove the ghost of Nazi guilt involved a rejection of Hinduism, which they had associated with Aryanism. Vivekananda became a convenient whipping boy to vent their anger as they launched a campaign to discredit Hinduism.

More or less contemporaneously with these developments, the Harvard professor of comparative religion W. Cantwell Smith wrote: 'There are Hindus, but there is no Hinduism.'[10] In other words, while there are people who call themselves Hindus, there is no coherent religious position which they share. Hinduism is thus a bogus category. *The Harvard Gazette* characterized Smith as one of the most influential figures of the past century in the field of comparative religion.

Another early participant who deepened the theory of neo-Hinduism was the British Indologist Ursula King, who, like the others, shifted her focus from her earlier general study of Hinduism to target neo-Hinduism as an artificial and dangerous construct. Her importance is considerable, both in her own right and because she groomed the young Indian scholar Anantanand Rambachan, who is instrumental today in perpetuating the thesis. Ursula King chaired his Ph.D dissertation committee, and it was in this dissertation that many of the prevailing myths of neo-Hinduism became solidified.

Rambachan became the first scholar in Hacker's school of thought who used the teachings of moksha in Shankara's Advaita Vedanta as the criterion for judging modern Hinduism. Shankara is widely acclaimed as one of the greatest Hindu philosophers, and as the founder of the Advaita Vedanta system. This was the first time any prominent scholar in the Western institutions engaged in religious studies had stood on Shankara's shoulders to fire against contemporary Hinduism. In this manner, Rambachan advanced the neo-Hinduism thesis to a deeper philosophical level. His allegations are far more serious than those of his predecessors, for he argues, on the basis of a philosophical comparison with Shankara, that Vivekananda's core ideas are fundamentally flawed and borrowed from Westerners.

Rambachan likes to note that under colonial influence, the upper strata of Indians had become disconnected from their own traditional sources of knowledge and were increasingly dependent on European accounts of their own history and culture. He points out correctly that the 1800s was a time when Protestant and Catholic missionaries constantly denigrated and criticized the Hindu scriptures. Their attacks against the Vedas had become troubling for Hindu reformers of the Brahmo Samaj prior to Vivekananda.

Under these conditions, Western Unitarians arrived in India as a welcome relief, for they interpreted Hindu theology as being open, rational, experiential and science-friendly, compared with how orthodox Protestants had portrayed it. Unitarians adopted a positive approach to Hinduism, albeit still from a Western perspective. Sensing a good fit, the Brahmo Samaj sent its bright youth to Unitarian seminaries in England for training to become Samaj leaders. As a result, the Samaj started to adopt the framework of Unitarian Christianity in order to identify alternative sources of authority within Hinduism that would support this kind of universal and 'scientific' ideology based on experience.[11] This, according to Rambachan, laid the groundwork for the way in which Vivekananda incorporated the principle of direct experience and intuition into his newly invented Hinduism. He claims that such notions were derived from Unitarian sources and had no real precedent in classical Indian thought.

Hacker, Rambachan and others from this school of thought also accuse Vivekananda of introducing Western scientific inquiry and direct experience in order to bring Hinduism on par with Western thought, and in the process downgrading the textual authority of the Vedas.

Rambachan's harshest allegation is that Vivekananda did an illicit reinterpretation of the famous dictum of Vedanta, tat tvam asi, or 'that art thou', as the basis for the Hindu social ethic. Its original meaning, he argues, had nothing to do with social ethics and was strictly about private mystical unity. Similarly, he claimed that Vivekananda's emphasis on *ahimsa* as social non-violence differed from its traditional meaning. Thus, Vivekananda becomes, somewhat anachronistically, the culprit for an artificial construction of a new religion with proto-fascist tendencies.

Rambachan directly attacks Vivekananda's unified approach to the four major paths of yoga—jnana yoga (knowledge), raja yoga (meditation), karma yoga (selfless service) and bhakti yoga (devotion). He argues that three of these (raja, karma and bhakti) violate Shankara's ideas on attaining moksha (enlightenment) because he insists that only jnana is capable of leading to moksha. He further alleges, based on extensive argumentation, that these four systems lack consistency and coherence. He faults this four-path system for its inability to explicate the fundamental problem of *avidya*, or ignorance, as the major bar to moksha. Rambachan writes that in Vivekananda's work 'there is no attempt to carefully relate the nature of each method to the assumptions of avidya as the fundamental problem'.

He adds that Vivekananda is vague and obscure in connecting them to moksha.[12] But Rambachan is too narrowly fixated on moksha and disregards the fact that vast majority of practising Hindus pursue goals of dharma that are not limited to moksha per se. The issue of Hinduism's unity and legitimacy cannot be based solely on whether all its lineages agree on the same approach to moksha.

Rambachan concludes that because Vivekananda desired to engineer a rapprochement with the West, his idea of Hinduism lacks intellectual rigor, promotes yogic mystification and spiritual experience over reason, and weakens the Advaita Vedanta founded by Shankara. Rambachan's implicit assumptions are that Shankara is the sole authority on Advaita, Advaita Vedanta speaks for all Vedanta systems, and Vedanta represents all Hinduism. It will become clear later that both Shankara and Vivekananda are being oversimplified in order to highlight and exaggerate a disagreement within Hinduism in order to demonstrate its lack of unity and coherence.

I must clarify that Rambachan's views are, technically speaking, in line with the traditional interpretations of Shankara's Advaita Vedanta, which Rambachan has studied under the tutelage of very important Vedanta teachers. My disagreement with him is not over the technical interpretation taken in a literal sense. It is over the very nature of the debate he has led in academic religious studies and as the Hindu voice in prominent inter-faith forums. The internal differences he is fixated on are well known and relate to the means for attaining *moksha* (ultimate liberation). They reflect the inter-lineage and inter-darshana debates within Indian traditions. But most Hindus are not pursuing moksha per se in *any* lineage. Their relationship with Hinduism is much more mundane and concerns legitimate pursuits (*purusharthas*) that are more pragmatic than moksha.

I find it problematic to represent Hinduism in international forums that aim to undermine its legitimacy on the grounds of disputes among lineages over technical issues of moksha; issues that do not affect the practice of Hinduism by its vast majority of followers today. The final section of the Introduction chapter is titled 'Framing the debate in three disciplines'. Had Rambachan made his points strictly within the scope of inter-lineage debates in philosophy, it would not have been turned into a political campaign against contemporary Hinduism. But bringing in contemporary Hinduism's history and politics has expanded its scope and changed the character of the debate. It is this expanded scope that this book responds to. I am concerned about the effect his posture has had on the wider discourse on Hinduism as I will explain below and further in Chapter 7.

The Chorus Line

The myth of neo-Hinduism has spread far and wide beyond the academic circles where it began. It has entered mainstream media, government policy-making, and even popular cultural portrayals of India. It is often the official version of Hinduism taught in American school textbooks. It is increasingly assumed by cosmopolitan Indians who imagine they are the well-informed, proud citizens of an emerging superpower. This myth has clear social and political ramifications, as we shall see.

Soon after Rambachan's Ph.D dissertation appeared, Romila Thapar, an eminent historian of India, wrote a widely cited article in which she states that the Hindutva political movement had created a new form of Hinduism by artificially collapsing the earlier pluralistic and variegated realities of India into a neo-Hinduism monolith. She labels this monolith 'syndicated Hinduism', and this term has now become popular.

Thapar believes this 'syndication' to be a reaction to the encounter with Semitic religions that occurred during colonialism. Neo-Hinduism, she argues, is an attempt to restructure the 'indigenous religions' into a homogeneous one, paralleling some of the features of Semitic religions. She sees this as a fundamental departure from the essentials of the indigenous religions.[13] Thapar concludes that 'Hinduism' was created 'for purposes more political than religious, and is mainly supportive of the ambitions of a new social class'.[14] She characterizes Hinduism as something that 'ends up inevitably as a garbled form of Brahmanism with motley "values" drawn from other sources. The call to unite under Hinduism as a political entity is anachronistic'.[15] Thapar seems more comfortable with a history centric religion or one that is defined as being a 'reaction' to history. She writes:

> Unlike the Semitic religions (with which the comparison is often made), which began with a structure at a point in time and evolved largely in relation to and within that structure, Hinduism (and I use the word here in its contemporary meaning) has been largely a reaction to historical situations. The attempt to delineate a structure relates to each such situation.[16]

Thapar comes close to understanding that in order to find unity in Hinduism, a different approach is needed, but she fails to go further in that direction:

What has survived over the centuries is not a single, monolithic religion but a diversity of religious sects which we today have put together under a uniform name. The collation of these religious groups is defined as 'Hinduism' even though the religious reference points of such groups might be quite distinct.[17]

Internet discussions have further spread this myth. For example, a Canadian web site on Perennialism features articles from ex-followers of the Ramakrishna Mission who have converted the Mission's ideas first into Western Perennialism, then into Transpersonal Theory, and now into something called Integral Christianity. One such article, titled 'The Neo-Vedanta of Swami Vivekananda', describes the Swami and his influence as inauthentic.[18] Also available on the same site are the writings of activist Meera Nanda, who links Vedic science to oppression by Hindu nationalism.[19]

Some senior scholars trusted by the Hindu diaspora have echoed these ideas. Take, for example, the work of John Stratton Hawley, who for many years headed the programme in Hinduism studies at Columbia University, and leads many initiatives on Hinduism in India and the U.S. In his influential article on Hinduism, Hawley begins with the following sarcastic statement:

Hinduism—the word, and perhaps the reality too—was born in the nineteenth century, a notoriously illegitimate child. The father was middle-class and British, and the mother, of course, was India. The circumstances of the conception are not altogether clear.[20]

Many Indians have noted the racist and sexist overtones in this statement, and it is shocking how easily the peer reviewers and editors of the most prestigious academic journals let such slander pass through in the name of 'scholarship'. In the same article, Hawley claims that 'political interests in India have attributed to contemporary Hinduism the character of a "world religion"'. The implication is that it is *not* a world religion, and has no claim to be properly represented at the table when world religions are being discussed.

Earlier, in a similar vein, J.A.B. van Buitenen had written in the *Encyclopedia Britannica's* entry on Hinduism:

> As a religion, Hinduism is an utterly diverse conglomerate of doctrines, cults, and ways of life ... In principle, Hinduism incorporates all forms of belief and worship without necessitating the selection or elimination of any ... A Hindu may embrace a non-Hindu religion without ceasing to be a Hindu.[21]

More bluntly, Frits Staal states that, 'Hinduism does not merely fail to be a religion; it is not even a meaningful unit of discourse. There is no way to abstract a meaningful unitary notion of Hinduism from the Indian phenomena.'[22]

Another well-known scholar, Robert Frykenberg, agrees: 'There has never been any such thing as a single "Hinduism" or any single "Hindu community" for all of India ... The very notion of the existence of any single religious community by this name has been falsely conceived.'[23] Claiming that Hinduism lacks any 'concrete elements or hard objects', he asserts that it has been used by those who 'have tried to give greater unity to the extreme cultural diversities that are native to the continent'.[24]

David Kopf focuses on the fashionable 'orientalist' critique:

> The work of integrating a vast collection of myths, beliefs, rituals, and laws into a coherent religion, and of shaping an amorphous heritage into a rational faith known now as 'Hinduism' were endeavors initiated by Orientalists.[25]

I do agree that Western orientalists distorted India by seeing it through their lenses. But I disagree that Vivekananda merely copied those ideas. Most of the ideas of Vivekananda are derived from prior indigenous systems and traditions.

Gerald Larson, a prominent scholar who receives funding by the Hindu diaspora, has a friendly demeanour but his positions are opposed to Hinduism's unity. He supports the Aryan invasion theory, and claims that the neo-Hindus created their own version of Hinduism as a reaction against what the Western Indologists had romantically imagined earlier. He writes:

> Modern Indian notions of religion derive from a mixture of Christian (and mainly Protestant) models, Orientalist and largely Western reconstructions of India's religious past, and nineteenth-century indigenous reform movements most of which were defensive reactions against the onslaught of Westernization and Christian missionizing.[26]

Heinrich von Stietencron claims that prior to the nineteenth century, there was no notion of a unity of practice or doctrine among the people who are now called 'Hindus'. His entire case rests on the analysis of a single eleventh-century text, according to which, he claims, all the religious groups now classified as Hindu were previously antagonistic toward one another.[27] All non-Shaivists, for example, were told that they must convert to Shaivism in order to attain liberation. The text describes a ritual for achieving this conversion. Stietencron generalizes this single text to make sweeping conclusions about the nature of religious life across India prior to the colonial influence.

Julius Lipner, another influential scholar of Hinduism, recommends that the term 'Hinduism' be used (at least in the humanities) only to refer to Hindu culture and *not* to a single unified faith.[28] P.J. Marshall writes similarly that colonial scholars and administrators 'invariably made a distinction between "popular" Hinduism, which they did not deem worthy of study, and "philosophical" Hinduism, which they tried to define as a set of hard-and-fast doctrinal propositions and to place in current theories about the nature and history of religion'.[29]

David Lorenzen, a professor of South Asian history at the College of Mexico's Center for Asian and African Studies, notes that a number of Indian academics teach that Hindu unity did not exist before the nineteenth century. Among these, he cites Bipan Chandra, Gyanendra Pandey and Veena Das, and names several Americans as well.[30]

One of the mainstream's loudest critics of this so-called nationalist neo-Hinduism is the journalist Pankaj Mishra, who has written for *The New York Times* and published widely acclaimed international works. Mishra has a direct, journalistic style using plain and simple words. His opinions influence English-speaking Indians who regard them as authoritative. However, he does not offer any independent analysis of his own, instead merely parroting the standard Western discourse about Hinduism that I have been describing.

In his article 'The Invention of the Hindu', he articulates his thesis that 'Hinduism is largely a fiction, formulated in the eighteenth and nineteenth centuries.' He regards Hinduism as a construct of colonialism that was enthusiastically and dangerously endorsed by Indian modernizers and reconfigured as a global rival to the three big monotheisms. Hinduism, according to him, abandoned 'the tradition of toleration which lies in its true origins'.[31]

In another high profile article, Mishra claims that the British, as part of their divide-and-rule policy, indoctrinated Hindus to hate Muslims. Towards this goal, they spread the idea that pre-Islamic India had been great but that the Muslims had devastated it, and that the Brahminical past was tolerant and free from the cruelties of caste.[32] Mishra goes on to explain that as a result of their pride, Hindus started to aspire to 'the European idea of nation—of a cohesive community with a common history, culture, values and sense of purpose'.[33] This process, he says, was encouraged by the colonialists in a manner that would create a Hindu / Muslim divide.

While Gandhi and Nehru started this nationalist trend, Mishra blames Veer Sarvarkar and Guru Golwalkar (founders of the political Hindutva movement) for propagating the notion of 'Hinduism = India' at the expense of Muslims. He writes that these men saw India as exclusively 'the sacred indigenous nation of Hindus' and that it could only be revived by 'forcing Muslims to give up their traditional allegiances' and embrace Hindutva, itself a product of orientalism.[34]

Of special concern to Mishra is that Hinduism, starting with its alleged origin in British rule, was designed to be antagonistic to Muslims. Hinduism, he claims, did not even exist prior to the arrival of Muslims in India, and then it got crystallized by the British. He writes:

The bewildering diversity of people who inhabited India before the arrival of the Muslims in the eleventh century hardly formed a community, much less a nation; and the word 'Hinduism' barely hinted at the almost infinite number of folk and elite cultures, religious sects and philosophical traditions found in India.[35]

The neo-Hinduism myth is even being communicated in sensational and sexualized terms in journalism and social media. An op-ed piece in *Indian Express* by leading scholar and columnist, Ashutosh Varshney, states that in neo-Hinduism, 'a singular national identity was also equated with masculinity by Hindu nationalists. Vivekananda, whose sayings Narendra Modi tweets, came to promote 'three Bs' for Hindus: beef, biceps and the Bhagavad-Gita'.[36]

Although the thesis of a pernicious and distorted neo-Hinduism acquired the aura of academic respectability only after India's independence, the seeds of it are also found in the views of prominent Indians who could not understand a coherent Hinduism. 'Hinduism, as a faith', wrote Jawaharlal Nehru in his monumental, *The Discovery of India*, 'is vague, amorphous, many-sided, all things to all men. It is hardly possible to define it.' Ironically, the patriotic writer, B.G. Gokhale, writing on Indian nationalism in 1958, also adopted the position that Hindu ethics were formed under the colonial influence of Christianity.[37] Such leaders did not intend to undermine Hinduism or the concept of Indian unity, but they inadvertently perpetuated the myth that Hinduism has appropriated Western constructs and hence it lacks legitimacy.

Proponents of the neo-Hinduism thesis are surprisingly consistent and homogenous in their views. Rarely, if ever, does one encounter any internal disagreement among them. The starting point implicit in many of their writings is a socio-political ideology of the current political fragmentation. This gets projected back in time to emphasize how one group of Indians exploited another and to conclude that there was never a unity and historical continuity. This is correlated with highly exaggerated philosophical conflicts. The end result is to claim that Hindu practices are senseless, abusive and dangerous.

3

Paul Hacker's Construction of 'neo-Hinduism'

Initial romance with Advaita Vedanta and its personal influences on Hacker

Paul Hacker's enduring mark on the study of Hinduism started with intense interest in Shankara and Advaita Vedanta, which he initially represented with great respect in many publications. But starting in 1953, this fascination with Indian non-dualism turned into a fierce critique on both historical and theological grounds.

The shift, though seemingly sincere, also seems to have boosted his career: after spending a year as a professor at Mithila Postgraduate Research Institute in Darbhanga, India, he returned home to occupy the prestigious Indology Chair at the University of Bonn, which had been established in 1818 as Germany's oldest chair for Indian studies.[1]

Having spent many years researching Shankara, Hacker began to mine Hinduism for the renewal of Christian theology. In a 1969 article, he compared and contrasted Shankara and Thomas Aquinas. He also wrote extensively on the *Puranas*. His serious interest in reading Indian texts as a source for creative ideas is clear from his statement that 'India is the classical land for the study of source materials in the history of religion.'[2] His personal faith was influenced by his encounters with Vedanta, and he wrote that its 'theological thought can open the religious scholar's eyes for realities which would otherwise remain hidden from him'.[3]

William Halbfass, Hacker's heir, admirer and peer, has noted Hacker's desire to make use of Hinduism in his personal explorations as a Christian. Hacker felt that Christianity and in particular Roman Catholicism provided a 'vantage point', and an 'antenna' for his study of such figures as Shankara, with whom he wished to engage 'at a commensurate level of discourse'.[4] Halbfass explains how Hacker's dramatic conversion from Lutheran Protestantism to Catholicism in 1962 was partly motivated by the need to critique Hinduism from a firmer Christian footing. He writes,

> Europeans who are confined to the secularity and modernity they have brought about will remain confined to a kind of monologue. To overcome modernity's monologue with itself was one of Hacker's deepest aspirations. The choice of a firm religious and theological position was, paradoxically, a step towards dialogue.[5]

In other words, Hacker developed a fascination for Advaita Vedanta during his study of Shankara and this eventually raised serious doubts in his mind about Christianity; he thought he could address these doubts better from within Catholicism than from within Lutheran Protestantism. This was a factor in his conversion to Catholicism, according to Halbfass.

Hacker starts his attack on contemporary Hinduism

To a certain point, Hacker's engagement with Hinduism could be seen as a kind of *purva paksha* in the Indian tradition of studying the other side in open-minded inquiry. This picture, however, is incomplete because his positive engagement with contemporary Hinduism was limited to what he viewed as 'pure' traditional Advaita. Halbfass uses the term 'confrontation' to describe Hacker's engagement. After first appearing to genuinely want to understand Advaita on its own terms, there came a tipping point when Hacker began to dismiss altogether modern Vedanta as exemplified in the works of Swami Vivekananda and Radhakrishnan. Now these thinkers were suddenly considered to be falsifying the tradition for political gain. Once he took this turn, Hacker became a harsh critic and considered so-called 'neo-Hindus' to be inauthentic and their ideas to be corrupted by the Indian encounter with Christianity and Western science.

In other words, after mining traditional Hinduism as a foil for his own personal explorations in Christianity, Hacker started making allegations that contemporary Hinduism was the result of Indian nationalists wanting to appropriate Christian ideas. Hacker posed the following question, and supplied his own answer:

> The student of the history of Indian thought must ask himself whether this modification is a straight prolongation of the lines traced out by the ancient masters of the monistic Vedanta, or whether there is a break between the ideas of the old school and Vivekananda's presentation of the Vedanta. The result of such scrutiny is that there is actually a break.[6]

Hacker increasingly indulged in a veritable anti-Hindu campaign on behalf of Christianity while continuing to present his work as objective scholarship. The following evidence is illustrative: He developed the thesis of the invention of Hinduism in ten articles published between 1954 and 1978, all of which were in German and reprinted in a volume of his collected writings for his 65th birthday. These were presented as scholarly contributions to a scientific debate. However, acting on Hacker's wishes, the editor of his collected works excluded the author's polemical Christian writings from the compilation. Among the articles that were left out was one that was published only posthumously, in 1983. Many such polemical writings also appeared in fringe religious pamphlets and propaganda literature which are unknown to most scholars. Hacker's Christian bias and intolerance toward contemporary Hinduism were evident in his intense exchanges with the Indian bishop Amalorpavadass and the Jesuit theologian Karl Rahner.[7]

Hacker's suppression of this material compromised his integrity as an objective scholar, as it misled readers into thinking his writings on Hinduism were objective evaluations when in fact they were, in Andrew Nicholson's words, the work of a 'Christian polemicist'.[8] In his posthumously published writings, Hacker is as explicit in his support for Christianity as he is in his attack on contemporary Hinduism.

There is an inherent contradiction here: Christianity is allowed to be renewed through contact with Indian sources, but Hinduism must remain fossilized in the past in order to be considered 'authentic'. No one has suggested the term 'neo-Christianity' for the kinds of revision that were undertaken in Christianity during the same period Vivekananda was active; and yet the Hindu revisions are branded in this way.[9] In fact, if the same criteria were applied to Christianity as are applied to 'neo-Hinduism', we would have to conclude that virtually every Christian theologian since Thomas Aquinas has been a 'neo-Christian' and that there is 'no such thing' as Christianity per se.

The Indian philosopher J.N. Mohanty took issue with Halbfass precisely on whether a double standard was being used to judge modernization in Hinduism when the same kind of development in Christianity was seen as normal. In a commemorative book published in honor of Halbfass's contributions, Mohanty writes:

> The distinction (between Traditional Hinduism and Neo-Hinduism) would be significant if it were a special feature of the history of Indian—more specifically, of Hindu—civilization. But is it? Can

one not, in a similar vein, distinguish between 'fortlebendem trädionellem Christentum' and 'Neu-Christentum'! Is not there a noteworthy difference between the new self-understanding of (Protestant) Christianity and the classical Christian self-understanding?[10]

Mohanty goes on to argue that all cultures evolve in response to circumstances and that such an adaptation by Hinduism is therefore a healthy sign of its resilience:

> If a culture's self-understanding is always, as a rule, caught up in a process of historical development, in response to historically confronted challenges, the response of neo-Hinduism is what it should be (despite minor aberrations, exaggerations and/or enthusiasms). What is more, if no cultural phenomenon, religion including, remains tied to the original formulations and the classical statements, then it is not Hinduism alone that is guilty of evolving into a 'neo-form'. To the contrary, that such varieties of response to the new challenges (from the West) were forthcoming, demonstrates the resilience of Hinduism.[11]

Halbfass responds in the same book as follows:

> What is the significance and legitimacy of the 'Neo' in expressions like 'Neo-Hinduism' and 'Neo-Vedanta'? Could we speak of 'Neo-Christianity' as well? In fact, I have used this term in *India and Europe*, and not all of my Christian readers and reviewers were entirely happy about the term. Concerning the expression 'Neo-Hinduism': I have, over the years, distanced myself increasingly from Paul Hacker's somewhat simplistic use, most explicitly in the introduction to my recent collection of Hacker's Vedanta studies. Still, I believe that 'Neo-Vedanta' and 'Neo-Hinduism' are useful and legitimate as convenient labels. They are simply abbreviations for important developments and changes which took place in

Indian thought since the period around 1800, i.e., the relatively unprepared opening to foreign, Western influences, the adoption of Western concepts and standards and the readiness to reinterpret traditional ideas in light of these new, imported and imposed modes of thought. We have, however, to emphasize that the demarcation of these modernist trends against 'surviving traditional Hinduism' is more problematic than it appears in Hacker's dichotomy.[12]

Mohanty questions whether the new self-understanding of Protestant Christianity should be called 'neo-Christianity', but Halbfass only says his Christian readers are not all happy with the term. Essentially, he evades the real issue, which is that the two faiths are being treated in an unequal manner by academic scholars who are supposed to be impartial in their approach.

Regardless of his personal religious views, Hacker's main achievement, according to his supporters, was to assert that Hinduism's claim of unity is a fabrication. Hinduism as a unified entity was 'essentially inspired by apologetics and nationalism'.[13] So-called 'Hinduism', Hacker claimed, is basically no more than a collection of amorphous religions that co-exist in the same region and have some commonalities, but these commonalities are far outweighed by divisions and mutual antagonisms. Western scholars are also to blame for this artificial unity, he says, insofar as they insist on applying a simplistic 'collective label' and description to this divergent phenomenon.

Above all, Hacker wants to convince us that what he dismissively calls 'neo-Hinduism' was the product of Christian and colonial influence. He gives no credence to the way basic values in Hinduism arise organically from within the tradition and how they get churned and debated before each successive new variety emerges. After alleging that the key principles are borrowed from Christianity, he dismisses 'neo-Hinduism' as being primarily Western in its 'intellectual formation'.[14]

Alleging political motives and appropriations from the West

Hacker cites the writings of many Hindu leaders of the late nineteenth and early twentieth centuries to the effect that traditional Hinduism was considered too weak and that this weakness led to the downfall of India. According to him, Indian leaders suffered a deep inferiority complex about the weakness of India compared with Europe, and attributed this weakness to Hinduism's inability to adapt to the modern era. By 1894, Vivekananda was expressing alarm and humiliation at the impoverishment of Indians. Neo-Hindus, in Hacker's view, felt that Hinduism caused Indians to become resigned and complacent.[15] Radhakrishnan had also attributed India's failure to Hinduism's incoherence and ethical rottenness. Hacker read this as a sense of inferiority caused by the encounter with European civilization, especially science, technology and rationality, as well as the stressful challenges posed by Christian missionaries.

Hacker theorized that inferiority was the chief impetus for creating a new religion that would bring pride among Indians; Hinduism had to be conceived as being on par with modern science and indeed superior to it in spiritual terms. Citing Vivekananda's calls for Indian unity and the inner resolution of tensions, Hacker writes that 'such ideas reveal clearly that nationalism is the origin and driving force of the Neo-Hindu conception of unity'.[16]

After this astounding allegation, Hacker makes it very clear that there was no foundation on which Vivekananda could build, except a purely political construct. In other words, the unity is not spiritual but political. He goes on to say:

> After all, the Hindu group of religions is little more than a geographic entity. Within it we find many common denominators, but even more antagonisms, rivalry, and division. Hinduism, according to Vivekananda's demand, should understand itself as a unity so that India can become a nation.[17]

Hacker asserts that the unity which Vivekananda seeks can be built only on one school of Hindu thought and practice; it cannot at any point be pluralistic:

> However, this idea of unity can be maintained only insofar as one of the Hindu systems, i.e., the monistic Vedanta system, is considered to be universally superior; all other types of religion found within Hinduism are recognized as its preliminary stages and as having a relative validity only. In short, Vivekananda's idea of the unity of Hinduism amounts to the proclamation of the superior and universal authority of Advaita Vedanta. And this authority has to prevail for the sake of nationhood. For Vivekananda, religion and nation are one.[18]

In other words, Vivekananda distorted traditional doctrines so that they conformed to his new Westernized idea of Advaita Vedanta and used this as his template to create a bond among all versions and branches of Hinduism—a bond that had not existed before. He did so for purely instrumental and pragmatic reasons, to introduce new ideas from the West and put them in Indian clothes, using Sanskrit words with new meanings.

In Hacker's view, this use of philosophical and religious ideas as a means for achieving political ends was typical of Indians. Modern Indians found themselves to be in a state of paralysis and apathy and regarded Hindu ethics as irredeemable, powerless and inferior. Prominent leaders such as Bankim Chandra (1838-94), Vivekananda and Radhakhrishnan also felt paralysed, he claims, and it could only be cured by reference to Christian and Western values.[19]

Hacker's overall thesis on the Western origins of ideas that were digested into Hinduism is summarized below:

> We can even state it as a rule that up till now the essential impulse and influential elements of Neo-Hindu thought have always come from the West or from Christianity, in such a way that an idea coming from those sources appears so powerful in a particular

situation that its adoption is inevitable; that these impulses and elements are then hastily attached to inherited ideas or identified with them at the price of logical incongruity and even a kind of dissimulation; and that on the other hand—in typical Neo-Hinduism, as opposed to surviving traditional Hinduism—ideas inherited from the Hindu tradition hardly ever become significant or effective as such. We can see this also in the realm of language. Literary Hindi nearly always uses Western concepts, and yet uses hardly any loanwords; instead, it uses Sanskrit words as shells in which the Western concepts are inserted. In the realm of political ethics, we should remember that the duty of non-violence, which Tilak, and Aurobindo in his political period, did not recognize, but which has now become a universally binding ideal, was first discovered by Gandhi in Leo Tolstoy's writings before he attached it to the traditional Indian idea of ahimsa. The Neo-Hindu dogma of the equality of all religions, however much it can be supported by certain Hindu traditions, emerged originally at the beginning of the nineteenth century, probably from the ideology of the European Enlightenment. The Neo-Hindu concept of dharma was clearly prompted by the philosophy of Augustus Comte and John Stuart Mill, but was then expressed in completely Indian terms. In Haribhadra's ethic of love, and in Vivekananda's amalgamation of Western and Indian forms of ethical relativism, there is an attempt to fuse inherited Hindu ideas with concepts taken from Christianity or from Western philosophy, which provide the impulse for this attempt, and to fuse them in such a way that the result appears to be genuinely Hindu.[20]

Hacker on Vivekananda and the West

Hacker claims that the watershed event in this massive appropriation of Western ideas by Indians was Vivekananda's visit to the West in 1893. He writes: 'After his encounter with Ramakrishna, the second great event in Vivekananda's life was his exposure to the Western way of life, i.e., the United States of America and Europe.'[21] The principal reason for Vivekananda's visit was, in Hacker's view, entirely conditioned by a sense of inferiority. He wanted to learn Western ways and borrow ideas to formulate his own brand of Hinduism. He admired the West's technology, science, industry, vigor and work ethic. He appreciated its social order, particularly the educational systems and the traditions of philanthropy, altruism, and collective action. He was impressed by the self-confidence and national pride of Westerners. He wanted Indians to have these attributes, albeit cloaked in Hindu religiosity.

After learning from the West, claims Hacker, Vivekananda formed his ideas of nationhood. He realized that Westerners had ideas of a shared civilization that had permeated their education, but as this was not the case with India it was easy for the British to conquer India. Hacker extensively quotes Vivekananda's writings on loss of national pride and lack of mass education in India. Upon returning home to India, he founded the Ramakrishna Mission with the principal aim of philanthropy and education. Again, Halbfass restates Hacker's thesis clearly: 'The link which the "Neo-Hindus" find to their tradition is, one may say, an afterthought; for they first adopt Western values and means of orientation and then attempt to find the foreign in the indigenous.'[22]

According to this thesis, Vivekananda tried to give a worldly and practical dimension to Hinduism and portray it as 'the expanding religion of which his national pride was dreaming'.[23] Hacker interprets the swami's strategy as follows:

1. Previously, Vedanta was entirely metaphysical, unworldly and abstract. Vivekananda draws it into the practical realm of the individual's life. The doctrine of the divine essence of man gets turned into a nationalistic, political agenda as a result of advocating a certain kind of education in service of the nation.

2. He utilizes ideas from European positivism. Since the sum total of all humanity is God, he equates divine service as service to mankind. Thus, identifying the totality of humanity with God becomes a device for teaching altruism. This European influence derives from the secular philosophers of Europe.

3. He interprets *tat tvam asi* ('that thou art', a fundamental axiom found in the Upanishads) to mean every individual should be

seen as one's own self, thus reflecting the Christian idea of 'doing good unto others ... ' Prior to this adaptation, *tat tvam asi* referred exclusively to the individual's identification with Brahman, and not to any identification with other individuals for the purpose of ethical actions (selflessness, compassion, etc.).

4. He positions Vedanta as the universal world religion because it is based on spiritual experiences which may be seen as similar to scientific experiments.

I shall now address the main areas in which Hacker claims neo-Hinduism deviates seriously from traditional Hinduism and appropriates its core ideas from the Christian West. The purpose here is to clarify Hacker's position, and only briefly indicate my rebuttal which will be elaborated in later chapters.

Allegation 1: Importance of Direct Experience

A major distortion charged by Hacker is the elevation of direct experience over traditional, text-based doctrines. Before Vivekananda's rise to prominence, Debendranath Tagore, father of the poet Rabindranath Tagore and a leading thinker of the Brahmo Samaj, had already questioned the degree to which the Hindu scriptures should be taken as authoritative. To him this authority exists in the experiential confirmation of truth rather than in texts. He felt that the ancient rishis had empirically tested their insights and that the Upanishads were thus accounts of the experiences of ancient yogis. Debendranath Tagore felt that the ancient rishis wanted each of us to realize these truths and confirm them experientially. Truth is therefore not to be found by reading any text; it is to be *experienced,* which in turn confirms what the text states.

Hacker and his followers claim that even though mystical traditions proliferated in Bengal at the time, Debendranath Tagore's important ideas derived from modern European thought. Tagore sought Indian equivalents for the Western principles of self-certainty and common sense.[24] In Hacker's view, Tagore reversed the priority established by the sage Kumarila and other orthodox commentators: self-evidence and intuition became primary sources, and the Vedic texts became secondary. Western empiricism had helped Tagore formulate his ideas of mystical empiricism, according to which spiritual truths must be empirically verified through spiritual experience. However, Tagore rejected the Western notion that empiricism is limited to the senses, believing instead that experience can transcend sensory limits. This idea later entered into the thinking of other Indians.

Hacker acknowledges that Vivekananda was deeply immersed in mystical experience and that 'through mystical experience, Narendra [i.e., Vivekananda] learned that there was indeed religious experience in the form of direct experience of the religious object as something real'.[25] As I shall show in Chapter 6, Vivekananda's emphasis on direct experience has become Rambachan's weapon for attacking him.

Hacker claims that the twentieth-century philosopher Sarvepalli Radhakrishnan also developed neo-Hinduism in this direction that departed from tradition. Radhakrishnan allegedly went on to reformulate Vedanta by borrowing ideas of mysticism from the American philosopher William James along with other great Christian and Muslim mystics. Hacker writes:

> Like William James, however, Radhakrishnan pits experience against dogma. Hindu sages, mystics, and doctors, on the contrary, have ordinarily been quite dogmatic in their outlook. So it would be hard to disprove that in Radhakrishnan's philosophy the primacy of experience was only secondarily connected with ideas of the Hindu tradition.[26]

Thus, in Hacker's analysis, Radhakrishnan inverts the priority between sruti and experience from the order found in *Mimamsa* philosophy. For him, experience ranks higher than sruti.[27]

Allegation 2: 'Tat Tvam Asi' ethic

Swami Vivekananda's innovation, which he called 'Practical Vedanta', was meant to address the needs of his time using Vedanta principles. One such practical application was in the realm of ethics. Since we know that we are all inseparable from Brahman, we should therefore spontaneously love and care for others. Sharing love with others expands our being and helps us transcend the limited, individualized ego. This is the ethic of altruism that helps us rise above negative conditioning. It also forms the basis for unity-in-diversity insofar as one's self is manifested in every creature and in every entity. Before Vivekananda, the German philosopher Arthur Schopenhauer had proposed such a system of ethics in which he cited Hindu texts for support. He used the Upanishadic notion 'tat tvam asi' to assert that a good person recognizes that his self is the same as that which is manifested in every other person, and this notion grounded his ethics.

Hacker harshly disputes that this approach to ethics is in any way in alignment with traditional Vedanta. He claims that 'tat tvam asi' originally referred to the merging of the individual self with the ultimate Self, i.e., Brahman. It was not a prescription for achieving a certain ethical attitude toward one's fellow human beings. Hacker argues extensively that the ethics in the Upanishads and the Bhagavad-Gita are different from what Vivekananda, under Western influence, had construed them to be. In Hacker's view, the original Vedanta idea of ethics was introverted and intended only as an aid in achieving moksha, and not for action in the external world. This original conception of ethics did not serve any social purpose or support any nationalistic activism; instead it caused Indians to be apathetic and socially uninterested. Hacker claimed that Vedantic monism 'has explicitly banished all volition and all action to the realm of the unreal'. Schopenhauer's reinterpretation was a serious mistake, he argued.[28]

Hacker does not spare Gandhian ethics, asserting that Gandhi's principle of ahimsa was borrowed from Christianity's teaching of loving one's neighbour as oneself:

Gandhi's notion of ahimsa had some aspects which are foreign to the Hindu tradition. First, he made ahimsa a norm for political action which it had never been in the Hindu past. Second, he extended the meaning of ahimsa so as to include selflessness, goodwill toward all life, and even charity in the broadest sense, including of one's enemy. It is clearly the Christian ideal of love of one's neighbour which Gandhi denoted by the old Hindu term. In the traditional doctrine, ahimsa had the purely negative meaning of abstention from killing or injuring living beings.[29]

Hacker contends that Gandhi's foremost follower, Vinoba Bhave, advocated altruism and helping the needy and that he based these values solely on ideas that had been imported from Christianity into Hinduism.

To make his case, Hacker quotes the Gita's statements on ethics but conveniently omits the fifth chapter of the text where Krishna instructs Arjuna in the practical importance of taking action. Verse 7 of that chapter refers to *sarva-bhutatma-bhutatma,* which means one who has attained identity with all the selves of the world. Verses 18-20 extol one who is established in unity-consciousness and sees every creature with an equal eye. Verse 25 explains that such a person takes delight in bringing good to all creatures. So it is incorrect to say that such an ethic was lacking prior to colonialism.

Yet Hacker insists that *only* after Schopenhauer did the neo-Hindus formulate the idea that one must have an ethical attitude toward another person because we are all essentially one. Prior to this adulteration in the nineteenth century, he claims, Vedanta lacked ethics. According to him, 'non-dualism ethics' is a 'logical impossibility' and a 'monstrosity'.[30] He refers to this as a 'distortion' that is being called the 'tat tvam asi ethic', and considers it to be derivative thinking. Hacker claims that through this invention propagated largely by Ramakrishna Mission, action 'acquired … an intrinsic value' in Hinduism that it never had before. He concludes:

It is understandable, then, that the pseudo-Vedantic ethic became widespread. It is also understandable that in the urgency of the situation no one should have paused to consider whether this ethic was traceable to historical Vedanta, and whether it fitted the nature of Vedanta as a monism of consciousness.[31]

Another German Indologist, Paul Deussen, one of Schopenhauer's most important followers, is credited with having directly inspired Vivekananda into the practical interpretation of Vedanta. Hacker makes of him the 'smoking gun' which ties the thought of Vivekananda directly to Western influences. Hacker cites what Deussen had said in Bombay,

> The Gospels quite correctly establish as the highest law of morality, 'Love your neighbour as yourselves.' But why should I do so since by the order of nature I feel pain and pleasure only in myself, not in my neighbour? The answer is not in the Bible ... but in the Veda, in the great formula 'That art Thou', which gives in three words the combined sum of metaphysics and morals. You should love your neighbour as yourselves because you *are* your neighbour. [Emphasis mine][32]

Hacker alleges Vivekananda copied this interpretation from Deussen who in turn had learned it from Schopenhauer. Hacker even claims to know the precise date when Vivekananda appropriated the idea, though he could not cite concrete evidence that Vivekananda was aware of Deussen's ideas. Hacker writes that 'Vivekananda became the first Indian exponent of the pseudo-Vedantic *tat-tvam-asi* ethic.'[33] He then criticizes many other neo-Hindus for adopting a practical, positive approach to Advaita for worldly life.[34]

My response is that even if Vivekananda got this from Deussen, it would not change the fact that the idea lies within Hindu text; after all, Schopenhauer and Deussen explicitly referred to Hindu texts (and only to Hindu texts) when they explained this idea. So whether contemporary Hindus got the idea on their own, or whether it was triggered by Deussen, the conclusion would remain the same, namely, that the idea resides in Vedanta texts. Furthermore, Hacker conveniently sidesteps Deussen's explicit comment that the philosophical explanation for loving one's neighbour as oneself is not to be found in the Bible but in the Upanishads!

Allegation 3: Nationalist agenda

As a result of bringing ethics into Vedanta, Hacker argues, a dramatic shift came about that also helped bolster nationalism. Vivekananda taught the socio-political implications of his new Advaita: that once man realizes his identity with Brahman, this identity will give him boundless confidence and power, making him 'capable of working efficiently for the spiritual recovery of India, and [bringing] about a national reconstruction'.[35] One reason this might have upset Hacker is that he was rooted in Christian fundamentalism, and Vivekananda's Practical Vedanta had dampened the fire of Christian proselytizers.

Hacker also attacks the concept of dharma, as taught by Vivekananda, claiming that this was a distortion and reinterpretation by Bankim Chandra Chatterjee and various others in the nineteenth century. He accuses them of appropriating Christian concepts to construct dharma as a category that can compete against Western notions of religious egalitarianism and social justice. In his essay 'The Concept of Dharma in Neo-Hinduism', Hacker argues that modern Western ideas such as positivism (from Comte and Mill), and scepticism and agnosticism (from Hume and Comte), have been appropriated by Indians in such a way as to show neo-Hinduism's superiority to Christianity.

He explains how a lot of Sanskrit words acquired new meanings under Western influence, citing examples from the publications of Gita Press in India. In particular, he asserts that the term 'dharma' has been 'reinterpreted according to Western models', adding that 'scarcely a trace of the old concept of dharma is left in this doctrine'. In Hacker's view, 'only the word "dharma" is left'.[36] He elaborates:

The efforts of Neo-Hinduism to develop a new concept of dharma are an attempt, using principles borrowed from European positivism and modernism, to find a new norm for ethical and social relationships, such as traditional Hinduism had in its countless rules of dharma—a new norm, expressing both the essence of the national religion as it is interpreted today, and the requirements of a new age.[37]

Furthermore, in order to downplay the rigidity of birth-based caste, these neo-Hindus reinterpreted the Gita to shift from the physical to the mental sphere and thereby replace caste with inner qualities. Hacker insists that caste and traditional notions of duty are the areas in which neo-Hinduism departs from tradition most freely, again, under Western influence. He argues that Sri Aurobindo (and later, under his influence, Radhakrishnan) redefined dharma as social activism and *svadharma* (or 'one's own' dharma), in accordance with the Western sense of personality. Hacker is scornfully dismissive of these understandings, asserting with magisterial certainty that all traditional Hindus 'know very well' the opposite: that svadharma is completely determined by caste and stage of life and ultimately by karma. Neo-Hindus, he claims, are completely out of touch with their traditions and have 'no active or living connection' with them.

The Bhagavad-Gita's idea of dharma was reinterpreted in such a way as to contradict the traditional notion of dharma, and this involved a shift in the notion of svadharma. The original idea had been based on boundaries with respect to castes and stages of life, which did not work in modern times and was seen as an obstacle to achieving unity. Therefore, nationalists reinterpreted svadharma so that its basis became individual qualities and not birth. The newly formulated dharma then became increasingly individualistic in accordance with Western ideals and got turned into the version of svadharma advocated by Sri Aurobindo, Radhakrishnan, Gandhi, and their followers.

Hacker fails to consider that *varna* (not 'caste', which is a term that was imported by Portuguese colonizers and was absent in Indian traditions) is based on the *guna* theory of the *Samkhya* system. According to this theory, varna is the psychological makeup of individuals based on the mixture of the three gunas present in that person, and this mixture, in turn, is determined by the person's own karma. A person who goes beyond the three gunas is called *trigunatita*, and he or she is essentially a yogi; a yogi has no varna or caste.

Allegation 4: Inclusivism and sameness

There is an aspect of Vivekananda's thought that has been termed 'inclusivism'. It is the insistence that Hinduism contains or anticipates all that is good in disparate religious points of view. Inclusivism is criticized on two grounds by Hacker. First, neo-Hindu inclusiveness is the tendency to appropriate everything good from disparate Indian traditions that had been fragmented and disunited, and label it Hindu. Prior to these neo-Hindus, he claims, there was no such tendency and hence the various fragments were never unified.

Halbfass defines 'inclusivism' as the 'model, which presents other, competing religious and philosophical views as being ultimately included in one's own'.[38] He notes that Shankara manages to avoid the worst pitfalls of inclusivism, concluding that 'Sankara is obviously aware of the relativistic dangers in using the inclusivist model and the potentially confusing effects ...'. In other words, inclusivism is not evident in Shankara's approach. Halbfass supports Hacker's claim that inclusivism is a new device created to bring fictional unity to Hinduism which had been absent.

Hacker criticizes neo-Hinduism for its tendency for accommodation, easy compromise, and assimilation. Halbfass explains: 'What he [Hacker] is ultimately concerned about is [neo-Hinduism's] distinction from the Christian approach to other religions, which presupposes, in his view, a clear recognition of others in their otherness.'[39] Hacker therefore rejects the 'doctrinal tolerance' in India. Inclusivism, in his view, is 'typically Indian'.

The second problem is fear that inclusivism poses a threat to Christianity. Hacker, on the one hand, admires Indian openness and writes: 'Yes, there is something to learn for us. We should be put to shame by the Indian openness for religion which is still very much alive in our days.'[40] But he prefers Christianity's clear delineation of boundaries between itself and others and repeatedly argued in favour of open confrontation, and genuine acknowledgement of the otherness of Hinduism (as perceived through a Western lens). In short, he prefers openly acknowledged differences to attempts at finding sameness.

Hacker thinks Vivekananda was advocating inclusivism in the worst way when he spoke about the 'infinite arms' of Vedanta, which would in theory be able to embrace and include all present and future developments in science, religion and philosophy.[41] Hacker found this threatening and argued that neo-Hinduism is more open than traditional Hinduism and hence more assimilative and dangerous.

Hacker further asserts that neo-Hindus have claimed that their Vedanta is the ultimate level to which all religions eventually evolve and that all faiths will be united within it. He considers this view of Vedanta as only superficially tenable and so vague as to cause it to lose all distinction. The pioneers of neo-Hinduism claim that all religions are equally valid paths that lead to the same goal. Hacker speaks scornfully and sarcastically of such a notion.[42]

I agree with this particular criticism by Hackers and others in his camp. It is inaccurate to say that all faiths lead to the same goal. There are serious differences in their perceptions of the human problem and in the goals to which they aspire. This artificially imposed sameness is a disservice both to Hindus and to the adherents of other faiths. I have explained this point in considerable detail in *Being Different* and will return to it in the Conclusion.

4

Agehananda Bharati on Neo-Hinduism as a 'Pizza Effect'

A European convert to Hinduism who took formal vows as a sannyasin, Agehananda Bharati (Leopold Fischer) was an influential scholar. He was fluent in German and clearly influenced by Hacker's writings. The shift in his thinking on contemporary Hinduism into a negative direction occurs in his widely influential paper, 'the Hindu Renaissance and its Apologetic Patterns', published in the *Journal of Asian Studies* in 1970.[1] There he targets the contemporary Hinduism movement as a purely political and artificial fabrication, calling it 'the linguistic medium of the modern Indian apologetic'.

Echoing Hacker, Bharati insists that this new brand of Hinduism is inauthentic and disconnected from the past. He writes that it 'is neither what the scriptures of the commentators say, nor what the villagers and the pandits may aver'. He considers contemporary Hindus 'to be "marginally relevant"'.[2] He further alleges that 'the modal attitude of the [Hindu] Renaissance is anti-scholarly and anti-intellectual' and devoid of scholarly dialogue within the Indian tradition. Bharati uses the same two-pronged attack as Hacker: he criticizes contemporary Hindus both for imitating Westerners and for deviating from their own traditions to become modern.

Pizza Effect: Indians copy Westerners

One of the lasting influences of this article by Bharati is his coining of the phrase 'Pizza Effect' which has gained considerable currency. He explains the metaphor as follows:

> The original pizza was a simple, hot-baked bread without any trimmings, the staple of the Calabrian and Sicilian contadini from whom well over 90% of all Italo-Americans descend. After World War I, a highly elaborated dish, the U.S. pizza of many sizes, flavors, and hues, made its way back to Italy with visiting kinsfolk from America. The term and the object have acquired a new meaning and a new status, as well as many new tastes in the land of its origin, not only in the south, but throughout the length and width of Italy.[3]

Bharati uses this concept to claim that the scientific approach and terminology used by contemporary Hindus is an instance of the Pizza Effect, i.e., Indians adopting Western concepts but giving them Sanskrit names. Though drawing on the ancient language, these are, in Bharati's view, 'true neologisms', invented by Western Indologists and then copied and re-marketed by Indian scholars who displace the old pandits with this newly minted coinage that is now in vogue in the Indian legislature, media and educational institutions.[4]

The Pizza Effect, according to Bharati, accounts for the popularity of Maharishi Mahesh Yogi and Swami Vivekananda, among modern Indians. Bharati writes: 'Mahesh Yogi's attraction for his Indian disciples derived from the pizza-effect, as did Vivekananda's and the other swamis' who had inspired Western audiences, and who made it known in India that they had done so.'[5]

Furthermore, the contemporary Hindu work ethic has been appropriated from Western norms, he alleges. While Gandhi did stress the dignity of physical work, citing the Gita's promulgation of karma yoga, Bharati cites another scholar and writes that 'respect for physical work is a purely Western import, like so many ideological items'.[6]

One of the most significant claims of the neo-Hinduism thesis is that Gandhi and others followed the lead of Western Indologists in their praise for the Bhagavad-Gita. It was the British who gave it the stature of 'the Hindu Bible' when it previously had no such stature. Bharati remarks that the Gita is *smriti* (human-constructed), not *sruti* (authorless), but that neo-Hinduism makes it seem canonical. He claims that it was only when Gandhi read this text in English translation in London, and not in his Vaisnava childhood, that he made it the center of his political creed. 'Historically seen, the suzerain status ascribed to it is another paradigm of the pizza-effect', Bharati remarks, crediting the English translation of Annie Besant for educating Gandhi on the Gita.[7]

Bharati sees the same Pizza Effect in the case of Balgangadhara Tilak (1856-1920), one of the first leaders of Indian nationalism, who he alleges was merely copying the Europeans' glorification of the Gita when he drew on it for inspiration. Bharati insists that Tilak made the Gita prominent in his work only because of its prestige among Western orientalists, and that he deliberately suppressed mention of its final message, which 'extolls' bhakti (devotion) and *prapatti* (surrender), rather than action, per se. This gives the Gita 'chauvinistic underpinnings', says Bharati.[8]

He claims that Wilhelm von Humboldt's praise of the Gita calling it the 'profoundest and most sublime [text] which the world had to show' had influenced Tilak's choice of it, as did the praise given by Warren Hastings and several other Europeans. This revaluation of the text shows the Pizza Effect at work; had it not been for European praise, the Gita would not have enjoyed such a high stature among Indians.

Bharati ignores the fact that long before any European exerted influence, many important Hindu thinkers, such as Shankara, Ramanuja and Vallabha, had written commentaries on the Gita. Hence its importance is hardly a European gift.

Hinduism deviates from Indian tradition

Bharati sharpens his attack on contemporary Hinduism by creating a wedge between traditional sadhus and the modern 'scientific sadhu' of which Swami Vivekananda is, according to him, an exemplar. Bharati insists that contemporary Hindus reject past sadhus; he claims that they make the traditional ritual specialists into scapegoats for all that is wrong with India. He alleges the traditional sadhu is seen as a 'worthless parasite' whose sole aim is to 'nurture and perpetuate outdated traditions and anti-scientific attitudes, in order to preserve his place in society, as one who feeds off people without working'.

In other words, neo-Hindus are said to have reinvented the idea of sadhu in a modern, scientific light, with Vivekananda as the prototype, in order to measure up to Western norms, while the real sadhus of the past get rejected and blamed for various problems.[9] Bharati writes that monks who identify with contemporary Hinduism see themselves as different from other sadhus. In his view, they are not 'that sort of sadhu' because 'the modern [Hindu] apologetic does not see them as part of sadhuism'.[10]

I disagree with this assessment. Traditional sadhus are not hated by contemporary Hindus. Quite the contrary; contemporary Hindus are often in awe of them and seek out traditional sadhus for rituals. Their reduced numbers are due to secularism's reallocation of priorities in education and funding, and not due to hatred by practising Hindus.

Bharati's antipathy for what he perceives as the mistaken cult of Vivekananda is clear from the manner in which he explains the latter's popularity:

Yet, all 'modernites' overtly or covertly admire and venerate the 'scientific', 'modern' man who wears monastic robes: Swami Vivekananda is an undisputed culture-hero not simply of all modern Bengali Hindus when they reflect on their heritage; his photogenic poses adorn the walls of homes, theatres, tea shops, and offices of the subcontinent, as well as many Hindu homes in Africa and Southeast Asia.[11]

He even criticizes the continued popularity of mantras that Vivekananda stressed, such as *'om purnamadah ... purnamudacyate'* and seems vexed that no other mantras have been deployed to take their place since that time.[12]

He is bothered by the amount of respect modern Indians give such leaders: 'To my knowledge', he says, 'no Indian political leader has ever tried to downgrade Vivekananda, Aurobindo, Sivananda either overtly or covertly.'[13] But, I wonder, why on earth *should* they attempt to downgrade these major figures?

Bharati also regards those Indians who teach Indian philosophy in English as suffering from the Pizza Effect insofar as they merely repeat what has been learned from European Indologists. Even the famous Radhakrishnan is dismissed as one of the many Indian 'chroniclers' of the modern Hindu movement, who rewrite and teach what European Indologists had already formulated about Hinduism.[14]

Fear of sexual impotence drives neo-Hindus

Bharati suggests a much deeper psychological cause of this Hindu reform movement which draws in millions of modern, Westernized Indians. He theorizes it is the Hindu fear of sexual impotence that accounts for it.

In a passage so strange as to be comical, Bharati writes that the source of this new movement lies in Hindus' fear of loss of power, 'epitomized by the fear of the loss of semen'.[15] He suggests that recent scholars are 'alert' to this 'reality'.[16] He refers here to a number of recent highly sexualized and Freudian readings of *Tantra* which are themselves misguided, to say the least. What he refers to as 'reality' is a Western psychological fixation strangely projected onto Indian traditions. Here is Bharati on the subject:

> Historically, this syndrome is not new at all—Patanjali and the classical yoga spoke of ojas, a sort of hierogenetic power residing in, or embodied by, the semen which has not been shed. Recently, scholars of very different interests have become alert to this all-India

syndrome, shared by Hindus and non-Hindus, but no doubt derived
from a Hindu matrix ... If we want to use psychologisms, it can no
doubt be said that the Hindu 'cathects his libido on his semen'.[17]

Bharati's definition of neo-Hinduism tenets

The entrance of European ideas into India, as Bharati describes it, caused
contemporary Hindus to become alienated from their own tradition,
and this in turn shaped the Hindu reform movement that he calls neo-
Hinduism. He offers the following characterization which is similar
in spirit to that of Hacker and concerns the beliefs of contemporary
Hindus. The words he puts into the mouths of contemporary Hindus
are worth quoting at length:

India has forgotten her marvelous past; this past contained not only
material and cultural wealth, it also offered a complete solution of
all problems of the individual and of society. There is nothing—
material, spiritual, or cultural—which ancient India has not brought
forth. All this was lost, partly through the apathy of her people,
partly through hostile conquest from outside. India was the home
of perfect men—men who owned wealth and renounced it for the
quest of wisdom and purity. The modern world—the West, that
is—has usurped the things India has lost. India has to go to the
West to learn its techniques ... [Although] these techniques were
borrowed they echo ... what had long been lost in India. In matters
of the spirit, India has retained its superiority—the West has failed,
it has misused its powers. India now can and should have both the
worlds: She can learn the tricks of the West, but she must live the
teachings of perfection as only her ancients knew it. Hence, the
man who lives and preaches these truths in a new language must
be sought out and honored. What is the gist of those total-solution
yielding teachings? It is all contained in the Vedas and in the Gita,
it is all in the words of Vivekananda, Aurobindo, Sivananda, etc.:
All religions are one, and the theological differences, the varying
concepts of God are unimportant; yet, of all these concepts, the

Indian concept is the noblest and the most profound; it is the most 'scientific,' it is universal. Society is corrupt: The Indian social system is bad, because misinterpretations and willful manipulations of the ancient lore have made India a slave to its divisive tendencies—the true teachings of India deny divisions, deny caste by birth, and teach that one must live in the world and yet seek the truth which is hidden beneath the modern Indian's diffidence. To this final quest everything is of secondary importance—yet, because karma yoga is the call of the day, Indians must cast off their slothfulness and achieve the divine through active social engagement.[18]

I, too, criticize such views of Hindus for their chauvinism and reduction into sameness. But Bharati caricatures all contemporary Hinduism this way, and ends up throwing out the baby with the bathwater. He ignores the centuries of thought and reflection that led up to the latest Hindu thinking, as will be explained in Chapters 8, 9, 10 and 11.

5

Ursula King's Bridge from Hacker to Rambachan

noted in earlier chapters how Hacker (in Germany) started the
initiative to undermine and de-legitimize contemporary Hinduism and
its founder, Swami Vivekananda, how Halbfass (in the U.S.) sponsored
and promoted his work to bring it into mainstream academics, and
how Agehananda Bharati (also U.S.-based) fuelled it beyond the limited
circle of Indologists. This chapter explains how this thesis spread widely
into the academic circles well beyond a small coterie of Indologists of
Germanic ethnicity.

The scholar who provided this push was Ursula King, based in
Britain. Her role is especially important for a number of reasons.
She did not merely restate Hacker's thesis in her own words; rather,
she deepened the claim that the prevailing ideas on karma yoga, as
commonly taught in Hinduism, are of recent origin since they differ
significantly from the way karma was traditionally interpreted in Hindu
texts. She also sharpened the formulation of 'neo-Hinduism' as a new
religion, citing its indebtedness to the Europeanized ideas transmitted
in the nineteenth century.

Before discussing King's work on neo-Hinduism, I wish to point out that I first started studying her writings in an entirely different context. One of the major thinkers I have researched for my ongoing work on Westerners' appropriation and subsequent rejection of Indian thought (a phenomenon I call the 'U-Turn') is the Catholic theologian, Teilhard de Chardin.

It was as a result of reading King's 1981 book on Teilhard that I learnt that he had travelled to India, studied Ramanuja (an Indian philosopher in the eleventh and the twelfth centuries), and appropriated many ideas from Hinduism to formulate his own, now famous though unorthodox, Christian theology.

I decided to write about what he learnt from Hinduism and how his followers today are in denial of that important influence. Thus, in my early experience of reading her, King was one of the foremost scholars championing Teilhard's theology while drawing attention to its Indian influences. I found it ironic, then, that her later work on Hinduism had shifted to undermine the very tradition from which her hero, Teilhard, derived so many of his ideas for the enrichment of modern Christianity.

There are three major works in which King critiques contemporary Hinduism. She wrote the first of these—'True and perfect religion: Bankim Chandra Chatterjee's reinterpretation of Hinduism'—in 1977, in an attempt to show how the Bengali thinker had appropriated Western Enlightenment ideas and Christianity into his own proposals for a new Hinduism. In 1980, King expanded Hacker's and Bharati's thesis about contemporary karma yoga being a new construction which deviates from the tradition. This is the central thesis of her paper 'Who is the ideal karmayogin?' In 1989, her next paper 'Some Reflections on Sociological Approaches to the Study of Modern Hinduism' solidified the view that contemporary Hinduism was a socio-political construction.

Needless to say, King references Hacker's writings in German on the same subject and amplifies them, making them available to English-speaking academics before Halbfass's volume of English translations of Hacker's works came out in 1995.

King starts her 1977 article by pointing out that Bankim Chandra Chatterjee's work is a cornerstone of the movement which she believes can rightly be called 'neo-Hinduism'. 'We have here a precisely dated example', she writes, 'of the transformation of traditional Hinduism', where, under the influence of a new culture, 'past elements are selectively emphasized and related to new ideas arising in a different context'.[1]

According to King, Chatterjee is intimately familiar with major Western thinkers, and under their influence he reinterpreted Hinduism using Western notions of the social, the historical, and the scientific. She notes that his fundamental principles were mainly taken from Comtean and Utilitarian writings. Chatterjee follows late nineteenth-century liberal Protestantism, which presents Jesus as the perfect and ideal man, divested of all supernatural features and hence seen as natural and scientific. This view of Jesus was compatible with the Vedas and the philosophical schools of India, which she insists do not support any notion of a personal God.[2] And so Chatterjee needed to put ideas about Jesus in Hindu clothing in order to reinvent Hinduism.

As King tells the story, Chatterjee saw himself as positioned between the wholesale acceptance of Hinduism by the Indian masses and the wholesale rejection of it by the Anglicized Bengali intelligentsia. He wanted to invent a new Hinduism that could be positioned between extreme forms of traditionalism and Westernization, so he selected Krishna as the only authentic avatar who possessed all the qualities needed for the human quest. He claimed Krishna possessed them to a greater degree than Buddha or Christ or Muhammad or any other religious figure. The personality of Krishna became a vehicle through which Chatterjee could incorporate whatever qualities of the ideal person he imported from Western influences.

Even though Bankim Chatterjee's ideas did not get turned into an institution similar to the Ramakrishna Mission, they had a long-term impact, writes King. In his universalization of the dharma, his emphasis on the Bhagavad-Gita as a call to action, and his celebration of God as Mother, he paved the way for later reformers to make Hinduism available to both east and west. King says Chatterjee influenced such different figures as Tagore, Vivekananda, and particularly Aurobindo, who she thinks took the concept of the Divine as Mother from him.[3]

King goes into great historical detail to argue that, 'works from Western sociology, philosophy, and theology were an important factor in [Chatterjee's] re-interpretation of Hinduism which helped to lay the foundations for a Hindu revival'.[4] She accuses Chatterjee, just as Hacker accuses Vivekananda, of changing traditional dharma from being merely an obligation to one's family and caste to becoming an obligation to society, one's country, and the entire world.

Her most innovative claim is that starting with Vivekananda and continuing with Radhakrishnan, Gandhi and others, a new ethic called 'karma yoga' was formulated by restating Western liberal values and ethics using Sanskrit terminology.

King credits Christian missionaries with having inspired the new definition of karma: 'Under the influence of Christian missionaries, the idea that *karma = seva* (understood as social duty and service to others) was articulated earlier in the nineteenth century.'[5] She points out that at first the idea of karma was only ritualistic and referred specifically to the sacrificial actions prescribed by the Vedas; only later, in the Gita, did it come to mean performing one's duties according to caste. Traditionally, the position of the karmayogin was secondary to that of the jnannayogin, who achieves moksha by withdrawing from the world. In modern times, she concludes:

> The Bhagavad-Gita has so displaced the orthodox vedic scriptures, at least in popular thought and practice, that some speak of a new Hindu orthodoxy based on the modern interpretations of what is now considered to be the central message of the Bhagavad-Gita. … Although karma means more than merely ritual action in the Bhagavad-Gita, karma yoga as path of human action is still closely confined there by the limits laid down by the traditional varnashrama-dharma system.[6]

King is willing to admit that the Gita is open to multiple interpretations. The Gita, she says, did not define the karmayogin precisely because it vacillated as to who exactly he was supposed to be, which allows for a great deal of philosophical and ethical engagement with modern views. In fact, she says, the idea of karma is now sometimes so widened as to lose all specific content as formerly circumscribed and defined by the shastras (texts). The idea of karma as understood today is not found in traditional Hinduism, she alleges.[7]

King identifies Vivekananda as the pioneer of this re-formulation of karma and claims he recognized his own departure from tradition. She feels he departed under Western influence, probably during his three years of travel to the West (1893-1896). She notes that he developed the concept of karma yoga first in his lectures to Western audiences.[8] She summarizes his views thus:

> The human goal of perfection is now seen in the path of action, understood as duty but achieved without bondage to the fruits of action. Such action, performed in the spirit of devotion and sacrifice, is real renunciation. That is the true meaning of the message of the ideal karmayogin who is none other than Krishna on the battlefield at Kurukshetra, especially as portrayed in the second and third chapters of the Bhagavad-Gita. Quite contrary to the accepted view of the past, the traditional path of renunciation is now considered to be inferior to the path of action.[9]

King further claims that both karma yoga and jnana yoga are modern inventions by neo-Hindus, with the former meant for Indians and the latter intended for Westerners, and that neither is authentic to the tradition, which is primarily bhakti, or devotion, oriented.[10]

She goes on to echo Bharati in saying the Gita had not been so popular before colonial influence but that neo-Hindus have made it mainstream today. Unlike the earlier, world-negating emphasis of Hinduism, this newly interpreted Gita emphasizes the

> active, world-affirming teaching of the ideal karmayogin, symbolized by Krishna teaching at Kurukshetra. This extraordinary emphasis given to the Krishna-figure and his partly new, actively

understood message of karmayoga, blended with the age-old bhakti tradition of the Indian masses, has become the mainspring of an activist and theistic Neo-Hinduism of the present.[11]

Even the iconographic image of Krishna depicting him as karmayogin on the battlefield of Kurukshetra is modern, according to King. She claims this image was not found in earlier art wherein Krishna is depicted in a bhakti context only. The modern depiction was used on the cover of Sri Aurobindo's weekly review *Karmayogin* in early twentieth-century Calcutta. Sister Nivedita continued this publication in which 'religious and political nationalism are closely intertwined', says King.[12] The publication and its reprints became a major political influence and hence the Gita got utilized for social and political activism. In Chapter 9, I respond to King's view of karma yoga as being a Western-inspired invention, and I do so by showing its pre-colonial origins.

King concurs with Bharati in asserting that Gandhi read the Gita for the first time in England in 1888-89, and she references Bharati's analysis, noting that the British influence led Gandhi to a consideration of karma yoga as being the central message of the Gita. She summarizes her own thesis on the origins of contemporary karma yoga:

> The changed emphasis on karma yoga as an ideal path of action for individual and society has come about through the socio-cultural transformations of the nineteenth and twentieth centuries and is given religious legitimation through certain passages of the Bhagavad-Gita. The adaptation of traditional teachings to modern needs allows for the development of a dynamic spirituality, at least partly new, which preaches the ethic of work and service as a form of worship leading to liberation. The symbol of the karmayogin brings together and fuses into one the classical Krishna of the Bhagavad-Gita with the puranic Krishna of myths and legends as well as with exemplary religious figures of the present.[13]

She goes on to say that the choice of Krishna himself is contradictory to this myth, for the Krishna of the Gita remains outside of the action and engages only in philosophical dialogue about it. She claims, too, that in traditional Hinduism there are contradictions between the ideals of the householder and those of the ascetic.[14]

As for the Gita's call to action, she says it applies only to the *Kshatriya*, or warrior caste, and not to human beings as a whole. Hence, teaching karma and using the Gita to support this teaching are modern fabrications by neo-Hindus. King explains that neo-Hinduism's image of God includes a new message of grace which is inspired by Christianity. She credits the Europeans for such new ideas through their translations of the Gita and asserts that this scripture would not be important in India today were it not for India's contact with the West.[15]

King ends her 1989 paper by proclaiming that the study of neo-Hinduism as a radically new kind of religion with political implications needs to be researched and that she intends to map the territory that such research should cover. She makes it clear that she belongs to the current consensus which sees no unity or coherence in Hinduism as a religion. She writes,

> Instead of seeing Hinduism as a religious system, it would perhaps be more accurate to view it as a multi-dimensional socio-religious process which has undergone some radical transformations over the last hundred years and continues to change, providing in turn a basis for the religious legitimation of large-scale social and cultural change.[16]

King asserts that Hinduism itself is a vague term that is 'heuristically almost useless for analysis'. It is 'primarily not a religious concept, but one of geographical origin'.[17] Before 'Hinduism' came into use, the natives of India referred only to *sampradayas* (lineages), which were orthodox and narrowly defined. As King sees it, there was no central, church-like authority that might ensure that Hinduism qualified as a proper religion.

Like Bharati, she believes considerable inspiration came from the Protestant Reformation in Europe and its aftermath, in which neo-Hindus had been educated. This strong Protestant influence led to sweeping changes which included a shift from the search for otherworldly liberation to the reform of Indian society, coupled with a prescriptive approach to Hinduism influenced by Western models. She concludes:

> In the past, Indian religious reformers had always primarily been concerned with the search for liberation or moksha; the social consequences of their teaching occurred mainly as unintended by-products. By contrast, Hindu reformers of the nineteenth and twentieth centuries consciously planned and willed the reform of Indian society and religion as an end in itself. Hindu writers of this period did not so much describe what Hinduism is but, influenced by a western model of religion, they prescribed what Hinduism ought to be. ... Whereas Hindu religious practices were traditionally local, regional, sectarian, and exclusive, rather than unitary and universal, the search of the reformers concentrated on the unifying elements of the tradition which could be universalised and applied to people all over India, as well as related to religion outside it.[18]

The notion of the unity of the Godhead based on the Upanishads 'would not have been but for the presence of Christianity in India'.[19] While it is true that the Arya Samaj based its ideas on the Vedas, King writes that both it and the Brahmo Samaj were reacting competitively to Christianity by trying to create a church-like institution. Both these nineteenth-century movements were instrumental in reviving Hinduism in their own separate ways. Later on, the Gita was utilized to forge a unified identity that could stand up to the West.

As we shall see in the next chapter, what makes King important, besides her own contributions to the myth of neo-Hinduism, is the fact that she groomed the young Hindu from Trinidad, Anantanand Rambachan, into his present position as one of the main proponents and expositors of the thesis that contemporary Hinduism is merely an inauthentic 'neo-Hinduism'.

6

Rambachan's Argument to Fragment Hinduism

Using Shankara to shoot down Vivekananda

Anantanand Rambachan is perhaps the foremost exponent of the neo-Hinduism theory today, and his influence extends well beyond the academic circles. He was a student of Ursula King; indeed, it was under her guidance that he came to the University of Leeds to write his Ph.D dissertation. It bears the title 'The Attainment of Moksha according to Shankara and Vivekananda with Special Reference to the Significance of Scripture (Sruti) and Experience (Anubhava)',[1] and this forms the foundation for all his subsequent writings.

Since he is arguably the leading scholar in the myth of neo-Hinduism, it is important that we grasp fully his arguments for de-legitimizing Swami Vivekananda and other leaders of contemporary

Hinduism. A scholar of high reputation, he has devoted much of his life to defending what he takes to be the real and authentic Vedanta tradition, and to lowering the legitimacy of Swami Vivekananda in the process. He is influenced by Halbfass and Hacker, and cites the former approvingly as saying that Vivekananda should be 'demythologized'.[2] Unlike many who parrot the myth of neo-Hinduism only for political reasons or to be fashionable, Rambachan has a scholarly case to make. It is, however, a case against which I argue forcefully.

Since 1985, Rambachan has been a professor of religion, philosophy and Asian studies at St. Olaf College in Minnesota, which is affiliated with the Evangelical Lutheran Church of America. He is the author of several books, all of which develop, in different ways, the thesis under discussion. He is heralded as the official Hindu spokesperson in several powerful international bodies, and for more than twenty five years he has been hoisted as the voice of Hinduism in interreligious dialogue at various national and international gatherings. For example, he is active in the World Council of Churches, a consortium of Christian organizations, where he was considered the 'Hindu expert' in the last four General Assemblies in Canada, Australia, Zimbabwe and Brazil. He is also a regular participant in the Vatican's Pontifical Council for Interreligious Dialogue; the Vatican considers him its Hindu expert.

Rambachan has served on the Advisory Board of the Centre for Studies in Religion and Society, Victoria University, Canada, and as a member of the Consultation on Population and Ethics. He is currently an advisor to Harvard University's Pluralism Project, a member of the International Advisory Council for the Tony Blair Faith Foundation, and a member of the Theological Education Committee of the American Academy of Religion. In 2008, at the invitation of the Archbishop of Canterbury, he delivered the distinguished Lambeth Lecture at Lambeth Palace, London. As well, he has contributed to the joint UNICEF-Global Network of Religions for Children project. In 1989, the government of Trinidad and Tobago awarded him the Chaconia Gold Medal in recognition of his public service. The British Broadcasting Corporation transmitted a series of twenty-five lectures by him around the world.

Hindus look at Rambachan's career and assume that he is their sympathetic voice in prestigious public forums, representing their views and aspirations. In several respects, he *is* sympathetic. But on closer inspection we can see that, in keeping with Paul Hacker and other leaders of this school of thought, Rambachan characterizes Vivekananda as the architect of an artificial neo-Hinduism that was manufactured under Western influence. He sees Vivekananda as the product of four influences:

1. The Brahmo Samaj project, which sought to Westernize Indians by constructing a contemporary Hinduism that would be scientific, rational, and 'clean' of old embarrassing baggage.
2. The nationalistic movement led by British-educated Indians who valorized Indian history and intellectual traditions, and created a unified Hinduism using primarily European translations and accounts as their source materials.
3. The profound mystical influence of Ramakrishna.
4. The desire to use Sanskrit terms to make Western ideas seem authentically Indian.

Out of these influences was born the new religion which Hacker, Rambachan and others have branded 'neo-Hinduism'. According to Rambachan's thesis, this new religion had little or no basis in tradition and was designed to serve as the backbone of the Indian national movement which later morphed into Hindutva politics. No assessment of Vivekananda by this camp is complete without claiming that India's religious conflicts today may be traced back to Vivekananda's so-called neo-Hinduism.

Rambachan's dissertation repeats statements by Western predecessors that leading Hindu intellectuals of the nineteenth century who influenced Vivekananda had serious doubts about traditional Hinduism (to the point, in some cases, of formally rejecting the authority of the Vedas) and hence they wanted to appropriate Western secular ideas and scientific inquiry.[3]

While other scholars in this genre focused on social, political or historical arguments to make their case, Rambachan was the first amongst the academia (and is still the foremost) to bring forth powerful philosophical arguments in support of this critique.

His main strategy has been to prove that there is a break between the Vedanta traditions of Shankara and Vivekananda, and that these two thinkers contradict each other in ways that are irreconcilable. His case is built on the purported philosophical incompatibility between their respective paths to moksha.[4] Rambachan thus deserves to be considered Hacker's heir. What is ignored by them is that there is a period of over a thousand years between Shankara and Vivekananda, and this period saw many new interpretations of Vedanta without any Western influences. They also fail to situate their issues concerning moksha in the much broader context in which Hindus practise their dharma.

In order to exaggerate the 'conflict' between these two prominent streams of Hindu thought, Rambachan seizes on an old and well-documented debate. The central issue here concerns the status of anubhava or direct realization and its relation to the study of Vedas (sruti) in the writings of Shankara. Given the importance of this philosophical point, I shall summarize it next.

Shankara states that because the *atman* (ultimate self) is free from all limitations, there is no real problem, no suffering, and no *samsara* (world as experienced by the senses), and that therefore we are *already liberated*. Our problem is simply that we do not know or experience ourselves as such. This ignorance is the whole reason for all the suffering, and so *brahmavidya* (knowledge of Brahman) is a state of being and not a solution as there is no *real* problem.

There *is* no problem, as it were, because the atman is self-illuminating awareness and self-evident existence and therefore does not require anything *outside of itself* to reveal itself. It is already present as the very substratum of one's being and sense of self, independently of any cause. Therefore, there is no problem to solve, only the need to remove ignorance and obstacles to brahmavidya, which is what moksha achieves.

Moksha is brought about by merely a 'cognitive shift', and this cannot be caused by any action, be it devotion or work. (The term 'cognitive shift' here does not refer to ordinary cognition but to a realization that indicates a shift in consciousness. It includes intellect but goes beyond intellect to superconsciousness.) The realm of causation cannot touch Brahman because Brahman is un-caused. It is impossible for any action in the limited realm of *samsara* to touch that which is eternal and un-caused and that which transcends samsara. This means that actions such as meditation, bhakti, and so on, are unable to 'cause' liberation.

Rambachan takes this position of Shankara to the extreme. Vivekananda's paths like raja yoga (emphasizing direct higher experience through meditation) and karma yoga are declared flawed by Rambachan because he feels these paths cannot lead to moksha. In other words, most of the paths advocated by Vivekananda and commonly taught today as aspects of Hinduism are within the realm of causation, and causation cannot touch the atman that is already liberated. Hence, the paths of contemporary Hinduism are incapable of resulting in moksha, the final goal. All contemporary Hindu teachers are, therefore, mere 'apologists' rather than legitimate teachers.

In his book the *Limits of Scriptures: Vivekananda's Reinterpretation of the Vedas*, Rambachan also deals with the ancient distinction between sruti and smriti, or, respectively, authorless Vedic texts as distinct from mere human constructions or 'remembered knowledge'. He emphasizes Shankara's position that sruti is primary and necessary in order to arrive at the self-validating source of knowledge. It reveals the already-present Brahman and yields liberation. Thus, in his view, sruti is not ancillary or subordinate but essential to direct experience (anubhava or *pratyaksa pramana*) for gaining knowledge of Brahman. Rambachan contrasts this with Vivekananda's view that sruti, or the Vedas, is subject to verification by experiential knowledge or anubhava. Rambachan considers Vivekananda's emphasis on anubhava to be a radical departure from the position of Shankara.

Rambachan explains the dichotomy in terms of different attitudes to anubhava and sruti. He says that unlike Vivekananda, 'who presented the affirmations of sruti as having only a hypothetical or provisional validity and needing the verification that only anubhava could provide', Shankara, by contrast, 'argued for sruti as the unique and self-valid source of our knowledge of absolute reality (Brahman)'. As I shall explain further in Chapter 10, Shankara's position is not as rigid as Rambachan would have us believe. Shankara has a great deal of respect for yoga; hence he must by implication also respect the anubhava that results from it.

Rambachan posits that Shankara subordinated all ways of knowing to sruti; he held that for the true seeker, moksha is the immediate result of fully understanding the teachings. Vivekananda held rather that sruti is verified by anubhava.[5] Rambachan insists that, 'for a qualified aspirant, nothing beyond a proper investigation of the meaning of those sentences in the sruti revealing Brahman is required'. To highlight the mutual contradiction between these two great Hindu thinkers, he goes on to say:

> If, as in the case of Vivekananda, the knowledge gained from inquiry into the meaning of the sruti lacks certitude and finality and must be confirmed by anubhava for moksha to be achieved, then the attainment of this experience becomes all important since liberation is impossible without it. In Vivekananda ... it is difficult to find an unconditional rationale for the sruti. If on the other hand, as in case of Sankara, the sruti is the valid source of knowledge (pramana) for brahman, the implications are that such knowledge can be neither derived from any other source nor contradicted by another means of knowledge. This knowledge does not need to be validated or confirmed by another source of knowledge. As understood by Sankara, moksha is identical with the nature of the self (atman), which is free from all limitations.[6]

Rambachan further expounds the view that, for Shankara, sruti is not simply a guide to spiritual practice to get the experiential result; it is an end in itself. For Vivekananda, however, 'any knowledge derived from sruti inquiry is not final knowledge'; instead, 'liberating knowledge is derived only through the direct verification afforded by a special experience'.[7]

To recap, Rambachan's contention is that, as per Shankara, a mere understanding of the sruti text is sufficient, that no further effort or realization is necessary or possible for attaining *brahmajnana* (knowledge of Brahman), and that the understanding itself should reveal the already-present Brahman; no meditation, practice, realization or action is mandated to attain liberation or moksha. Furthermore, no path based on anubhava alone is capable of bringing liberation.

While it is true that Shankara does not explicitly suggest anubhava as alternative or valid pramana (means of knowing), Rambachan makes Shankara seem dogmatic by insisting that anubhava is outright rejected. Contrary to what Rambachan would have us believe, Shankara does not interpret the Upanishads as merely analytical reasoning but also as intuitional knowledge. Shankara says that things not within ordinary perception are matters of direct experience of the rishis.

Furthermore, Shankara points out the limitations of sruti, indicating that it only reveals what leads to good acts and what leads to harmful acts. The Upanishad tradition is clear that sruti is informatory, not mandatory commands. Later sections below and all of Chapter 10 will present a more detailed, nuanced analysis of Shankara to show that the split between sruti and direct experience in his thought is far more qualified than Rambachan admits. Vivekananda's position is also more nuanced than Rambachan acknowledges.

Issues with methodology

Rambachan applies a methodology selectively to Vivekananda that draws on an analysis of contemporary socio-historical-political forces to explain how a system of ideas came about. He does not, however, apply the same reductive method to Shankara. In other words, Vivekananda's ideas are not examined as philosophical truth-claims within the broad spectrum of Hindu philosophy, but are rather seen as mere projections of, and masks for, social and political agendas of nationalism. For example, Rambachan is quick to assume that it was the attempt to impress Unitarians in the West (for reasons of personal and national pride) that induced Vivekananda to downgrade the scriptures and upgrade experiential realization. But as I shall explain, the experiential approach (anubhava) is old and deeply-rooted in Indian traditions.

Long before colonialism, there were numerous Indian thinkers and schools that advocated ideas similar to those of Vivekananda, but Rambachan ignores them all in order to credit European influence alone for giving birth to contemporary Hinduism.

What Vivekananda did was to harmonize various interpretations of Vedanta that had emanated from the Vedic source. His goal was to make the Vedas accessible to commoners without the need for a great deal of sophistication or without having to choose a specific lineage.

Rambachan does not approach Shankara the same way, but makes him an absolute criterion of orthodoxy as if he were independent of similar influences. He does not consider that many of Shankara's writings were in the socio-political context of debating Buddhists and the Samkhya dualists. Hence, the same kind of social influence could also be brought into the examination of Shankara as Rambachan applies to interpret Vivekananda. In short, Rambachan applies a double standard in his treatments of these two Hindu leaders.

Rambachan argues that the upper strata Indians were increasingly influenced by the Unitarian form of Christianity, a liberal denomination that does not affirm the Trinity and purports to be based more on reason than historical revelation. Westernized Indians found this denomination to be amenable to their views and admired the compatibility of Unitarian thought with science, including their acceptance of unmediated individual exploration. Rambachan writes that Vivekananda got his ideas of anubhava from such Western sources:

> The idea of intuitive experience as an immediate source of spiritual knowledge, which rose to prominence at this time, became a leading idea of the period, and has become a dominant motif in the rhetoric of modern Hinduism. In Vivekananda, it became associated with the idea of a scientific method of arriving at religious verification.[8]

And again:

> In particular, they seized upon the concepts of intuition and nature
> as such sources and sought, with very little success, to construct a
> theology on the basis of what could be known through these means.[9]

This is how, according to Rambachan, Vivekananda incorporated the
principle of direct experience and intuition into his newly invented
Hinduism when it allegedly had no real precedent in classical dharmic
thought.

But Rambachan must then deal with an obvious contradiction,
for Vivekananda's guru was Ramakrishna, a very traditional guru
operating almost entirely without Western influence. Ramakrishna's
quintessential teaching emphasized a strong, even dramatic, emphasis
on direct experience. Rambachan admits that Ramakrishna had a
profound scepticism for, and mistrust of, scriptural texts: 'Ramakrishna
was derogatory and cynical about the value of scriptural study, and
negative in his views about their overall importance. He maintained
the primacy of direct personal experience. Vivekananda, of course, as
a direct disciple of Ramakrishna, was the heir to this legacy.'[10] So it is
a rash conclusion that Vivekananda got his ideas from the Unitarians
or other Western sources. Rambachan, a little too conveniently, does
not bother to examine Ramakrishna's legacy and rushes to credit the
Unitarians instead.

Another crack in the edifice constructed by Rambachan is that he
assumes Shankara to be the only legitimate Hindu thinker, and that any
deviation from his thinking qualifies as inauthentic. But why is it bad
to study and learn from other thinkers in the light of new knowledge
and circumstances? After all, the Hindu tradition has evolved numerous
times in its long history. Rambachan depicts Shankara as a sort of
messiah figure in the Abrahamic sense, as if his is the final word,
not to be questioned, challenged, superseded or even adapted based
on subsequent discoveries. The fact is there have been numerous
challenges to Shankara, even from well-known Vedantins right from
his own lineage.

It is also important to remember that Shankara and Vivekananda were addressing different audiences, at different times, and in different cultural contexts and circumstances. Rambachan would seem to prefer a Hinduism that is frozen in time, unable to move or develop in response to an ever-changing world.

Rambachan tends to deny the existence of Hinduism as a coherent entity and applies Western reductionism to make his case. Because of the Western influence of normative thinking, and its limited view of what a 'religion' is, there is often triple-reduction at work among such scholars:

1. **Hinduism → Vedanta:** This conflates Hinduism with Vedanta and ignores numerous other approaches to Hinduism, such as Kashmir Shaivism and Tantra, to name just two major ones.

2. **Vedanta → Advaita Vedanta:** This reductionism ignores the other schools of Vedanta that are different from Advaita Vedanta, such as *Vishishta-advaita Vedanta, Bhedabheda Vedanta, Dvaita Vedanta*, and various sub-schools of these.

3. **Advaita Vedanta → Shankara:** This reductionism assumes that there has been no further development in Advaita Vedanta after Shankara. The fact is that the *mathas* (centers of Vedanta learning) established by Shankara have themselves evolved Shankara's thoughts further and reinterpreted many of his works.

One needs to put the different interpretations of Vedanta in their proper contexts. Shankara emphasizes jnana (knowledge) as the means to liberation, whereas Ramanuja and Madhava emphasize bhakti (devotion). The difference here is one of priority: whether bhakti prepares one for jnana or vice versa. But all the interpretations agree that jnana and bhakti are both important, regardless of priority, and all of them accept that karma yoga is also important for preparing the individual for liberation. As long as an individual takes care of all three (and he is required to do so by all the lineages), he is on the path to liberation.

Thus, for a practitioner, the theoretical disputes are not so important because he is asked to engage in all these practices regardless of the particular theoretical model he follows. Shankara does not consider these methods to be in conflict, because purity—via any method, textual, bhakti, meditation, or any combination of these—opens the door to jnana and moksha.[11]

Although Vedanta is important to Hinduism, and the Advaita school is perhaps its most widespread interpretation, and although Shankara was undoubtedly a great figure, the Hindu tradition is much vaster than any one thinker, yogi, rishi or founder of a specific lineage. This is because it is not history centric in the way the Abrahamic religions are. It is even larger than any individual avatar, be it Rama, Krishna, or any specific deity. Hinduism has been vibrant and alive, changing many times, before Shankara, during his lifespan, and after him.

Vivekananda was indeed critical of Shankara at times, as well as of other prior thinkers. But this does not disqualify him as a legitimate interpreter of Hinduism for his times. Shankara's own writings are not pramana or sruti. They are open to criticism like any other interpretation. Hence, Shankara's interpretation cannot be seen as the only one within Advaita Vedanta; nor can Advaita Vedanta be seen as the only legitimate interpretation of Vedanta; nor, for that matter, can Vedanta be seen as the only authentic version of Hinduism.

Furthermore, Rambachan incorrectly assumes that: Hinduism → political Hindutva. This reduction collapses millennia-old Hinduism into mere modern politics. These political forces are important to study as separate phenomena, but one cannot take one's conclusions about modern Indian politics and project them back on to Hinduism in order to make sweeping dismissive conclusions. For one thing, Hinduism has never been limited to the political boundaries of modern India. And it has had a long history of change.

In summary, Rambachan skips the entire history of Hinduism before and after Shankara and jumps straight from Shankara to colonial times, ignoring the numerous adaptations, offshoots and innovations that have occurred in the thousand years between Shankara and colonialism.

Essentializing Shankara

Most Indologists focus only on Shankara's philosophical arguments. The topic of yoga (a term which covers a wide range of spiritual practices, including meditation) is dismissed quickly on the grounds that Shankara did not believe realization to be the product of any action or activity and that he has often pointed out limits to the efficacy of action. According to these thinkers, Shankara regards knowledge as the only valid means for achieving moksha; yoga is downgraded as a form of ritualistic mental action that cannot lead to liberation.

But when Shankara's relationship with yoga is examined closely, it turns out to be more complex than any 'for' or 'against' stance would imply. Neil Akshay Dalal is a young scholar whose recent Ph.D dissertation at the University of Texas was on the topic of sruti and anubhava as paths to moksha.[12] Dalal nuances this controversy nicely by noting that Advaita Vedantins have had a long debate among themselves over whether texts are the ultimate authority and primary method for liberation, or whether *sadhana* (which could include meditation and/or bhakti) can lead to the experience of liberation. He explains that this type of debate also exists in other religions:

> The tension between the external dependence on texts, tradition, and culture versus an internal dependence on self-inquiry, insight, and religious experience is found in some form within many traditions, such as Christian official doctrine and Christian mysticism or the Koran traditionalist and the Sufi mystic or between the Buddhist focused on interpreting the Buddha's word and the Zen Buddhist meditator. The difference between the specialist in textual study and specialist in practice alludes to a number of other dichotomies, such as the tension between knowledge and action, theory and practice, conceptual knowledge and direct experience, intellectualism and anti-intellectualism, and externalism and internalism.[13]

Clearly, the debate is an important one in the case of Hinduism where the paths of experience (i.e., yoga, meditation) have achieved great maturity as compared to Abrahamic religions; hence, to exclude yoga from Hinduism would be a mistake. What is at stake in this debate is the relative importance between the text expert (pandit or shastri) on one side, and the experiential guru (yogi, mystic or bhakta) on the other. Some of the most noteworthy teachers of Advaita Vedanta, post-Sankara, have been both at the same time.[14]

Those in the camp of emphasizing experience point out that textual study is inherently limited to theorizing and intellectualizing and that such objectification cannot grasp non-duality or Brahman, which is beyond concepts. Indeed, the *Mundaka Upanishad* proclaims that a guru must have both knowledge of shastra (texts) and experience of enlightenment.[15] Sankara himself confirms this principle in his commentary on the Bhagavad-Gita (4.34), describing the teachers as wise ones 'who have realized the truth' which they will impart.

On the other hand, those like Rambachan who insist that the proper study of sruti is a necessary and sufficient means for moksha, rely on selective textual references to claim that the path of experience is not valid. Dalal is much more balanced than Rambachan. He admits that Shankara did not dismiss *samadhi* (the highest state of consciousness in Patanjali's system) and that he sought a harmonious interaction between texts and meditation.

A related point is that not everyone is ready to attain moksha. Many people are simply not interested in moksha, because they have mundane needs and interests. What is the Hindu teaching for them? Should Hinduism abandon them and limit itself only to a select few who are pursuing moksha? Vivekananda's appeal is to humanity at large; it is not limited to the miniscule minority that seriously pursues attaining moksha. Therefore, his methods cannot be evaluated against the narrower paths recommended for those who are focused only on moksha.

Rambachan often translates moksha as salvation (incorrectly in my opinion), and therefore unconsciously assumes the Christian tenet that without salvation one will go to hell. But in Hinduism's case there are other legitimate pursuits besides moksha; those who do not attain moksha in this life get reborn rather than going to hell. Hence, the notion that 'getting saved' is the sole criterion for being a Christian cannot be applied to Hinduism by considering moksha as the sole criterion for being a Hindu.

In this regard, I wish to quote a passage from one of Advaita Vedanta's core texts (Shankara's commentary on the *Brahmasutra*), that says that Brahman possesses 'a double nature' depending upon whether it is the object of ultimate knowledge or not. Those who are ignorant of ultimate knowledge (i.e., the vast majority of the population) experience Brahman by seeing themselves as devotees and Brahman as the object of their devotion. The text then explains the various grades of experience applicable depending upon the condition of a given person:

> The different modes of devotion lead to different results, some to exaltation, some to gradual emancipation, some to success in works; those modes are distinct on account of the distinction of the different qualities and limiting conditions. And although the one highest Self only, i.e., the Lord distinguished by those different qualities, constitutes the object of devotion, still the fruits (of devotion) are distinct, according as the devotion refers to different qualities. Thus Scripture says, 'According as man worships him, that he becomes;' and, 'according to what his thought is in this world, so will he be when he has departed this life.'[16]

Shankara goes on to clarify the grades of conditioning and corresponding experiences:

> Although one and the same Self is hidden in all beings movable as well as immovable, yet owing to the gradual rise of excellence of the minds which form the limiting conditions (of the Self), Scripture declares that the Self, although eternally unchanging and uniform, reveals itself in a graduated series of beings, and so appears in forms of various dignity and power.[17]

The point here is that for the vast majority of humanity, meditation and devotion as espoused by Vivekananda are beneficial. It is inappropriate to use criteria that are applicable only to those who have attained or are pursuing the attainment of ultimate knowledge.[18]

Further clarification of Shankara's intentions is provided by his direct disciple and one of his most important followers, Sureshvara, who writes:

> The performance of daily obligatory rites leads to the acquisition of virtue; this leads to the destruction of sin, which in turn results in the purification of the mind. The purification of the mind leads to comprehension of the true nature of Samsara or relative existence; from this results Vairagya (renunciation), which arouses a desire for liberation; from this desire results a search for its means; from it come renunciation of all actions thence the practice of Yoga, which leads to a habitual tendency of the mind to settle in the Self, and this results in the knowledge of the meaning of such Shruti passages as 'Thou Art That' (Tat Tvam Asi) which destroys ignorance, thus leading to the establishment in one's own Self.[19]

Thus, Shankara and his direct followers embrace a natural continuum that includes both yoga and sruti. There is no rejection of yoga, contrary to what Rambachan asserts.

Challenging the direct experience of the rishi-yogi

Rambachan opposes the idea that adhyatma-vidya or inner science is supported by Advaita Vedanta (or any aspects of Hinduism for that matter). To demonstrate the error of this approach, Chapter 11 includes a section describing adhyatma-vidya as an established method of scientific inquiry in Indian traditions.

He notes correctly that Western science 'was enjoying considerable prestige among the Bengali intelligentsia in the nineteenth century. It was widely felt that all systems of human thought, including religion, had to be validated by the scrutiny of science and reason.'[20] But he is incorrect to insist that Vivekananda reformulated his views of sruti and anubhava, based exclusively on the prestige accorded to the Western scientific method.

Rambachan is critical of Vivekananda's view of the empirical nature of the rishis' discoveries and therefore their verifiability. Rambachan uses his own understanding of the conventional scientific method as the basis for his critique. (He seems to be uninformed of the post-modern philosophies of science that are proliferating in the West; ironically, these are inspired by Hindu and Buddhist ideas.) He writes that Vivekananda portrays the rishis as only discoverers of spiritual laws, which can be verified by any serious investigator, and which bypass the need for faith and belief:

> Vivekananda portrays the aptas or rishis as only the 'discoverers' of spiritual laws. Like a scientific manual then, the Vedas, as books, are just the written records of these spiritual laws discovered by different persons in different times. The representation of the Vedas as records or reports of spiritual findings and the rishis as discoverers provide the foundation for the deepening and development of the scientific paradigm. One is not obliged, according to Vivekananda, to accept scientific propositions as valid because of faith in the individual scientist. As a method of gaining knowledge, he sees science as being distinguished by the fact that it offers the possibility of verification.[21]

Vivekananda had indeed been clear in his emphasis on direct experiential realization, but this emphasis was based on rishis who had had such experiences; it was not based on Western scientific methods. The proponents of Mimamsa, even before Shankara, had argued for a similar view of the rishis of the Vedas, namely, that they were the discoverers and not the authors of the Vedas. Even the exact word order of a hymn in the Veda was 'seen', not authored, by the rishi. Shankara would seem to suggest that the *mantra-drashtas* ('seers' of mantras) were drashtas because of their yogic insight into reality.[22] Also, Shankara regarded Krishna's statements in the Gita as a key component of shastra, and the Gita is known as a means to liberation. Since the Gita is considered to be smriti, clearly sruti is not the only means.

But Rambachan provides a sharp critique of Vivekananda's application of the scientific paradigm, writing:

> In an age when science, in the enthusiasm and arrogance of its youth, seemed ready to subject all the areas of human knowledge to its criterion and methods, Vivekananda felt that faith in the sruti as the source of brahmajnana was irrational. He sought to posit a process of attaining brahmajnana which he felt had satisfied the demands of science. It not only fails to do this, but, in a much wider perspective, his analysis is unsatisfactory and unconvincing. It is true that faith (sraddha) in the sruti as a pramana is indispensable for Shankara, but this is not a faith which proscribes all use of human reason.[23]

Vivekananda had written that the state of a rishi is the ideal for Hindus and everything else is a means for preparation, including the Vedas, grammar, astronomy, etc. Vivekananda translates the Sanskrit word 'rishi' as a seer of mantras, one who has realized certain truths available to the superconsciousness, and recorded them. He explains that:

> Rishi is the name of a type, of a class, which every one of us, as true Hindus, is expected to become at some period of our life, and becoming which, to the Hindu, means salvation. Not belief in doctrines, not going to thousands of temples, nor bathing in all the rivers in the world, but becoming the Rishi, the Mantra-drashta— that is freedom, that is salvation.[24]

It is important to note that Vivekananda combines anubhava and sruti rather than rejecting one or the other, the way Rambachan wants us to do. Vivekananda equates sruti with a map that can create curiosity and guidance for first-hand knowledge but can communicate only an approximate idea of reality for most persons because they lack the purity of consciousness. Sruti consists of records of the anubhava or spiritual discoveries of others and the methods by which such discoveries have been made. Each person must purify his mind to be able to rediscover the reality for himself, i.e., have his own anubhava.

The truth of sruti is in the availability of the direct knowledge, not as a disembodied propositional text.

Therefore, everyone should become a rishi, which means someone capable of such a direct apprehension of truth. Sruti was not meant for the ordinary intellect; it is not concerned with any process of rational inquiry. Sruti becomes meaningful only when one has advanced to the same heights of consciousness as the rishis.

Rambachan is wrong in saying that Vivekananda disrespects sruti. As Rambachan acknowledges, Vivekananda honors and respects the rishis as the discoverers or seers of the Vedas. It follows that if discoverers are considered so great that all of us must aspire to be like them, if they are put on a pedestal as the ultimate role models, then we must certainly respect what they have discovered. Hence, it would be a contradiction for him to have such high regard for the rishis while having a low regard for the Vedic mantras they brought to us.

When Vivekananda says we must eventually transcend the Vedas and certify their claims by our own experience, he is, of course, speaking to his contemporary society, which presumably had fallen to a much lower level of consciousness than what prevailed in Shankara's time. Yoga and sadhana, as preliminary practices on the path of jnana, may therefore be more important today than was the case in Shankara's time.

Is Rambachan fixated on Christian assumptions?

Rambachan's position implies that all higher states of consciousness (i.e., adhyatma-vidya, or inner sciences) are inauthentic. In taking this view, he is asserting that the experience-based systems of Patanjali, Kashmir Shaivism and Tantra (to name only a few) are all irrelevant. He offers cover to Westerners like Ken Wilber who are busy appropriating and digesting these Indian sources into their own concoctions, because Rambachan makes such Hindu practices look like artificial constructions.

The possibility of becoming a rishi—indeed, the requirement that every individual become one—is what differentiates Hinduism from

Abrahamic religions. In the latter traditions the ultimate truth is limited to a few select prophets, through whom, in turn, truth is made available to the many. Vivekananda writes:

> Truth came to Jesus of Nazareth, and we must all obey him. But the truth came to the rsis of India—the mantra-drastas—the seers of thought—and will come to all rsis in the future, not to talkers, not to book-swallowers, not to scholars, not to philologists, but to seers of thought.[25]

This is an important distinction, which I have turned into my thesis on the history centric character of the Abrahamic religions. While the prophet Mohammad had a certain experience that is documented in the Qur'an, no other Muslim who is considered credible has claimed a similar experience, and nor is it ever possible to have that experience, according to Islam. In fact, it is considered blasphemy to claim that such an experience is possible for anyone other than the prophet Mohammad.

Likewise, Jesus is claimed to have had a direct and complete experience of God, amounting to an identity, as both Father and Son. But Christians today do not aspire to have this complete experience. Such a claim is often regarded as the worst kind of idolatry. We must be allowed to ask: Is Rambachan unconsciously projecting a Christian bias, namely a bias against the path of anubhava which gives humans the rishi experience?

Since nothing akin to complete superconscious perception is available in Christianity and since not even partial knowledge of God can be attained by 'natural' means alone, the only way to attain religious truth in the full sense is through revelation given to a small number of prophets and inherently unavailable to the rest of us by any direct means. Rambachan wants to reduce the Vedas to the same status as Biblical revelation by denying that every human is endowed with the rishi potential. He therefore exaggerates the difference between sruti and anubhava in order to make them seem contradictory.

Let us examine Rambachan's writings to further uncover the Christian biases that might unconsciously be limiting him. About Vivekananda he writes:

It is clear that, for him, the Vedas do not possess any intrinsic validity. Consistent with his views on their origin and the personal foundations of their authority, he envisages them as simply recording the spiritual discoveries of others, and the methods by which such discoveries have been made. These findings, however, must be personally rediscovered by every individual before they are valid for him or her ... A scriptural text is represented by him as a second-hand religion. As a record of the experiences of others, it may stimulate our own desires, but even as one person's eating is of little value to another, so also is the record of another person's experiences until we attain to the same end. The imperative therefore, for Vivekananda, is that everyone should become a rishi.[26]

Rambachan is accurate in claiming that for Vivekananda, genuine knowledge, including religious knowledge, is based on experience. Claims based on faith and belief trouble Vivekananda, especially those which are not repeatable and are considered unique to certain people only. What Rambachan fails to emphasize sufficiently is that Vivekananda identifies direct knowing with superconscious perception, and Rambachan argues against the possibility of higher states of consciousness through direct experience. He offers the following logic:

Brahman cannot be known through sense perception because it is nirguna (quality-less). It is free from all the qualities (form, taste, smell, touch and sound) through which the various sense organs apprehend their respective objects. In addition, the sense organs can only know the nature of things by objectifying them. Brahman, being the Knower, the Awareness in the sense organs, can never become the object of their knowledge. It can never be the object of any organ or kind of perception. This is one of the major inconsistencies of Vivekananda's use of the analogy of perception to describe the gain of brahmajnana in samadhi. Even if it is superconscious rather than ordinary perception, Vivekananda still posits the mind as the organ of knowledge and ends up postulating brahman as an object. To claim any kind of experience as the means through which the knowledge of brahman can be gained requires proof that this is possible without presupposing brahman as an object. Vivekananda has failed to offer any such proof.[27] [Emphasis mine]

Vivekananda's stance is based firmly on the Vedic sutra 'manasaivanu drashtavyam' (it is to be seen by the mind alone), which Shankara cites frequently. Rambachan does not appreciate that in higher states of consciousness the knower, the knowing and the known are unified and there is no separate 'object of knowledge'. Hence his issue with Vivekananda in the above passage is based on a flawed assumption. Rambachan frequently refers to the rishi state as 'ordinary perception'. Here and elsewhere Rambachan is confusing perception in the ordinary sense with the rishi-state in which they 'see' sruti.

Rambachan seems to be superimposing the Abrahamic idea of prophecy onto the rishis and thereby treating sruti as another 'revelation' that came via the rishis. The superconscious cognition is better referred to as the indescribable rishi-state. One cannot apply ordinary logic about cognition to examine it. Hence Rambachan cannot assume that in the rishi-state there are the same limitations of objectified knowledge and separation of knower from known.

Rambachan simply avoids the important question: Who are rishis? How do they differ from prophets? What is meant by their 'knowing' or 'seeing' the sruti?

Furthermore, Rambachan's artificial and unnecessary dichotomy between anubhava and shruti pramana is an example of slipping into the Aristotelian binary logic of the 'excluded middle' which is different from the Indian logic of 'this as well as that'. It is a reductionist understanding of anubhava to see it as third-person cognition only, i.e., external perception. Such reductionism isolates us from our own true nature and our interconnections as symbolized by Indra's Net.

Allegation that yoga makes people less rational and intelligent

In a strange twist, Rambachan attributes the lack of intellectual depth in contemporary Hindu scholarship to the popularity of views on the primacy of yogic experience. He feels that Vivekananda's characterization of shruti as 'second-hand religion' contributes to a low estimation of the value of scriptural scholarship. It makes the study of shruti and right interpretation less important. The upholding of the samadhi experience as a source of brahmajnana has led to intellectual decline, he claims.

> The championing in contemporary Hinduism of personal experience over the authority of scripture ... has contributed to the divorce of scholarship from spirituality. Examples of scholarship without religious commitment and religious commitment lacking the self-critical insights of scholarship abound. [...] The decline of the significance of the Vedas as a pramana and its characterisation as secondhand religion have contributed to the devaluing of scriptural scholarship. Its study, exegesis and interpretation are not of utmost significance. Vivekananda contemptuously dismisses scriptural scholarship as an activity at the theoretical and intellectual level. With an emphasis in contemporary Hinduism on the gain of knowledge through the transcendence of reason and not on its mediation, reason, argument and intellectual activity, all important qualities of interreligious dialogue assume more of an obstructive character.[28]

Rambachan has his argument backwards: yoga is not weakening intellectual power of the Indian tradition; rather, it is the loss of yoga that is dulling the intellect. Far from discounting reason, Vivekananda held many successful discussions with scientifically minded Westerners and, in turn, influenced some of the greatest Western minds of his time.[29]

The alleged lack of intellectual creativity among modern Indians is not limited to Hindus but is characteristic of secularized intellectuals as well, such as those pursuing post-colonial and subaltern studies. These persons are mainly engaged in regurgitating Western theories and forcing their validation in Indian contexts. Rambachan himself often comes across like a product of Christian training averse to embodied knowing.

Rambachan would find it hard to refute that the monks of Ramakrishna Math combine scholarship and religious commitment with great rigor and go to great lengths to inculcate this combination in their students. Although Rambachan relies on Shankara, he fails to note that many of the best available translations of Shankara into English are those produced by the Ramakrishna Mission monks, and that many scholars studying Shankara would have first encountered Advaita Vedanta through these translations and commentaries.

In essence, he fails to appreciate the difference between first-person and third-person approaches to sruti, thereby limiting his approach to sruti in the third-person. This prevents him from seeing sruti in the context of the huge amount of research into non-dualism that has been going on in Western neuroscience, cognitive science, philosophy and religion. The irony is that while Westerners at the cutting edge of such research are frantically appropriating Hindu and Buddhists ideas and practices for their first-person research, Rambachan is fighting the fact that Hinduism ascribes great honor and legitimacy to first-person empiricism.[30]

Political allegations

Rambachan contrasts the statements Vivekananda made in the West with those he made in India, and sees the differences as a problem. But it is common in Hindu teaching to create balance in a given student by emphasizing an aspect that is deficient. And so Vivekananda emphasizes spirituality to Westerners because he finds them to be too materialistic in their outlook, whereas he feels that Indians had abrogated their material and social affairs to the British rulers and hence, to Indians, he emphasizes social and economic responsibility.

Rambachan is also troubled that Vivekananda wants to reconcile various schools of Vedanta. But many prior thinkers also integrated multiple schools of Hindu thought, such as Vijnanabhikshu. This pre-colonial unity of Hinduism will be discussed in Chapter 8.

Another serious issue Rambachan picked up from Hacker is that 'Vivekananda adopted the position that there was no bar of sex, race or caste to realization.'[31] Rambachan here seems to be blaming Vivekananda for advocating the liberal view that everyone has the right to study the Vedas! Yet it must be remembered that the neo-Hinduism school sees Hinduism as the source of several social ills of India. Rather than appreciating the social adaptations as a valid undertaking, he sadly chooses to attack these improvements.[32]

Rambachan criticizes those who defend Vivekananda, accusing them of being products of political circumstances. For instance, he criticizes Radhakrishnan for supporting Vivekananda on the issue of textual analysis and anubhava.[33]

Western scholars' support for Rambachan

As might be expected, Rambachan is well-supported by Western scholars of Hinduism. For instance, the well-known American academic Harold Coward praises Rambachan precisely for developing the philosophical arguments to undermine Vivekananda. In his review of Rambachan's work, he positions him as the successor to Halbfass in continuing this genre of work, writing that, 'While others have highlighted Vivekananda's influence on Indian nationalism and the impact of the Ramakrishna mission, this is the first critical assessment of his thought and its influence on contemporary Hinduism.'[34] Coward applauds Rambachan for exposing Vivekananda as the man who fabricated 'the direct supersensuous *samadhi* experience of *brahman* as a parallel to the perceptual verification of knowledge offered by modern science', and he accuses Vivekananda of wanting to make Hinduism 'seem compatible with modern science'. Citing Rambachan as his expert on the matter, he concludes that Vivekananda has left Hinduism a 'flawed legacy' which needs to be refuted and that 'Rambachan's book is a first and most important step in this direction'.[35] Coward shares Rambachan's complaint that 'in spite of its radical inconsistency with Shankara, Vivekananda's thought has been uncritically adopted by Hindus of this century and is not serving them well'. He also praises Rambachan for endeavoring to answer the question as to why Hindu scholarship in this century has become so flabby. The implication is that contemporary Hinduism's own exemplars have been producing 'flabby' scholarship and that Rambachan is the competent scholar who has arrived to set things right.

The list of scholars who support Rambachan's ideas is extensive. Clearly, given his power and visibility, Rambachan has gone a long way in shaping opinions, not only amongst a significant section of academics but more widely, in the media and the public sphere as well.

Many scholars disagree with Rambachan

But several other scholars are troubled by the neo-Hinduism thesis. Jonathan Bader, for instance, asserts: 'It is difficult to see how Hacker can claim that Sankara has rejected the practice of constant meditation. Neither does it appear that Sankara has "discarded remnants of yoga".'[36] Bader summarizes Shankara's position on meditation and yoga as follows:

> The yoga element in Sankara's work must be accepted as an integral component of his thought. The significance of yoga is recognized in the Bhagavadgita, the Brahmasutra, and even in the older Upanishads. If these authoritative texts accord a place to yoga, then it is little wonder that Sankara follows suit.[37]

Bader is critical of scholars who force Shankara into their own limited concept of what a philosopher is. One must separate out Shankara's teaching on moksha from his concern to defeat opponents in arguments. The former project is about attaining the 'lived experience' called 'jivanmukti', as expressed in the mahavakyas. This was meant for the practitioner, not the academic. Unlike his *Upadesasahasri* (which is a 'how to' guide for the practitioner), Shankara's *Brahmasutra-bhasya* discusses meditation as exegesis. Although he does list the meditation steps involved in Brahmasutra-bhasya, his central concern is to show a coherent metaphysical view across the Upanishadic texts.[38] In his various commentaries, he is concerned with philosophical argumentation against opponents and does not give extensive treatment to meditation practices. This should not be seen as indicative of a lack of interest in meditation, and certainly not as evidence of opposition to it.

Bader feels that the neo-Hinduism line of thinking superimposes European idealism onto Shankara and that this leads to a wrong interpretation that he is an 'illusionist'. Such scholars see yoga and Advaita as mutually exclusive camps, and hence want to place Shankara in one camp or the other, but they fail to see the unity of Advaita-Yoga that Shankara propounded.

In a similar vein, Madeleine Biardeau writes: 'There is, perhaps, a danger in wishing to over-systematize the thought of an author and to perceive relationships between different aspects of his work which appear as being independent because they respond to different problems.'[39] Vidyasankar Sundaresan suggests that in order to appreciate Shankara's coherence, we must see his various writings as linked to each other, just like web pages, and then follow these links in ways which printed books cannot allow. This is better than counting how many times certain words appear and other mechanical methods often used by philologists.

Sundaresan clarifies the difference between Shankara and those who, like Vivekananda, hold that sruti as pramana is bolstered by yogic experience, or who see yogic experience as its own pramana. He feels that Rambachan belongs to the group that is anxious to save sruti pramana from the idea that *nirvikalpa samadhi* verifies liberation, and they wish to purge Advaita Vedanta of developments from the post-Sankara schools of Vivarana and Bhamati. Vidyasankar Sundaresan's overall assessment of Rambachan is clear and explicit:

With all due respect to Anantanand Rambachan ... the difference between one who does an academic study of Sankara's works and one who lives and breathes Advaita Vedanta is the following. The former thinks that Sankara was like a university professor of philosophy and thinks that both the traditional and neo-Vedantins have deviated from Sankara. The latter uses yoga as an upaya, in line with what Sankara describes as 'upakurvantu'.[40]

Douglas Skoog also refutes Rambachan, saying he 'has apparently confused the content of sruti statements with the experience that sruti can occasionally engender'.[41] His paper opens by saying that its specific purpose is to critique Rambachan's views on sruti versus anubhava.

There is a key Advaita philosophical distinction between higher and lower levels of truth/reality which Rambachan has omitted. According to Advaita, on the level of paramarthika (ultimate reality and awareness), there is only knowledge of brahman, a state of awareness devoid of all mental and perceptual distinctions, in which even the usual distinction of knower and object of knowledge fall aside. This state of awareness or knowledge is referred to as moksa (liberation) or anubhava (direct awareness) or brahmajnana (knowledge of brahman). In contrast, on the level of vyavahara (practical reality and knowledge), there exists multiplicity, cogitation, duality. One knows an object (conceptually) as apart from oneself, possessing distinct qualities.[42]

T.S. Rukmani states her position as follows, which is very much in line with my thinking:

One can conclude by saying that Sankaracarya was very much a yogin at heart, incorporating wherever possible the vocabulary of Yoga in his Advaita Vedanta, and speaking approvingly of even the siddhis or supernormal powers that are described in the Yoga tradition. His conviction of the reality of Brahman to the exclusion of everything else forces him to interpret nididhyasana-dhyana in a manner commensurate with his metaphysics and epistemology. He, in no way, admits the dual principles of purusa and prakrti as the ultimate realities and remains a staunch opposer of the dualistic metaphysical stand of both Samkhya and Yoga.[43]

Arvind Sharma writes that Rambachan should not essentialize the term 'pramana' as it is used by Shankara. He notes that it is used at least three different ways and that Rambachan himself is inconsistent in the way he refers to Shankara's position.[44] While agreeing with Rambachan that Shankara considered sruti to be the primary authority, he disagrees that sruti represents the only authority.[45]

Furthermore, Sharma disapproves of the fact that Rambachan has replaced the term 'shastra' (texts) in Shankara's writings with the term 'sruti' (Vedas). He shows that Shankara's notion of shastra includes not only the four Vedas, but also *Itihasa* (major narratives of the past), Purana (folk narratives), *vidya* (science), Upanishad, *sloka* (verses), *sutra* (aphorisms), *anuvyakhyana* (explanations), and *vyakhyana* (commentaries).[46] Rambachan's mistranslation was used to boost his case for the exclusivity of sruti and thereby undermine Vivekananda's use of a wider range of texts.

Sharma also demonstrates that Shankara declares Brahman to be knowable, but not as an object of sense-perception. Here, Shankara implies that *indriyas* (senses) and *pratyaksha* (direct perception) are limited and he does not use the word 'anubhava' to denote this limitation.[47] In other words, it is an incorrect understanding by Rambachan to limit anubhava as sensory perception and fail to appreciate anubhava at higher states of consciousness.

I disagree with Rambachan on the issue of the primacy of a narrowly conceived Advaita Vedanta. I also disagree with his interpretation of Shankara, who is far more open to, and embracing of, anubhava and the utility of yoga and sadhana than Rambachan allows. Furthermore, he takes Shankara out of his historical context and makes him into the kind of absolute authority of the kind one sees in Western religions. Rambachan displays a limited understanding of the historical evolution of Hindu thought. Had he read the books that compare various yoga systems in the classical period, he would not be so prone to essentialize yoga and pigeon-hole it the way he does.[48]

For instance, a prominent Jain scholar named Haribhadra (dated sometime between the fifth and seventh centuries) wrote extensive comparisons of various Indian systems, including Vedanta, Tantra, Shaivism, Vaishnavism, as well as Buddhism and Jainism. He organized them as somewhat equivalent and generally complementary approaches leading to the same goal. In doing so, he liberally interpreted traditional texts his own way, often refuting older interpretations, and in this manner reconciled them into a coherent spectrum. Yet the coherence and compatibility across multiple systems do not negate their distinctiveness. 'The wisdom gained from discipline is singular in essence', he writes, 'though heard of in different ways.'[49] Such harmonizing across various Indian systems has been frequent since early times.

Rambachan underestimates the degree to which Vivekananda is rooted in traditional Hinduism, and fails to see how contemporary Hinduism is a reasonable adaptation of this tradition. Vivekananda's contribution to changing national self-consciousness involved re-aligning and reinterpreting the cultural, metaphysical, political and spiritual heritage of India. His important contributions include lifting the prominence given to adhyatma-vidya, or systematic inner exploration, and his emphasis on karma yoga. Not only is Vivekananda perfectly respectful of the textual tradition as an important dimension of spiritual realization, but Shankara himself validates direct experience and the active practices of meditation, Tantra and karma yoga more than might at first appear.

I wrote an extensive response to Rambachan in a recent issue of the *International Journal of Hindu Studies*, and I elaborate my arguments further in Chapter 10 to this book.

7

The Myth Goes Viral

One of the characteristics of a hegemonic discourse is that a large coterie of writers produces material that reiterates a given supposition as common knowledge. The group relies on references to each other's works so as to give the semblance of credibility. As the process unfolds, the core thesis is increasingly taken for granted and requires ever-decreasing rigor to prove it. In this fashion, the academic literature is filled with assertions and re-assertions of the myth that Hinduism is a modern invention, both implicit and explicit. I will refute this in greater detail in the chapters to come, but here I shall show how widespread this view has become.

What follows is a discussion of some of the more recent scholars who are propagating the myth that there is no such thing as Hinduism, that what we call Hinduism is a construct of the modern period made only for political advantage and in order to impose a top-down homogeneity that suppresses the rights of women, non-Hindu religions, and minorities.

Many of these scholars' assumptions about the nature of religion and spirituality are shaped by the Abrahamic traditions. Their claims about the exact process by which this artificial Hinduism came about may differ, but all see it as a process that rests historically on a chaotic pre-colonial condition which defies categorization. *Being Different* argues at length that this sense of chaos attributed to Hinduism and deeming it conceptually incoherent is a projection of Western anxiety and of the need to control. In dharmic thought, de-centralization is not the antithesis of unity and one need not fear it as 'chaos'.

Richard King

One of the important current scholars of the myth of neo-Hinduism is Richard King. His work is worth examining in detail because it is presented as a critique of colonialism and hence it impresses many Indians. Like his cohorts, he believes 'the notion of "Hinduism" is itself a Western-inspired abstraction, which until the nineteenth century bore little or no resemblance to the Indian religious beliefs and practices'.[1] King's critique is typical of those who apply the history of the word 'Hindu' interchangeably to the entity itself. In showing that the name itself was imported or coined only relatively recently, the claim is made that the religious and philosophical movement itself has not existed until recent times. He actually extends this critique to the classical term 'sanatana dharma', which roughly means 'eternal dharma as a common base' and pre-dates colonialism. King, however, writes to the contrary, insisting that,

> to appeal to the Indian concept of dharma as unifying the diversity of Hindu religious traditions is moot, since dharma is not a principle that is amenable to a single, universal interpretation, being in fact appropriated in diverse ways by a variety of Indian traditions (all of which tended to define the concept in terms of their own group-dynamic and identity).[2]

King disqualifies the existence of a unified dharma because he is unconsciously applying the Judeo-Christian normative idea of religion as 'one way, one path and one absolute history'.

King shares a wide consensus among many scholars as to the artificial nature of contemporary Hinduism. He pinpoints the commencement of this artificial Hinduism with a purely political date: 1947, the year of India's independence from Britain. He writes:

> Before the unification begun under imperial rule and consolidated by the Independence of 1947, it makes no sense to talk of an Indian 'nation', nor of a religion called 'Hinduism' which might be taken to represent the belief system of the Hindu people.[3]

King's purpose is made clear in his book's final chapter where, in addition to denying any unity in India's past, he actually recommends what amounts to a balkanization of India in the future! He proposes doing so along the lines of a subaltern project, by dissolving the nation back into a collection of local communities, especially Dalit ones. He refers to Dalits as 'tribal people', and claims that 'modern Hinduism represents the triumph of universalized, brahmanical forms of religion over the "tribal" and the "local"'.[4] Then he introduces his solution: 'The subaltern project is characterized not only by its critique of the colonialist but also by its rejection of the "nationalist" model of Indian history that is seen to be a product of European colonial influence.'[5]

According to this view, Europeans are to blame for bringing the concept of the modern nation-state into Asia; to achieve true de-colonization, India must revert back to when it was a collection of hundreds of separate and fragmented groups. He writes:

> The modern nation-state, of course, is a product of European sociopolitical and economic developments from the sixteenth century onwards, and the introduction of the nationalist model into Asia is a product of European imperialism in this area.[6]

India needs to undergo this reversal, he explains, because it has become a nation of elitists. As a result, 'the people' are denied the ability to participate in their own governance.[7] He confesses that as an Englishman, he bears this 'white man's burden' to reverse the colonial impact, by wanting to return India to its pre-colonial state. He writes: 'My own work is to be seen as a response to the colonial past of my particular field of interest and an attempt to come to terms with the colonial legacy of the England in which I was born',[8] adding that, 'as a scholar specializing in the study of ancient Indian philosophy and religion, I am invested with the authority to "speak about" or "represent" such phenomena'.[9] He never identifies who these 'tribal people' are and what their own faith is like. They are voiceless, and *he* intends to be their voice.

Many of the neo-Hinduism school of scholars, like King, feel proud to be doing their bit to rescue India from colonialism. According to them, much of the self-understanding of India is derived from the influence of colonialism and Christian missions. By 'blaming' colonialists for having 'invented' Hinduism, they see themselves as doing the 'real' Indians a great favour by convincing them to reject Hinduism.

What they fail to see is that they are further weakening the Indian position by suggesting that the West is its only agent of change, or at least the dominant agent of change. Furthermore, they undermine the capacity for change in dharma itself by demonizing Sanskrit as oppressive and fossilized.

This is characteristic of what I have called the 'whiteness syndrome' which consists of seeing itself as universal, seeing non-white civilizations as lacking agency, and elevating itself as the 'voice of the downtrodden'. This may be an attempt at alleviating white guilt, but it has the opposite effect of substituting a more sophisticated kind of colonization. King's work provides a good example of this tendency. As with all such works, his initial position is descriptively accurate. He notes, for instance, and correctly so, that colonial academics and administrators in India emphasized the teaching of Protestant religious texts and that this emphasis skewed their understanding of Indian culture. The emphasis was placed on translating texts and compiling critical editions of Indian works, which had the effect of homogenizing fluid narratives into a rigid canon and imposing Western frameworks and methodologies. The oral and folk traditions were often ignored, or even denounced as superstitious, because they did not fit the Western norms.[10] Unfortunately King's and similar analyses by others often end up blaming Sanskrit for this process, when in fact, during the pre-colonial period, there was never any attempt on the part of Sanskrit writers to impose the language on others or to replace other languages with it. In modern times, it is the English language that is hegemonic and is causing the demise of other languages. The charge that Sanskrit is the culprit when it comes to damaging other Indian languages is false.

In the same vein, King claims that Christianity was the first religion to develop abstract religious ideas. It then imposed them on Indian subjects through colonialism. Even mysticism, he claims, was first defined by Christian and European power politics, romanticized, and superimposed on to Indian beliefs in colonial times. Again, there is some truth to this description. But King ignores the influence in reverse: that considerable influence from Hinduism and Buddhism had already come into European Enlightenment thought and had, to some extent, shaped this category of mysticism. King joins his cohorts from this school of thought in claiming that as a response to European colonial hegemony, Western-influenced Indians 'constructed' Hinduism using universal ideals borrowed from Judeo-Christian concepts. Therefore, he concludes, Hinduism did not exist in antiquity.[11]

King also posits that the claim that the Vedas, Upanishads and Bhagavad-Gita hold universal ideas and ethics is false. Instead, these values were actually planted by modern Western-educated Indians who copied from their colonial rulers in order to build a nation that could appear legitimate by Western standards.

He then indulges in some pop psychology, asserting, as does Agehananda Bharati, that leaders such as Vivekananda developed this new kind of Vedanta in order to 'counteract Western discourses about the effeminacy of the Bengali male'.[12] Furthermore, Gandhi is alleged to have used Vedanta's passiveness to turn 'Bengali effeminacy' into an 'organized, non-violent, social protest'.[13]

Here is how King alleges that Vivekananda appropriated Western ideas to formulate an idealized Vedanta that had never existed:

In Vivekananda's hands, Orientalist notions of India as 'other worldly' and 'mystical' were embraced and praised as India's special gift to humankind. Thus the very discourse that succeeded in alienating, subordinating and controlling India was used by Vivekananda as a religious clarion call for the Indian people to unite under the banner of a universalistic and all-embracing Hinduism.[14]

Once this Vedanta had been formulated, 'Vivekananda's neo-Vedanta became an ideal Asian export to the disaffected but spiritually inclined Westerner searching for an exotic alternative to institutionalized Christianity in the religions of the "Mystical East".'[15] The goal of the neo-Hindus was to claim parity with Western religions by refashioning their faith in order to reform 'their decadent religion'. As a result of this, 'Hinduism in the twentieth century is allowed to enter the privileged arena of the "world religions", having finally come of age in a global context and satisfying the criteria for membership established by Western scholars of religion!'[16]

King is simply unwilling to grant even the slightest validation to the mystical dimension in traditional Indian sources. He claims that this sense of the past as imbued with the value of direct superconscious experience was merely a projection of the Western 'Romanticist conception of India'. He writes that this has not just 'become a prevalent theme in contemporary Western images of India' but that it has 'exerted a great deal of influence upon the self-awareness of the very Indians which it purports to describe'.[17]

According to King, mysticism is inherently flawed, as it is nothing less than a strategy for male domination: the soul is seen as feminine and in need of surrendering to the divine seen as masculine. His somewhat naïve view of meditation comes out in dismissive statements such as the following:

Try practising intense meditative concentration on an image of Amitabha Buddha for seven days in a row and you too are likely to have some kind of 'vision' or experiences of Amitabha—if only in your dreams![18]

His critique of Christian mysticism in such major Western figures as Meister Eckhart may or may not be valid, but here it gets applied too glibly and forcibly to Vedanta, where the divine feminine has, in any case, a different valence. He cites Eckhart's Christian mysticism as his standard and indicates that Eckhart's experience was superior to that of the Hindu mystics because it offered the potential for ethics whereas Shankara's Vedanta lacks ethical application.[19]

King goes on making sweeping statements, such as his claim that the elevation of the experiential above all else is 'a product of the modern era'.[20] He is quite plainly wrong about this, for in India the experiential use of meditation to achieve higher states of consciousness is an ancient discipline. He is also wrong to claim that giving importance to mystical experience leads to suppression of the ethical dimension.

King ends on a patronizing note, saying he wants to make sure that 'credit' for this recent manufacturing of Hinduism is also shared by the natives of India: 'To ignore the indigenous dimension of the invention of "Hinduism" is to erase the colonial subject from history and perpetuate the myth of the passive Oriental.'[21] Although Western influence was necessary, he says, we must also note 'the crucial role played by indigenous Brahmanical ideology'.[22]

I do agree with King that the European Enlightenment's ideal was to eradicate mystical subjectivity in favour of an 'objective' view without emotional bias, and that this was to be achieved strictly through rationality as opposed to revelation. This position glorified secular reason at the expense of truths revealed by Judeo-Christian prophets and messianic figures. The problem is that King is fixated on this European 'internal conflict' between history centrism and reason, and applies it to India. He does not consider the method of spiritual knowing which is based neither on historical texts nor on reasoning alone, but rather on the rishi's inner science of adhyatma-vidya. This method transcends the European conflict between historical dogma and reason. (For an overview of history centrism, see the section in the Conclusion chapter. A more elaborate treatment is in *Being Different*.)

Whereas I maintain that freedom from history centric revelation has been characteristic of dharmic spiritual thought from the beginning,

King accuses Brahmins of manufacturing this non-history-based premise. He writes, 'The Sanskritic "brahmanization" of Hindu religion … remains profoundly anti-historical in its postulation of an ahistorical "essence" to which all forms of "Hinduism" are said to relate.'[23]

Abrahamic religions regard historical revelation—that is, the participation of God in history—as essential to spiritual progress and the gold standard against which mystical states, already suspect, must be measured. Consequently, knowledge becomes a prisoner of historical dogma. These religions have not developed experiential methodologies for discovering spiritual truth. For spiritual confirmation, they rely entirely on ancient historical events and third-person testimonies. Insisting on the validity of such history therefore becomes dogmatic.

Indian traditions, on the other hand, are alive with fresh insights emerging from meditation. That's because these traditions do not depend on fixed, unique events in history but rather on the evolution of discoveries as an ongoing process. King perpetrates his own version of orientalist violence to this Indian creativity by positing that it is a construct of Brahminical imposition and by fossilizing, as it were, the spiritual experience recorded in the textual tradition of the past.

King does acknowledge that some scholars support the idea that one could regard dharma as the unified concept underlying Hinduism. He cites Halbfass as making the point that the variety of dharma reflects 'elusive, yet undeniable' coherence.[24] However, Halbfass does not explain what the basis of this cohesive dharma is, or what its shared tenets are. King therefore dismisses Halbfass's willingness to see unity because Halbfass cannot articulate the basis of that unity. Also, King alleges that Halbfass 'fails to appreciate the sense in which the postulation of a single, underlying religious unity called "Hinduism" requires a highly imaginative act of historical reconstruction'.[25]

It is easy to see that King opposes all attempts to identify common principles across a diverse range of dharma traditions. He is explicit on this point:

> The prize on offer is to be able to define the 'soul' or 'essence' of
> Hinduism. My thesis has been that this 'essence' did not exist (at

least in the sense in which Western Orientalists and contemporary Hindu movements have tended to represent it) until it was invented in the nineteenth century.[26]

Brian Pennington

Another established and influential scholar in this echo chamber is Brian Pennington, to whom I also responded in a recent issue of the *Journal of Hindu-Christian Studies*. Pennington's book bears the provocative title *Was Hinduism Invented?* However, it lacks a cogent argument and mostly restates the view shared by earlier myth-makers, which is that Hinduism was a fiction created by nineteenth-century Europeans and copied by Hindu activists. While the book claims to be about Hinduism, most of it is in fact concerned with the British experience in India. The information it contains is presented in a random and sensational manner.

Pennington spends most of his book on minute biographical details of several leading missionaries such as William Ward, William Carey, Abbe Dubois and Claudius Buchanan, as well as other influential colonial officers such as James Mill, William Jones, H.T. Colebrooke, et al. He shows that there was a church-academic nexus as well as an academic-government nexus among British institutions that studied India. For example, Cambridge University established a prize named for an essay competition on the topic: 'The best means of civilizing the subjects of the British Empire in India, and of diffusing the light of the Christian religion throughout the eastern world.'[27] The British missionary press, Pennington argues, constructed the Hindu heathen in derogatory terms and used him as a foil to construct the superior Christian self. Pennington says the memory of Druid paganism and of other pre-Protestant religions was superimposed on India to form a cognitive map of Hinduism. Also, the intense rivalry between Catholics and Protestants included vilification of Catholics as foreign savages, and this negative imagery overflowed into India. The British authorities issued pamphlets with titles such as 'Human Sacrifices in India'.[28]

The most prominent idea in connection with Hinduism revolved around satanic idols which could be blamed for subverting reason and piety among Hindus. Pennington says, 'The evangelical missionary's confrontation with the Hindu idol encoded so many other contrasts critical to the crystallization of a British sense of national self: reason vs. irrationality, Christian vs. pagan, mind vs. body, freed vs. enslaved, and so forth.'[29] There was widespread suspicion of Hindu rituals, which the British associated with evil idols, and missionaries fanned the flames by sending back sensational reports of their encounters with them. These reports detailed the missionaries' own heroic 'accomplishments' in destroying heathenism, and they proposed a roadmap for what must be done in India.

All this is well and good. It is standard post-colonial scholarship restated. The problem comes when Pennington argues that Vivekananda copied this colonial material and, together with various Indian Brahmins, jointly created what is now known as Hinduism. Pennington sees this as a joint construct of Britain and India, Hindus and Christians, who devised 'something that the later nineteenth century would take for granted: a coherent, cohesive, pan-Indian Hinduism'.[30]

Pennington does acknowledge, towards the end of his book, that most modern religions have similar qualities of change, reform, and ruptures caused by the events of recent times. 'Continuity and the triumph of historical memory over sustained, deliberate, and widely dispersed interventions are also parts of the story we must not overlook', he writes.[31] He also offers other disclaimers, for example that new evidence shows that there were similar Hindu movements prior to colonialism. This disclaimer comes in light of numerous criticisms against his thesis, which show that ideas of Hindu unity had existed prior to colonialism. However, this is 'new evidence' only to those scholars who have been out of touch with Indian sources and have thrived on parroting the myth. In any case, Pennington's disclaimers notwithstanding, it is clear that his thrust is to reduce and essentially dismiss contemporary Hinduism.

The following disclaimer toward the end of his book shows that Pennington does understand what is at stake in his thesis. In fact, he articulates the 'case against' his view quite well. But this is merely to cover himself and is disconnected from any argument he has made.

> To narrow the focus and put the matter somewhat bluntly for clarity's sake, if religion is not a real thing, then likewise it is not meaningful to speak of Hinduism or any other 'religious' faith as if it were a real thing. This claim in turn denies and devalues the lived experience of, in this case, Hindus and hits at the very heart of what many regard with the greatest reverence as the core of their received identity. Moreover, this claim excludes their voices from the centers of knowledge production about their defining experiences and emotions on that very basis. The arguments that religion is a meaningless category and Hinduism a bungled western construct best dispensed with effectively undercut the geopolitical aims of some Hindus to be taken seriously after centuries of stereotyping, misrepresentation, and demonization at the hands of the Christian West. To seek to deny, moreover, entrance to a conversation about the social and political character and effect of religion to those who espouse religious points of view on the argument that such voices represent not the scholarship of religion but data for scholars of religion, and to claim this at the same time that one claims that religion is a misleading category for cross-cultural comparison, signals an attempt to trump the self-representation card that some non-Christians might now play.[32]

Despite wanting to appear to acknowledge the influence of both sides on each other, Pennington insists that 'colonial modernity' dominated the exchange between the British and the Indians. 'The religious categories and social practices of both British Christians and Indian Hindus were transfigured by a colonial modernity', he says.[33]

Pennington is also among the members of the neo-Hinduism camp who claim to know the exact point of origin of neo-Hinduism. He suggests it originated in a reference in an early nineteenth-century Hindu newspaper. The newspaper notes 'the emergence of an enduring modern and popular Hinduism that rejected the rationalist monotheism of nineteenth-century Hindu reformers and embraced instead a programme carried forward to this day by the slow ascendancy of Hindu nationalism'. The paper, published out of Bengal, was *Samacar Candrika* (Moonlight News). Pennington states: 'Manufacturing this Hinduism proved to be an act less of promoting particular items of doctrine or sites of authority ... and more of patterning a general structure for Hindu action, social and ritual.'[34] The paper took up contemporary issues to discuss the role of Sanskrit and the other Indian languages, caste, rituals and image worship in an age of science. The editors, according to Pennington, wanted to build a bridge between the past and the modern age:

> Its 'construction of Hinduism' was an undertaking far closer to the literal meaning of the phrase, a manipulative as well as an imaginative construction. The Candrika sought not just to craft a public image of Indian religion but also to promote openly Hindu unity and identity by patterning religious activity for Hindus while decentering potentially divisive issues of belief and Hindu sectarianism. It targeted the actual morphology of ritual, caste, and gender relations to foster a unified and normative Hindu practice.[35]

This newspaper was the first sustained effort to construct Hinduism in a manner different from the discourse advanced by British and Indian reformers of the Ram Mohan Roy variety. Even though its circulation was only a few hundred in a city of a few hundred thousand, many of its readers belonged to the influential elite. It represented those Hindus who wanted to oppose the missionaries and reshape Hinduism without sacrificing its traditional character. Thus it opposed both the *Samacar Darpan*, the newspaper of the powerful Christian seminary at Serampore, and the group of Eurocentric Indians represented by Ram Mohan Roy. Under the heading 'Constructing and Manufacturing Hinduism', Pennington writes that Bengali elites were caught between colonialism and their desire to control their own social structures, while bringing change that would be relevant for the times.

Turning to more recent times, Pennington lashes out at the proponents of Hinduism for being politically motivated in a sinister sense. He picks up on the term 'syndicated Hinduism' that was initially coined by Romila Thapar in India, and writes:

> In the twentieth century, Hindu nationalists, it has been regularly observed, awoke to the political fruits that the concept of a nationally and historically cohesive tradition could yield. Nationalist groups have pieced together a 'syndicated Hinduism' in recent historical memory to suggest a monolithic, ancient religion and have thereby sought to manufacture a certain historical integrity and communal unity for all of India.[36]

Brian K. Smith writes that there are stakes involved in making such portrayals of Hinduism:

> The history of modern 'constructions' (and 'deconstructions') of Hinduism, both in India and in the West, seems to demonstrate that all such representations have had a stake in portraying this religion as more or less indeterminant, unbounded, pluralistic to the point of all-embracing—as, in other words, distinct and different from other religions.[37]

Peter van der Veer, Sheldon Pollock and others

Another scholar, Peter van der Veer, gives full expression to the thesis that colonial constructions became internalized by Indians. He stresses how these constructions provided a bulwark for Brahmins, writing:

> What orientalism has done is two things. It gave crucial support to the Brahmanical contention that Indian civilization is a unified whole based on a shastrik, authoritative tradition of which Brahmin priests and sectarian preceptors are the principal bearers.[38]

He speaks of the role of Indologists in forming a kind of 'Hindu canon' on Judeo-Christian models, with critical editions of the *Mahabarata* and *Ramayana* and with projects involving the stabilization of the texts of the Puranas. He repeats a constant drumbeat of his peer group against Gandhi, namely, that Gandhi only valued the Bhagavad-Gita as a result of Western influence.[39]

I agree with van der Veer that Western Indologists developed a view of Indian society based primarily on the study of Sanskrit texts which they interpreted in collaboration with 'a Brahmin elite'. The Indologists assumed that Brahmins represented the entire society. He is also right in saying that this led to the impression of Indian society being static with no development over time.[40] However, if a similar disqualifying criterion were applied to Europe's learned class of thinkers and writers of the past, one would also have to dismiss the credentials of Western civilization and its history as nothing more than the product of some elites.

Such one-sided approaches to cross-cultural influences permeate his works even when he claims otherwise and seems conscious of this risk. For instance, in a subsequent book, van der Veer starts off by admitting that the influence between India and Europe was felt in both directions. The aim of his book, he says, is to 'disturb the complacency' of national histories, both Indian and British.[41] But the book fails in its stated purpose because it is mainly about how the British influenced Hinduism and not the other way around. The Indian influences upon the British that are covered are superficial, and do not include India's impact on the Industrial Revolution (supplying manufacturing know-how in steel, textiles, etc.) or her impact on Western philosophy, psychology, linguistics, literature, and even modern Christianity. There is a line drawn by such scholars when they admit to India's influence on the West, and they try to emphasize areas of impact that do not undermine the superiority of 'the West' as such.

Van der Veer is also among the most insistent of the scholars who claim that Hinduism was created for sinister political motives and characterizes Swami Chinmayananda (founder of the widely popular Chinmaya Mission) as one of these nationalists. He writes:

Vivekananda's work has also inspired Hindu nationalists with a somewhat different gloss on Hindu spirituality. One of the most important of them is Swami Chinmayananda, a religious leader who is the founder of the Vishva Hindu Parishad (VHP), an organisation that attempts to 'reclaim' India for the 'Hindu majority'. The VHP is at the forefront of an anti-Muslim movement in Indian politics in the 1980s that assails the secularism of the Indian state and attempts to make India into a Hindu nation-state.[42]

Furthermore, he blames the Indian diaspora for feeding this unified Hindu identity:

> The construction of a unified Hindu identity is of utmost importance for Hindus who live outside India. They need a Hinduism that can be explained to outsiders as a respectable religion, that can be taught to their children in religious education, and that can form the basis for collective action ... In an ironic twist of history, orientalism is now brought by Indians to Indians living in the West.[43]

To sum up, van der Veer's thesis is that Europeans and Brahmins elevated Vedanta's importance for mutual gain. This later backfired on the Europeans because Indians used the constructed idea called Hinduism in order to: (a) arouse nationalism against British rule, and (b) dupe the West into adopting many Indian ideas into Western philosophy and popular culture (which the author calls the 'reverse colonization' of Europe). The implications in India went further, because Hinduism: (c) denies the tribal people (the 'real Indians') their authentic beliefs, and (d) has culminated in the Vishva Hindu Parishad, which is anti-Muslim and anti-secular.

The politicizing of Hinduism and of Sanskrit is fashionable and can even result in awards from the government of India. A good example is the career of Sheldon Pollock, a well-known scholar of Sanskrit at Columbia University. The Indian government awarded him the Padma Shri Award in 2010, following which he received a massive grant from Infosys Foundation to promote Indian classical languages.

One has to delve deeply into his work to understand his ideology on the subject. In an interview, Pollock was asked why caste prejudices persist in Indian culture even as Sanskrit is disappearing, whereupon he answered by separating out 'secular Sanskrit' from 'religious Sanskrit' in order to strike at Hinduism. The culprits, according to him, are the mantras of Sanskrit. He sees Sanskrit mantras as anti-secular and causing caste-based oppression. On the other hand, 'secular Sanskrit' represents the flowering of culture, the arts, and sophistication.[44]

Pollock wants to protect Sanskrit by recovering what he sees as the 'emancipatory, egalitarian, empowering' aspects of the Indian tradition, and by rejecting Hinduism, which represents oppression. When the interviewer asked him about *shabda* (sound, speech) and mantras that go beyond literal meaning, he shrugged off the idea and remarked flippantly that 'energy is in the eye of the beholder'.[45] I have written at length in *Being Different* on such demonizing of Sanskrit.

Recently, he has formulated his new doctrine called 'Liberation Philology' which turns the study of Sanskrit into activism to break up India into a zone of conflicts. He describes it a project of 'supplementing postcolonialism with postcapitalism, or a concern over past wrongs with a concern for future rights; and finding way[s] to meet, from our small philological locations as specific intellectuals, the obligation to construct "a planet-wide inclusivist community"'. Using this jargon, he is busy spreading a reinterpretation of Sanskrit texts to expose that oppression is built into them. Sanskrit studies for him is a political weapon to help 'liberate' the Dalits, minorities and women from its horrors. It is worth noting that Hacker also started out as a Sanskrit philologist of considerable competence before turning his knowledge for political use.

Another prominent Indian social scientist in the Western academy, Jayant Lele, traces the origins of neo-Hinduism to the desire of Brahmin administrators to protect their position of privilege and augment their prestige vis-à-vis the British by casting their work in terms of liberal Christianity or utilitarianism. He writes: 'The presence of an ancient and highly sophisticated civilization could not be ignored, although admitting its presence in the simple folk wisdom and everyday life practice of a peasant would have been contrary to the project of control and exploitation.' This helped the Brahmins' 'hegemonic agenda dating back to Manu' to construct 'a new explanatory narrative'.[46]

More recently, Reza Pirbhai, associate professor of South-Asian Studies at Louisiana State University, writes that, 'reading between the lines' of the Bharatiya Janata Party's modern Hindutva politics, he can see that the European Orientalists had invented Hinduism. First the Europeans constructed this ideology with Brahmins as conspirators, and then Vivekananda adopted it, followed by the further developments of Gandhi, Aurobindo, and others. He concludes that Hinduism is one of the youngest religions in the world, being a nineteenth-century production of dubious parentage. Pirbhai reads through Westernized filters and writes with great certainty:

> The doctrines and practices presented as 'Hinduism' by colonial-era Hindu intellectuals and their postcolonial heirs did not exist prior to the British colonization of South Asia. Instead, a vast array of Sanskrit texts, supplemented by variegated vernacular and oral traditions, were the norm.[47]

Christophe Jaffrelot is a French expert on Hindu nationalism who also writes extensively on this subject. He sees Gandhi as the central player in politicizing neo-Hinduism, writing: 'Indeed, Hindu nationalism crystallized as an ideology and as a movement exactly at the time when the Congress became imbued with Gandhi's principles and grew into a mass movement.'[48]

Jaffrelot feels that Balgangadhar Tilak (a prominent freedom fighter and a contemporary of Gandhi) took the nationalist discourse in the direction of violent action in the name of Hinduism, away from Gandhi's harmonious ideal of equality for all faiths. Gandhi's India was defined in terms of a certain geography and culture, even though he acknowledged religious identities. Then Nehru took Gandhi's idea in the opposite direction, toward European secularism and away from religion. Thus, Gandhi occupied the middle ground in Hinduism, with Tilak and Nehru as the two poles opposing each other. Jaffrelot concludes that from this 'churning' of political ideas emerged Hindu nationalism's attempt to redefine Indian culture as Hindu, and determined to assimilate all the minorities.[49]

Meera Nanda is yet another scholar who has joined the deluge against contemporary Hinduism. She builds on Rambachan's criticism of Vivekananda's association of anubhava with scientific empiricism. She is a Marxist who is especially critical of Vivekananda for wanting to see Hinduism in scientific terms, which she regards as an enterprise solely motivated by the 'nationalist urge' to declare Hinduism as a religion of reason over Christianity and Islam.[50]

Nanda claims that 'the naturalistic and empirical theories of modern science' contradict Vedanta, and she suggests that Vedanta is worse in this regard than the Abrahamic religions. She writes:

> Unlike the Abrahamic religions which are wary of epistemological relativism out of the fear of relativizing the Word of God revealed in the Bible or the Koran, Brahminical Hinduism (and Hindu nationalism) thrives on a hierarchical relativism to evade all challenges to its idealistic metaphysics and mystical ways of knowing.[51]

This is a highly tendentious way of characterizing an important difference between Abrahamic religions and Hinduism, a difference too complex to analyse here in any depth but one that goes far beyond some weak desire to 'evade' challenges.

An example of how pervasive the myth of neo-Hinduism has become may be found in the recent public campaign by Goa's Christian priests to preach that 'there were no Hindus in Goa before the Portuguese landed'. This claim came in the midst of an election season heavily based on religious identity politics.[52]

One of the side-effects of such discourse has been that many Hindu ideas and practices such as yoga are being demonized or else removed from Hinduism and turned into secular and/or Christian practices. For example, David Gordon White is a well-known scholar of Hinduism who is highly regarded by many naïve Hindus. His latest book, *Sinister*

Yogis, claims to be a well-researched history of yoga according to which yoga, in its original form, was a system of exploitation that entailed heightening one's power over others, including for purposes of sexual exploitation. His recent books along these lines have been widely acclaimed by scholars. According to White, the benign and humanistic form of yoga we find today is a recent invention.[53]

Contributing to this genre of scholarship are writers such as Mark Singleton, whose book, *Yoga Body*, claims that modern yoga teachers got their ideas from the West. According to him, it was men like Sri Yogendra (1897-1989), T. Krishnamacharya (1888-1989) and Swami Kuvalayananda (1883-1966) who developed yoga practices based on Western gymnastics and YMCA influence in India. Indians felt they were physically weak, and such leaders brought these Western practices to help boost their physical strength to match the Western masculinity. Singleton especially targets B.K.S. Iyengar, who is now in his mid-90s and regarded as the man who brought yoga to the West. He holds Iyengar accountable for 'packaging' these Western systems to fit into old Hindu texts and make them seem indigenous to India.

Thus, after Hacker, Halbfass, King and Rambachan had established the foundations of the myth of neo-Hinduism, various other writers have expanded it. Neo-Hinduism is considered the vehicle by which Hindu nationalists oppress Dalits, minorities and women. It has become entrenched in the Marxist and subaltern studies view of Hinduism as the scourge that is causing all of India's social problems.

Hindu leaders echo the chorus

Hindu sympathizers often repeat the myth, sometimes unwittingly. Shamita Basu, for example, intends a sympathetic treatment of Vivekananda, but her ideas of Indian nationalism are inspired by Antonio Gramsci and by subaltern and cultural studies. Basu quotes Rambachan's arguments against Vivekananda's claim of yoga as a science.[54] She underscores Rambachan's view that scientific experience (grounded in the senses) cannot be equated with spiritual experience (which is transcendental and subjective). However, she fails to note that

Rambachan misses the point by equating outer (third-person) and inner (first-person) sciences, collapsing the latter into the former.

Despite showing sympathy for Vivekananda and his cause, Basu maintains that 'as a unitary tradition Hinduism was a political strategy that nationalism surreptitiously introduced into the neo-Hindu discourse'.[55] Unable to study the philosophical issues independently, she merely parrots the opinions of well-known scholars with Western credentials.

Frank Morales is another example of voices speaking for what they regard as the 'pure, traditional Hinduism' while criticizing contemporary Hinduism. He writes that 'there are really two distinct and conflicting Hinduisms today, Neo-Hindu and Traditionalist Hindu'. The criticism is basically a rehash of the Hacker-Rambachan position, except that here it is offered as an attempt to rescue the 'real' Hinduism of a bygone era from the clutches of the modern era.[56]

Many other Hindu leaders also see contemporary Hinduism as destructive of traditional Hinduism, and inadvertently they have exacerbated the internal divisiveness. They often seem more concerned with defending the 'purity' of a given Hindu sampradaya or philosophical school. They fail to see the hard reality that Hinduism, across the board, faces heavy challenges for its survival.

Such voices, in their attempt to claim the role of orthodoxy, are over-playing the colonial influence on the natural evolution of Hinduism. I take a more balanced and nuanced view of this evolution as it occurred over the past two centuries, noting both what has weakened it as well as what has enlivened it and made it relevant for today.

Ironically, Hindu groups that attempt to promote their tradition often give grants to the very same scholars who are attacking Hinduism's unity. A good example is the funding provided by the Dharam Hinduja Institute of Indic Research in Cambridge, U.K., established by a billionaire in the memory of his deceased son. Among the main scholars directing the institute's strategy were scholars who propagate the myth of neo-Hinduism, such as Julius Lipner, Julia Leslie, Ursula King and Elizabeth de Michelis.

De Michelis, for instance, writes in her book *A History of Modern Yoga* that 'Western esoteric ideas' of the eighteenth century had entered into Bengali intellectual circles and later got turned into Vivekananda's 'Neo-Vedantic occultism', which Vivekananda allegedly renamed 'Raja yoga'. She claims that the origin of yoga as practised by contemporary Hindus took place only after Vivekananda published his 'Raja Yoga', in which he 'reconfigured the *Yogasutras* of Patanjali along the lines of a then-emerging New Age occultistic style of secularised and individualistically oriented religiosity'. Her subsequent work has deepened her claim that yoga is essentially not Hindu but rather a secular practice with health benefits which neo-Hindus have appropriated from the West to boost their own chauvinistic identities.

Some academic defenders of contemporary Hinduism

Arvind Sharma is among several scholars who have serious problems with the position of the Hacker-Rambachan camp. Thus, when Brian Hatcher[57] claims that contemporary Hinduism's quest for eclecticism departs considerably from tradition, Sharma responds that 'efforts to sustain such a claim tend to exaggerate the discontinuity between neo-Hindu and orthodox Hindu positions on certain issues'.[58]

Sharma also takes exception to Hatcher's use of 'eclecticism' as the lens through which to perceive Hinduism and portray it as fragmented and lacking coherence. Sharma points out that there is a double standard at work when one finds others' religions to be 'eclectic' but not one's own:

> I know of no person who accepts his own religion or culture in toto without individual preferences (choices). Why is such *internal* selection not called eclectic and does not set the same discourses in motion as when the choices are external?[59]

In the course of pointing out Hinduism's fragmentation, Hatcher claims that the 'knowledge of Brahman [as] accessible to everyone …

is somewhat against the traditional grain'.[60] He is referring to the claim that lower castes are excluded from having knowledge of Brahman. Sharma argues that even in traditional Advaita such knowledge is accessible to everyone through smriti, and that direct experience of Brahman in this life is also possible without recourse to sruti.[61]

Brian Smith is another important scholar of Hinduism who challenges the attack on the contemporary Hinduism project. There is nothing wrong with this project per se, he notes. Theologians of all faiths tend to make such reinterpretations, and there is 'certainly no reason'

> to single out the theologians of Hinduism. Such an enterprise, if set into motion, should be directed equally at all of the 'religions'. 'Buddhism,' 'Christianity,' 'Islam,' and 'Judaism' are all, at least in part, the conceptual products of their theologians. 'Hinduism', from this point of view, is hardly a unique case.[62]

He goes on to say that if scholars decide to decenter the theologians of a religion, they should be

> mindful of the ethical and intellectual consequences of such interventions. We should carry out this self-appointed task in our study of all religions and not just a selected few. Religions do of course change over time; and the conceptualizations of any particular religion will inevitably be altered by history. The contours of modern indigenous (that is, 'Hindu') views of 'Hinduism' have also undergone such change, especially in light of the interactions Hindus have had with the West.[63]

There is nothing new about reinterpreting a faith; nor are such reinterpretations and conceptualizations necessarily unorthodox or separate from tradition. Smith argues that all religions have changed in ways similar to how Hinduism has changed, and that neo-Hinduism is, in one respect, a natural consequence of changes that have occurred in society and politics. He writes:

All religions, at various points in recent history and under varying circumstances, have adapted to the modern world and the accompanying intellectual trends of modernity. 'Hinduism' (or 'Neo-Hinduism') is not unique in this regard either; the Neo-Hindu movement shares many commonalties with developments in other religious traditions around the world over the past several hundred years. The study of religion is the study of traditions in constant change.[64]

Smith warns his academic peers that a 'form of "essentialism" occurs when one period of change is somehow constituted as a deviation or inauthentic swerve from some supposedly more or less timeless norm'.[65] The important point he wants scholars to note is that contemporary Hindus have 'by and large, constructed a vision of their religion no less open-ended than the definitions put forth by the mainstream of Indology'.[66]

Smith also reminds scholars 'that religion has always had a political dimension'.[67] He criticizes recent scholars for their tendency to deny contemporary Hindus the agency to redefine themselves for modern times, just as people of all other religions have been doing. He writes: 'That "Hinduism" was "constructed"—by Orientalists, Neo-Hindus, Hindu nationalists, separately or in concert—is not some kind of epistemological revelation, nor is it a historical anomaly, nor is it a feature common only to this entity. One might equally, and with as much validity, argue that all such designations for world religions are "constructs".'[68] He concludes with an important statement that aptly supports many of my arguments:

> This kind of indifference to indigenous conceptualizations of self-identity is one unfortunate end result of the argument that Indology and Orientalist concerns singlehandedly 'constructed,' 'invented,' or 'imagined' a unified religion called Hinduism. This position is especially problematic in an age where Western scholars often claim to be concerned to allow the 'natives to speak' and 'assume agency' over representational discourse. [...] Denying the legitimacy of any

and all 'Hindu' representations of Hinduism can easily crossover into a Neo-Orientalism, whereby indigenous discourse is once again silenced or ignored as the product of a false consciousness delivered to it by outside forces or as simply irrelevant to the authoritative deliberations of Western Indologists. While there are many reasons for scholars to feel uncomfortable with the claims some Indians have and are making regarding 'Hinduism,' it is perhaps equally dangerous to deny them the legitimacy to declare what, for them, is 'Hinduism'.[69]

Smith is also suspicious of the academic fashion for deconstructing Hinduism in the name of saving its 'victims' and positioning scholars as the saviors. (I mentioned this tendency in my discussion of Richard King earlier in this chapter.)

A Jewish scholar points out that Judaism faces essentially the same problem, i.e., academics are systematically fragmenting Judaism to the point where it is made to seem non-existent:

So there is no possibility of claiming there never was, nor is there now, such a thing as 'Judaism,' but only 'Judaisms'. For once we take that route, there will be no 'Judaisms' either, but only this one and that one, and how we feel from day to day, and this morning's immutable truth and newly fabricated four-thousand-year-old tradition.[70]

Krishna Prakash Gupta is another scholar who defies the hegemonic discourse on contemporary Hinduism amongst the 'Neo-Hinduism' circle of academics. Speaking of Vivekananda's legacy in general and of the Ramakrishna Mission in particular, Gupta insists that they cannot be explained simply as a response to Western challenges. On the contrary, he argues, they were conceived and designed 'strictly in terms of conventional Hindu thought categories'. He goes on to argue that Western influence cannot possibly explain the trajectory of the Ramakrishna Mission movement, and insists that Vivekananda's reformulated Vedanta was 'Western only in appearance'. In concept and organization, it was Hindu.

The charge that contemporary Hinduism's major figures and institutions are a 'native' response to Western challenges is clearly misleading, according to Gupta. He views the Ramakrishna Mission as 'an internally consistent evolutionary manifestation of India's pre-modern religiosity' and not merely as a native response to some Western challenge. He suggests we abandon the current sociology-of-religion framework and analyse the genesis and evolution of the Mission on its own terms.[71]

Will Sweetman argues that many biases about the non-existence of such a thing as Hinduism can be traced back to the assumptions built into Protestant Christianity. He argues that:

> Even where such Christian models are explicitly disavowed, the claim that Hinduism is not a religion can be shown to depend upon a particular religious conception of the nature of the world and our possible knowledge of it, which scholars of religion cannot share.[72]

In other words, failure to fit Hinduism into the category of 'religion' should not be seen as a problem for Hinduism. Nor should we accept the ridiculous claim that no such entity exists. Rather, it should lead scholars to reject the very category of 'religion' as something universal. 'Religion' should be seen as a Judeo-Christian theological view that projects itself as being universal when it is not.

What is interesting about Sweetman's thesis is that he finds that many scholars who criticize Christian categories are themselves using Christian assumptions of cosmology. He cites R.N. Dandekar and S.N. Balagangadhara as examples of such scholars, i.e., their attempts to rescue Hinduism from Christianity are based on using Christian ideas unconsciously. I tend to agree with him. Scholars of post-colonialism typically lack a sufficient understanding of Hinduism from which to embark on their critique of the category of 'religion'. To remedy this situation, the Conclusion shall utilize the notions of 'astika', 'nastika' and 'poison pills' as concepts from where a better approach can start.

PART 2

UTTARA PAKSHA
(My Response)

8

Historical Continuity and Colonial Disruption

A major cause of the distortions discussed in the foregoing chapters has been the lack of adequate study of pre-colonial Indian thinkers. Such a study would show that there has been a historical continuity of thought along with vibrant debate, controversy and innovation.

A recent book by Jonardan Ganeri, the *Lost Age of Reason: Philosophy in Early Modern India 1450-1700*, shows this vibrant flow of Indian thought prior to colonial times, and demonstrates India's own variety of modernity, which included the use of logic and reasoning. Ganeri draws on historical sources to show the contentious nature of Indian discourse. He argues that it did not freeze or reify, and that such discourse was established well before colonialism.

This chapter will show the following:

- Indian thought prior to colonialism exhibited both continuity and change.
- A consolidation into what we now call 'Hinduism' began *prior* to colonialism.

- Colonial Indology was driven by Europe's internal quest to digest Sanskrit and its texts into European history without contradicting Christian monotheism.
- Indologists thus appropriated selectively whatever Indian ideas fit into their own narratives and rejected what did not. This intervention disrupted the historical continuity of Indian thought and positioned Indologists as the 'pioneers'.
- Post-modernist thought in many ways continues this digestion and disruption even though its stated purpose is exactly the opposite.
- Swami Vivekananda's innovations were based mainly on pre-colonial sources within Hinduism and were not based on copying Western ideas.

This demonstrates that there was a wealth of internal resources to bring change without having to depend on colonial imports. In fact, colonial intervention is what caused disruption in this flow. Rather than seeing colonialism as the force of innovation, it would be more accurate to see it as a disruptive force.

Traditional categories of astika (those who affirm) and nastika (those who do not affirm)

Hinduism has long defined itself on its own terms, in part through a long-running distinction between 'astika' and 'nastika'. These terms need to be understood in their historical context in order to appreciate the existence of movements that sought internal unity and philosophical coherence. The very existence of these old philosophical categories is clear evidence that people we later started calling Hindus did indeed have an awareness of collective unity and coherence regardless of whether or not they had a name for their identity. The history of this awareness may be tracked by examining how these terms were used over time.

The terms 'astika' and 'nastika' have had broad meanings, wherein astika is someone who says 'there is' while the nastika says 'there is not'. Of course what is being affirmed or denied is left out of this etymology. The set of criteria for affirming has varied over time, and from one thinker to another. As a result, the terms are elastic and dynamic, and not easily translated into English.

Astika and nastika cannot be simply equated with theist and atheist, respectively; some schools that were considered astikas have propounded a form of atheism. Nor can astikas be equated with those who affirm the Vedas in every case.[1] In other words, to put too defined a predicate onto 'there is' or 'there is not' would be misleading, and that may be one reason why the ancient sages left these terms open.

These terms have served to classify and stratify various philosophical positions. Their exact meaning has changed to correspond with the continual negotiation and re-negotiation of philosophical principles. While the astika concept consolidated the 'insiders' of a metaphysical system, the nastika concept helped create a boundary with 'outsiders'. This indicates tension amongst rival philosophies, as well as flux and continual competition, and hence the emergence of new systems. The nature of this rivalry must be contrasted with the sectarian history of the West because of two significant factors that were absent in India, and this absence created a space that made the flux and dynamism possible:

- In the Indian context, there is no totalizing, absolute history of prophets and revelations that serves as the litmus test of the kind that dominates a given Abrahamic religion. In other words, Indian systems did not carry the burden of having to reconcile their latest ideas with a standard, canonized, non-negotiable history.
- There was no continuous central ecclesiastical institutional authority with judicial or quasi-judicial powers to adjudicate and enforce theological truth, at least not for any sustained period and not over any large portion of the population.

The absence of these two kinds of constraints helps to explain the dynamism that is appreciated as a signature quality of Hinduism.

Along with this absence of closed-minded forces, there has been a unifying base to which Hindus could refer, an underlying structure which, again, I like to think of as an open architecture. Rival schools had ongoing serious debates with one another based on a common vocabulary and related metaphysical quests. Here was an active ecosystem which nurtured numerous theories of varying life-spans. These movements often merged, bifurcated, competed, died or evolved in their shared intellectual soil. The astika/nastika distinction comes as close as anything to defining the boundaries of these shared assumptions. These schools were never dogmatic or policed since their positions were always debatable and subject to change.

In his excellent study of the pre-colonial coherence of Hinduism, titled *Unifying Hinduism*, Andrew Nicholson explains that prior to the medieval period there was no single way to define what 'astika' meant. One principle that prevails in many definitions is that ethics—rather than metaphysical propositions or doctrines—be used as the criteria for being astika. This could explain why astikas were traditionally mentioned as praiseworthy whereas nastikas were seen as a threat. The charge of someone being a nastika was considered severe. Naturally, the Buddhists and Jains were unwilling to be branded as nastikas. No one wanted to be called nastika. Many kinds of groups have considered themselves astika, while defining nastika as some disqualifier applicable to other schools. One school's criteria for nastika may be another's criteria for astika. The mere fact that such a line was drawn, even though subject to negotiation and change, proves my point about having a quest for a coherent sense of collective self.

The criteria for determining which systems are astika and which, are nastika depended on the thinker and the period. One criterion, which made sense in some contexts, was to identify the astika as affirming the ritual authority of the Vedas. But this earlier meaning changed when the emphasis moved from performer of correct *rituals* to holder of correct *views*. Thus, Manu (one of the foremost writers of smritis) defined a nastika as any twice-born who disregards sruti and smriti on the basis of logic; such an individual, he felt, should be excluded by the righteous and considered a reviler of the Vedas.[2] This definition itself required debate and analysis, and it was later superseded.

In fact, there have been many criteria for membership into the astika family. For Sanskrit grammarians in the seventh century through to the seventeenth century, 'astika' meant someone who believed in an afterlife.[3] Another example is Medhatithi (a ninth-century south Indian writer) who defined astika as one who 'affirms the value of ritual'.

The Jain scholar Haribhadra developed a classification system according to the criterion that astika requires one to 'affirm the existence of virtue and vice'. Haribhadra also included Jains and Buddhists as astikas, because his criterion was based on affirming the existence of another world (*paraloka*), transmigration (*gati*), virtue (*punya*), and vice (*papa*). His definition has nothing to do with theism or Vedas. He lived in the era when there was a proliferation of Puranas, Tantra, Shaivism, Vaishnavism and early bhakti movements. Born a Brahmin, he later became a Jain monk. As a prolific writer on many subjects including catalogues that summarized the philosophical positions of others, he is considered a highly reliable source of various philosophical positions prevalent at that time. Even though he concludes that Jainism is his most preferred system, he is highly respectful of the other Hindu and Buddhist systems of thought.[4]

Haribhadra illustrates that it was common for thinkers to organize the various schools' positions *not* into a binary of astika/nastika but into a hierarchy of grades of truth. The boundaries were still soft and porous. Today, scholars have become too sweeping in applying these terms as normative categories that are assumed to be fixed and uniform. I agree with Nicholson that:

Modern historiographers of Indian philosophy have largely been blind to the numerous intertextually related definitions of the terms astika and nastika. This oversight is further evidence of our own credulity and overreliance on a handful of texts for our understanding of a complex situation in the history of ideas.[5]

Only much later did thinkers assert that the differences between astikas and nastikas were too large to be bridgeable, whereas the internal differences among the various astika positions were deemed to be less significant. At first, schools such as Samkhya and Mimamsa did not explicitly state that they had commonalities that differentiated them from non-Hindu philosophies of the Jains and Buddhists. But over time, there emerged codifiers who consolidated what became known as the six systems of Indian philosophy and gave them prominence over the rest. Later still, these six got further consolidated with a shared commitment to Vedic authority, by which they differentiated themselves from Jains and Buddhists.[6]

The grand consolidation into what we now call Hinduism evolved only after Shankara's death, when his own followers incorporated the rival schools into a 'Vedic family' which included the Samkhya and Yoga schools. A number of venerable sages played an important role in the consolidation and crystallization of the astikas as a well-bounded category, including Madhava (fourteenth century), Madhusudana Sarasvati (sixteenth century) and Vijnanabhikshu (sixteenth century). Madhava was important not only because he was a minister of the powerful Vijayanagara Empire, but also because he became the head of the Sringeri matha founded by Shankara. Madhusudana even argued that some of the astikas were deliberately teaching in ways that would keep people from following the nastikas such as Jains and Buddhists.[7] Vijnanabhikshu, in the sixteenth century, continued the consolidation further.[8]

It is fair to say, however, that by the sixteenth century, astika had crystallized and solidified to correspond roughly to today's Hinduism and that nastika meant Buddhists, Jains, and materialists. This sense of being a Hindu continues to this day. The goal of each of these thinkers was to organize, classify and rank different philosophies in order of merit, thereby showing them to be part of the astika family. The Sanskrit term for such a compendium is 'samgraha' or 'samuccaya' (collection).

Many intellectuals within what is now considered the Hindu family developed their own organizing principles in which all astika schools were neatly arranged in a hierarchy. The specific organization and hierarchy differed, but there gradually emerged a growing consensus that astika was one who 'affirms the Vedas as the source of ultimate truth'.[9] While this served as the big tent now called Hinduism, competing authorities differed on the ranking inside the tent among the various ideas, paths and practices. Each group formulated its own hierarchy of validity among various astika systems. For instance, Madhusudana espoused Advaita Vedanta as the highest level of his hierarchy, while Vijnanabhikshu espoused Bhedabheda Vedanta, but both shared the desire to reconcile all the astika schools.[10]

The consolidation of Hinduism involved moving towards an expanded sense of astika with many more schools of thought and lineages gradually being absorbed into it. This process required selectively co-opting from those who had been previously rejected and admitting some of their ideas into the hierarchy of legitimate means for spiritual advancement.

Despite all the apparent contradictions among the astikas, they were seen as sharing in the higher cosmic unity expressed by the dharmic traditions as a whole. The astika/nastika evolution was the mechanism by which medieval compilers and classifiers assimilated the terminology and ideas of Samkhya and Yoga into their own frameworks.

This method of the evolution of ideas is not a problem for the dharma traditions. The history centric religions are another matter, for they operate by a single standard involving the historical record. Criteria for compliance are hard, and policing is both constant and ecclesiastically sanctioned. The whole dogmatic enterprise would fall apart if there were flexibility of the kind found in dharma.

Pre-Colonial Hindu Unifiers: Example of Vijnanabhikshu

Andrew Nicholson places the growing consolidation of Hindu 'big tent' unity in roughly the fourteenth to sixteenth century CE period.[11] He shows that the categories of astika/nastika were fluid previously, but in this period they became solidified and hardened. He sees the medieval consolidators of contemporary Hinduism as analogous to European doxographers. A doxography is a compilation of multiple systems of thought which are examined for their interrelationships, and sometimes new classifications are proposed. It is like a survey of various philosophies from a particular point of view that is looking for relationships across various systems. Often the bias of the doxographer is expressed by the set of schools that he includes and the ones he excludes, and the criteria by which he ranks them.[12]

Nicholson goes into great detail to show that the writings and classifications by rival Indian schools changed during the medieval period, with many cross-borrowings and new alliances.[13] He argues that this Indian genre, akin to European doxography, served as the means to cross-fertilize among traditions, thereby making each tradition more accessible to others.

The scholar Vijnanabhikshu is a good example to illustrate that there was continuity in Hinduism prior to colonialism. He and his sixteenth-century contemporaries were precursors to an evolving pre-colonial Hinduism that culminated in Vivekananda's movement. This was not a break from the past, nor was it based on imported ideas. It brought many streams together in a creative manner.

Vijnanabhikshu claimed that there are two paths to final liberation. The first, the path of knowledge (jnana) offered by Samkhya and Vedanta can lead to enlightenment, but the follower will have to endure continued embodiment during the state of jivanmukti (living in a liberated state).[14] However, the second, the path of yoga as the Vishnu Purana suggests, brings immediate liberation, destroying *prarabdha* (past life) acts and bypassing jivanmukti altogether.[15] Yoga in this discussion includes many spiritual practices, including meditation. This makes yoga the 'fast track' to complete liberation. (Note that Vijnanabhikshu was not following Patanjali's Yogasutras in every respect.)

Therefore, he advocated yoga as practice, but at the same time he did not discard Vedanta's method of inquiry into the nature of Brahman, nor Samkhya's technique of discrimination between purusha (being, self) and prakriti (nature, matter). He could mix and match all three systems and did not see them in contradiction. He believed that the terms, 'purusha' and 'jivatman', although from different traditional texts, are synonyms, as are 'kaivalya' and 'moksha'. They were merely meant to serve different kinds of persons.

Vijnanabhikshu explains how all systems culminate into yoga at the highest level: 'Just as all the rivers, beginning with the Ganges, exist as parts of the ocean, so too the philosophical systems, beginning with the Samkhya, exist entirely as parts of this Yoga system.'[16] He treats various Hindu systems as parts of the greater whole which is yoga. His ideas were later elaborated by others such as Swami Vivekananda who continued the work of clarifying, updating and expanding Hinduism by building on past ideas.

Vijnanabhikshu did not found a new school but merely compiled, organized and classified other schools, and showed approximate equivalences and correspondences among them. His writings were influential in understanding Hinduism both in the West and in India. European Indologists such as T.H. Colebrooke (1765-1837), A.E. Gough (1845-1915), Paul Deussen (1845-1919), and Richard Garbe (1857-1927) were looking for a system of classification to understand Hindu thought in a manner they could deal with. Vijnanabhikshu, along with other medieval Indian compilers of traditional systems, became a good source for them.

However, given the power of colonial Indology, these Westerners assumed they had become the intellectual inheritors of Vijnanabhikshu's thought. As is often the case when Westerners digest Indian ideas, these colonial Indologists positioned themselves as the originators of the ideas; in actuality they had picked up these ideas from Indian thinkers such as Vijnanabhikshu. Nicholson's view is that the medieval scholars such as Vijnanabhikshu became the pathway for Western Indology. Nicholson writes how a new kind of unified view of Hinduism emerged:

> Between the twelfth and sixteenth centuries CE, certain thinkers began to treat as a single whole the diverse philosophical teachings of the Upanishads, epics, Puranas, and the schools known retrospectively as the 'six systems' (darsana) of mainstream Hindu philosophy. The Indian and European thinkers in the nineteenth

century who developed the term 'Hinduism' under the pressure of the new explanatory category of 'world religions' were influenced by these earlier philosophers and doxographers, primarily Vedantins, who had their own reasons for arguing the unity of Indian philosophical traditions.[17]

Vijnanabhikshu's writings on Samkhya, Yoga, and Vedanta suggest that, in harmony with Patanjali, he understood yoga to be both a philosophical system and a practice of self-transformation. As such, yoga was amenable to adaptations and interpretations. His integration involved some innovative philosophical arguments concerning the relationship between difference and non-difference, between parts and whole, and so on. He believed that Bhedabheda Vedanta was superior because it was best able to reconcile all the schools consistently with the Upanishads.

From Vijnanabhikshu to Vivekananda

The foregoing overview of Vijnanabhikshu shows that Vivekananda's project was in many ways a continuation of what the medieval Hindu doxographers were already doing. Vivekananda wanted to harmonize the major strands of yoga. Toward that end, he treated separately each of the traditional four expressions of yoga that are also explained in the Bhagavad-Gita—raja, bhakti, karma, and jnana—but kept them on an equal plane, as four options that can be mixed and matched by an individual rather than seeing them in an absolute hierarchy. He felt that yoga was compatible with Vedanta. The former he saw as a practical technique that confirmed spiritual liberation (or self-realization recorded by the rishis in the Veda) through personal experience (anubhava); the latter he saw as the standard of reference for self-realization in line with Vedic testimony (sruti-pramana).

Vijnanabhikshu had contributed to the emergence of a proto-Hinduism to which Vivekananda became a worthy heir. In the same manner, Vivekananda established common ground between yoga and Vedanta. He regarded the practices of the Vedanta, Samkhya, and Yoga schools to be different but reconciled as complementary paths. While yoga is the most direct of those paths, the practices of the Vedanta and Samkhya schools are also means to the same end. He regarded the goal of all these systems to be identical: it is the reuniting of the individual self with Brahman, in its natural state of non-separation.[18]

Vivekananda's challenge was also to show that this complementarity model was superior to models that emphasized conflict and contradiction. He showed great philosophical and interpretive ingenuity, even to those who might not agree with all his conclusions.[19] The intellectual position of Bhedabheda, which is a suitable foundation for his Practical Vedanta, is not as well known today as Advaita Vedanta.

Although Vivekananda was a passionate advocate of a Vedanta-Yoga unity, he was not averse to drawing on elements of Western philosophy and metaphysics that were popular at his time. His predilection for Herbert Spencer and others was generally to borrow English terminology as a way to present his own ideas more persuasively because of the influence of colonial and Orientalist polemics.[20]

The colonial disruption

What I have shown thus far in this chapter is that long before the colonial influence in India, there were new kinds of thinkers (such as Vijnanabhikshu) who were comparing various Hindu schools and integrating them in novel ways to develop unified Hindu thought. I shall now show how the continuity of the Hindu tradition and the dynamic equilibrium among Indian thinkers were severely disrupted by colonial interventions.

Underlying this disruption were several factors. A great deal of colonial understanding of India was shaped by the European need to use India as raw material to formulate arguments for their *internal* intra-European debates. Some of these debates concerned the problem of pantheism, the pagan assumption of the complete immanence of divinity in the world of nature—which was seen as a major threat to Christian monotheism. There was a strong desire to prove that the origins of European culture were 'pure' and free from the taint of 'nature worship'.

Europeans had begun to believe that their own ancestors were Aryans who spoke Sanskrit, but at the same time these ancestors could not be seen as pantheists. On the one hand, the worthy progenitors of Europeans had to be Sanskrit-speaking Aryans so as to prove their superiority as a race. But on the other hand, they had to be shown to be not pantheistic, so as to protect and ensure their Christian identity. Hinduism presented a problem in that it had both pantheist *and* Aryan aspects, as per the Europeans' understanding. This complexity and contradiction could only be resolved by interpreting Hinduism in such a way that it would conform to the European quest for identity.

One of the effects of using the European lens in dissecting Indian thought was to render rigid the various Indian philosophies, as though they were mutually exclusive and irreconcilable. The fossilizing of the six 'schools' of Indian thought helped to break up Indian culture into static, manageable pieces that could be taken out of context, played one against the other, and selectively appropriated or rejected. The end result was that what was considered worthy and useful could be 'digested' into the West or controlled by it. The project of digesting Hinduism into Western universalism thus requires seeing Hinduism

Figure 3

Causes of these distortions

1. European lenses mapping India onto pantheism and Aryan theory
2. Rigid classification into 'Indian schools of thought'
3. Post-modern mappings
4. Lack of attention to pre-colonial sources

Results

1. Digestion into Western Universalism
2. Reduction of Hinduism and stereotyping of Hindus
3. Post-modernist mappings leading to distortions

as an incoherent collection of fragments and contradictions. Later on, Indian ideas were mapped onto post-modern concepts, which further distorted Hinduism's portrayal.

Figure 3 shows the four colonial causes of distortions and the three consequences of this. I will elaborate on some of these below.

European debates: Are the Hindus Aryans or Pantheists?

Many European Indologists believed that a race referred to as the 'Aryans' shaped both Indian and Western pre-history. These Aryans were assumed to be monotheistic, thus providing Christianity with a sort of ancient warrant. Their language was Sanskrit, and they were seen as Europeans who had migrated to India and also formed the precursors of what we now call Hinduism. Sanskrit was regarded as the mother of the Indo-European family of languages, and hence the ancestral language of Europeans. Classical India was thus made to fit neatly into the quest for the origin of European bloodlines. Indology became a central part of Europe's enterprise to discover its *own* pre-history.[21]

But this picture created a serious theological problem. In the nineteenth century, the pantheism debate (called 'Pantheismusstreit') had become central in European intellectual life. The earliest and most highly appreciated Sanskrit works—considered by many Europeans to be far superior to the Western theological classics—were the Vedas and other texts of Hinduism. These were seen as pantheistic in their theology and practices and hence incompatible with the monotheism of Christianity.

The Indologists' charge that Vedanta was pantheistic rested on a crude interpretation of the Advaita principle that 'all is one'. The notion of God's immanence was seen as a dangerous one because it would undermine the exclusivity of history centric revelation and lead to a new rise of paganism, Christianity's ancient enemy, within. Because pantheism was considered a serious threat, such a view of Vedanta could not be allowed to be part of the idea (or myth) of Aryan purity.[22]

The history of Aryans and their Sanskrit texts in India had to be carefully interpreted so as not to undermine the authority of Christianity. Indologists therefore promulgated the view that Aryans had become corrupted by Indian Brahmins who sneaked pantheism into the originally pure monotheistic philosophy of the Aryan race. So it was proposed that the pre-Aryan Indians had been pantheistic just like all other tribes that were being 'discovered' in the non-European world; further, the Brahmins of India had polluted the pure Aryan invaders, resulting in the unfortunate pantheistic references in Sanskrit texts. This meant that Brahmins had to be vilified as the bad guys, and they've been used as scapegoats ever since.

This opposition to what some saw as a pantheistic Vedanta made the Samkhya metaphysics seem more attractive to many Indologists. They first argued that Samkhya was theistic and then argued further that it was of the monotheistic type (by mapping Purusha = Christian God).

Another issue before Indologists was to decide whether Indians were a moral race or not. If Indians were originally atheistic, they would have had to be inherently immoral, whereas if they had been theistic (especially as per a dualist monotheism which resembles Christianity), then they had the moral capacity to understand God, even though, later on, the Brahmins had corrupted them.[23] The questions as to whether Samkhya or Vedanta was older and which was closer to Western monotheism thus had sweeping implications for the history of 'European Aryans' and their relationship to Indians.

Competing Indology camps emerged, each striving to fit all the pieces of the puzzle together. One side believed in the 'indigenous aboriginal origins' of Indian thought while another believed in the 'foreign Aryan origins'. Those who wanted to redeem Indians from the charge of being originally immoral posited that Samkhya was the original system of the foreign Aryans and that it had been polluted by the Brahmins in a subsequent period. Such Eurocentric projections continue to this day. For example, the important Indologist and scholar of Hinduism, Gerald Larson, supports the theory of European Aryans invading India, and sees Samkhya as the original Indian school of thought and superior to Vedanta.[24]

Those Indologists who supported the Vedanta camp valorized the monism of Advaita Vedanta because it resembled Kant and Schopenhauer's transcendental idealism. In other words, by mapping onto some Western system it could be digested and thereby rendered non-threatening to the West. This helped Advaita Vedanta get accepted by the colonial administrators and Orientalist scholars as the essence and culmination of Indian philosophical systems. Bhedabheda Vedanta was seen as threatening because its notion of God's immanence was seen as similar to pantheism. Indologists started attributing the rise of Bhedabheda Vedanta to the decline of the true monistic Vedanta of the Upanishads, and also to the contamination from non-Vedic forms of worship in the Puranas and Tantras.

Even though the very same European Indologists had extensively mined Vijnanabhikshu for knowledge, they eventually marginalized him because of this fear of Bhedabheda Vedanta. Advaita Vedanta was thus assigned greater importance. Colonialist historians also marginalized Vijnanabhikshu in order to boost European Indologists as the eminent thinkers of Indian philosophy. This explains why it is important for them to claim that Vivekananda was borrowing his ideas of Hinduism from European sources. It is a high priority for them to break up the continuity that actually existed from ancient tradition, via Vijnanabhikshu and others of the pre-colonial era, to Vivekananda and his followers.

Reduction into 'Indian schools of thought'

A related aspect of European Indology was the over-emphasis on the separate strands and lineages of Hinduism. As I have noted, in the pre-colonial period there was no single definition of 'astika' and 'nastika'. Various traditional ways were (and still are) practised by Hindus without any sense of rigid boundaries separating them. However, some scholars have assumed astika/nastika to be fixed, rather than fluid categories, and this in turn has caused Hinduism to be essentialized into binaries of rival schools in a way that makes them seem mutually contradictory. This feeds their claim of Hindu incoherence, discontinuity, and fragmentation.

An example of Western reductionism may be found in the Wikipedia entry on 'astika' and 'nastika', which are essentialized as follows:

> By this definition, Nyaya, Vaisesika, Samkhya, Yoga, Mimamsa and Vedanta are classified as astika schools; and some schools like Carvaka, Ajivika, Jainism and Buddhism are considered nastika. The distinction is similar to the orthodox/heterodox distinction in the West.

The giveaway here is in the final sentence: this classification system is described as 'similar to the orthodox/heterodox' distinction in the West. But the dharma traditions do not operate in terms of this orthodox/heterodox binary. There is no institutionally enforced and normative position of 'orthodoxy' in them, nor any absolute history (comparable to the history centrism of Jesus) with which Indian philosophers are obliged to comply.

Since colonial times, scholars have cranked out one work after another on Vedanta versus Samkhya, and on other 'conflicts' within Hinduism. The effect of this reductionism into separate schools is felt to this day. One fixation of such scholars is to pit sruti against experience, using Shankara as their authority for this division.[25] The artificial problem of reductionism of 'Vedanta versus Yoga' is addressed at length in Chapter 10.

Daya Krishna, a recent and very prominent scholar of Indian metaphysics, criticizes the tendency to essentialize Indian thought into 'schools' that are fixed into mutually exclusive cocoons. He writes:

> [The schools of Indian philosophy] are treated as something finished and final. No distinction, therefore, is ever made between the thought of an individual thinker and the thought of a school. A school is, in an important sense, an abstraction. It is a logical construction springing out of the writings of a number of thinkers who share a certain similarity of outlook in tackling certain

problems. Samkhya, for example, is identified too much with Isvarakrishna's work, or Vedanta with the work of Sankara. But this is due to confusion between the thought of an individual thinker and the style of thought which he exemplifies and, to which he contributes in some manner. All that Sankara has written is not strictly Advaita Vedanta. Nor all that Isvarakrishna has written, Samkhya. Unless this is realized, writings on Indian philosophy will continuously do injustice either to the complexity of thought of the individual thinker concerned, or to the uniqueness of the style they are writing about.[26]

The Western fixation on 'schools' of Indian thought has, in effect, made them seem frozen, homogenized and isolated. This treatment is a form of reifying different dogmatic points of view and considering them at war against one another in a manner typical in Western history. It makes the different Indian 'schools' appear irreconcilable, and the emphasis has been to prove that these thinkers were each other's enemies.

Andrew Nicholson, whose work on the coherence and antiquity of Hinduism is the positive exception to many of these trends in scholarship, further explains this problem as follows:

In the west, our understanding of Indian philosophical schools (as the word darsana is generally translated) has been colored by our own history. The default model for the relationship between these schools is often unwittingly based on models derived from Western religious history: the hostilities between the three religions of the Book, the modern relationship of the various Christian denominations, or even the relation between orthodox and heterodox sects in early Christianity.[27]

Nicholson is also concerned about making sure that Indian thinkers are studied as individuals and given their due, and not simply lumped together into frozen 'schools':

Once the theory of the British invention of almost everything in modern India has been properly debunked, we can look realistically at the ways that such thinkers creatively appropriated some Indian traditions and rejected others. This is not the only reason to study premodern India, but it is one of the most important. Sanskrit intellectual traditions should be approached not as a rarefied sphere of discourse hovering above everyday life and historical time but, rather, as a human practice arising in the messy and contingent economic, social, and political worlds that these intellectuals occupied.[28]

Nicholson suggests that other models are available for Westerners to appreciate the distinction of each thinker, such as the one used in science. Different scientific disciplines operate in separate domains. They discover in parallel, and they continually try to reconcile their differences. But they are not mutual enemies. In the same manner, we can say that different Indian systems have focused on different domains: Mimamsa focuses on exegesis of Vedic ritual injunctions; Vedanta on the nature of Brahman; Nyaya on logical analysis; Vaisheshika on ontology; Yoga on the embodied human potential; and so on. Nicholson writes:

One of the important differences between the analytical terms darsana and vidya is that 'sciences' are not inherently at odds in the way that 'philosophical schools' are often depicted. Instead, they can represent different, and often complementary, branches of knowledge, much in the way that modern biology, chemistry, and physics are understood as complementary.[29]

This way of proceeding is illustrated in the story of the blind men feeling different parts of an elephant. Each draws a different conclusion and some of these appear to contradict each other. In Indian thought different views can also be appreciated as complementary.

Post-modern and post-colonial distortions

Post-modernism and post-colonialism have further distorted and fragmented classical Indian thought. The attack on the coherence of Hinduism (and likewise on the unity of India and on other 'big' collectivities and concepts) is a signature of post-modern and post-colonial scholarship, where it typically goes unquestioned. In the laudable effort to take apart and de-fang large and oppressive entities, armchair academics tend to go on a witch hunt against any large metaphysical concept whatsoever. They often do this mechanically and unconsciously, without regard for the differences between their various targets, or for the effects of their views on the ground. Thus, their attacks on the concept of a unified Hinduism with a distinct spiritual mission indirectly support the very Western hegemony they are purportedly combating.

Despite the fond hopes of post-modernism, the competition between large collective identities is not fading away; rather, it is intensifying. Post-modern thought has influenced many Indian intellectuals to view their own heritage as incoherent, and further to imagine that all other nations must also blur their identities to the same extent. They do not realize that the sense of incoherence leaves them no place to stand when defending their tradition. Also, the post-modern deconstruction of grand narratives has been vastly asymmetrical with respect to its effects; the deconstruction of the West is less devastating than the deconstruction of the non-West.[30]

Rather than dividing Hinduism into fixed and competing schools to solve the 'problem' of apparent inconsistencies between various strands and lineages, let us be reminded that these apparent inconsistencies, which are actually less profound than many scholars make them appear, can be explored in other ways. There can be many reasons for these differences, including the following:

- Different audiences may be served by different works, including audiences that are followers of rival schools who need to be approached in their own vocabulary. Some works may have been written in response to a specific situation or challenge.

- The 'author' of a given work is not always a single individual, so differences within a text are bound to occur. There are sometimes multiple individuals representing a lineage, and the lineage was systematized only after their time by presenting the sum of their works as though it were that of a single individual. The very notion of an individual author in India differs from that in the West, and composite authorship is frequent.

- When metaphysical systems differ, their soteriological processes often remain shared partially or entirely. For instance, certain yoga practices are shared across many metaphysical systems. Hence, for instance, Shankara may endorse yoga's benefits and, at the same time, disagree with the dualist metaphysics of Samkhya with which yoga has been coupled. This means we must understand the context in which he disagrees with it and the extent of his disagreement. This would nuance our understanding of his statements that appear contradictory.

- Teachers at times may have wanted to shock students into accepting their approach by appearing to reject something else by way of contrast. Sometimes, for instance, a given meditation technique is rejected because it is associated with an opposing metaphysics, and an alternative is suggested that is similar to the one rejected, but this alternative is couched again in a new metaphysics. Again, Shankara, as we shall see in Chapter 10, provides an example of this.

- Many philosophers assert a unity when they speak of higher states of consciousness, but less so when they are discussing ideas pertaining to ordinary states.

Challenging the Neo-Hinduism thesis

This chapter has argued that the neo-Hinduism camp is wrong in claiming that Vivekananda copied Western ideas and put them in

Sanskrit to make them seem Indian. On the contrary, there had been a vibrant flow of Indian ideas prior to colonialism, and it was the colonialists who disrupted this for their agenda to construct an ancient history for European civilization. Most of Vivekananda's unification of Hinduism was already being carried out by pre-colonial thinkers like Vijnanabhikshu.

The next chapter will continue my rejoinder by showing that even in the domain of social activism and worldly progress there were pre-colonial Hindu pioneers who provided resources for contemporary Hinduism. Hence, it is inappropriate to credit colonialists as the sole source of Hinduism's social consciousness.

9

Traditional Foundations of Social Consciousness

One of the major allegations with which Hinduism is constantly being bombarded is that it lacks social consciousness and historical processes of development. The common critique is that such consciousness and agency were imported into India in Swami Vivekananda's time. Prior to that time, Hindus lacked cohesiveness, social consciousness, and sense of advancement through time. They were otherworldly, frozen in a mode that was devoid of practicality. This allegation has been devastating, especially since many Hindus accept it and propagate it.

Critics cite a certain interpretation of Advaita Vedanta that since the world is an illusion, there is no such thing as progress or social consciousness. The condition of this world and the people in it, the argument goes, is a pure illusion (*maya* or *mithya*); why then concern ourselves with issues within the illusion? In this view, Hindu teachings are meant only to emphasize the attainment of moksha and liberation from the illusory world. It is a philosophy of escapism rather than engagement with the world. Therefore, it is irrelevant for a Hindu to have compassion for others. If this alleged mindset has changed at all, it is said to have changed only under Western influence because contemporary Hindus sought to emulate Christian ethics and social practices.

This view of Hinduism as indifferent to suffering had originated in colonial times. There is, for instance, an influential book by J.N. Farquhar written a century ago, *Modern Religious Movements in India* (1915), which is still used by many Western scholars as a major reference on Hinduism. Farquhar advances a clearly tendentious Christian missionary thesis, claiming that Western society is inherently dynamic because of Christianity, and that Indians lack ethical and historical consciousness because of Hinduism, leading to their neglect of economic, social and technical progress. The claim being made is that Hindu *seva* (social service) was appropriated from Western and Christian ethics and did not exist within the Hindu tradition.

To refute this portion of the neo-Hinduism thesis, this chapter will make the following points:

- There are plenty of *textual* references in Hinduism supporting social action, without having to appropriate such ideas from the West.

- There are several examples of grass-roots level social movements in India prior to colonialism.

- Western social theory of religion has resulted in erroneous conclusions about Hinduism.

- Christianity, contrary to widespread belief, did not originally have social responsibility of the kind it later developed as a result of non-Christian influences.

- The 'world-negating' model of Hinduism which leads to such allegations is false.

- Vivekananda did not develop his interest in social activism only after his visits to the West.

I shall argue not only that Hindu society prior to the colonial and post-colonial period encouraged compassionate action towards others, but also that Hindu thought is rich in Indian resources to draw upon. There has always been a debate between the role of *pravitti* (positive engagement with the world) and *nivritti* (withdrawal from the sense of doing external work), and there have been plenty of advocates for each.

Although moksha (liberation) is often cited as the ultimate goal, Hinduism has many kinds of legitimate pursuits other than moksha, including pleasure and worldly success. Each pursuit has its own ethics associated with it. The Mahabharata and Manusmriti are full of examples of social ethics for *different* contexts. Raja dharma, for example, is the dharma for social governance. The ancient principles of Hinduism include the concept of 'pancha maha yagna' which exemplifies a dharmic social consciousness. One of the five duties every human must undertake is '*manushayagna*' (serving human beings by feeding them, etc.).

Philosophically, the idea of reincarnation undermines the importance which the Abrahamic religions give to bloodlines, race, and historical identities. Because each of us has been born into many races, bloodlines and histories in prior lives, there is nothing absolute and permanent about one's body, and we now experience merely one of many lifetimes and many bodies we have had. Reincarnation also means that one need not be obsessed with one's biological relatives, because one's future birth could be in any culture or ethnicity in the world. Hence, it is better to be loyal to humanity and to the cosmos at large.

The shanti mantras, many of which hail from the Vedas, wish peace not only to all humans but to all sentient beings, to all planes of existence, and to all planets in the universe. This is in the spirit of the interconnectivity of Indra's Net. Such ethics tend to argue against selfish loyalties and encourage harmony with society and nature.

The quest for realizing one's higher self involves detachment from materialism. And seeing the world as God's lila (divine play) is taught as the model for performing one's pragmatic roles selflessly. All these are good foundations for ethical behavior. Furthermore, in any assessment of Hinduism's track record in social and political areas, one must note that *sanskriti* (Indian culture and civilization) were not spread for purposes of conquest, imperialism, taxing other nations and the like. It was always a cultural exchange with other nations carried out with mutual respect.

Unfortunately, Hinduism's theories and traditions of social responsibility have been obscured, once again, by the imposition of Western methodologies in the sociological study of religion.

Western methodological straitjacket misapplied to Vivekananda

Krishan Prakash Gupta shows how the theories of religion propounded by sociologists such as Max Weber, Emile Durkheim and Bronislaw Malinowski have made it standard practice to explain new religious movements in the non-West as reactions to deprivation and helplessness. Of the supposed defensive reactions to outside forces, Gupta writes: 'Through these reactions, religion was supposed to be serving a very useful function in crisis-management.'[1]

He explains that contemporary Hinduism was analysed in these terms on the basis of a 'simple need-fulfillment framework' involving assumptions such as the force of the Western influence, native impotence before it, and nationalist reaction to crisis.[2] Gupta writes:

> In this scenario, non-Christian religions were as a rule not viewed as internally-evolving systems but merely as anxiety-resolving defence mechanisms used by the people concerned to meet the Western challenge. [...] Viewed in this paradigm, these movements can be easily explained as transitional, imitative, and non-rational. The Ramakrishna Mission movement itself can be considered a response to the missionary challenge in the late nineteenth-century India, and Vivekananda's Practical Vedanta merely as an impassioned attempt at Westernization of Hinduism. The impact of the total movement can then be seen simply in the reaffirmation and revitalization of a dying tradition. In fact, most analyses of the Ramakrishna Mission,

irrespective of their widely divergent ideological perspectives, have not been able to go beyond this framework.[3]

Naturally, Vivekananda repeatedly becomes the target of such investigation. Hinduism's internal resources before colonialism are not examined as causal factors in the modernization. As Gupta explains, 'Hinduism is reduced to play the role of a transitional defence mechanism. Such an explanation, I think, seriously distorts the meaning of Vivekananda's breakthrough.'[4]

If one were to apply Max Weber's criteria to evaluate the Ramakrishna Mission, one would conclude that it failed for not turning its monks into rational theologians in the Christian sense. Gupta explains why Weber's Protestant Ethic fails as a theory for understanding the Ramakrishna Mission:

> The Mission has neither produced a Vedantic church, nor a Vedantic nation, to say nothing of supplying an ethic to support industrialization. Logically extended to its ultimate implications, this failure would suggest that the Mission has indeed been only an irrelevant mix of reaction and revivalism, having no potential for effecting any evolutionary breakthrough in India's transition to modernity.[5]

Gupta is dissatisfied by such trendy application of Western models to Hinduism. He concludes:

> Pre-modern Hindu religious movements are expected to perform the same role which the pre-modern Christianity supposedly performed in Europe. Vivekananda-type reforms are valued in this response not as symbolic expressions of an evolving Hindu tradition but primarily as transitional vehicles for bringing India closer to Westernized modernity.[6]

The reason for the failure of Western sociological models lies in the very nature of Hinduism, as he explains:

Hindu scriptures, unlike their Christian counterparts, do not act as a straitjacket but primarily as a leaven in society. The believers are bound only in conscience; rules of law are derived from customs, not sacred books. Religious functionaries can technically provide legitimation to any custom provided it is dictated by contemporary efficiency. There is at no point any cognitive conflict between Reason and Religion. This stands in sharp contrast with Christianity.[7]

To understand how continuity and change function in Hinduism's history, one must consider that there have always been dominant views as well as various kinds and degrees of dissent. The dissenters at times directly confronted the dominant view, as the Jains and Buddhists did. At other times they simply bypassed the received teaching to develop an independent approach of their own, as in the case of Tantra, yoga, etc. In some of these instances, it is the Vedas themselves that are being challenged or bypassed. In other instances it is ritual privileges that are challenged by developing a direct personal approach to the ultimate reality without mediation by priesthood; this form of bypass is found in yoga and Tantra.

Seen in this manner, Vivekananda was not at all the first leader to challenge the received views. Nor was this challenge inspired from external sources. It was from his guru, Ramakrishna (whose indigenous credentials no one contests), that he learned to transcend the orthodoxy of rituals, sects and dogmas. This contradicts the claim that he appropriated the Western notion of challenging orthodoxy as had been done by Europeans against the church. Gupta clarifies:

Vivekananda's pre-modern revaluation of Hinduism occurred in this pre-Western-impact historical context. By attacking caste parochialism and ritual efficacy and by enlarging the sphere of religiously-relevant action, his Practical Vedanta reasserted once again the specific Hindu form and substance of protest. His selective acceptance of the West played only a minor supportive role in this reform. The West became meaningful to him only in providing an occasion to use a new vocabulary; otherwise, the old medium persisted.[8]

Vivekananda thus utilized old Hindu ideas which emphasize that spiritual pursuits had to be meaningful and pragmatic in the lives of individuals. He was not attempting the kind of revolt against a centralized authority that characterizes movements in the Abrahamic traditions. He used the concept of self-realization based on direct experience, and emphasized only those aspects of the Vedas and other Hindu systems that he considered relevant in his context. There was nothing unprecedented about this.

The notion of contextual dharma for each community and individual is also very powerful in Indian traditions. This means Vivekananda was able to apply Vedanta differently for his audiences in India and the West. Gupta explains how he adapted Vedanta in two different places, as a matter of appropriate emphasis and not contradiction:

> In America, Vivekananda drew a portrait of Krishna, the divine object of surrender, who was immersed in his Lila (divine play) with the gopis (milk-maids). In India, this image was changed to project a fighting Krishna, the charioteer of Arjuna, who was vigorously pleading for an activist affirmation. These distinctions became much more sharp in Vivekananda's total relativization of ethical demands. In America, he told his audiences to practise Yoga and renunciation, instead of supporting missionary humanitarian work. In India, he exhorted his followers to practise a little (indulgence), inculcate some rajas (materialism), and engage wholeheartedly in altruistic services. In America, he criticized the machine culture because, instead of solving the problem of poverty, it created only new wants. In India, he not only upheld the necessity of a material civilization but even thought of organizing monks for industrial purposes.[9]

Gupta goes on to say that Gandhi took many of Vivekananda's original ideas and applied them socially. One was the principle of limiting one's consumption and materialism. Gandhi's idea of *swaraj* (self-rule, or independence from the British) was not about creating an Indian government that would impose the same ways as the British did. Instead, it meant that purified individuals engaged in their svadharma (personal dharma) would be ruling their lives from within.

The 'world-negating' misinterpretation of social problems

In order to deny the very existence of a Hindu social ethic, the philosophical basis being advanced is that Hinduism advocates a world-negating outlook. India's modern conditions of relative poverty and social depravation, compared with conditions in the West, are explained as the result of an emphasis on escaping from the mundane world. The Hindu, according to such interpretations, wants to run away from worldly challenges rather than developing solutions. He abandons those who suffer because they and their suffering are ultimately illusory. But, as I will show in this chapter, there is a good deal of evidence from pre-colonial Hindu movements to disprove the claim that Hindu ethics emerged only from colonial influence. The concept was in fact indigenous.

The scholarly basis for making the claim that Hinduism is world-negating is that a number of traditional scriptures depict the world as *mithya*, a term Western Indologists have mistranslated as illusion. The Western understanding of mithya is seriously flawed, and this flaw has fed the misconception that Hinduism regards the world as illusory. This, in turn, feeds the stereotype of a world-view predicated on otherworldliness, social irresponsibility, fatalism, and the like.

A better way to explain 'mithya' would be to appreciate that the conception of reality in Vedanta is always comparative. Relative to a particular material, an object made out of that material is considered 'less real'. For example, a bucket made out of plastic is unreal *relative* to the plastic itself. A cause is considered to be relatively 'more real' than its effect, because the reality of an effect depends on its cause.[10] It follows that anything which has a material and/or efficient cause can be described as a dependent reality, i.e., mithya. The 'cause of the world' is thus ascribed a greater degree of reality than the world itself. When we say that the universe is mithya, we mean it is unreal when seen as an independent reality; however, it is surely real when seen as caused by Brahman and dependent upon Brahman.

In addition to 'mithya', there are two important Sanskrit words which one must understand in this respect. They are *sat* and *asat*. These two words are often mistranslated as 'real' and 'unreal', respectively. The English language does not allow for a category that is between real and unreal, making it impossible to conceive of mithya as a type of reality that is different than either sat or asat. Such a limitation precipitates the conflation of asat and mithya and creates the misconception that mithya is illusion.

To understand mithya correctly in relation to sat and asat, one must appreciate that sat is that which does not depend on anything else for its existence, whereas mithya *does* depend on something else for its existence, and asat is that which *cannot* exist at all.

The profound points of distinction between these Sanskrit terms become blurred by mistranslation into Western languages that simply cannot support the categories they wish to appropriate. This ultimately leads to distorting notions such as: traditional Hinduism lacked the ethics of charity, social activism, and worldly progress because it sees the world as unreal. Once this error in dismissing Hinduism as otherworldly and escapist has been understood, the ground is cleared to delve deeper into Hindu ethics. I will discuss mithya further in Chapter 11.

There is, indeed, a large volume of evidence that demonstrates a positive emphasis on ethics and human rights in Hinduism. The following statement in the Mahabharata illustrates this emphasis:

> One should never do that to another which one regards as injurious to one's own self. This, in brief, is the rule of dharma. Yielding to desire and acting differently, one becomes guilty of adharma.[11]

Both in the Bhagavad-Gita and elsewhere, acceptance of the theory of karma and of the world as mithya does not imply social escapism.

The Gita (in verse 6.32 and elsewhere) explains the basis for the Hindu principle of charity as *Narayana-seva*, i.e., serving God by serving one's fellow human. Every major commentary on this verse (including Shankara's) emphasizes this teaching. This is also the basis for Gandhi's concept of ahimsa. Krishna asserts that generosity (*dana*) and compassion (*daya*) are qualities that arise 'from me alone'.

At the practical level, there have always been co-operative welfare activities within one's *jati;* Hindu role models have exemplified personal acts of charity such as giving food and making donations for general public amenities. Examples of such actions in Puranic sources include the gifts of food, medicines and hospitality; construction of public works such as water supply, irrigation, parks and shelters; planting trees and the building of public halls, temples and maths. The svadharma based on one's varna, ashrama and other individual variables also has corresponding acts of charity associated with it.[12] This includes prescriptions for the way in which charitable action should be performed, i.e., governed by qualities of purity. Hinduism definitely recommends disinterested charity.

Origin of Christian philanthropy

A distortion of historical facts makes Christianity seem to be the major force for social action whereas Hinduism is made to appear static and lacking a social consciousness. But contrary to the belief that Christianity is progressive, many Western scholars of Christianity find the theology and socio-political record of Christianity to be devoid of social responsibility. Kristen Southworth is among them. She writes:

> Within Christianity we find some of the most striking theological rejections of 'this world', along with a focus on a resurrected life in another world. For many, resurrection is representative that the end goal is the afterlife, and this has become the most central tenet of the faith for many people, one which has given rise to a consistent ethical dilemma throughout Christian history: why should I work to improve conditions in this world when my home

is ultimately elsewhere? In many popular Christian cosmologies, this 'other world' is seen as utterly elsewhere, entirely separate from this world. As such, ascetic monks and lay Christians alike have, throughout history, struggled to find the motivation to engage in restorative social efforts that bring about positive change in this world. I think we should be very careful about applying the same cosmology of salvation, and thus the same problem, to Hinduism.[13]

Gwilym Beckerlegge has written similarly on the other worldliness problem in early Christianity and the corresponding de-emphasis on service to others:

> Within the Christian tradition, the expectation of a fleeting passage through this world, a mere prelude to the eternal life to come, at times has given rise to ambivalence about political and social responsibility and a balancing act between meeting what have been felt to be the conflicting demands of piety and more temporal imperatives. For some, withdrawal from the world has provided a solution to this dilemma.[14]

By the early fourth century CE, the church had permeated the mainstream of Roman society. When the Roman state started falling apart, the church inherited many of its welfare functions with the full support of the state. The church-state nexus was powerful, and the church became the state's agent in charitable matters and was subsidized by it. That is why the scope and resources of the church's charitable activities expanded throughout Europe in the medieval period. The church was also the largest holder of material assets. Social activity was not theologically grounded but linked to the church's power in the public square.

A better notion of social service evolved in the West as a result of the inadequacies of earlier Christian forms of charitable practice. The human rights movements of the West were based, in large part, on the humanist criticisms of Christianity. In other words, Christianity was seen as the problem, not the solution. Beckerlegge concludes:

'There is nothing inherently "Christian" in the characteristics of social service.'[15] Thus, one cannot simplistically claim that 'Philanthropy = Christianity', because one must consider the historical and sociological forces that were secular.

In the case of India, the colonial church-state-mercantile nexus was driven by many factors which contradicted Christian ideals like 'love thy neighbour'. India suffered socially and politically when the British ruled, including a breakdown of public institutions and economic structures. The British imposed drastic changes in the methods of revenue collection, and these devastated local economies which had earlier thrived. Many traditional industries were destroyed in order to create large new markets for British manufactured goods. Draconian levels of taxation were imposed in India to suck out the wealth in order to fund Britain's industrial revolution.

The history of economic and social ruin caused by the British is well-documented and I shall not take the time to delve into the details here. Dharampal has documented this extensively, and a book titled *Late Victorian Holocausts* by Mike Davis explains the famines caused by the British rulers, and shows the British being complicit.[16]

The charity that was offered to non-Christians in India was often driven by the goal of proselytizing; education and orphan care became strategies for soul-harvesting. Christian education in India was funded by the East India Company's loot and later the British government stepped into this role.

Conditions that led to the revival of Hindu seva

Before the British rule, between the eleventh and thirteenth centuries, the Islamic conquest of northern India had already wrought havoc on traditional Indian society, and reduced India to two main classes: a small but rich aristocracy (made up of new Muslim and old Hindu nobles) and the common labourers and peasants who led miserable lives. There is abundant evidence of this problem.[17]

The systematic impoverishment of the masses became even worse when the British displaced the Muslim rulers. The modern academics find it politically incorrect to criticize the devastation under Islamic rule, even though post-colonial scholars have amply exposed the ruin created by the British.

Indian intellectuals and nationalists such as Dadabhai Naoroji (1825-1917) and G.K. Gokhale (1866-1915) pointed out that the ordinary Indian was reduced to a life of struggle merely to satisfy the basic material wants. Naoroji ridiculed British attempts to dismiss the mass poverty of Indians as accidental, natural or causal.[18] Gokhale rejected the explanation that it was the result of laziness, inferiority and lack of education of Indians or, still more unfortunately, the result of a blind, inexplicable fate.[19]

It was under Islamic and then British rule that the Indian 'subalterns' emerged as the large population of poor we find today.[20] Although earlier Hindu tradition must also be examined for causing social ills, it cannot be blamed as the sole cause, as is often alleged. In fact, Indians before colonial rule were not only better fed than their European counterparts, but in terms of philosophical grounding, key Hindu texts have always placed great emphasis on feeding the public. A nice compilation of such textual references was carried out by Jitendra Bajaj in an important book.[21] It shows the large-scale charitable activities of feeding the poor at various times and places. It also shows the British amazement at this native Indian phenomenon, as well as the manner in which British rule transformed a society of plenty into a society of poverty.

In response to what is being called the Hindu holocaust suffered under foreign rule, various indigenous movements arose, such as the Swaminarayan and Radhasoami lineages. These were *not* based on copying Christian ideas of charity but are clear examples of traditional Hindu ideas at work in modern times. Here the sannyasin adopts seva to the public as his role, besides his traditional role as spiritual teacher.

Looking at the ground reality for evidence, one finds that jatis have practised collective works of seva long before colonialism. Buddhist social work and the organization of monasteries are well known, and in fact these influenced early Christianity. Guru Nanak (1469-1539), founder of the Sikh dharma, was another sadhu active in political and social affairs. Sikhs worldwide are known for their generosity and sharing with others in need.

Vivekananda was influenced by such local models, and there is reason to believe that he might have taken the vow to a life dedicated to serving others (sevayoga) during his year-long tour of Gujarat in 1892. Gandhi, Tagore, Aurobindo, and others subordinated the goal of individual moksha to promoting collective well-being.

Sahajanand Swami and social activism in contemporary Hinduism

The example of Sahajanand Swami (1781-1830) illustrates the role of traditional Hindu leaders and organizations in launching large-scale seva movements without importing any colonial models.

Gujarat had become ravaged by wars, social decay and economic distress resulting from numerous incursions and disruptions. The British were in the early stages of filling the military and political vacuum that existed, and their policy was not to interfere with the religious practices of the Hindus. These were the conditions that existed when a young man named Sahajanand Swami arrived.

Sahajanand Swami had renounced the world as a *brahmachari*, a wandering young ascetic in the Hindu tradition, and had travelled in the Himalayas. He studied yoga under a guru, went to several prominent centers of Hindu pilgrimage in north and south India, and became a follower of Ramanuja's Vishishta-advaita Vedanta. He was also taken by his father to Varanasi to engage in the tradition of philosophical debate, and is said to have defeated many rivals.

Upon being appointed leader of his satsang community, he made sweeping changes based on ancient Hindu ideas. For instance, his male followers had to take a vow which included the following precepts: not to steal, not to commit adultery, not to eat meat, not to consume intoxicants, not to commit violence, to be away from women, and to remain completely unattached to material luxuries. Simplicity and inner discipline were seen as the bedrock on which a strong, healthy society could be built.

One of the core principles he demanded of his students was ahimsa (non-harming), a principle which he shared with the large Jain community in Gujarat. (This was a major source of inspiration for ahimsa as taught by Gandhi, another native of Gujarat.) Sahajanand Swami taught that ahimsa was necessary to be able to give up worldly attachments and to serve humanity in a dharmic manner. He also convinced people to end superstitious rituals and magic.

It is important to note that the East India Company had turned Gujarat into their hub for opium production for sale to China. But in direct opposition to these British vested interests, Sahajanand Swami ordered that opium be strictly forbidden, declaring it a serious vice. Certainly, nobody can accuse him of succumbing to Western influence.

At the same time he was pragmatic.[22] Sahajanand Swami utilized traditional asceticism in new ways entirely through his own innovation. Such responses by ascetics to external challenges are well-documented. David Lorenzen's article 'Warrior Ascetics in Indian History' gives numerous examples of warrior ascetics in traditional India long before colonialism. In fact, the Sikh dharma started as a Hindu mobilization of ascetics willing and able to encounter the mighty centers of power. Hence, Hindu political and/or social activism was not learned from colonialism; there were plenty of indigenous reference points and role models.[23]

Sahajananda Swami's ascetics were organized for collective projects of social welfare, partly as a means of restoring order which had disintegrated. This kind of work was unconventional for ascetics who renounce the world and take vows of poverty and celibacy. Using a new approach, Sahajanand Swami ordered the ascetics to do manual labour, including digging wells and reservoirs, repairing old ones, building and repairing roads, opening kitchens to feed the hungry, and so on. His followers were responsible for major construction projects (some remnants of which can still be seen) and the swami himself is known to have carried bricks to the sites.

This practice changed the public image of ascetics, which had earlier depicted them as parasites and a burden on society. Now they were seen as social servants helping society with great integrity and making no personal demands in return. Thus, a traditional form of Hinduism was modernized. It is widely acknowledged that Sahajanand Swami's path of dharma was very successful in bringing prosperity and cohesion to Gujaratis. The historian R.C. Majumdar calls his movement 'the greatest of the reforming sects of Gujarat'.[24]

Sahajanand Swami also organized Swaminarayan Satsang, a large Hindu organization which is thriving worldwide today. The work ethic that includes Hindu simplicity and self-discipline is now visible among Gujaratis worldwide—a combination of hard work, organization, and simple, frugal living. His projects made no distinctions based on caste or sect. Many persons of lower social demographics joined his organization once they gave up eating meat.

Although the primary devotion was to Narayana or Krishna, in his teaching he instructed followers to worship Shiva, Ganapati, Parvati, and Surya also. In addition, his movement promoted the Sanskritization of Hinduism in Gujarat, while at the same time encouraging local languages in festivals and theaters. These devotional groups transcended jati boundaries.

Sahajanand Swami was a major figure in the period after the great bhakti saints and before the onset of British influence. At least one Western scholar, Raymond Williams, agrees that this was an example of indigenous Hindu social activism. He notes that, 'The effects of Western education were not directly felt in Gujarat in Sahajanand's lifetime',[25] so the West could not have been the inspiration for Sahajananda Swami's vision. Indeed, while the British were busy working top-down to gain control, he was busy bottom-up rebuilding a society from the grass-roots using his own tradition.

He created a cohesive Gujarati identity by proudly establishing sacred places, great temples and social institutions. These activities also resulted in the integration of the various dialects into what has become today's standardized Gujarati language. For these and other reasons Sahajananda Swami is considered a true founder of the Gujarati ethos and identity.

Mohandas Gandhi, another Gujarati, is quoted as saying: 'The work which Sahajanand could do in Gujarat, the [British] rulers by their might could not do and would not be able to do ... The era of Sahajanand has not yet passed away.'[26] Raymond Williams summarizes his impact thus:

> He began his career in the midst of medieval India. His teachings hold fast to the ancient traditions. His worldview, manner of life, and the devotional path he set forth are in continuity with the famous medieval saints of Hinduism. The reforms he instituted, based, he believed, on the correct interpretation of the ancient tradition, make him the best early example of Neo-Hinduism.[27]

It is interesting to note that Williams cannot help using the term 'neo-Hinduism' in the above quote, even when the substance of his position is that this Hindu movement was *not* based on colonial borrowings. This is how the reckless use of the 'neo' prefix has allowed the mischievous thesis of neo-Hinduism to slip into general use.

Beckerlegge is another scholar who acknowledges that Sahajananda used traditional Hindu sources for his emphasis on seva:

> Standing in the visistadvaita tradition, the assumption upon which Sahajananda Swami based his ethical demand for service to others has been stated briefly as follows: 'Man is the microcosm of God who is the macrocosm and hence the service of humanity is the service of the almighty God.' Determined to purify the institution of sannyasa, which had fallen prey to popular abuses, Sahajananda Swami detailed ascetics in the fellowship to offer service to the people. Acts of service included providing food and water to the needy, building and repairing wells and tanks, offering spiritual teaching without making any demands on villagers, and building temples; activities largely within the traditional. ... It is evident from the chronology of the Sahajananda's life that his mission ended almost as British influence was slowly starting to make an impact in the area where his teaching took deepest root. Consequently, there is little evidence to suggest that the origins of Sahajananda's commitment to an extended form of seva can be traced back to

any other source than that of the Vaishnava bhakti tradition which nurtured him. The broad consensus shared by students of the Swaminarayan movement is that the assumptions and motivations underlying its practice of service are derived from traditional Hindu religious roots and specifically those of Vaishnava bhakti.[28]

Centuries before Sahajananda Swami, the tradition of serving the poor as worship to the Lord had already been solidified in Vitthala, a traditional deity seen as protector-of-the-lowly (*dinanatha*) and merciful-to-the-lowly (*dinadayala*). Vitthala became a very popular devotional deity.[29] Another movement that included social service for the poor as an intrinsic part of mystical experience was Basavanna's Lingayat Sampradaya, which existed as early as the twelfth century. There are many similar examples of Indians using their own resources.

Swami Vivekananda's sevayoga

Vivekananda continued this tradition of adapting Hindu ethics independently of Western influences or models. Contrary to the allegations that the West taught him the idea of seva for one's fellow human being, he was directly influenced by Sri Ramakrishna in this regard. Swami Shantatmananda of the Ramakrishna Mission explains this direct influence as follows:

'Swami Vivekananda's idea of service is largely based on Sri Ramakrishna's idea of Service of God in Man i.e. *Shiv Gyan Se Jiv Seva*. One day at Dakshineswar in Sri Ramakrishna's room the basic tenets of Vaishnava religion were being discussed. It seems they are (1) taste for God's name (*Nam me ruchi*); (2) compassion for jivas (*Jiv par daya*); and (3) service to Vaishnavas (*Vaishnava Seva*). After uttering the first tenet, Sri Ramakrishna uttered the words Jiv par daya and immediately went into Samadhi. When he came out of that state, he said, "What! How can man who is a lowly creature or insignificant like a worm show compassion or daya to another person. No, it is not compassion, but service to God in Man or *Shiv Gyan Se Jiv Seva*." Among others Sri Narendranath Dutta was also present in that room. He said, "Today I have heard something very new and if God gives me an opportunity I shall proclaim this before the world." This is what he developed as the concept of service and also incorporated it in the aims and objects of the Ramakrishna Mission, etc. Although the underlying idea is Advaita or all-pervading Brahman or consciousness which can also be stated as Tat Twam Asi, Swamiji gave greater emphasis on the idea of service to God in Man.'[30]

It is in fact quite likely that in addition to the influence Sri Ramakrishna, Vivekananda also received first-hand experience from the social work that disciples of Sahajananad Swami were carrying out in the areas of Ahmedabad, Junagadh, and Bhuj.[31] His subsequent visit to the United States helped nourish this indigenous vision of service to others into what is called 'sevayoga', but his visit to the U.S. was not the origin for this vision. As we have seen, this was a central teaching of Sri Ramakrishna; and Sahajanand Swami had 'preserved the best of the beliefs and practices from the past and forged a new form of Hinduism well suited to the modern period'.[32]

Vivekananda was not an armchair theorist. He taught that self-development involved an active relationship with others. He developed what he called Practical Vedanta, based on the creative application of his tradition to modern circumstances. He interpreted the famous *mahavakya* (great saying) of the Upanishad, 'tat tvam asi', as universal connectedness, taking it to mean that in every heart there is Brahman.[33] Since the world is Brahman, worldly activity is sacred and selfless work is worship. This became a cornerstone of his social philosophy of alleviating poverty. He said: 'I do not believe in a God who cannot give me bread here, giving me bliss in heaven.'[34] In a lecture delivered in the United States he declared:

In this world of many, he who sees the One, in this ever changing world he who sees Him who never changes, as the Soul of his own soul, as his own Self, he is free, he is blessed, he has reached the goal.

Therefore know that thou art He; thou art the God of this universe, 'Tat Tvam Asi' (That thou art).[35]

Bhaktiyoga is an effective instrument for acknowledging this relationship. Vivekananda's social outlook also combines knowledge and action, or jnanayoga and karmayoga. Karma, or helping others, is thus ultimately bhakti of the divine since everyone's ultimate nature is divinity. This is how he became a promoter of sevayoga, the yoga of service to people. Clearly, the philosophical and theological basis of his sevayoga differed from the basis of social action in Christianity.

He started the Ramakrishna Mission as another example of seva in response to the plight of the people. Each similar Hindu movement did its own independent reassessment of the role of the sannyasin, and these roles were pragmatically redefined. In the Swaminarayan, Radhasoami, and Ramakrishna movements, the traditional notion of seva provided sufficient flexibility, and yet each movement improvised its own distinct path based on the practical qualities in Hinduism. Vivekananda used examples of great Indian leaders like Chaitanya, Kabir, and Nanak, as well as movements such as Buddhism, as sources for his inspiration.

A combination of traditional Hindu social ethics was being reformulated for modern times in a way that also responded to what Christian missionaries offered. This did not constitute the 'Westernization' of the Hindu tradition. Beckerlegge's argument is again more reasonable than that of many of the promulgators of the neo-Hindu hypothesis:

The choice facing Vivekananda and those Hindus who had access to new ways to intercede in the face of human misery, therefore, was not one between 'Westernisation' and holding to an 'authentic' Hindu code of action. The transformation, sought by Swami Vivekananda, of existing expressions of Hindu charitable action into a form of social service was a result of the recognition of both the ineffectiveness of earlier types of charitable activity and the conviction that the nature of society in India was subject to forces which would make established styles of philanthropic action

increasingly ineffective. As such, the transformation of Hindu
charitable activity, which Vivekananda helped to effect, may be
compared legitimately to the transformation of Christian charitable
practice in the West which had begun to take place during the
previous half century, although triggered by different economic,
political and social factors.[36]

Swami Vivekananda contextualized the dharma for his time by
formulating the concept of 'Daridra-Narayana', which means Vishnu (as
Narayana) manifesting as Daridra (the poor, suffering). He applied the
teaching of oneness implied in 'tat tvam asi' and in Krishna's injunction
in the Bhagavad-Gita to 'worship me in all beings', and shaped the
metaphor and imagery of Daridra-Narayana. This provided a broad
basis for service of one's fellow beings.[37] Doing service was not a break
from the traditional meaning of this mantra but an expansion of its
meaning.

In the present age of poverty, scriptures must be reinterpreted as
referring to Narayana (in Daridra form) symbolizing divinity in the
form of the poor. Narayana must therefore be seen in the context of
the socially and economically oppressed people of India. Vivekananda's
perspective of God from the vantage point of the suffering of the poor
was thus based on the traditional Hindu image of Narayana's presence.
It was not an import of Christian ideas.

In an address delivered at the great temple of Rameshvaram on
27 January 1897, Vivekananda explained his Practical Vedanta: 'He
who sees Shiva in the poor, in the weak, and in the diseased, really
worships Shiva: and if he sees Shiva only in the image, his worship is
but preliminary.'[38]

In 1901, at Belur Math, Vivekananda personally fed a group of
poor Santal labourers and addressed them: 'You are Narayanas, God
manifest; today I have offered food to Narayana. The service of Daridra-
Narayana—God in the poor.' Then turning to his fellow monks he
said, 'Sacrifice of everything for the good of others is real Sannyasa.
Narayana, the God of the poor, is the God of the Samhita, Brahmanas,

Upanisads, Puranas, and the Bhagavadgita.'[39] Service of the poor thus became for him a means to God-realization. Later on, many others such as Gandhi adopted this notion to fight poverty and social injustice.

In coining the term 'Daridra-Narayana', Vivekananda introduced a new hermeneutics of engagement for reinterpreting dharma within the framework of the widespread poverty in India. He felt that traditional scriptures of Hinduism must be read in the context of the social, economic, and historical situation and not as speculative, fossilized ideology. Since every age has its own dominant set of questions and problems, an ancient text must be understood accordingly.

Vivekananda's solution arose, however, from tradition and was entirely consonant with tradition, not only in terms of a long-standing concern for others, but in terms of a theoretical understanding of seva *as a path to moksha*. The social consciousness that grew out of this understanding was promulgated in the Ramakrishna Mission; it expressed a view that was Vedantin as much as it was practical.

The neo-Hinduism camp chooses to dismiss the emphasis on service to humanity by claiming that Vivekananda started this project only *after* he had travelled to the United States. This is said to prove that he capitulated to Western influence and was not acting under the influence of Ramakrishna or other Hindu traditions. Following this premise, Agehananda Bharati wrote that 'the parable of the Good Samaritan plays no very great role in Hinduism' prior to Vivekananda, and that Vivekananda was under Western influence to start his new philanthropic ideal.[40]

But Vivekananda's urge to identify himself with the poor reached its zenith at Kanyakumari (the southernmost tip of India) in 1892 when he went around personally acquainting himself with the dire conditions. This investigation, it should be noted again, took place before his trip to the West. His published correspondence and reports of his views in newspapers before departing from India state clearly that he travelled to the U.S. in order to find financial support for his plans for Hindu seva, not that he went looking for a social theory that was absent in his own tradition.[41] The Western influence was more in the methods of implementation to get money and build institutions and was not the philosophical impetus for doing seva, which he knew was already present in his own tradition.[42]

Gupta considers it misleading to assume that Vivekananda's ideas came from the West just because he had at times expressed his appreciation for Christianity. Although he often referenced Western thinkers in his talks overseas, these were general references to the prevailing controversies in the West, into which he wanted to bring Hindu ideas, not the other way around.

He expressed surprise and contentment when he found that certain Hindu ideas—such as renunciation and bhakti—*also* existed in Christianity, i.e., there was an affinity. In the following private letter cited by Gupta, Vivekananda explains why he praised Christianity in the West. The reason is not that he wanted to mimic Christianity in order to reformulate Vedanta; rather he wanted to find a place for Jesus of Nazareth within a Hindu context.

I am here amongst the children of the Son of Mary and the Lord Jesus will help me. They like much the broad views of Hinduism and my love for the Prophet of Nazareth. I tell them that I preach nothing against the Great One of Galilee. I only ask the Christians to take in the Great Ones of India along with the Lord Jesus, and they appreciate it.[43]

Although scholars also claim that his American travels impressed Vivekananda with America's apparent altruism and highly developed social organization, Gupta cites numerous instances from the historical accounts that seriously question this view. Gupta says:

His experiences in America were actually profoundly disturbing: denial of hotel rooms because of his skin colour, letters threatening his life, humiliating discourtesy of his presumed hosts, condescending behavior and arrogance of his Christian friends, and cheating, hypocrisy, and fanaticism in the name of religion.[44]

Challenging the Neo-Hinduism thesis

This chapter has refuted the thesis that traditional Hinduism lacks social consciousness and that Vedanta has an otherworldly outlook in which worldly challenges are seen as mere illusions. Besides citing textual references that contradict this misinterpretation, the chapter gave concrete examples of grass-roots social movements prior to colonialism—the most notable example being that of Sahajanand Swami.

I also argued that Western social theories of religions, based as they are on Christian assumptions, are flawed in their applicability to India. Furthermore, Christianity's own claim to charity is put in doubt when its history is examined under the microscope.

Clearly, Vivekananda had plenty of internal resources, both theoretical as well as practical, on which to base his social activism. He did not depend on Western imports as alleged by the neo-Hinduism scholars.

The following chapter returns to Rambachan's core allegation that Shankara's philosophy prevents any unification of Hinduism because Shankara allegedly rejected yoga. I will argue that this is a narrow-minded reading of Shankara. The harmonizing of Vedanta and yoga is central to Bhagavad-Gita's multiple paths that include jnana yoga, raja yoga, bhakti yoga and karma yoga. This will seal the case against the neo-Hinduism camp's attempt to debunk contemporary Hinduism.

10

Harmonizing Vedanta and Yoga

This chapter goes into greater philosophical depth on one specific issue: the relationship between Vedanta and yoga. A large part of contemporary Hinduism involves both these aspects combined in a seamless manner. Hence, it is important to answer the following question: Are these two systems compatible (as Swami Vivekananda claims) or incompatible (as the neo-Hinduism camp claims)? If they are compatible then contemporary Hinduism comprises of a legitimate unity of diverse principles and paths. If they are incompatible then my opponents are right in claiming that contemporary Hinduism is a fabrication and a sham. We must note that compatibility is not to be based solely on whether they have the same approach to moksha, but on a much broader view of the multiple goals of life that Hinduism enriches.

Since Rambachan utilizes Shankara as his main weapon to debunk Vivekananda and contemporary Hinduism, one of the main questions we will address is: What is Shankara's view on yoga/meditation? The topic is philosophically complex and also controversial. There are numerous scholarly books and articles on this specific debate. But it is at the heart of the issue concerning the legitimacy of contemporary Hinduism.[1]

By its very nature this issue is very technical. Many non-academic readers might want to skip this chapter (at least in their first reading) because it mainly reinforces the arguments already presented in Chapter 6. However, I will try to make it more accessible for the ambitious non-academic reader. It is helpful to first introduce a few terms that are used frequently in this chapter:

- <u>Yoga</u> will be used to refer to a wide range of experiential techniques including meditation. These include practices derived from Patanjali's yoga system and from various other yoga systems. Shankara imposes limits upon the yoga systems because he considers them to be based on dualism, but at the same time he espouses his own kind of yoga (without calling it 'yoga' per se), which is based on his non-dualist metaphysics. Much of the controversy and confusion among scholars is due to the semantics of 'yoga' in a given text.

- <u>Anubhava</u> is a very important term. It means experience of any kind, mundane or in a higher state of consciousness. Experiences of higher consciousness are the goal of a wide diversity of Hindu paths. *My own use of the term refers to direct mystical experience in the <u>rishi state</u>*. This is the state of super-consciousness and not one of ordinary cognition. Every human has the potential to attain this state, even though in practice it is rarely achieved (see Chapter 11 for more on this). The contention being discussed here is whether or not Shankara allows room for anubhava in his system. I claim that he does, and therefore Vivekananda's teachings do not contradict Shankara's.

- <u>Nididhyasana</u> is the term Shankara uses to describe the Upanishadic system of meditation, yoga and anubhava.[2] This is the subject of Shankara's important text called *Upadesasahasri*. This system of Shankara is sufficiently similar to many methods of anubhava espoused by others, though he bases his meditation system on using sruti.

- <u>Sruti</u> refers to the Vedic texts. These are *a-purusheya* (authorless) and hence not human constructions, which would be subject to time, place and context. The other category of text often referenced is <u>smriti</u>, which are human constructed texts. Naturally, all commentaries on sruti are smriti because they are, by definition, human constructed.

- <u>Pramana</u> refers to the means of knowing. Different schools of thought accept different lists of pramanas as valid. The debate here concerns whether or not Shankara considers mystical experience (anubhava) to be one of the valid means either by itself or in a supportive role. Shankara places great emphasis on sruti as the pre-eminent pramana. My theory is that he did this in order to differentiate himself from the Buddhists who did not want to rely upon the Vedas (i.e., sruti).

In formulating my position, I have studied several primary and secondary sources. The main primary sources I utilize include the following works by Shankara himself where his authorship is undisputed:

- Shankara's commentary on his mentor Gaudapada's major work called <u>Mandukya-karika</u>. This work is on the mantra 'Om' and its use in meditation. (Shankara continued the intellectual foundation established by Gaudapada, but his direct guru was Govinda, and Govinda's guru was Gaudapada.)

- Shankara's commentary on the <u>Upanishads</u>, which are the philosophical parts of the Vedas. Various Upanishads are located at the end of each of the four Vedas. *Each Upanishad is a different rishi's direct experience of the ultimate reality.* This record of the rishis' experiential 'vision' is considered '<u>sruti</u>'.

- Shankara's commentary on the <u>Brahmasutra</u>, also known as the Vedanta-sutra. Brahmasutra is the classical exposition of the Upanishads that systematizes the various approaches and styles found in the Upanishads. Its author was Badarayana, and every interpretation and school of Vedanta refers to this as a primary text. Shankara's commentary on this text is called <u>Brahmasutra-bhasya</u>.[3]

- Shankara's commentary on the <u>Bhagavad-Gita</u>.
- Shankara's own original text called <u>Upadesasahasri</u>, which is his manual on meditation theory and practice. It explains Shankara's own kind of yoga, which he calls <u>nididhyasana</u>.

I realize that this terminology will be unfamiliar to many readers, but it is vital for ascertaining whether, and in what ways, contemporary Hinduism is a legitimate continuation of the tradition. I will try to provide simple explanations as we proceed.

In addition, the writings of several contemporary scholars—Jonathan Bader, Michael Comans, T.S. Rukmani, Arvind Sharma, Kim Skoog and Vidyasankar Sundaresan—have been useful to me as secondary sources.[4]

Based on my own investigations, I am convinced that:

1. Shankara made room for anubhava, but he advanced his own approach to it. His approach differed from the classical yoga systems such as the Yogasutras of Patanjali. Differences between Shankara and Patanjali have been exaggerated by the neo-Hinduism camp to imply that Shankara rejected all meditation.

2. Other thinkers of Vedanta before and after Shankara went even further in closing the gap between Vedanta and yoga. Clearly, Vivekananda had resources available from within the Indian traditions to shape his ideas.

3. Given the above two points, Vivekananda's system based on the unity of Vedanta and yoga was a valid continuation of tradition.

Vedanta's evolution at the time of Shankara

In popular accounts of Advaita Vedanta, it is often presumed that Shankara developed it out of thin air, or else that the system was nothing new and had been in place since time immemorial. Both these views are contestable. He was an innovative thinker who responded to the hegemonic discourses of his time by introducing his original Vedanta interpretation. The systems he opposed included Bhedabheda Vedanta, Samkhya dualism, the ritual-dominated Purva Mimamsa, and Buddhism.

Shankara was not disconnected from prior thinkers, and so his work was not done in isolation. A characteristic of Indian thought is that change and continuity co-exist, and that is because there is no mandate to burn or destroy what has been superseded, or to impose conversion upon adherents of other schools. Hence, new interpretations continue alongside old ones, leading to the pluralism we find across various schools of thought.

To show this change and continuity, I have developed the flowchart in Figure 4. In the middle, running from top to bottom, is a vertical trajectory of time which shows how Advaita Vedanta evolved in Shankara's milieu. The left and right sides show the influences from two major opponents, as a result of which his new system was crystallized. On the left side are shown the Samkhya dualists; their rigorous system is based on the ultimate difference between Purusha (roughly equivalent to the self, both individual and universal) and Prakriti (roughly equivalent to the world of matter in a broad sense). On the right are the Buddhist non-dualists.[5] In considering Shankara's approach to yoga, these are the most important competing views he contested.

The vertical trajectory in the middle shows that the predominant Vedanta discourse prior to Shankara's mentor Gaudapada had been Bhedabheda (difference-nondifference), wherein Brahman is held to be simultaneously identical to and yet different from the individual atman. Shankara strongly refutes this interpretation and proposes the complete identity of Brahman and atman, an absolute and unqualified non-dual view of reality.

It is important to note that both Bhedabheda and Samkhya were severely challenged by Buddhism, which was powerful in Shankara's time. This was the climate in which Shankara's movement was born. (This does not mean Advaita Vedanta did not exist in some form or other prior to such time.) The originator of what is considered Shankara's Advaita was Gaudapada, and Shankara followed in his footsteps. As a result of Shankara's victories in prestigious debates with the leading Buddhists of his time, Advaita Vedanta took many intellectuals away from Buddhism. In fact, Shankara's place in history is due to his success in challenging Buddhism and replacing it with his Advaita Vedanta as the dominant system.

Shankara's Advaita Vedanta was designed to satisfy the following criteria:

- It argued against Samkhya's dualism.
- Within the Vedic intellectual space, it argued against Bhedabheda Vedanta. For this purpose it included many Buddhist ideas.
- Yet it was not the same as Advaita Buddhism, and it argued strongly against Buddhism by staying rooted in Vedic sruti, which Buddhism rejects.

The two boxes shown at the bottom of the diagram indicate how Shankara incorporated certain elements from his two main opposing camps. As the lower left box indicates, he rejected Samkhya metaphysics because it was dualistic. Since Samkhya and yoga were integrated as one unified darshana, he also had to criticize yoga in many places as part of his broader criticism of Samkhya. But, as I shall explain later, these criticisms of yoga are not attacks on the practice of yoga per se; they are attacks on the dualistic metaphysics of Samkhya.

He de-coupled yoga from the Samkhya metaphysics, which enabled him to incorporate many elements of yoga into his nididhyasana system described later. This incorporation of yoga into Vedanta is an example of samarasata (sharing of nutrients with others, as I shall describe in Chapter 11). It utilized a new vocabulary rather than relying upon the earlier terms, such as 'samadhi' that was used by Patanjali and others. As shown below, Patanjali's terms such as 'samadhi' were present only on the margins of Shankara's discourse, and usually were interpreted in ways different from Patanjali's usage. Shankara's yoga relied on its own terminology.

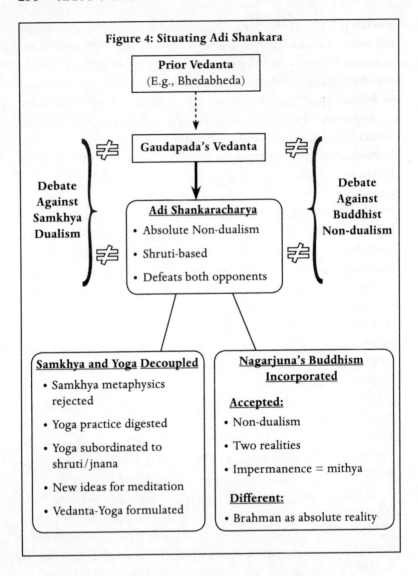

Figure 4: Situating Adi Shankara

Prior Vedanta
(E.g., Bhedabheda)

Gaudapada's Vedanta

Debate Against Samkhya Dualism

Debate Against Buddhist Non-dualism

Adi Shankaracharya
- Absolute Non-dualism
- Shruti-based
- Defeats both opponents

Samkhya and Yoga <u>De</u>coupled
- Samkhya metaphysics rejected
- Yoga practice digested
- Yoga subordinated to shruti/jnana
- New ideas for meditation
- Vedanta-Yoga formulated

Nagarjuna's Buddhism Incorporated

Accepted:
- Non-dualism
- Two realities
- Impermanence = mithya

Different:
- Brahman as absolute reality

Shankara made the practice of yoga subordinate to his path of jnana for attaining moksha, claiming that as a smriti, yoga must be subordinated to jnana which is based on sruti. Just as the smriti tradition of Patanjali yoga needs to be understood in subordination to sruti, so also the practice of yoga according to Shankara is subordinate to, and not independent of, the path of jnana. This subordination limits the extent to which yoga can independently benefit a practitioner. But that does not make yoga useless and is certainly not in contradiction to Advaita Vedanta.

At the same time, Shankara was also debating the Buddhists—in fact so successfully that it set in motion the long-term decline of Buddhism from the intellectual mainstream in India. (Buddhism continued to be an important system of monastic practice until its monasteries and universities, such as Nalanda, were later destroyed by Muslim invaders.) He simultaneously rejected Buddhism but digested several key elements from it. This is evident because some of his key ideas resemble the philosophy of Nagarjuna, who was arguably the most important thinker in Buddhism after Buddha himself.

Like Nagarjuna, Shankara negated the self-existence of any object, though unlike Nagarjuna he based all existence on Brahman (which is not an object). Hence his negation was accompanied by the positive essence of a non-object (Brahman). Nagarjuna's negation, by contrast, led to *sunyata* (absence of all essences). At the same time, like Nagarjuna, Shankara posited a two-level reality, one ultimate (which is Brahman in Shankara's system) and the other provisional (mithya). And Nagarjuna, in turn, could well be described as having digested Yajnavalkya's teaching of non-duality found in the *Brhadaranyaka Upanishad* while rejecting the Upanishads' commitment to the atman as the supreme Reality.

In short, Shankara demonstrated the unity of the Upanishads in a coherent metaphysics that would defeat certain hegemonic discourses of his time, and thus he established Advaita Vedanta as the new dominant discourse, replacing Buddhism in large parts of India.

The relationship among the three competing systems is summarized in the table below. Clearly, all three systems have meditation practice built into them, but each has a distinctive metaphysics, as well as a specific stance on the Vedas (sruti). The table makes clear where Shankara disagrees with both Samkhya and Buddhism and where there are commonalities among them. This also explains why he criticizes the specific kind of yogic practice Samkhya teaches, as that would confuse the student with respect to his cosmology. While rejecting Samkhya, he upholds non-dualist meditation (which we may refer to as 'Advaita Vedanta-Yoga'). In contrast with Buddhism, he upholds sruti meditation.

	Sruti Based	Non-Dualist	Yoga/Meditation
Samkhya-Yoga	No	No	Yes
Buddhism	No	Yes	Yes
Shankara	Yes	Yes	Yes

Theory of two realities

The Upanishads talk of both *Nirguna* Brahman (without attributes) and *Saguna* Brahman (with attributes). Shankara wanted to bring these into a single coherent framework. For this, he needed to solve the problem of the relationship between the world of karma, which is subject to causation, and the ultimate reality, which is untouched by causation.

Shankara achieved this reconciliation by following Gaudapada's idea of a two-level reality: (a) 'paramarthika', absolute Reality or Brahman; and (b) 'vyavaharika', empirical or conventional reality that is relative, i.e., the world as we ordinarily experience it.

However, this division creates another issue, because, according to such a division, the world is both real (*sat*) and unreal (*asat*)—an apparent self-contradiction. Advaita Vedanta tries to resolve this by saying the world is different from both sat and asat; it is *mithya*, a third category, between real and unreal, which defies the laws of logical thinking (*anirvacaniya*).[6] Figure 5 shows how Shankara resolves these issues.

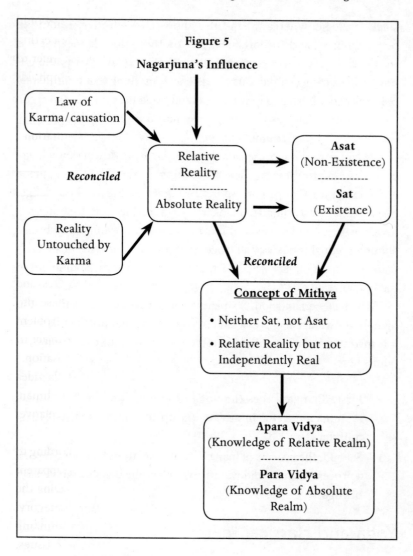

Figure 5

Nagarjuna's Influence

Advaita Vedanta's two-level theory is often compared to Nagarjuna's theory of two levels of truth: conventional and absolute.[7] Many Vedantins accept that Gaudapada and Shankara were influenced by Nagarjuna, and that they took his theory and integrated it with the Upanishads as their non-dualist view.[8] However, Nagarjuna's approach is radically negative (leading to 'emptiness' of substance) and based solely on logic, whereas Shankara's approach is positive (leading to purna, fullness) and anchored in sruti. Another principle they share is the doctrine of non-origination (*ajativada*), which says that nothing is born into existence or dies out of existence. Anything that is ultimately real was never born and never dies. Gaudapada uses this idea to argue that anything that has a point of origination must be mithya since whatever is sat (real) cannot change.

Vedanta interpreters use *para* (higher) and *apara* (lower) knowledge to correspond to these two levels of reality. In this framework, jnana and conventional yoga correspond to higher and lower knowledge, respectively. According to Shankara, yoga enables one to attain the lower realm only. However, this is not useless or wrong, for it brings about a gradual process of advancement towards moksha. Shankara's jnana teachings on '*neti neti*' and '*tat tvam asi*' are for the attainment of the higher reality.

As I shall explain soon, Shankara's jnana process for attaining the highest knowledge includes a kind of yoga or meditation. On this basis, it is incorrect to say Shankara rejected yoga. I wish to emphasize two points here:

- First, Shankara sees the yoga of Patanjali and other similar systems as useful in advancing up to a point that is below moksha.
- Second, the process of jnana for attaining moksha itself contains a process (called nididhyasana) which is Shankara's own version of yoga.

Yoga and classical texts

This section explains how Shankara treats yoga and direct experience in his various writings. Contrary to Rambachan's analysis, Shankara holds a positive view of others' yoga systems, even though he regards his own system as superior to theirs, and sees limits in what other yoga systems can accomplish.

Shankara's mentor's writing

Gaudapada's major text, *Mandukya-karika*, is centered on Om, and half a chapter is devoted to discussing methods for controlling the mind. He calls this confluence of yoga and Advaita '*asparsa-yoga*', where the word 'asparsa' means 'untouched', suggesting that the non-dual Brahman is free from conditioning of senses and mind. The importance of direct experience is clear as he explains his asparsa-yoga:

> The mind is the perceiver of duality. When the mind is held still, duality is no longer apprehended. But this cessation is not like that of deep sleep, in which the mind is simply dispersed. The mind must be awakened. It should be restrained from its tendency to become distracted by the objects of desire. This is to be effected by the constant recollection of the non-dual Brahman in conjunction with the recollection of the suffering inherent in the world of duality.[9]

Gaudapada also makes clear that this yoga is different from what Patanjali's system teaches, because the latter system had become part of dualist thought. Shankara's first Advaita work was a commentary on *Mandukya-karika* in which he uses 'samadhi' in a positive sense as a synonym for the Self.[10] He clarifies that the ultimate reality as described in the Upanishads, 'is hard to be attained by the yogis who are devoid of the knowledge taught in the Vedanta philosophy'.[11] This means that yogis must also have knowledge of Vedanta; thus yoga is not rejected but considered incomplete by itself.

Upanishads

The term 'samadhi' is absent in the ten major Upanishads. This is cited by one scholar, Michael Comans, as evidence that samadhi was not considered important as a means for experiencing Brahman. Other terms for experiential practice do occur, but these correspond to the Yogasutras' '*dharana*' (one-pointedness) and not to samadhi, the highest state. Several experiential processes are described in the Upanishads, even if they differ from the Yogasutras.[12]

The word 'samadhi' first appears in the Hindu scriptures in the *Maitrayani Upanishad*,[13] which is a later Upanishad, in which five of the eight limbs of classical yoga are mentioned. It also occurs in some of the later Upanishads of the Atharva Veda. So the term samadhi seems to have entered from yoga into the later Upanishads. Shankara uses this term in multiple ways, leaving its exact meaning unclear. He acknowledges that it has a role in Vedanta, but not as central as the role in Yogasutras. Samadhi is insufficient by itself for attaining moksha. In one statement Shankara sees samadhi as similar to deep sleep and notes that deep sleep is temporary because false knowledge has not been permanently overcome as it is in moksha.[14]

In Shankara's framework, there are three states of consciousness: the waking state, the dreaming state, and the state of deep dreamless sleep. Then there is '*turiya*', which is not another state of consciousness but the substratum of all the states. It is in *turiya* that a person becomes one with Brahman. Samadhi is merely a state of consciousness; therefore moksha cannot be within it.

Regarding yoga more generally, there seems to be cross-fertilization between it and the Upanishads. I agree with Eliade's remark on this cross-fertilization and on the somewhat distinct target audiences of the Upanishads and yoga:

> It is true that the Upanisads remain in the line of metaphysics and contemplation, whereas yoga employs asceticism and a technique of meditation. But this is not enough to halt the constant osmosis between the Upanisadic and yogic milieus.[15]

The Upanishads do describe yoga, though not as a formal system in the way Patanjali does. References to yoga in the early Upanishads on which Shankara commented are scarce, but they indicate his generally positive attitude.[16] The first Upanishad to mention yoga is the *Katha Upanishad*, which explains a type of yogic meditation: 'Let the intelligent man sink speech into mind, sink that into intelligence, and intelligence into the great atman, and sink that into the peaceful atman.'[17] Shankara introduces this sutra with the comment that the text presents 'a means for the ascertainment of that Self'. Another place says of this sutra that it is 'just for the sake of the clear understanding of the Self that the sruti enjoins meditation, viz. "the discriminating person should restrain speech in the mind"'.[18] Shankara's commentary gives a detailed explanation of this sutra, clearly indicating that he regards it as offering a method of meditation leading to Self-knowledge.[19]

In another place in his *Katha Upanishad* commentary, Shankara starts by explaining the method of withdrawing the mind and intellect from all activity in order to realize atman. But then he clarifies that yoga here means not joining (as in union), but *dis*-joining or withdrawal from all superimpositions that are other than Brahman.[20]

In his commentary on the *Chandogya Upanishad*, Shankara explains *dhyana* as 'the continuous flow of a conception which is not interrupted by different types of conceptions'. He praises those who have achieved this as persons who are endowed with calmness, who never betray their divine character, and says that its effects are visible in such persons.[21] Clearly, this is not an attack on yoga. Shankara does not consider the practice of yoga as referenced in many Upanishads to be a problem.

Some scholars look for the exact same words as in Patanjali's Yogasutras to determine whether or not he encouraged experiential practices. This is a misleading approach because one cannot use Patanjali's system as a universal canon of yoga to judge all other systems.

Bhagavad-Gita

If one wants to search for similarity to the Yogasutras texts, Chapter 8 of Shankara's Gita commentary provides ample material wherein he uses exact words and phrases from the Yogasutras and the Yogasutra-bhasya in close juxtaposition to one another. In this commentary, Shankara frequently replaces the word 'yoga' in the original text with 'samadhi'. He considers samadhi a key factor in yoga. For instance, he comments that one apprehends the Self by means of a 'mind which has been purified through samadhi'.[22] But this is a temporary state, according to him, and not a permanent liberation as moksha.

The provocative question we must address is: According to Shankara, is it possible to attain knowledge of Brahman through the Bhagavad-Gita solely? If the answer is negative, the implication would be that modern Hindus are misguided because the Gita would be incapable by itself to lead to knowledge of Brahman. If the answer is positive, it would disprove Rambachan's claim that only sruti can lead to knowledge of Brahman, because Gita is not part of sruti. To answer this question, Arvind Sharma quotes Shankara's introduction to the commentary on the Bhagavad-Gita, which concludes as follows:

> The Gita-Sastra expounds this twofold Religion, whose aim is the Supreme Bliss. It expounds specially the nature of the Supreme Being and Reality known as Vasudeva, the Parabrahman, who forms the subject of the discourse. Thus the Gita-Sastra treats of a specific subject with a specific object and bears a specific relation (to the subject and object). A knowledge of its teaching leads to the realization of all human aspirations. Hence my attempt to explain it.[23]

Sharma finds it abundantly clear that, according to Shankara, the Bhagavad-Gita by itself suffices as a valid means of knowledge about Brahman. The implication of Shankara's above quote is that though he sees the Vedas as the ultimate means, they cannot be the only means. The Bhagavad-Gita reflects this sentiment when it says: 'What utility there is in a reservoir by the side of an all-spreading flood of water, the same (utility) there is in all Vedas for an enlightened Brahmana.'[24] Here, the person with direct experience is like the all-spreading flood of water, whereas the person with knowledge of the Vedas is like a reservoir with limits. In other words, direct experience is important and not just the Vedas.[25]

In some places in his Bhagavad-Gita commentary, Shankara appears to equate samadhi with the nididhyasana part of his own system, which I shall discuss next.[26]

Shankara's own kind of yoga: cognitive shift without action[27]

Jonathan Bader sees Shankara as a great unifier: 'For the most part, Sankara tends not to reject outright those traditional Vedanta teachings which are incompatible with his Advaita. Instead, he subordinates them.'[28] Shankara was not simply a metaphysician concerned with the purity of his intellectual arguments; he was also a teacher who brought about real transformation in people, and yoga had practical value for achieving this. Both dimensions of his work need to be appreciated, not just his intellectual debates with opponents.

His system is remarkably similar to the teaching in the *Brhadaranyaka Upanishad* and Shankara describes it in detail in Upadesasahasri, which is accepted as one of his original works. It is a guide book on Advaita Vedanta using his three-fold process of *sravana-manana-nididhyasana*, leading to moksha. These three steps are:

- *Sravana*: First the aspirant hears the verses from the teacher.
- *Manana*: Then he reflects deeply upon them.
- *Nididhyasana*: Finally, he becomes absorbed in constant meditation on what has been learned.

The three chapters of *Upadesasahasri* are arranged to correspond to this three-fold process, with each chapter elaborating on one component. The first chapter has mainly citations from sruti, and Shankara explains how the sruti is to be heard. The second chapter is intended to help the advanced student engage in rational argument with a teacher who leads him to the understanding of the Self. The last chapter is devoted to explaining *pari-samkhyana* meditation, i.e., nididhyasana.

Systematic withdrawal from particular to universal

Shankara's method involves withdrawal from the particular and identification with the universal, culminating in the experience of the ultimate universal, the Self. The Upanishadic mahavakyas (the four great mantras of sruti) are repeated to act as triggers to create a uniform and continuous cognition of non-duality. This brings a radical cognitive shift such that objects are seen as non-separate from Brahman, the ultimate (and only) universal.

The student directly realizes the Self as continuous non-dual existence. What previously used to be cognized as reality now consists of impermanent entities called 'nama-rupa'. Shankara says that only the Upanishadic mahavakyas can achieve this cognitive shift. This makes them unique. Hence, he places great emphasis upon sruti.

Nididhyasana does not produce anything new; the identity of Self with Brahman was always the reality. Nididhyasana merely neutralizes the conditioning (sanskaras) which distort reality into a sense of finite entities that are separate from Self. The Upanishads do not directly designate and objectify Brahman but indirectly point the student to Brahman.

The teacher must use verbal methods to unlock the meaning of the Upanishads, and the student must have gone through rigorous preparations. Shankara's system directs the student to 'pull his mind back' from the world (similar to pratyahara in Patanjali's yoga) and 'withdraw' his mind into the Self. This is a process of subsuming 'particular' entities (visesa) into their 'universal' categories (samanya), such that particular entities are eventually cognized as non-separate from their ultimate substratum. This process is meant to negate conceptual entities in a sequence going from particular to less particular and more general. It culminates in reaching one's true Self by going through a succession of higher stages.[29]

Shankara's commentary on the Brahmasutra explains such a process:

> Thus the sage identifies himself, by stages, with the vital force that comprises everything. Then withdrawing this all-comprising vital force into the inner self, he next attains the natural state of the Witness, the transcendent Self that is described as 'Not this, not this'. This self which the sage thus attains is that which has been described as 'Not this, not this'.[30]

Comans explains this step-wise withdrawal process as follows:

> For example, diverse sounds are merged in the sense of hearing,
> which has greater generality insofar as the sense of hearing is the
> locus of all sounds. The sense of hearing is merged into the mind,
> whose nature consists of thinking about things, and the mind is in
> turn merged into the intellect, which Sankara then says is made
> into 'mere cognition' (*vijnanamatra*); that is, all particular cognitions
> resolve into their universal, which is cognition as such, thought
> without any particular object. And that in turn is merged into
> its universal, mere Consciousness (*prajnana-ghana*), upon which
> everything previously referred to ultimately depends.[31]

Dalal explains Nididhyasana as 'a process of intentionally remaining
in an awareness of non-duality, and maintaining or repeating
that knowledge to the exclusion of other thoughts and types of
consciousness'.[32] This is a negative process used merely to remove the
false superimpositions. Shankara is emphatic that any liberation gained
as a result of any action would be impermanent, summarizing all this
nicely for us:

> Liberation is not an effect—it is but the destruction of bondage,
> not a created thing. As we have already said bondage is ignorance,
> which cannot be destroyed by work, for work can function only
> in the visible realm. Production, attainment, modification and
> purification are the functions of work. In other words, work can
> produce, or bring within reach, or modify, or purify something; it
> has no other function besides these, since nobody knows about it.
> And liberation is not one of these; we have already said that it is
> simply hidden by ignorance.[33]

Dissolving the text/experience gap

Nididhyasana is Shankara's technique in which the practitioner forms
a dynamic relationship with the Upanishads, and this relationship
naturally expands as one proceeds. The boundary between text and

practice dissolves: from the fixed written words, the boundaries expand to include the spoken word, logical reflection, and the internal process of nididhyasana. Dalal explains this:

> [Shankara] expands the domain of textual study so that it ultimately absorbs contemplation. This move allows him to include all methods directly leading to liberation as modes of textual study. In doing so he breaks the false dilemma of studying texts versus self-inquiry, so that they come together. For him, texts expand with self-inquiry. The notion of text is much larger than what many scholars and practitioners assume when approaching the study of Advaita and has been largely misunderstood. ... It is closer to the general sense of gazing thoughtfully at something for a long time.[34]

> Sacred texts possess a receding horizon. At first there appears to be a clean distinction between texts and contemplative practice. However, if one enters the methodology prescribed by Sankara, the notion of text expands and continues to grow the deeper one studies. Sacred texts stretch beyond conventional boundaries of words, not only to encompass contemplation, but knowledge of non-duality and liberation as well. One never catches the boundary of the boundless text.[35]

Nididhyasana leads to a culmination where there is no difference between the pandit as text specialist and the guru teaching spiritual practice. It is a way to internalize the structure and content of sruti. Dalal reconciles the text and the practice by proposing an expanded view of what we think of as text:

> For advanced practitioners without obstructions, nididhyasana happens naturally and spontaneously without any willed effort. Sankara's orientation blurs the differences of reading, listening, teaching, contemplation and their respective experiences to the texts alone. ... In Sankara's view one should not make a distinction of texts and their performance. His Advaita system makes no room

for a difference between the specialist in the study of sacred texts and the specialist in spiritual practice. ... Properly understanding Sankara's nididhyasana may come down to our own notions of what constitutes a text. ... I believe Sankara holds an orthodox yet fluid interpretation of what constitutes the Upanishadic texts. On one hand the Upanishads are a set of sacred texts that are eternal, unchanging, fixed, and carefully handed down through the generations. On the other hand, even though the words stay the same, he sees them in a dynamic relationship with the student's progression along the Advaita path. In this conception, the boundaries of the text expand beyond the fixed written words to include the spoken word, logical reflection, and the internal process of nididhyasana.[36]

Difference from Patanjali's Yoga

Shankara does not say all thought forms must be restrained in the manner of the famous *citta-vrtti-nirodha* of the Yogasutras, in order to attain moksha. (The term 'citta-vrtti-nirodha' refers to cessation of mental activity.) But he does not reject citta-vrtti-nirodha itself. Rather, the cessation is the effect of nididhyasana and is not the practice itself. Sundaresan explains Shankara's position: It is not as if practising yoga to achieve citta-vrtti-nirodha independently of Advaita Vedanta will lead to Self-knowledge. It is Self-knowledge, obtained through Vedanta, and its recollection that directly leads to what the yoga system describes as its goal of citta-vrtti-nirodha.[37]

Shankara's goal is not the attainment of samadhi as in the Yogasutras, because, according to his metaphysics, there is nothing new to be accomplished that does not already exist. All ordinary yoga, meditation, prayer, karma, etc., are in the domain of action and subject to causation, and causation cannot touch Brahman. Only nididhyasana is outside the domain of action and not subject to causation, because it uses the sruti mahavakyas. What is required is merely a cognitive shift to know what is already present. Causation cannot produce any such result because Brahman is not something to be 'caused'.[38]

No causation is involved

No amount of personal practice without the mahavakyas and no amount of cultivation of karmic merit can suffice for this cognitive transformation to occur. Shankara insists that the realization of Brahman is *not* to be viewed as an action. No action is 'done'; rather, one dispels ignorance, a cognitive correction. Any action and its effect are finite, i.e., with an end. If moksha were the effect of an action, it could not be permanent. This is why Shankara avoids explaining knowledge of Brahman explicitly in terms of anubhava, because that would give his opponents a chance to misconstrue moksha as an 'event' or effect resulting from action.

Nididhyasana is thus a non-causal process in which the teacher plays a role in oral transmission of the mahavakyas. It is not functioning at the level of conceptual knowledge of texts or logical analysis or direct experiential Self-knowledge in the Christian mystical sense. Skoog differentiates this from Christian mysticism in an important way:

> The Christian does not recognize mystical realization or liberation from worldly ignorance and sin as a necessary culmination of one's spiritual life … The Indian view of revelation stands in contrast to the current Western 'Heilsgeschichtlich' conception of revelation where it is viewed as a series of historical events. Specifically, during a certain segment of history—beginning with the origin of the Jewish state and ending with the development of the Christian community—God's presence and nature were exhibited through a series of events involving select prophets and apostles. Christians establish their faith on these events that happened in the world and which were documented by men knowledgeable of the events. In the Indian context, sruti covers a vast array of different literary formats.[39]

Flexibility on anubhava

I shall now discuss whether anubhava is a pramana (valid means to knowledge) according to Shankara and how it is related to sruti. The term had at least three different meanings in the classical philosophical schools of Nyaya and Samkhya in Shankara's time.[40] Arvind Sharma notes that Shankara has also used the term 'anubhava' in three different ways, which are: (1) to refer to experience in its widest connotation,[41] (2) to refer to empirical experience,[42] and (3) to refer to non-dual experience.[43] The third sense is applicable to our discussion on the role of anubhava.[44]

To illustrate Shankara's positive attitude towards anubhava, Radhakrishnan paraphrases a sutra by Shankara as follows: 'How can one contest the truth of another's possessing knowledge of brahman, vouched for as it is by his heart's conviction?'[45] Here, one's 'heart's conviction' of possessing Brahman's knowledge may be seen as validating one's direct experience.

Shankara's commentary on the Brahmasutra also seems to accept that direct experience may be a means of attaining liberation, and sruti is not the only means to knowledge of Brahman.[46] There is even further evidence from Shankara's commentary where he makes clear that scripture (i.e., sruti) is not the only means for knowing Brahman:

> In the case of religious duties, i.e., things to be done, we indeed entirely depend on Scripture. But now we are concerned with Brahman which is an accomplished existing thing, and in the case of accomplished things there is room for other means of right knowledge also ...[47]

Sharma concludes his analysis of Shankara's position on anubhava as follows: 'In the case of sruti by itself, one "knows" about Brahman because one cites the scriptures; in the case of anubhava, one cites the scriptures because one knows.'[48]

In a somewhat similar manner, Jonathan Bader explains Shankara's position as follows: 'The sruti serves as the basis for anubhava', and yet 'one must not rely solely on sruti but also upon a direct experience of the truth: scriptural texts on the one hand and intuition on the other are to be had recourse to according to the situation'. In other words, 'sruti serves as the source of knowledge, while anubhava is the final result of the pursuit of knowledge'.[49]

True knowledge is anubhava, which the aspirant derives initially from sruti and makes it his own direct experience. Furthermore, Sharma argues that Shankara sees jivanmukti as a state of direct experience.[50] A jivanmukta is one who has attained knowledge of Brahman with bodily existence. This differs fundamentally from Christian salvation, which is only freedom in heaven after death.

Although Rambachan was on Dalal's Ph.D dissertation committee, and Dalal articulates nicely Rambachan's line of thinking and adds further depth to his arguments, in the end Dalal distances himself and adds nuance that is missing in Rambachan's radical and absolute stance. I shall quote two extensive passages from Dalal where he leaves room for fluidity in interpreting Shankara, and does not try to 'box-in' Shankara the way Rambachan does:

> [Shankara] leaves open a number of questions about contemplation. He is ambiguous about the specifics of nididhyasana practice and does not set out a clear definition or how it functions in his soteriology. He does not label the types of self-knowledge encountered in the Advaitin's study, such as a distinction between propositional and non-propositional self-knowledge. We have also repeatedly seen problems in trying to formulate a chronology of listening, contemplation, and liberation for his view. Does the wise person who practises nididhyasana already possess brahmavidya? Is repetition possible prior to brahmavidya? Is there any further requirement for contemplative repetition if one has immediate brahmavidya? Does instrumentality for brahmavidya necessarily lie **in** the Upanishads and not in the individual's mind, or in both? All too often scholars and Advaita practitioners accept stock answers for such questions, but upon closer inspection these answers evade our grasp due to Sankara's silence or to subtle non-committal shifts in his writing.[51]

Dalal is flexible on this controversy and keeps the door open, as illustrated in his conclusions below:

I interpret Sankara's silence as meaningful and intentional. ... Shankara likely recognized the many ambiguities, paradoxes, and unsolvable issues in Advaita formulations of jivanmukti and thus of nididhyasana. Furthermore, Shankara is aware that the Advaitin is trying to solve a problem that does not truly exist according to the philosophy. In a sense, the whole pursuit of liberation is illogical. It is therefore questionable whether he believed the underlying theory of a contemplative approach to an apparent delusional problem must be logically watertight. While we can formulate a picture of nididhyasana's practice, function, and relationship to textual study, it also holds a nonverbal and non-rational position in Shankara's soteriology. Perhaps we may conclude that the meaning and Shankara's interpretation of nididhyasana is fluid in order to help us embrace the complexity and paradoxes we encounter in attempting to bridge non-dual metaphysics and lived practice. It is fluid, in that our view of nididhyasana changes depending on shifting perspectives. From one perspective it looks like a meditation practice, but from another it is a mode of textual study. From one perspective it may be propositional knowledge and from another it may be direct brahmavidya. From the self-ignorant standpoint nididhyasana is practiced before liberating brahmavidya, but from the standpoint of the liberated person brahmavidya is present during nididhyasana. Allowing our formulation of nididhyasana to shift depending on context and perspective is I think the most appropriate understanding of its place in Shankara's thought.[52]

Traditional Advaita practitioners do not accept stock answers for the sruti-anubhava relationship, and that is because the exact mix lies in each seeker's anubhava. According to Vidyasankar Sundaresan, scholars after Shankara have disagreed on whether instrumentality lies in the texts or in the mind; the gap narrowed over time as the text-based approach increasingly incorporated yoga practices. Shankara has room for both, thereby accommodating the past rishis' experiences as well as one's own individual experience.[53]

Summarizing Shankara's posture on anubhava/yoga

Shankara's position on the yoga systems of others may be summarized as follows:

1. The need for yoga is not denied, but the dualist metaphysics of the Self is rejected.
2. Yoga is not by itself a necessary or sufficient means to liberation.
3. Yoga does help to regulate the flow of ideas in the face of disturbances caused by past conditioning.

This is explained below.

Respect for yoga

Vidyasankar Sundaresan notes that Shankara had great respect for yoga and that at the same time he also wanted to differentiate his own system from it. In Shankara's system, yoga cannot be applied independently of Vedanta to realize moksha. Shankara quotes the Yogasutras as saying that the ancient rishis directly perceived (*pratyaksha*) the devatas and that the various powers acquired through the practice of yoga cannot be refuted by mere denial. He says that even the Vedas tell us of the greatness of yoga and concludes that the abilities of the ancient rishis, who themselves revealed the Vedas, should not be compared with our own, more limited abilities.[54] Shankara refers to those who know the Self as yogins, indicating his overall high regard for yoga. One may infer that, in Shankara's view, the reason the rishis were able to reveal the Vedas is that they had yogic powers, though he does not say so explicitly.

It is interesting to note that numerous texts on yoga existed prior to Patanjali who turned these into a systematic compilation. Shankara was influenced not so much by Patanjali's Yogasutras as by Vyasa's commentary on it and on various other yoga texts that are now unknown. He quotes and references yoga texts in many places, though there is some dispute as to whether he is referring to Patanjali or some other text. But this detail is not relevant to our discussion. What matters is that Shankara's overall attitude toward yoga is positive, as is reflected in his statements like 'scripture also proclaims the greatness of yoga'.[55]

Yoga as preparation for higher practices

Shankara also accepts various sadhanas as a preliminary discipline for removing the prior conditioning caused by past karma. He does not accept them as a stand-alone complete means to liberation but as useful practices for those whose minds are in a state of dualism. And he regards asparsa-yoga (from his mentor Gaudapada) not as the highest path but as a means towards it.

Although Brahman is beyond verbalizing and the role of sruti is therefore not conceptual, one must prepare oneself in specific ways before pursuing liberation. These are as follows: ability to discriminate between the real and the unreal, indifference toward all petty desires and sensuous ends, mental tranquility, self-control, dispassion, endurance, faith, and passionate longing for liberation. According to Shankara, only after preparing oneself in these areas does one attain liberation upon hearing the mahavakyas. In various places, Shankara explains how practices generally associated with yoga help one advance toward realization.

After the preparation, sruti is the catalyst for those who are near liberation, and the mahavakyas can then 'push' one into liberation.[56] Without the preparation, sruti is merely a conceptual rendering, as the following passage from Shankara makes clear:

> Scriptural text, etc., are not, in the inquiry into Brahman, the only means of knowledge, as they are in the enquiry into active duty (i.e., in the Purva Mimamsa), but scriptural texts on the one hand, and intuition [anubhava], etc., on the other hand are to be had recourse to according to the occasion: firstly, because intuition is the final result of the enquiry into Brahman; secondly, because the object of

the enquiry is an existing (accomplished) substance. If the object of
the knowledge of Brahman were something to be accomplished,
there would be no reference to intuition, and text, etc., would be
the only means of knowledge.[57]

By Shankara's time, Vedic rituals had already become transformed
into *upasana* as meditation with a deity. The term 'upasana' means
relating to a deity in a prescribed manner.[58] There are many kinds of
upasanas in different sects and lineages. In numerous places, Shankara
describes upasanas as a way to attain identity with a deity. Hence one
cannot dismiss them as unimportant in Advaita Vedanta on the grounds
that they are within the realm of action.[59] The *Chandogya Upanishad's*
second chapter is almost entirely devoted to describing upasanas based
on Vedic mantras.

Shankara speaks approvingly of self-discipline and sitting meditation
(practices similar to *yama*, *niyama* and *dhyana*).[60] He says that yoga
teaches certain postures to help attain steadiness, one-pointedness,
and the continuous, uninterrupted flow of identical thought. This is a
reference to yoga as an aid to the upasana, which he sees as preparation
for experiencing the Self. There are many similarities between
Shankara's understanding of upasanas (which his system utilizes) and
the Yogasutras' dhyana.[61]

Shankara also uses the notion of upasana in his own system, but
gives it a new interpretation in which 'tat tvam asi' becomes the basis
for a meditative process to discriminate between Self and non-Self and
to affirm the unity of atman and Brahman.[62]

It is clear that there are great similarities between Shankara's
nididhyasana and other systems of yoga, even though he considers other
systems of yoga to be of limited value. His nididhyasana system is a kind
of yoga designed in a careful manner so that it complies with sruti.[63]

Comparing different levels of meditation, dhyana

Patanjali's Yogasutras describes two kinds of meditation systems. Those
systems that reject all contact with objects are deemed to be superior,

the goal being to stop mental fluctuations by removing the self from objects. This has similarities with Shankara's approach, even though Yogasutras teaches the attaining of silence by cessation while Shankara teaches witnessing and withdrawal. The other system—meditation based on object-centered consciousness to establish identity with the object—is deemed to be at a lower level.

In Yogasutras, dhyana involves focus on 'something' as *alambana* (support). But Advaita Vedanta does not consider anything other than Brahman to be real, and it cannot accept that focus on (and support of) an unreal object can lead to Brahman. So Shankara cannot posit a false object as support for meditation. At the same time, Brahman is not an 'object', and hence Shankara cannot accept Brahman as a support for meditation. This is where Advaita Vedanta's dhyana and yoga's dhyana differ. However, Shankara accepts meditation on Saguna Brahman, even though this is deemed inferior and suitable for lesser minds. And Om as Brahman is admitted as an alambana in many Upanishads.

Shankara is also flexible as to the specific rules for meditation and allows the teacher to decide what works best for a given student.[64] Bader gives a technical comparison between Shankara and yoga and also cites instances where Shankara's Brahmasutra-bhasya is very close to Vyasa's commentary on Yogasutras.[65]

Even though the Gita holds karma yoga in high esteem, Shankara emphasizes jnana yoga instead. Still he concedes that karma yoga can be a means to prepare for jnana yoga.[66]

Reasons for rejecting yoga at times

Despite their overlap, Advaita Vedanta and yoga are two distinct darshana systems with common elements. Each claims to supersede the other and may at times accommodate the other as a means along the way. Their mutual tension arises from yoga's historical links to Samkhya and hence to dualism, whereas Advaita Vedanta is uncompromisingly non-dualistic. Shankara accepts Samkhya and yoga partially—where they do not conflict with the Vedas—and rejects them where they do.[67]

In the Yogasutras, the practice functions independently of texts and culminates as an immediate experience of one's own Self that is identified as liberation.[68] Shankara rejects this because it neglects the primacy of the Upanishads as the source of knowledge of Brahman. He clearly states that his criticism of yoga is based on his attack against the Samkhya system, which he feels also applies to the metaphysics of yoga as understood in his time. He says that 'by the refutation of the Samkhya-smriti the Yoga-smriti also is to be considered as refuted for the latter also assumes, in opposition to sruti ... '[69] Therefore, he criticizes the yoga school for not basing itself on sruti texts and analyses the differences between these to highlight that Vedanta must be based on sruti. He says, ' ... the sruti rejects the view that there is another means for liberation apart from the knowledge of the oneness of the Self which is revealed in the Veda'. He then makes the point that 'the followers of Samkhya and yoga are dualists; they do not see the oneness of the Self'.[70]

Some of Shankara's criticisms of yoga also concern the risk of adopting it as an end in itself and becoming fixated on it. This is consistent with Patanjali's own warnings of similar risks.[71] It could also be conjectured that Shankara asked the students to renounce all ritual and karma yoga as a form of shock treatment, to prevent them from becoming stuck in action as the 'easy way'; this might have been his way of pushing the aspirant into jnana.

Advaita Vedanta beyond Shankara

Paul Hacker was the first Westerner to study the connection between Shankara and yoga.[72] Even Comans, who is sceptical of those who find yoga in Shankara, admits that gradually Advaita Vedantins have expanded the role of samadhi:

> Clearly the modern Vedantins, in their expectation that samadhi is the key to the liberating oneness, have revalued the word and have given it a meaning which it does not bear in the yoga texts. And, we suggest, they have given it an importance which it does not possess ... in the writings of Sankara.[73]

Four historical periods

It is important to understand that Advaita Vedanta developed through four historical periods.[74] This will keep us from fixating too much on Shankara as the only standard criterion for judging the authenticity of contemporary Hinduism. These periods are as follows:

1. **Advaita of the Upanishads**, which are experiential and not yet turned into a single philosophical system in a unified manner. These texts may be regarded as the raw experiences of several rishis, hence their diversity of context, style and content.

2. **Shankara's Advaita**, wherein he formalizes a new view of absolute non-dualism, and introduces the notion of maya.[75] This is heavily influenced by Buddhism and yet is a rebuttal to Buddhism at a time when it had great influence. Simultaneously, it is in response to dualistic Samkhya, which was also popular at the time.

3. **Post-Shankara Advaita**, which goes from the ninth to the sixteenth century CE and includes many great thinkers such as: Padmapada, Sureshvara, Vachaspati, Prakashatman, Vimuktatman, Sarvajnatman, Sriharsha, Chitsukha, Madhusudana, etc. Advaita Vedanta develops into three distinct streams at this time.[76]

4. **Contemporary Advaita Vedanta**, which is based on the experiences of Ramakrishna and crystallized by Swami Vivekananda and others that followed.

There has been an old debate on the relationships between contemplation, textual study, and liberation, both within the Advaita camp and among the various Vedanta traditions. Such tensions existed during Shankara's time and have continued ever since. Examples of this controversy are found in Mandana Misra's *Brahmasiddhi* and in the views of Suresvara. The balance between textual, philosophical and practical concerns has been continually contested.

Soon after Shankara's death, Bhaskara harshly rejected Shankara's concept of liberation, saying: 'Some of us would rather be jackals in the forest than have your kind of release.'[77] In the centuries following Shankara, the importance that Advaitins give to yoga techniques has gradually increased. For example, the popular fourteenth-century text *Pancadasi* combines Vedanta and yoga, though it stays faithful to Shankara's perspective by noting that meditation is for those who lack the intellectual acuteness to undertake Self-inquiry.

Another example of this shift is the *Vedantasara*, a late Vedanta text by Sadananda (fifteenth century CE). This text adds samadhi (having reinterpreted it to make it conform to Advaita ideas), along with sravana, manana, and nididhyasana.[78] Nirvikalpa samadhi is now described as the state where there is no distinction of knower, knowledge, and object of knowledge; the mind has become totally merged in the non-dual reality. All the eight limbs of yoga practice mentioned by Patanjali's Yogasutras are reinterpreted to conform to Vedanta.[79]

The main points of innovation in modern Advaita Vedanta are as follows:

- Greater emphasis is placed on the aspirant's attaining direct experience just as the rishis did.
- Various schools, both Advaitic and others, are not rejected outright but seen as a spectrum, each being relevant at some stage of an aspirant's journey.
- Vedanta is seen as relevant to the needs of society in modern times, and there is more emphasis placed on the immanent aspects of reality than in the past. Vedanta is now made relevant to householders in their lives in the world, and not just a means for sannyasins to attain moksha.
- Contrary to the Judeo-Christian religions of the late nineteenth century that were fighting against the discoveries of modern science, Vedanta is positioned as a science in its own right, because its claims can be experienced and validated here and now, i.e., reproducible and not contingent on some non-verifiable history centric event long ago.

- Since it is not history centric, this system may be seen as a threat to the Abrahamic religions which are boxed into history centric dogmas.
- While it has been pejoratively called 'neo-Vedanta' as some sort of phoney system by some, it is more appropriate to call it 'Integral Vedanta'.

Vivekachudamani

Kundan Singh has been studying Rambachan's attacks against Vivekananda for many years and wrote an unpublished paper arguing that Rambachan does not represent Advaita Vedanta's position accurately.[80] Singh brings evidence mainly from *Vivekachudamani*.[81]

Though there are credible claims that this book was not written by Shankara himself, even scholars who take this view, for example Comans, acknowledge that it had to be written by someone in the direct lineage of Shankara, most probably in Sringeripitham (which was the first of four seats of learning established by Shankara).[82]

Bader is another scholar who has examined the authorship of this text and opines:

> While the historian and philosopher may be tempted to simply reject the Vivekachudamani as a 'spurious' work, one studying the traditional approach has little choice but to examine it closely. This medieval text which is not only philosophically coherent, but profound in its interpretation of Vedanta, cannot be so lightly dismissed.[83]

So let us examine what this text has to say on the relevance of direct experience. For example, verse 54 of Vivekachudamani says clearly:

> The true nature of Reality is to be known by a first-hand personal experience through the eye of clear understanding, and not through the report of learned men. The beauty of the moon is enjoyed through one's own eyes. Can one appreciate it through the description by others?

Furthermore, verse 4 mentions 'srutiparadarsanam' which basically means gaining mastery over sruti. The question then becomes whether mere intellectual knowledge suffices as mastery, or whether transcendence of intellect into a higher state of consciousness is what constitutes mastery. Verse 6 provides an insight on this and states that despite all sorts of rituals, altruistic deeds and worship, moksha cannot be accomplished without experientially knowing one's unity with Brahman (atmaikyabodhena vina). Thus, though the study of scriptures is extremely important, additional efforts have to be made in order to experience unity with Brahman. Until then, the knowledge of the Vedas and Upanishads is provisional and must be confirmed in one's experience. The knowledge gained from sruti must be applied to accomplish the already-existing moksha.

Verse 474 says: 'Perceive the nature of the Self with the eye of perfect Knowledge through samadhi, where the mind has been brought to complete quietude.' Here the prescription of samadhi is quite explicit. The next verse 475 says:

When the Self, the Existence-Knowledge-Bliss, is realised, through liberation from one's bondage of ignorance, then the scriptures, logical reasoning, the words of the Teacher—these are proofs; the internal realization of one's own concentrated mind is yet another proof.

Verse 478 says that under the guidance of a teacher one comes 'face to face before the Self', clearly implying direct realization and not mere conceptual reasoning. We can find further support for direct experience in verse 365, which praises samadhi: 'Reflection should be considered a hundred times superior to hearing, and meditation a hundred thousand times superior even to reflection, but the Nirvikalpa samadhi is infinite in its results.'

The next verse 366 also advocates samadhi: 'By the Nirvikalpa samadhi the truth of Brahman is clearly and definitely realized, but not otherwise, for then the mind, being unstable by nature, is apt to be mixed up with other perceptions.' Verse 358 says that the upadhis (conditionings of the mind) cause one to think of diverse entities existing separately. 'Hence, until the dissolution of conditionings, let the wise person remain devoted to the practice of Nirvikalpa Samadhi.' (This differs from Shankara's works where he does not advocate the dissolution of upadhis on the grounds that the upadhi is essentially unreal and therefore all one needs is a cognitive shift.)

Clearly, by the time this major Advaita Vedanta text had been written—which was certainly long before colonialism, regardless of its precise authorship—the posture towards anubhava was consistent with Vivekananda's views. This refutes Rambachan's claim that Vivekananda was mimicking European ideas on direct experience.

Other later texts

Yogavasishtha is another work integrating elements of Vedanta, Jainism, yoga, Samkhya, Shaiva Siddhanta and Mahayana Buddhism. It therefore constitutes a Hindu text par excellence, comprising an amalgam of diverse and sometimes even opposing traditions. It provides an example of Hinduism's ability to integrate seemingly opposite schools of thought. The text emphasizes the common goal of attainment of

> a state that is the void, Brahman, consciousness, the Purusha of the Samkhya, Ishvara of the Yogi, Shiva, time, atman or self, nonself and the middle, and so forth. It is that state which is established as the truth by all these scriptural viewpoints, that which is all.[84]

Thus, it uses terms from several systems and tries to show equivalences across them. The text also includes Yogachara Buddhists and Sunyavadins among those who teach the same goal via different paths. Such harmonizing of Indian traditions has prevailed several times in Indian history.

Yogasutra-bhasya-vivarana is another work from Shankara's lineage. A commentary on Patanjali's Yogasutras, it states that meditation is, 'a continuous flow of a single conception, unsullied by other conceptions of a different type'.[85] Even though this text might have been written by someone other than Shankara, the author would have to be a serious thinker from the Advaita Vedanta lineage.[86] Later texts of Vedanta have continued this trend.

Challenging the Neo-Hinduism thesis

By Vivekananda's time, there was good harmony between Vedanta and yoga.[87] One can conclude that there has been an evolution within Advaita Vedanta on this issue.

Shankara considered that specifically the words of the Upanishads provide the necessary and even the sufficient means to engender this liberating knowledge. Other practices such as yoga served as helpful preparation and had their own place but were not sufficient by themselves. But the later Vedantins downgraded the importance of specific sruti mantras and upgraded the importance of yogic samadhi by presenting the latter as sufficient for liberation.

Using the writings from Shankara's own followers, it becomes clear that Rambachan is being narrow when he writes:

> Scrutiny of Vivekananda's statements on the Vedas and scriptural revelation, in general, reveals a point of view that is unqualifiedly opposed to Sankara's position ... Vivekananda has argued that the assertions of the Vedas are to be considered only provisionally true and that they become valid knowledge only when verified by direct apprehension.[88]

The next chapter will consolidate the arguments given thus far and present the case for Hinduism's unity and continuity on a solid philosophical platform. The Introduction presented an overview of my vision using Indra's Net as the poetic metaphor. The next chapter articulates this more specifically, consistent with my goal to cover as broad a range of Hindu diversity as possible.

11

Mithya, Open Architecture and Cognitive Science

Having addressed various technical issues point by point, I will now present my big picture vision of Hinduism. This will set the stage for the Conclusion where the breadth of Hinduism will be consolidated under the category of 'astika'. (I will redefine astika in the final chapter for this purpose.)

The view of the big picture uses the following three principles, each of which will be covered in a separate section.

Principle of the unity of existence:

- Everything that exists—divinity/God, individual creatures, and the material world—constitutes an integral unity. Included in this web are not only physical entities but also everything mental, conceptual, emotional, linguistic, and so on.

- This unified existence is not a homogeneous and undifferentiated mass (contrary to some reductive interpretations of Advaita

Vedanta). Rather, it includes infinite diversity within it; all diversity is contained within this unity.

- Many methods of understanding the relationship between unity and diversity revolve around the important notion of mithya discussed earlier. This *unity-in-diversity* is what I have referred to as integral unity. It is captured in the metaphor of Indra's Net.

Principle of the common toolkit and open architecture:

- There are vast differences between dharmic and Abrahamic traditions in the *human access* available to understand this reality. The Abrahamic religions depend on studying what they regard as the absolute history of God's interventions with man; it is only through those exclusive revelations given to the prophets that ordinary people learn the nature of God's commands, what man's duties are, and the ultimate truths and purpose of life.

- In the dharmic traditions, on the other hand, each individual may gain direct access to the ultimate truths using a variety of embodied tools and methods. Every human is endowed with this capacity and no one need depend on history to exercise it. Rishis and yogis have achieved this potential which is also available to each of us.

- Modern cognitive sciences have heavily borrowed from these Hindu and Buddhist tools (adhyatma-vidya) and used them to reinvent the mind sciences, neurosciences and psychology. This digestion has been taking place at a frenzied pace over the past few decades.

- Hinduism may be defined as a unified portfolio of ideas, practices and traditions which uses a 'toolbox' for discovery and a certain meta-language for expression. This definition gives it a lot of flexibility and freedom to evolve over time.

- In the dharmic traditions the use of such 'tools' has led not to a dogmatic belief but to a framework with an 'open architecture' that welcomes debate, mutual respect, evolution, and fluidity. At the same time, these traditions have to protect themselves from becoming too elastic and falling into fragmentation and relativism, i.e., the attitude of 'anything goes' or 'sameness'.

Principle of change and continuity of the ecosystem:

- It is directly as a result of the open architecture, and as a correlative to it, that Hinduism has changed and evolved. These changes have, over time, become increasingly coherent, as opposed to disconnected and violent. Debates and innovations have persisted over a range of distinct issues and the positions adopted have resulted in the rich diversity of systems within Hinduism.

The rest of this chapter elaborates these three principles encapsulating my vision of Hinduism based on which the Conclusion will present the defence of Hinduism and the way forward.

The unity of all existence

Purna

Given the nature of reality as expressed in the metaphor of Indra's Net, it is natural that the central concern of Hindu philosophers has been to understand how and why seemingly separate entities emerge out of such a unity. They do not want to unify separate entities but to understand how separation (or rather, the sense of being separate) comes about from unity in the first place.

This approach is inverted in Western religions, which often start with the assumption of atomistic separateness—of matter, life and the divine. The Judeo-Christian faiths presume intrinsic cleavages: God and humans are separated by sin and utterly removed from one another, the universe is an agglomeration of atomistic particles, and so forth. Furthermore, the reliance on historical and prophetic revelation ties humans to the past while the lure of salvation keeps them fixated on the future, resulting in dissonance in the present moment.

The Sanskrit word *'purna'*, often interpreted as 'completeness' or 'infinity', is a good starting point for understanding the Hindu metaphysics of the interconnectedness of all reality, physical and non-physical. Sri Aurobindo often uses the word to mean 'integral'.

The *Purna Stotra* is one of the most prominent mantras from the Upanishads. It says: 'That is purna. This is purna. Purna comes from purna. Take purna from purna, still purna remains.'[1] The word 'purna' occurs seven times in the original Sanskrit of this short text. It says: '"That" transcendent divine and the cosmic macrocosm are purna, and "this" microcosm is purna.' Mathematically expressed, it says: if you take away purna from purna, you still have purna. The micro and macro are each purna and are inter-contained, and, if you remove purna, what remains is still purna. The purpose of chanting this is to attune the listener to integral unity.

In the Introduction, the term 'bandhu' was used to understand purna in the way all things are correlated. By appreciating the bandhus (correspondences) among various entities that might appear independent, one gains appreciation for purna.

The coherence of Hinduism is rooted in this integral unity. We ordinarily experience dualities such as 'exterior' and 'interior', body and mind, spirit and matter, individual and collective. But the two poles in each of these dualities are mere aspects of an integral whole. Because everything is interrelated, it becomes natural to start the quest for ultimate truth using what is always immediately available, namely the embodied self. Hence, great importance has been given to yoga and similar embodied processes.

This approach accommodates various Hindu metaphysical systems as part of a family, and is not limited to Advaita Vedanta or any other specific system of Vedanta.

Mithya as Relative Reality

At the heart of integrality is the relationship between various *pairs* that seem like opposites, such as: relative and absolute; provisional and ultimate; particulars and universals; parts and whole; and dependent and independent. Among the various metaphysical systems, there are many ways of interpreting such pairs.

The relationship between the whole and its parts is an interesting one to appreciate how such pairs have been interpreted in many different ways, including the following interpretations:

- Only the whole is real and it is homogeneous; it appears falsely as a collection of parts that are actually illusory. (The 'whole' is conceptualized in several ways, including as *shuddha-chaitanya* or pure consciousness.) Many Advaita Vedanta scholars have interpreted pure consciousness to mean homogeneity of the absolute. The 'world is illusion' is an over-simplified view which has led many people to believe—quite falsely—that Hinduism has a negative outlook on life.

- The whole gets transformed into parts, which are therefore also real. The clay becomes the pot, so the pot is real, but *dependent* upon the clay for its existence.

- Parts are modes/attributes/qualities of the whole; hence the parts are real as well but not separable from the whole. The blueness of the lotus is real but only as an attribute of the lotus and cannot be isolated as having its own self-existence. Likewise, the smile on the face is real but only as a quality of the face and not separately existing as such. The interpretation of Vishishta-advaita Vedanta (one of the major schools of Vedanta), especially by Jiva Goswami, takes this kind of view. What is illusory is the *perception* that things exist separately. So maya is a false perception, not a false world.

- Vijnanabhikshu (mentioned earlier in Chapter 8) explained this notion of difference/non-difference using the arguments of a system known as Bhedabheda Vedanta. (See the end note for explanation.[2])

- Parts are co-dependent and co-originating, with no whole as the ultimate essence. This is the Madhyamika Buddhism view, according to which there is nothing like Brahman as the underlying unity. The unity consists of all existence with nothing transcendent beyond it.

The above is not a complete list by far, and serves to illustrate some of the metaphysical systems through which people have tried to explain Indra's Net and its integral unity. This book's purpose is not to get into a philosophical debate among the different metaphysical systems, on which numerous excellent books already exist. Rather, I am setting the stage for the Conclusion where I will solidify the broad category of 'astika' in which all such metaphysics can live harmoniously.

The Sanskrit non-translatable term 'mithya' is important to unpack these ideas. Figure 6 shows that mithya is a kind of relationship between the pairs mentioned above, and that it sits between two extremes. The extremes shown on the left and the right are two of the views concerning the relationship between a 'part' and the whole reality.[3] A part of the totality can be a physical object, an idea, an emotion, etc.,—anything we can perceive as an entity. The question we are addressing is: What is the status of such an entity in relation to the whole?

The position on the left of the diagram implies that each entity, or each 'part' of the whole, exists by itself, i.e., it has self-existence. This seems intuitively obvious to the ordinary mind. After all, the tree, the table, the keyboard, I and everything I experience seem to actually exist. This view is dualistic. It stems from the ordinary state of 'objectified' cognition, which is actually a projection of the ego, not a true perception of reality, as we often assume. The dharmic approach regards transcending this level of consciousness as being at the heart of the spiritual process.

The position on the right side represents the other extreme, which is that the entity or part does not exist at all, i.e., its existence is an illusion. As discussed above, this latter view has been advanced as a common interpretation of Advaita Vedanta, and it is one with which I strongly disagree. It leads to problems with ethics, since, if the world is illusory, then so are all its creatures and their conditions, and therefore there is no reason to be concerned about their welfare in the mundane sense.

I espouse the range of views in the middle, which is that any given entity has the *qualified* reality known technically in Sanskrit as 'mithya'. This word has no exact equivalent in English.

Figure 6

Object	Object	Object
exists independently	is mithya	is an illusion

One of the greatest misconceptions about the Hindu point of view stems from the common mistranslation of this word as 'illusion'. This mistranslation causes all diversity to be collapsed into the extreme position represented by the right side of the diagram.

According to the middle view (or views) shown in the diagram, every entity exists relative to something other than itself. One interpretation is that all entities exist, and 'really' exist but only relative to something other than themselves. Several of the various lineages of Hinduism take this view. Jiva Goswami's interpretation, for instance, is that all entities do exist but only as modes or forms of Bhagvan, or God, and not independently. In other words, since Bhagvan is real, his forms are also real, but they do not have independent self-existence. *Being Different* explains how mithya as relative existence also fits in with Buddhism's idea of mutual co-existence; however, this is different from Hinduism since Buddhism does not accept any equivalent to Brahman as an absolute.

A large part of the disagreement among the various Indian metaphysical systems centers on the interpretation of mithya. Those who interpret Vedanta as espousing a *homogeneous* Brahman with everything else seen as pure illusion, are depicted in the diagram's right extreme. Unfortunately, this has become the stock position of several scholars concerning Advaita Vedanta. My concept of integral unity is not to be conflated with such a view of Advaita Vedanta as the linchpin of that unity. In fact, Appendix A of *Being Different* explains integral unity with respect to several different dharmic traditions. Hinduism's integral unity is mainly illustrated there by Sri Jiva Goswami's *Achintya-*

Bhedabheda, which is similar to Ramanuja's Vishishta-advaita Vedanta.[4] That book's Appendix also explains integral unity from the perspective of Buddhism and Jainism. Integral unity, understood this way, is not homogeneous but includes diversity that is mithya.

Integral unity is not conceptualized in the same way in all dharmic systems. Given the paradoxical nature of mithya, there are multiple metaphysical systems, each of which has a different interpretation of integral unity. One can think of Advaita integrality, Vishishta-advaita Vedanta integrality, Tantra integrality, Aurobindo integrality, and many other kinds of integrality. The fact that each has integrality and yet is distinct from the rest is akin to several different objects being yellow, that is, the common quality of yellowness gives a family resemblance without making all yellow objects the same.[5]

Samavesha principle of integrality

Below is another way of conceptualizing the sense of a primal unity that underlies all dharmic traditions. It harmonizes the various metaphysical systems that interpret Indra's Net. Shrinivas Tilak explains integral unity using the principle of 'samavesha', which he says has three aspects:[6]

- **Samavaya** refers to two or more entities being in a particular relation as 'container' and 'contained', a relation of dependence and support. The whole is in its parts, and a quality or action is in a substance. Stated differently, the universal resides in the particulars. For example, the cloth is in the threads.
- **Samanvaya** (with an added 'n') refers to a relation of merging, accommodation or amalgamating. It assumes an underlying similarity or connection between ideas, concepts or even traditions which justifies the attempts to merge or reconcile them. This term occurs in the *Brahmasutra* and can be seen as a strategy for harmonization.
- **Samarasata** refers to the sharing of a common essence or life force. The result is a complex chain of existence in which all entities are bound together. This helps explain why trees,

plants, and animals are regarded as partaking of some of the characteristics of human beings. The specific nature of this essence is explained in different ways. In the *Samhita* texts, it is identified as fire or light; in later Vedic literature, it is atman, which is often identified with Brahman.[7] In yet other instances, it is vital essence or sap (rasa). Without the vital essence there would be no juice in the plants, no ghee in the milk, and no leaves on the trees.[8] Sap is the life force that is the mother of all things. According to Kaushitaki Brahmana (2:7), the essence of life flows out of one entity into all others and vitalizes each of them.[9] It also applies to the state attained by the yogin in which the world and one's life are experienced as a harmonious whole. In the Bhagavad-Gita (2:48), yoga is defined as that which promotes evenness. A mind infused with *samarasata* is open to include others or communicate truthfully with them because it is rooted in the sharing of a common force.

Thus, samavesha as described by the above three aspects, is the overarching framework under which a multitude of sects, philosophies, deities, modes of worship and other practices are united. This open architecture allows diverse practitioners to co-exist and mutually respect one another without compromising their own distinctiveness or impinging on someone else's. For instance, the embodied approach to experiencing unity is found in Vedanta and Saiva Siddhanta traditions without compromising their distinctness. There is sharing without claiming that all metaphysical systems are the same.

The evidence of Hinduism's own intuitive sense of coherence and unity is found not only in texts and teachings but also in Indian society. As noted earlier, the astrologically determined Kumbha Mela, the world's largest and arguably most ancient gathering of any kind, is testimony to the coherence and unity across Hindu society that defies the Western mindset. To give another example, Shankara started mathas in different corners of the subcontinent even though they had different languages and sub-cultures from each other—implying that there had to be an underlying sense of unity. Hindu sacred sites and narratives are filled with references to a shared set of pilgrimage places ranging from Mount Kailash, Mansarovar and the Himalayas in the north, to Ram Setu in the south. Various empires in India have spanned large geographies, sharing a deep sense of samavesha and respect for local cultures.

The point being made is that just because the unity and coherence were not of the same type as that in Abrahamic history centrism, and just because Indian political governance did not have a centralized 'state' in the modern sense, one should not assume that a society based on Hindu principles must necessarily be one of conflict and fragmentation.

Common toolbox and open architecture

To illustrate the distinction between Judeo-Christian and dharmic ways of approaching the divine, I shall use systems models as analogies. These models for the two civilizations are meant for readers with a scientific, technological or analytical mindset. As with any metaphor or analogy, they are not meant to be taken literally; their purpose rather is to suggest where the key differences lie.

Dharma metaphysics may be modeled as a meta-architecture applicable to numerous different schools which share common principles, symbols, and techniques, all of which are designed to help people gain access to higher states of consciousness. *Being Different* was written as the result of my quest to define this 'dharma architecture' in a way that does justice to its flexibility and diversity while, at the same time, avoiding the 'anything-goes' approach.

I will use the analogy of the computer industry to explain my approach. One can design and build any number of different kinds of computers by selecting from a vast range of components, including disk drives, screens, operating software, memory, printers, and so on. Each type of component is available from multiple vendors with different features, so there is a myriad of possible ways to configure perfectly legitimate systems, depending on the combination one selects. And yet they all have certain common standards and architectural principles.

Some sophisticated consumers are do-it-yourself types, who can build a system from these components, sometimes by trial and error. Others prefer to rely on a pre-packaged system supplied by a credible supplier—known as a 'systems integrator'—who selects the components for the client and puts the whole system together. The systems integrator is the intermediary who simplifies the enormous complexity of choices and tradeoffs for his specific clientele. His role is threefold: (i) to select, configure and put the whole system together, (ii) to install the system and train the user, and (iii) to be identified with a brand name (such as Dell, HP, Toshiba, etc.).

A Hindu sampradaya (lineage) or an individual guru is, as it were, a systems integrator who chooses the various components to build a 'total solution' for the spiritual life of a particular client. The client here could be an individual or a given target market. He installs this solution through initiation and training, and provides ongoing support. Many sampradayas are like brand names in that they are characterized by, or identified with, certain symbols, manner of dress, and so on.

Using this model, dharma may be seen as:

1. **An open architecture**: for spiritual quest, as well as guidance for one's mundane living.

2. **Modular**: a variety of components that fit into the architecture based on individual choice. One can choose one's own *ishta-devata* (personal deity of choice) and other *devatas,* rituals, day of the week to fast (if at all), pilgrimage sites, festivals, sacred texts, cosmological worldview, and so forth. The diversity of components that can fit into this architecture provides pluralism, and many of the components are 'customized' for each social context and/or period of time.

3. **Pre-packaged solutions**: pre-packaged 'religious' systems available from many competing sampradayas which provide total life solutions for the practitioner who does not want to, or simply cannot, configure his or her own spiritual path.

4. **Customization**: a do-it-yourself option for the sophisticated practitioner which bypasses all suppliers. This practitioner has

to be advanced in sadhana in order to be able to customize and configure a system in a responsible manner.

5. **Ongoing research and evolution**: various, ongoing R&D houses (individuals or sampradayas) who periodically come out with novel ideas and practices and introduce these into the marketplace; many innovations fail while others succeed.

6. **No centralized control mechanism**: like the Internet, there is no center, no owner, no founder, and alternative offerings are always subject to argumentation and change. There is no singular authority that has ever decreed and enforced what is 'right' for all practitioners. Nobody has been able to destroy the other options. There is no history of destroying rejected components (no burning of books); they simply fade away when newer ones get adopted by free choice. The marketplace of consumers and suppliers has always been dynamic, and nothing is resolved through the use of absolute force by theocratic rulers.

7. **Not history centric**: to participate successfully using this open architecture system does not require one to study the history of the system itself (for example, 'who created the Internet?', and other such trivia).

Such a culture is constantly being reworked based on numerous innovations which emerge in unpredictable ways and places. The system is self-correcting and adaptive, and avoids the problem of long-term exclusivity and fixations on history. The spirit of openness toward the multiplicity of possible answers to complex questions is why pluralism is deeply embedded in the dharma.

The Judeo-Christian religions lack the fundamental 'R&D culture' to be able to evolve in the same way that the dharma has evolved. They do not assert that the first principles of truth can be discovered by humans on their own; hence their obsession with claiming historically unique revelations as the only source of reliable truth about spirituality. This closed-mindedness leads them to insist that nothing is legitimate except their own product—a monopolistic mentality.

They lack the tools and technologies that the dharma traditions have developed over several millennia. When individual Western spiritual discoverers did make original claims, they tended to be persecuted by the establishment which saw them as a threat, rather than celebrating them as living masters the way they would have been in India. But the West is rapidly appropriating these tools, technologies and attitudes from dharma while, at the same time, denigrating the dharmic traditions.

Whereas the dharma traditions resemble Silicon Valley in their capacity for innovation and freedom, the Judeo-Christian religions come across like suppliers of controlled, state-supplied, monopolistic products. Like the Soviets, who believed in allowing only one airline, one brand of car, one toothpaste, etc. (despite the fact that consumers have many different needs), most Christians believe in allowing only one religion. Just as Christianity discouraged or outright banned mystics, the Soviets did not allow entrepreneurship as it threatened their monopoly.

The flexibility of dharma, however, comes with serious challenges. There is not just one Hindu book or one Buddhist book, but many, and each may give a different answer to the same metaphysical or ethical question. Since there is no single institutional authority to adjudicate such issues and provide command-and-control, on what basis is a practitioner to determine the right book to choose, or the right course of action to take?

The answer is that there are at least three approaches whereby a practitioner may determine the answer for a particular instance: scripture, lineage (which may mean sampradaya, or individual guru), and personal access to a higher state of consciousness. There are no canonized ethics—equivalent to the Ten Commandments—that can be applied blindly as 'universal'. It is important to establish this contextual basis of Hinduism (now seen as a post-modern idea) so as to avoid the frequent charge that Hinduism suffers from moral relativism.

The following section explains the principal tool of discovery that has been the signature quality of dharmic traditions.

Adhyatma-vidya

Adhyatma-vidya is the major tool for spiritual discovery and guidance in the dharmic traditions. It is the disciplined and systematic knowledge of the inner realm through precise observations made in a higher state of consciousness. This inner witnessing is done using disciplines wherein the mind itself is employed as an instrument for gaining insight. The human limits can be overcome by cleansing and de-conditioning the system of cognition, namely the mind, senses, memory and related faculties. The tradition posits that it is possible to achieve complete knowledge of all reality through such practices. This does not demand blind faith to a dogma; on the contrary, it requires that the practitioner detach himself from preconceived beliefs.

Sri Aurobindo explains that the experience of jnana (which he refers to as 'supramental cognition') makes it possible for one to know what exists as relative in the light of what is absolute: one sees, touches, feels, and knows the infinite by experience. Ordinary entities do not vanish, but rather are experienced as forms of the absolute. They are *not* experienced as existing separately by themselves. What vanishes is their separateness.

As a result of this extraordinary claim—that the relative limits of the ordinary mind can be transcended—Hindu and Buddhist meditation practice has been used as a form of scientific exploration. The yogi, as inner scientist, is himself the laboratory and the instrument of observation/experience.

Alan Wallace, who has spent his entire career studying the role of meditation in the dharma traditions and its relationship to the scientific method, explains that, although scientists seldom acknowledge this, the primary instrument they use to make any type of observation is the human mind. Therefore, it is the mind that must be fine-tuned and calibrated, and not just the external instruments found in a modern laboratory. Such a fine-tuned mind can also be turned inwards to observe itself. The ability to do this underscores the scientific importance of various kinds of yoga and meditation for improving one's cognition. The idea is to have clean cognitive instruments for discovering the deeper layers of reality. Wallace writes:

> Over the past three millennia, the Indic traditions have developed rigorous methods for refining the attention, and then applying that attention to exploring the origins, nature, and role of consciousness in the natural world. The empirical and rational investigations and discoveries by such great Indian contemplatives as Gautama the Buddha profoundly challenge many of the assumptions of the modern West, particularly those of scientific materialism.[10]

These contemplative scientists (rishis, yogis and buddhas) were, in effect, living human laboratories and they pursued the methods and techniques in order to refine and develop the inner sciences. Thus, the rishis pioneered the research in the area of experimental phenomenology. They discovered that in order to increase the resolution and clarity of the inner observations, it is essential to cultivate a simple lifestyle which minimizes mental perturbations and distractions. The more one reinforces mental concepts and desires, the more one strengthens the habitual mind and increases the obstacles to clear illumination. A silent mind is the equivalent of a clean laboratory.

Viewing themselves as navigators and explorers, the inner scientists developed, tested and constantly sought to improve the methodologies. Meditation texts were used as guidelines for comparing results and were continually enhanced by new discoveries. Some discoveries were more complete than others, some were better documented and communicated, and some were done with clearer and sharper instruments of knowing. Lineages evolved which continued the experimentation across many generations, all the while developing sophisticated conceptual models and epistemologies. The claims made were subjected to intense peer debates, many of which are well-documented. This methodology thus meets the standards of modern scientific empiricism.

The West has lacked the systematic techniques of yoga to be able to make reliable observations in the inner realm.[11] It is now catching up by digesting Indian theories and practices into this specialized domain of scientific inquiry.

The Sanskrit word 'vidya' from the root '*vid*' (meaning 'to know') has been used in India since time immemorial to denote systematic knowledge, learning, scholarship and intellectual pursuit in general. There are several classifications of vidya into distinct domains, including the following three:

- *Para vidya*, which refers to knowledge of transcendental realm;
- *Apara vidya*, which refers to knowledge of the external, material world as in physics and chemistry. The conventional study of Vedas and other texts, chanting, ritual, interpretations, astronomy, prosody etc., come under apara vidya, because perception is mediated by the conditioned mind (*paroksa jnana*); and
- *Adhyatma-vidya*, which refers to the science of yoga or the inner realm of humans. The term adhyatma means 'inner'.

The *Mundaka Upanishad* (1.1.4-5) defines para and apara vidya. It does not say that one is superior to the other, and traditionally both realms have been included in Indian education. *Isa Upanishad* (9-11), a very compact text, mentions both levels and makes clear that neither by itself suffices and both are important; they complement each other.

The seventh and ninth chapters of the Bhagavad-Gita are devoted to discussing the complex relationship between the empirical and the transcendent, or the natural world and the spiritual realm, respectively. These domains have also been termed *vijnana* and *jnana*, respectively. The Gita (9.4 and 3.40-41) says the empirical is simultaneously rooted, and culminates, in the transcendental.

There are two levels of reality in this view: one aspect of Brahman is manifest and the other is unmanifest, the point being that both are the same Brahman in different levels of experience. This double aspect of the God-nature relation has been expressed in various ways, including spiritual, secular, literary or metaphorical. The reality in its manifest (vyakta) form is accessible to sense perception and intellect, and this is the subject of scientific inquiry or vijnana. Knowledge of reality in its unmanifest (avyakta) form is available only as jnana or higher wisdom.

The pursuit of knowledge, especially the higher knowledge of the transcendent realm, is done through the theories and practices one may refer to as 'adhyatma-vidya'. This vast body of knowledge comes from many diverse traditions, each of which has perfected its own experiments and made its own discoveries. Adhyatma-vidya combines those aspects of para vidya and apara vidya that have a direct bearing on understanding the inner ecology of the human being at all levels— physical, emotional, intellectual and transcendental.

One may use the broad category of yoga and meditation to refer to these techniques. In the Bhagavada-Gita (10.32), Krishna says: *'adhyatma-vidya vidyanam (aham)'*, meaning Krishna is the spiritual science of the Self, where the quest for truth culminates. In *Katha Upanishad*, both the theoretical aspects (adhyatma-vidya) and the practical aspects (yoga-vidhi) are the subject of intense questions and answers.

The Gita (4.3) refers to the yoga tradition as *'puratana'*, or ancient, age-old and yet ever fresh. It describes yoga as consisting of four major paths, namely, jnana (knowledge), bhakti (dedicated love), karma (selfless action), and dhyana (meditation). Hence, meditation in isolation is not enough; it must be part of a total lifestyle in order to eliminate the mental patterns that bring interferences.

The goal of Patanjali's Yogasutras, one of the world's most coherent and widely used guidebook to inner spiritual exploration, is to bring the practitioner to his sva-rupa (innate or original nature) as mentioned in Yogasutras (1-3). Yogasutras (1.48-49) mentions that cognition in this stage differs from ordinary cognition which is based on the study of texts and reasoning. Patanjali's Yogasutras (7) says: 'pratyakshanumanagamah pramanani', which means proof by direct experience, inference, and competent evidence.

Vivekananda explained this principle as follows:

There are also three kinds of proof. Pratyaksha, direct perception; whatever we see and feel, is proof, if there has been nothing to delude the senses. I see the world; that is sufficient proof that it exists. Secondly, Anumana, inference; you see a sign, and from the sign you come to the thing signified. Thirdly, Aptavakya, the direct evidence of the Yogis, of those who have seen the truth. We are all of us struggling towards knowledge. But you and I have to struggle hard, and come to knowledge through a long tedious process of reasoning, but the Yogi, the pure one, has gone beyond all this. Before his mind, the past, the present, and the future are alike, one book for him to read; he does not require to go through the tedious processes for knowledge we have to; his words are proof, because he sees knowledge in himself. These, for instance, are the authors of the sacred scriptures; therefore the scriptures are proof. If any such persons are living now their words will be proof. Other philosophers go into long discussions about Aptavakya and they say, 'What is the proof of their words?' The proof is their direct perception. ... There is knowledge beyond the senses, and whenever it does not contradict reason and past human experience, that knowledge is proof. ... A man may be wicked, and yet make an astronomical discovery, but in religion it is different, because no impure man will ever have the power to reach the truths of religion. Therefore we have first of all to see that the man who declares himself to be an Apta is a perfectly unselfish and holy person; secondly, that he has reached beyond the senses; and thirdly, that what he says does not contradict the past knowledge of humanity. Any new discovery of truth does not contradict the past truth, but fits into it. And fourthly, that truth must have a possibility of verification. If a man says, 'I have seen a vision,' and tells me that I have no right to see it, I believe him not. Everyone must have the power to see it for himself. No one who sells his knowledge is an Apta. All these conditions must be fulfilled; you must first see that the man is pure, and that he has no selfish motive; that he has no thirst for gain or fame.[12]

Vivekananda went on to say:

He must show that he is superconscious. He must give us something that we cannot get from our senses, and which is for the benefit of the world. Thirdly, we must see that it does not contradict other truths; if it contradicts other scientific truths reject it at once. Fourthly, the man should never be singular; he should only represent what all men can attain. The three sorts of proof are, then, direct sense-perception, inference, and the words of an Apta. I cannot translate this word into English. It is not the word 'inspired', because inspiration is believed to come from outside, while this knowledge comes from the man himself. The literal meaning is 'attained'.[13]

Rishis and cognitive science

Clearly, even in Western cultural terms, the meaning of 'science' is once again expanding in scope. Science is now changing under the influence of Indian adhyatma-vidya, and the experiences in meditative states are being included as empirical evidence. The neo-Hinduism school rejects adhyatma-vidya and ignores its importance, because such scholars rely on an outdated paradigm of science. They tend to underestimate, for example, the significance of direct inner inquiry and first-person experience that is increasingly dissolving the barrier between subject and object in Western scientific exploration, which brings it closer to the Hindu metaphysics. Rambachan ignores these new scientific paradigms that are emerging in which contemporary physics and cognitive science challenge precisely the dualistic model of subject/object split—*and they present this challenge using precisely the ideas appropriated from the study of Hinduism and Buddhism.* It is first-person experience and experimentation that link dharma and cognitive science together.

I argue that adhyatma-vidya is closer to the spirit and substance of contemporary scientific inquiry than are the beliefs and practices of the Abrahamic religions. This convergence of dharma and cognitive science, and the inadequacy of Judeo-Christian theology to cope with it, are increasingly being recognized in the West, and are reshaping the discourse on 'science and religion'.

A century ago, today's Western vocabulary of cognitive science did not exist. It is important for us to re-discover the traditional Sanskrit vocabulary from which modern cognitive science has drawn so many of its ideas. This will help scholars understand the deep connections between the ancient sources and the new work going on in this area.

In simple terms, this 'new' scientific paradigm has been developing from the recognition of the role of the observer in cognition. The old Newtonian physics assumes an objective reality that is independent of consciousness. This dualist view is now considered reductionist and obsolete by scientists. Quantum mechanics has radically changed science in this regard. According to many interpretations of quantum mechanics, consciousness plays a role as the observer in 'creating' (by collapsing into) the state of the object that is observed. In other words, there is no particular state that the object is in *until* it is observed. Prior to an object's being observed, what we have are probabilities for its existence in various possible states. In a sense, the very act of observation 'creates' the state of the object in which it is found.

The link between this new physics and dharma has been noted since the discovery of quantum mechanics by Heisenberg and Schrodinger (both Nobel Laureates in physics). Each of these pioneers cited the Upanishads as the only source of philosophy known to them that was consistent with the paradoxical nature of reality according to quantum mechanics.[14] Western philosophical frameworks at that time (the 1920s and early 1930s) failed to accommodate any such possibility as quantum mechanics. This ushered in a new era of speculative research into the nature of consciousness and its relationship with the physical cosmos.

Most of the early philosophical explanations of quantum mechanics explicitly invoked ideas from Vedanta. There was a frenzied attempt to replace the disparate Western frameworks for consciousness and matter with a unified framework based on Vedanta. (In most dharma metaphysical systems, consciousness and matter were never separate frameworks.) The research literature on such ideas in the West has mushroomed and now spans many fields, including the philosophy of science, psychology, arts, neuroscience, religion, healing, and so forth. I shall not attempt here to present a tutorial on this vast terrain. Suffice it to say that the term 'first-person empiricism' is increasingly used to describe a means for knowing consciousness directly in non-dual states.

Although marginalized upon its arrival in the West, this new paradigm has become respectable and is seriously challenging old reductionist views of science.

What is most relevant to our discussion is that the pioneers in this science of consciousness start off by attacking the classical Western (Newtonian and Cartesian) models as being reductionist, and precisely for the reasons cited by Rambachan: the models are dualistic in their separation of subject and object and assume wrongly that objects have a separate self-existence. Rambachan, then, cannot very well accuse the new science of consciousness of the very problem it seeks to resolve, i.e., the reductionism intrinsic in 'objectification', as practised in orthodox scientific enquiry.

The recent scientific shift is toward a metaphysics that is closer to the cosmology of the Upanishads than to Christian theological constructs (based, as they usually are, on classical Greek models). This new insight involves cultivating the ability to experience reality in radically new ways. The new scientists of cognition know Hinduism to be closely related to their field, and adhyatma-vidya is being studied and practised as an important means of scientific inquiry. Yet there remains a broad disconnect between academic Hinduism studies and the emerging cognitive science.

I call adhyatma-vidya 'inner science' for a reason, which is to emphasize that after the rishis meditated and articulated what they 'saw', these first-person experiences were systematized and debated in peer reviews in India. This process has never been in tension with the scientific method because it is not bound to absolutist claims of history that are non-reproducible and hence non-verifiable.

Rambachan has not addressed the key question: *How did the rishis 'see' the shruti in the first place?* Unlike the Abrahamic religions, in which prophets hear from an external God, in the Vedas there is no external voice. There is no entity equivalent to Yahweh who speaks the Vedas to the rishis. Nobody says anything like: 'I am Brahma, the Creator, and I am giving you these covenants ... ' So Rambachan must explain how the Vedas were 'seen' by the rishis.

He cannot respond by saying that the Vedas were original compositions by the rishis, because Vedas are a-purusheya, i.e., beginningless and authorless. They existed before the rishis 'saw' them. So if the rishis neither composed them nor heard them spoken by an external person or entity, how is it that they were able to 'see' them? To the best of my knowledge, Rambachan, in his four decades of re-stating his position on the dichotomy between Vedanta and direct experience, has never dealt with this key question. What I am doing here, in effect, is sending the problem back to him and asking him for a solution in his own framework.

It is important to note that Hinduism does not regard the rishis as inherently different in substance or essence from the rest of us. Therefore, if the rishis had the capability of 'seeing' the shruti without any external God speaking to them, and without any previous textual tradition or 'revelation' on which to draw, why can't we do so as well? If Rambachan were to respond to this question by saying we are inherently incapable of 'seeing' as the rishis did, then he would be setting himself up for a massive contradiction with the core tenet: the atman is the *same* in everyone, rishi or not.

I am unaware of any way out of this problem other than by concluding, as I do, that each human has the same potential as the rishis, and that this potential is realized through disciplined sadhana (the inner sciences of adhyatma-vidya), even though very few of us are able to realize the ultimate result in one human lifetime; most of us will need to be reborn many times in order to evolve to the rishi state.

Robustness of the ecosystem over time

Figure 7 shows many of the issues that have been internally debated amongst Hinduism's various thinkers; it shows that the multiple positions in Hinduism have had extensive interactions. This dynamism negates all extreme or absolute views of the tradition, including the view that Hinduism is nothing but a random assortment of fragments with no unity, and the opposite view that essentializes Hinduism by attempting to establish that one school, and only one school, is 'orthodox' and hence authentic. (Indeed, the whole concept of orthodoxy is a Western one that distorts the nature of dharma.)

The debates over various issues show a complex and fluid relationship among the views. Some of the major questions that differentiate one Hindu system from another are the following:

- Which pramanas (means of knowing ultimate reality) are valid and in what priority?

- What is the nature of the ultimate goal—which could be *svarga* (loosely, a temporary heaven), moksha (loosely, enlightenment or liberation from the cycle of perceived birth/death), nirvana, co-existence with one's *ishta-deva*ta in a particular *loka* (realm), etc.?

- Are some forms of the divine superior to others and, if so, should they be the focal point of devotion? (For example, Vaishnavites prescribe worship of forms of Vishnu and Lakshmi; Shaivites prescribe worship of Shiva, and so on.)

- Which specific interpretation of karma-reincarnation should be embraced?

- What is the nature of jivanmukti (embodied liberation)? Does knowledge of Brahman or some other means expunge karmic effects that have already started producing results (i.e., *prarabdha-karma*)?

- In what way is adhyatma-vidya/yoga a useful path, and to what extent?

- Are Samkhya and yoga systems theistic or atheistic?

Such contentious issues comprise the fertile ground for producing many philosophies.

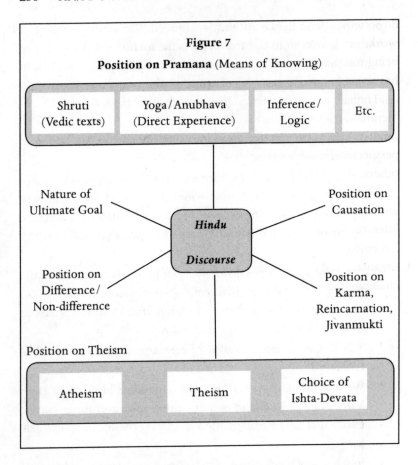

Figure 7
Position on Pramana (Means of Knowing)

Shruti (Vedic texts)

Yoga/Anubhava (Direct Experience)

Inference/ Logic

Etc.

Nature of Ultimate Goal

Position on Causation

Hindu Discourse

Position on Difference/ Non-difference

Position on Karma, Reincarnation, Jivanmukti

Position on Theism

Atheism

Theism

Choice of Ishta-Devata

The debates listed above cannot be equated with the conflicts among the Abrahamic religions. Among other things, they were relatively non-violent and they did not suffer from an obsession with historical details or an institutional obsession for 'order'. Nor did they establish a linear chronological sequence, with each school purporting to 'supersede' a previous one in a manner that every Hindu must accept in order to be a Hindu. There are many variations of each position shown in the diagram, and the examples I cite do not exhaust all of them.

My purpose here is not to get into a philosophical analysis of any of these views, much less into their histories or points of contention. To do so would require several volumes, and besides, such comparative works on Indian philosophy already exist in abundance. The point being made is merely that dynamism among and within these views has always existed.

The competing views of dharma can be seen in terms of multiple hierarchies. The ritualist, logician, grammarian, non-dualist, qualified-dualist, and experiential yogis represent some of the prominent perspectives; each view offers a framework in which it positions the others.

This multi-perspective view has been a type of dynamic equilibrium among the various thinkers, each holding its own truth and yet in active interaction with the others. Each of the following metaphysical theories has enjoyed prominence at some time in some place. The others were organized under it in some hierarchy of relative validity, in an ever-changing flux:

- Samkhya
- Yoga
- Bhedabheda Vedanta
- Advaita Vedanta
- Vishishta-advaita Vedanta
- Other systems of Vedanta
- Kashmir Shaivism
- Tantra, etc.

As the different thinkers argued against each other, they also learned from each other, and this equilibrium changed over time. They borrowed selectively from one another. Their arguments were shaped by their debates. This process led to the development of new genres and the further sophistication of old ones. Tension on certain issues can over time lead to cross-borrowings as a result of prolonged debates. Subsequently, there is re-integration of the various positions. This fluidity explains why Hinduism is an ecosystem in which new species are born and nurtured, older species adapt, and many die out naturally.

The Upanishads themselves demonstrate the diversity and evolution of various positions within Hinduism. The early Upanishads propounded various views which did not uniformly advocate monism or idealism the way some later Vedantins did. The Vedic insights were 'seen' by different rishis at various times and recorded in the Upanishads differently. Badarayana wrote his famous *Brahmasutra* precisely to offer a coherent system of thought that permeates all of the Upanishads, and this work became standard for all schools of Vedanta. Despite this being the case, a major disagreement in interpretations of Brahmasutra emerged between one group who saw the world as a real transformation of Brahman (*parinamavada*) and others who said the world is a relatively less real manifestation of Brahman (*vivartavada*). Other disagreements arose, even before Shankara's time.[15]

Buddhism and Samkhya had been dominant in India long before Vedanta's ascent. Even before these, there were numerous other philosophies. Within the Vedic tradition itself, the consensus shifted many times. Nevertheless, there has been a pervasive sense of samarasata, a sense of family commonality among the views, and none sought to establish any institutional or political control over the others.

Chapter 10 explained how Gaudapada reacted to Buddhism and selectively incorporated parts of it into his own Advaita Vedanta. Shankara was also reacting against earlier Bhedabheda interpretations of the Brahmasutra and the Upanishads. So this dynamic goes far back in time. By the sixteenth century, Samkhya had been partially incorporated into other schools. For example, the concept of *prakriti* in Samkhya became accepted by many Vedantins as roughly equivalent to *maya* in Advaita Vedanta. The trend is also clear in the works of Vijnanabhikshu and Madhavananda, who incorporated elements of various systems into newer integral unities.

Another fascinating example of cross-fertilization is yoga's historic relationship with other metaphysical systems. Yoga was a part of Samkhya but also existed separately as its own system. Over time, it has been incorporated into various other systems, each of which has its own adaptation and modifications. So it is fair to say that yoga itself has been a diverse, complex range of practices and theological reflections on those practices that evolved over time. Patanjali's Yogasutras was just one of many yoga systems, though his compilation has become the most popular one today.

Challenging the Neo-Hinduism thesis

The point of all this is to show that that a modern thinker such as Vivekananda was working within a long-standing, continually evolving tradition when he offered his own interpretation of it. Implicit in this was his understanding of the hierarchy of how the various systems fit under an overarching system. The neo-Hinduism camp mistakenly views this interpretation and compilation as a 'discontinuity' from the past and as a sign of Hinduism's incoherence, when it is actually nothing more than part of an ongoing adaptation.

The next chapter warns us that the openness and flexibility of dharma is also making it vulnerable to infiltration and digestion by predators. This will balance the present chapter's praise for the open architecture. The final chapter will then balance both these considerations. It will present a method for protecting the openness without being vulnerable to digestion.

12

Digestion and Self-Destruction

The integral unity of Indra's Net is under siege from something insidious. I refer to the widespread dismantling, rearrangement, and digestion of Hindu traditions into Western frameworks. The West is actually depleting and exhausting the very roots of Indian civilization on which it draws. Put another way, the programmes that seek to appropriate and misappropriate Hindu and Buddhist traditions are in fact distorting them, while enriching the predator host.

The metabolism of digestion

Digestion works in a series of steps and only by understanding the entire process can one understand its ultimate consequences. First the 'desirable' elements (such as a subset of yoga, for instance) are separated from the rest of the source tradition, thereby rupturing its integral unity. These separated elements then get 'scrubbed' to remove the dharmic contexts in which they are naturally found so as to 'secularize' them. Finally, they get re-contextualized either as Judeo-Christian or as Western science while the dharmic sources get erased, or else denigrated as inferior. As a result, the predator culture boosts its power at the expense of the source that is digested.

Thus, the adopted practices get distorted so as to make them 'digestible.' For example, Swami Vivekananda triggered an avalanche of Hindu influences in the West, but over time these became digested into various trendy 'Western thought' movements. My article in the volume published by the Ramakrishna Mission to commemorate the 150th anniversary of Vivekananda's birth gives an overview of his major influences that became digested over time.[1]

That article summarizes some of the key ideas now prevalent in the West that were transmitted to the West by him directly or indirectly. Once this snowball of Hindu influence on Western thought started rolling, it gathered momentum well beyond Vivekananda's ideas. The twentieth century thus witnessed the large-scale transfer of Hindu and Buddhist thought into the West, often without acknowledgement. Sometimes the sources were misunderstood or worse, misappropriated, and this trend continues to this day.

The article also points out the sleight-of-hand nature of many such appropriations and the efforts to develop and re-package them into marketable 'original' systems of thought. A prominent example is Ken Wilber's well-known and extensive empire, based on what he calls Integral Theory, which is heavily dependent on several Hindu and Buddhist sources in ways that Wilber does not acknowledge. There are also cognate enterprises such as 'Christian Yoga', 'Non-Dual/Integral Christianity' and 'Integral Judaism', all of which borrow heavily from Hinduism and related healing modalities, usually without attribution.

In an effort to boost their own status, scholars who serve as the facilitators of digestion typically map Hindu contributions onto the more limited frameworks of Judeo-Christianity. While many such digestions do enhance humanity's collective knowledge, many others cause serious distortions. In any case, the lack of formal acknowledgement contributes to a tendency to treat the Hindu sources as redundant and irrelevant. This limits the potential for Hinduism to continue to play its part on the world stage, and reduces it to an archaism, which is left behind because it is supposedly superseded by 'new' paradigms.

Many people ask me why it is bad for Hinduism to get digested in this way. After all, they say, the prey is absorbed into the life of the predator and can actually extend that life and contribute to its 'evolution'. To address this question, it is useful to contrast Western appropriations from Greece with Western appropriations from India. The modern conception of the West includes Greece as a subset, making it unnecessary to replace Hellenistic sources with other Western substitutes. Therefore, Hellenistic sources have retained their identity and distinctiveness as part of 'our Western past'. When such classical thinkers as Plato and Aristotle are treated as source material by modern Western scholars, they invariably receive proper attribution. (At the same time, the Hellenistic sources have been incorporated only selectively and their religious elements, which are of a 'pagan' nature, have been mummified.) In contrast, for many Western scholars, India remains the alien 'other'.

India is too different, too far away, and too massive to be included intact as a subset within the West in the way Greece has been. The inclusion of a unified India in the Western self-conception would threaten the very sense of what it means to be 'Western'. Therefore, what India offers must be broken into smaller parts that can be separately consumed and digested without attribution or preservation of the names of the sources. For this to become possible, the coherence and unity of India must be undermined so that it is made to appear fragmented and incoherent.

This intellectual breakup of India is akin to a predator's breaking up of its prey into morsels that lend themselves to digestion. It would not be feasible for a predator to swallow a large prey wholesale within its body. Instead, it must be cut into parts, and as each part passes through the predator's digestive system, it must be further broken down systematically, until every last protein and nucleic acid molecule has been processed by enzymes to yield raw material as nutrients for the predator's growth. Ultimately, no trace remains of the prey's own DNA; the raw-material nutrients produced by digestion are reassembled into the predator's cells, under the control of the predator's DNA.

The appropriation and absorption of non-Western sources into the West proceeds by a similar kind of digestive process so that the West may retain its sense of selfhood while capturing whatever aspects of India it seeks to own. This is why the mainstream Western academics does not teach Abhinavagupta, Aryabhatta, Bharata, Bhartrihari, Shankara, Kalidasa, Kapila, Kautilya, Nagarjuna, Panini, Patanjali and Ramanuja, among many other Indian greats on par with the great Greek thinkers. This violates the principle that the classical thinkers of all civilizations ought to be incorporated into curricula based solely on their merit and current relevance.

Just as the individual ego is at the center of one's narrative about oneself, so also is a people's collective ego at the center of its shared narrative. The West's expansive collective self ascribes a teleological role to its own coherence. Since it finds itself coherent, and views the other as incoherent, it seeks to digest the source of that perceived incoherence by breaking it into fragments and selectively mapping some of those fragments onto its own framework. Whatever it discards ends up being ejected as the waste product of the digestion process. This is why the act of bolstering one's own coherence, while aggressively undermining the coherence of others, is so central to the fight for world dominance.

It is unfortunate that Hindu and Buddhist ideas are routinely attributed to Western sources be they Hellenistic, early Christian or modern. This methodical re-mapping allows today's Western thinkers to co-opt the mantle of India's wisdom for their own. To protect what is called 'Western heritage' from the exposure of its vast indebtedness to Indian civilization, each successive generation promotes the further dilution and erasure of India's pivotal influence. Worse yet, it has become trendy among Western thinkers to reject Indian thought, while simultaneously espousing similar ideas clothed in Western vocabulary.

A good example of this dangerous pattern is the digestion of yoga. It is often remarked that this digestion of yoga into Western culture is being driven by globalization, consumerism and capitalism. But there is also a Judeo-Christian factor. The journey into Indian yoga begins with the seeker's open-minded immersion but may subsequently require re-contextualizing to comply with the Biblical constraints. Yoga gets reformulated either as a health programme, or a vaguely 'spiritual but not religious' programme in order to be digestible without damaging the DNA of the host. This puts it in neutral territory with respect to Judeo-Christianity, similar to the status of sports and health management. In the next stage one of the digestive tracts reconfigures it as Christian Yoga, replacing Hindu ideas and associations with Christian symbols and theology. A parallel digestive tract turns it into Western cognitive science, neuroscience, and other scientific bodies of knowledge.

The openness of Hinduism and Buddhism has helped these traditions spread and flourish across Asia for many centuries. But the export markets in Asia in those centuries were different from the present-day Western ones: The Asian recipients welcomed and integrated Hinduism/Buddhism into their own belief systems without feeling threatened. There was no need to distort them in order to make them fit. But today, Hinduism and Buddhism face a new kind of challenge when they encounter the Abrahamic religions whose claims depend on an exclusivist history of prophets. To bypass this challenge, the Indian gurus and/or their Western collaborators distort or dilute yoga to make it digestible for the Western consumer. To encourage this process many Indian gurus have been hoisted as prominent 'global' personalities.

The practical impact of this process of digestion is that, if unchecked, people who are attracted to yoga (including Hindus) will find it more easily available as part of Christianity or other Western movements which are savvier at marketing and have a positive 'brand' value. They will miss out on the authentic Hindu teachings. Hinduism will become obsolete and perhaps even extinct.

The flea market of modern gurus

For years, many Westerners have learned at the feet of Indian gurus or through secondary sources such as translated Indian texts, and have then appropriated or repudiated their teachers. On their part, many

Indian gurus have played this game with the American counter-culture and become market-driven, Americanized entrepreneurs, preferring to ignore or deny the exploitation of which they are a part.

The guru exporters and the Western importers have thus co-created many new 'products' for Western clients without fundamentally challenging the Western worldview. I have called this process of initial fascination and then rejection the 'U-Turn syndrome'.[2]

Figure 8 shows the multiple paths through which Indian spirituality and related knowledge have entered into the American mainstream. This 'digestive tract' proceeds from the left to the right of the diagram. The successive phases shown involve distinct processes whereby Indian traditions are turned into Western civilization's assets. The diagram gives a partial picture, showing only some of the flows during the past several decades and depicts the role that various intermediaries play. At the very bottom of the chart is an arrow going in the reverse direction— right to left—indicating the re-export of these repackaged 'Western' ideas back to Indians. It is intriguing that Indians are enthusiastically adopting ideas and practices which they see as American innovations, but which actually originated in their own culture.

The attempt to 'sanitize' what is called 'Eastern wisdom' and repackage it in Western secular terms has been going on for decades. The pattern is a recurring one: an intellectual entrepreneur 'goes East' in much the same way that the American frontiersman 'went West'. He or she may feel that the Abrahamic religions are too restrictive or oppressive, or that they are intellectually bankrupt in the face of new evidence in physics, psychology, and healing sciences. New treasures are unearthed during this process of Eastern exploration, and these are especially prized if they can initially be made to operate outside of accepted Western categories, including the category of religion itself.

At first, the Indian aspects of these new bodies of knowledge are noted and relished as the basis on which the entrepreneur/frontiersman can establish himself as an expert before his Western peers. But as that knowledge gets changed (re-packaged) for consumption in the West, the original contexts are removed and left behind as 'exotica'.

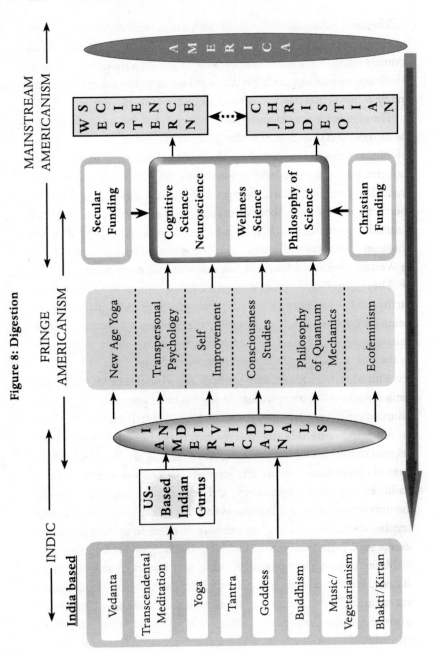

Figure 8: Digestion

The re-packaged knowledge generates new disciplines that supersede the old Western paradigms. Removing the original Indian contexts leads to forms of 'perennial philosophy' or secular scientism, which are supposedly value-free and operate outside of religious myths and devotional practices.

The column in the diagram called 'Fringe Americanism' lists some of the movements and areas of inquiry that were the first to become quasi-established inside America. Not yet in the mainstream, these fringe movements became part of the new 'frontier' of counter-culture that gradually became legitimized. Some of these movements have included the New Age trend in popular culture, as well as holistic healing as a satellite of medicine, transpersonal psychology as an outpost in academic Western psychology, and consciousness studies on the fringe of Western philosophy, neuroscience and cognitive sciences.

These embryonic movements served as preparatory stages for further digestion into the core of American thought and culture. Being on the fringes, the leaders of these movements could investigate courageously and experiment with ideas that were deemed too risky by the mainstream. Once the Indian sources had become validated and recognized on the fringes, there was a huge consumer demand which fuelled business opportunities. A range of institutions popped up to assimilate the digestible material deeper still.

A new generation of Americans has thus been falsely established as original thinkers. This is not merely a question of plagiarism but also a form of cultural and civilizational imperialism which takes the spiritual traditions of a people and distorts and dilutes them so as to appeal to the imperial palate. This exploitation of the source tradition stifles the organic evolution and development of these traditions. The Indian source gets depicted in one of two extreme ways: on the one hand, it is abusive to women, hopelessly backward, ridden with weird notions of caste, dowry, sati, etc., and ruled by some very strange-looking half-animal gods; on the other, it is full of romantic otherworldly 'mystical wisdom' that has great potential but lacks 'rationality', which the West must supply.

The cross-fertilization of ideas between different civilizations is inevitable, and indeed desirable. However, just as a tree disconnected from its roots cannot yield more fruit, a flawed re-packaging into new frameworks and nexuses deprives such ideas of their potential to affect further advancement. The gradual erasure of the history of Indian thought and its replacement with fashionable substitutes has led to a decline of interest in the subject at the serious level while making the same ideas popular at the superficial level.

Digestion and the neo-Hinduism thesis

The neo-Hinduism construct is another offshoot of the old story of Western universalism that sees the West as the driving force of progress in history. According to this view, all other cultures and civilizations are static and frozen in time, having, at best, exotic museum value for cultural, philosophical and religious tourists. This view ignores the fact that contemporary Hinduism is exactly the kind of diverse and freely evolving movement that could enable all great religions to change in accordance with today's world, provided, of course, that those religions are open to change in the first place. There is nothing 'inauthentic' about contemporary Hinduism.

The charge that Hinduism is incoherent helps to justify the fragmentation and re-packaging of Indian thought and practices into a kind of 'spiritual delicatessen': a buffet of disparate notions, from which Westerners can pick, choose, and digest individual elements for their own purposes. Enterprising new 'pioneers of Western thought' can claim this digested Indian knowledge as the product of their original discoveries; subsequently, the Indian sources are erased and replaced by Western ones. After all, if there is no such thing as Hinduism in a positive sense, how could one defend it against the digestion? The neo-Hinduism thesis facilitates digestion.

Conclusion:
The 'Poison Pill' for Protection
of Hinduism

The previous chapters refuted Swami Vivekananda's critics and provided various ways of understanding Hinduism's coherence, flexibility and diversity. This goal is part of a larger purpose, one which underlies most of my work: to establish the place of Hinduism among the world's traditions and to prepare Hindus to meet the challenges in an age of unprecedented threats and opportunities. This final chapter presents my strategy for this repositioning in a manner that extends the approach initiated by Vivekananda and other founders of contemporary Hinduism.

We live in a time of unprecedented inter-religious dialogue and encounters, one in which Western religions are rapidly digesting others as spare parts. The stark implication is that Hinduism itself—through these political and cultural forces, through historical revisionism, and through gross distortion of its tenets in the guise of academic scholarship—may become so weakened and mutilated as to not survive intact as a coherent tradition. Hindus themselves have been profoundly colonized; a radical 'repositioning for the future' is required to re-ground them in their tradition and create a viable way forward.

The questions that arise are: How can Hinduism be understood, practised and taken forward to withstand these forces of digestion? How can we 'take back' control of the discourse regarding the tradition and develop it on our own terms? This chapter first explains the predicament Hinduism faces, and then presents my proposal for securing it. I write with the humility that these are initial suggestions which will need to be debated and improved upon with the help of others.

Hinduism's predicament today

The typical understanding of Hinduism by many of its practitioners tends to be limited by virtue of one or more of the following: worship of a specific deity; teachings of a specific lineage; study of a specific book (shastra), or darshana/philosophy; or performance of a specific set of rituals. This suffices for most practitioners because they do not need to know anything beyond a specific path. One does not need to be a scholar in order to practise it. But this book is not aimed at explaining how to practise any one particular Hindu path. A person who is mainly interested in practising Hinduism should join an organization that teaches a specific path of his or her choice and make that path their base.

The book intends to portray the 'big picture' of Hinduism, a picture which is necessary to develop its leadership, defend it externally and also convince many of its own skeptical members of its integrity and coherence. The youth today look for answers to their big issues, and it is important that the representation of Hinduism in mass education, media and policy-making be positioned accordingly. The leadership skills that are meant for a given lineage or mode of practice alone are insufficient for performing this broader role.

Chapter 11 explained the notion of an 'open architecture' that positions Hinduism broadly enough to allow it to provide a framework for all kinds of views and yet grounds them in a coherent, unified manner. This open architecture is precisely what gave rise to such a rich and diverse array of Indian traditions which later coalesced into what we now call Hinduism, Buddhism, Jainism and Sikhism. These traditions best demonstrate the way in which this architecture works.

Let me stress again that Hinduism and Buddhism do not have an exclusive claim to this architecture; other faiths can also participate and draw on it. The open architecture presents a toolbox, not a closed program, and is certainly not dogma of any sort. Its extended usefulness lies in its applicability beyond the specific Hindu and Buddhist contexts from which it emerged. In other words, it is available to other faiths. But this creates a paradox. Chapter 12 explained that openness can go too far and lead to its own demise. It *is* being misused to appropriate selective parts of dharma into exclusivist religions.

This chapter proposes ways to safeguard against predators taking undue advantage of the open architecture by clearly establishing the core principles of Hinduism. The top half of Figure 9 shows the problems today. The confusion caused by some defining Hinduism too narrowly and by others, too broadly, results in its digestion into predator faiths. It has created the perception that there is nothing specific that can be called 'Hinduism' per se. The Introduction discussed the risk stemming from the simplistic 'way of life' description which excludes nothing, makes a mockery out of Hinduism, and turns it into an amorphous collection of raw materials available for digestion. Therefore, we must ask: how elastic is Hinduism, and when does it cease to be Hinduism if it is stretched too far? Specifically, what qualities must be preserved in order for it to still be Hinduism? The answers will guide us in achieving clarity on what must be non-negotiable.

The lower half of the diagram shows my proposed characterization and repositioning of Hinduism in order to address this situation. The left side shows open architecture for the expansion of narrowly defined Hindu sects and paths. The right side introduces another original notion which I call the 'poison pill', or, alternatively, the 'porcupine defence'. This is a high-risk, high-reward proposition which I will explain next.

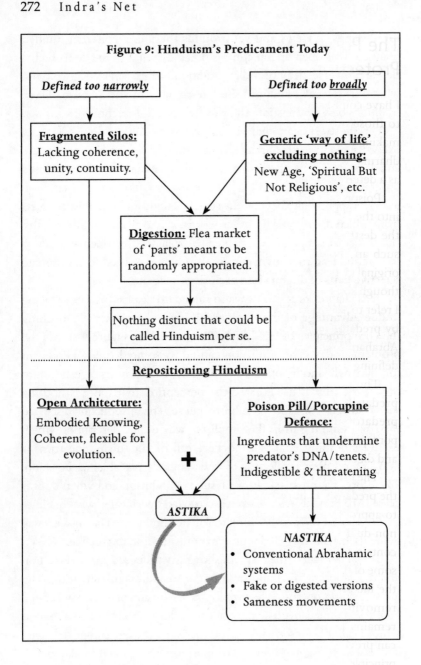

Figure 9: Hinduism's Predicament Today

The Porcupine Defence and the Poison Pill Protection

I have coined the terms 'porcupine defence' and 'poison pill' to refer to those qualities of dharma that the predators *cannot swallow*. By making these qualities explicit and including them in the definition of dharma, we can protect it from predators. These qualities then serve as a deterrent against digestion.

Poison pills are those elements or tenets that cannot be digested into the DNA of a predator, because consuming them would lead to the destruction of the predator's constitution. If a predator absorbs such an element, it will mutate so profoundly that it will lose its original identity and qualities. The predator, as such, will be dead, even though some new identity may have emerged in its place. The tenets I refer to as poison pills are intended to be dangerous for consumption by predators. This safeguards the dharma and can also provoke the Abrahamic religions to change dramatically from some of their current defining doctrines and dogmas.

The porcupine is an animal that does not intend to attack its predators, but for self-defence it has sharp quills which prevent predators from attacking it. If a predator were to try to eat the porcupine, there will be potentially fatal damage to the gustatory organs and digestive tract of the predator.

The presence of poison pills in Hinduism will create a conflict *within* the predatory culture: on the one hand members of that culture want to appropriate Hindu ideas and practices, such as yoga, meditation, non-dual philosophies, and so on. But on the other hand, as these contain poison pills (such as karma-reincarnation), they undermine some of the predator's core tenets. A clever predator will try to remove the inconvenient parts and digest the parts it wants—analogous to removing the quills of the porcupine and ingesting the body that remains exposed. The defence I suggest here will work only if we can prevent the subdivision of Hinduism into parts. That is why the principle of integral unity is vital to its survival. The skillful deployment of this device can equip Hindus for encounters with others, even those who do not see themselves as predators but whose approaches are, perhaps unintentionally, predatory.

Some people have complained that 'poison pill' has a negative connotation and should be replaced by something that sounds 'positive'. But I want poison pills to be seen in the same positive manner as Shiva's *trishul* (trident) which is a device for piercing the veil of falsehood, and thereby liberating us from the bondage of ignorance.[1] The poisoning I refer to is similar to killing the ego, except now it is the collective ego based on history centrism. Poison pills are like Zen koans, which use mental force for good.

In Ayurvedic medicine, many poisons are used to cure diseases. What is poisonous in one context can be a treatment in another. The poison pill metaphor is a positive one because it destroys and transforms the dangerous qualities found in certain religions. Since the ultimate essence of everyone is *sat-chit-ananda* (divinity) that cannot be destroyed or even scratched; what is to be destroyed is the false layers of the collective ego. The poison pill device is an act of *ahimsa* (non-harming) because it neutralizes the aggression of a predator who is committing *himsa* (harm) on a large scale.

Let us take the example of the 'Hindu Good News', which I have formulated as a potent poison pill. This fundamental Hindu principle cannot be reconciled with the commonly taught missionary slogan of the Christian gospel, or 'Good News of Christ'. The Christian Good News is that Jesus has come to save us from the Original Sin of Adam and Eve, whose disobedience to God caused Him to curse their future progeny (i.e., every one of us, individually and collectively, is born a sinner). Jesus's crucifixion was his personal sacrifice which absolved us of our sin. Hence, he is our savior who has arrived. That is the good news. But according to the Hindu Good News, we are all originally divine (*sat-chit-ananda*), and *not* originally sinners. There is no such thing as original sin. We simply do not have the problem that Christianity offers to solve. (See www.HinduGoodNews.com for an extended development of this point.)

The Christian cure being offered, in other words, is simply irrelevant, since we don't have the disease it purports to address. Furthermore, the notion of Jesus solving humanity's sins is not consistent with karma theory, according to which each of us is responsible for his or her past karmas. Therefore, whatever karma Adam and Eve might have done, they would suffer the consequences (*phala*) in their own future births, and this karmic debt could not get transferred to everyone else.[2]

One can see that the core definition of Hinduism must emphasize the principles of karma and reincarnation as non-negotiable, both for upholding the core principles of the tradition and for turning the Hindu Good News into a poison pill. This pill cannot be swallowed by Christian theologians since it would undermine the doctrine of original sin and hence void the need for a savior. In short, it would destroy the premise on which Christianity's Nicene Creed (i.e., its DNA) is sustained. The Nicene Creed is a list of historical-theological claims recited in most Christian churches as the basic affirmation or mission statement to which Christians must pledge allegiance. For those who doubt the centrality of history in Christianity, it is instructive to read this Creed, first composed in 325 CE when Christianity was adopted as a state-sanctioned religion of the Roman Empire.[3] What is important here is to understand that Hinduism as a whole, quite apart from the specific teachings of any particular lineage, is a package deal with certain non-negotiable elements that cannot be removed from it.

Another poison pill is the principle of reincarnation. This principle cannot be included in Christian mainstream doctrine, at least as currently articulated. Removing the notion of only one life on earth followed by a permanent heaven or hell would be a serious blow to Christianity. Its evangelical campaign is based on the fear of hell after this life and the infinite promise of paradise as the alternative. Even though at the superficial level of pop culture, many Westerners accept reincarnation, they have not thought through the deeper implication of how such views act as poison pills devastating the core doctrines of Christianity.

Reincarnation theory says that prior to this birth one has lived in numerous bodies belonging to diverse races, genders and social strata. This shifts one's thinking away from any racial basis for the concept of a 'chosen people', and the like. My past lives were not in the form of my biological ancestors, and my future lives will not be through my biological progeny. There is neither triumph nor guilt associated with my biological ancestors. My past and future are interwoven with *all humans of all kinds* everywhere—in fact, with all living creatures. We are all jewels in Indra's Net. This is the basis of Vivekananda's 'tat tvam asi' ethics—seeing divinity in all jewels, seeing oneself inseparable from everyone else.

Another devastating blow that a core principle of Hinduism deals is to the hegemony of the highly organized Abrahamic religions: by undermining the centralized corporate institutions and their stern authority over religious teachings, including their careful control on who can or cannot be counted as a theological or spiritual authority, a 'saint' or a member of the magisterium. The idea of living gurus and enlightened masters is seen as a serious threat by organized religions because a living enlightened master (jivanmukta) would be difficult for them to control. The decentralization of sources of authority is inherent in the phenomenon of living enlightenment. This, then, is yet another poison pill. The Hindu principle of embodied knowing has given rise to living masters, and this is a poison pill against the *dis*-embodied approach on which the Abrahamic religions are founded. Christianity excludes the notion that everyone <u>is</u> Christ in the exact same way as Jesus was—in the sense of 'aham Brahmasmi'.[4] This is why Christian saints can only be dead persons. Dead saints cannot threaten the established order of the church.

Visualizing Hinduism as a porcupine, I propose that one of its quills is the Hindu Good News (i.e., we are sat-chit-ananda), another is reincarnation, yet another is jivanmukti (living enlightenment), and so forth. Rather than providing here a long list of poison pills for the Hindu intellectual arsenal, I will suggest a few indigestible positions which may serve as the basis for formulating many such pills. These positions are rooted in the classical understandings of the Indian tradition, and have the capacity to destabilize if not deconstruct completely the exclusive truth claims of other religions. Such poison pills would serve as disruptive strategies against hegemonic monoliths.

I would like to point out that there is a subtle but important difference between the porcupine quill defence versus the poison pill offence, even where both refer to the same principle or tenet. The former is strictly defensive in that it prevents digestion by a predator. It acts as a deterrent and the desired effect is that the two sides leave each other alone. A poison pill, however, can also be sugar-coated to induce someone to swallow it. Once ingested, it can transform someone out of Judeo-Christianity—or cause adherents to revise the terms on which they embrace it in fundamental ways. Alternatively, it must be vomited out in case the person decides to remain an orthodox Jew or Christian as currently defined—i.e., such a person must stop appropriating from Hinduism in order to protect his established identity. In other words, the poison pill technique forces a choice one way or another. The confused and unstable state of dual-citizenship becomes unavailable as a long-term posture because its contradictions are not sustainable.

In this manner, the Hindu Good News and other poison pills can benefit Westerners who have immersed themselves in Hindu practices but who 'sit on the fence' with Jewish or Christian identities. Their gurus have failed to educate them on the irreconcilable differences. This is why many of them eventually 'U-Turn' back to their original faith, because they are unable to identify with the underlying presuppositions and theological views that subconsciously make them uneasy, and thus are unable to make a clear-cut choice.

After hundreds of interviews with U-Turners over the past twenty years, I am convinced that many of them would have given up Judeo-Christianity if their gurus had explained what in Hindu dharma is indigestible into their religion of birth. This is especially true in the early stages of romantic engagement when the seeker is overwhelmed by what Hinduism offers, and is willing to relinquish his or her earlier religious narrative, but does not yet have any idea what this would entail. The problem has been our gurus' frequent lack of understanding of the serious differences between Hinduism and the Abrahamic religions—or their desire to obscure or underplay these for purely strategic reasons—resulting in a lack of clarity and courage.

We must note that Christianity has its own arsenal of poison pills that are potent in undermining Hinduism's open architecture. The absolute and exclusive historicity of Jesus is the main Christian poison pill. I will return to this point shortly.

The next section will propose a way to fortify Hinduism by *blocking and excluding* certain dangerous tenets of the predators from entering the open architecture. To be clear, I intend to specify some of the tenets that ought to disqualify a given view from being incorporated into our otherwise big tent. I am aware that my discussion about specific aspects of certain religions, most often the Abrahamic ones, will be controversial, but again I offer this discussion in the service of clarity and in the hope that it will provoke further self-reflection on both sides.

Astika and Nastika: Redefining the terms of the interfaith debate

The defensive repositioning I am proposing draws on the terms 'astika' (affirmers) and 'nastika' (deniers) to classify the participants in interfaith relations. These terms have existed since classical times and have been used by major thinkers to define the coherence and unity of what has now become known as Hinduism. They were always used to draw a clear boundary, and the existence of such a boundary at a given time indicates that the thinkers appreciated the notion of shared identity.

Of course, the criteria for being astika have shifted. There has never been any one dominant philosophy or worldview in dharmic traditions that has established absolute hegemony consistently over time, for the simple reason that there has been no single linear history of events performed by God which every Hindu must accept, nor any central corporate authority that adjudicates canons, beliefs, injunctions, and so forth. Given this spirit of the evolving use of astika and nastika, I am extending the meaning of these terms beyond their traditional usage to apply them in a wider context.

Rather than speaking of Hinduism per se, or of any of the Abrahamic religions, I define my criteria such that the adherents to *any faith* may choose to affirm them in order to be considered astika; its opposite term nastika will refer to those who are disqualified by virtue of the nastika attributes I will explain.

My use of the specific terms 'Hinduism', 'Buddhism' and 'Christianity' is intended only to illustrate the astika/nastika qualities. An analogy may be made with ISO standards: they are not specific to any particular institution and serve as a basis for evaluating all organizations.[5] I intend my 'astika standards' to serve in this manner. Anyone and everyone may be evaluated based on this standard, regardless of his or her faith. They would either be classified as astika or nastika as a result of this assessment.

I wish to emphasize that this is merely a starting point for further discussion and evolution of the categories. The interfaith movement (or at least the Hindu participation in it) must proceed on the basis of such terms since they provide some clear criteria for locating different religions along a spectrum of beliefs and qualities and making distinctions among them. This is my way of throwing open the door for all humans to participate regardless of their religion of birth; this is how the open architecture has functioned in the past and must function now.

The overarching principle used in developing these criteria is the protection of the open architecture from getting usurped and hijacked by closed-minded dogmas. Once the rules are established, everyone qualifying as astika is invited. The appeal of being an astika is the freedom of belief and practice, the ability to achieve embodied knowing, and to customize one's own unique path. Those who do not enter the astika tent can of course meet us at the table of interfaith debate, but they should anticipate that we astikas will be strongly challenging many of their most fundamental principles, assumptions, doctrines and beliefs.

I could define the specific astika qualities first, and then extrapolate the nastika attributes as those that negate the astika. Conversely, I could start by defining the nastika first. I shall use the latter approach, i.e., define the nastika first. This allows me to focus on identifying the qualities that make certain beliefs harmful. I look for features that bring violence to other species within the ecosystem or that have a homogenizing impulse to reduce the diversity and preclude the flowering of faiths. For instance, I disqualify beliefs that impose closed systems and reject the freedom and flexibility of the open architecture. I reject exclusivity claims because these cause violence against others. And so forth. This approach is based on a clear understanding of what is problematic in the nastika's DNA. I will proceed by negation, in other words by defining nastika as the qualities by virtue of which certain systems ought to be rejected.

My definitions must sharply pinpoint the criteria for nastika. Whatever is not disqualified by these nastika criteria will be considered as astika. This leaves the door wide open to followers of every faith to enter the astika space, provided they have carefully expunged the nastika aspects of their faith.[6]

I want to clarify once again that no religion, such as Christianity, is being classified as nastika in total. Short of a wholesale revision of Christian church dogma, which is hard to envision at this time, it is up to each *individual* Christian to choose his religious preferences and define himself as astika or nastika by selecting or rejecting various tenets. Thus, a Christian may hypothetically reject history centrism (one of the criteria for being nastika) and reinterpret the life of Jesus in such a manner that he may qualify as astika. In doing so, if he is a member of a doctrinally founded Christian faith, he will probably be frowned upon by the religious authorities and in many cases be asked to leave the church in question. This is perhaps unfortunate, but he must realize that he cannot have it both ways.

There are numerous attempts going on to rehabilitate Judeo-Christianity as astika but without making the hard choices I demand. Ken Wilber's Integral Christianity is a prominent example of such self-deceptions. Just as the age-old Hebraic/Hellenistic conflict has never been reconciled, Wilber's movement to digest dharma into Christian history centrism is flawed. Major amendments to Christian doctrine are still necessary for it to become astika. My poison pills are exposing such fundamental and disqualifying flaws, including some that are disingenuous and even fraudulent, in the sense that they knowingly camouflage important distinctions.

This new approach offers a bridge from nastika to astika for those Jews, Christians and Muslims who find themselves 'boxed in' by their religions. Such a pathway is in accordance with Swami Vivekananda's proposal of an open Hinduism to be available as a template for Westerners. Since his time, many millions of Westerners have benefited from this openness in the form of movements that have sprung up in the West. This book's goal is to advance his ideas further in terms of these new astika and nastika categories.

Vivekananda did recognize aspects of other traditions that were not in accord with dharma; I have chosen to emphasize these even more strongly by adding "poison pills" and "porcupine quills" to the open architecture of contemporary Hinduism. I wish to accomplish two goals: make it difficult for aggressive religions to digest Hinduism, and reduce the U-Turns by Westerners back to their earlier religions. Poison pills and the porcupine defence fill a strategic gap here. The insights into digestion and the insistence on distinctions and differences, including the use of the strategy of poison pills to counteract attempts at digestion, are my humble innovations in the hope of taking Vivekananda's revolution forward. This exercise also consolidates Hinduism in a novel manner such that it becomes impossible to regard it as a collection of unrelated practices and disparate elements.

It is worth comparing my proposal with the way each of the Abrahamic religions protects itself. The history centrism of Judaism, Christianity and Islam cause them to be in mutual conflict with one other, as explained in Chapter 2 of *Being Different*. These religions survive as separate and distinct entities precisely because the history centrism of one is not digestible by the other. Many attempts have been made to construct a single hybrid but without success. Thus, history centrism is the main poison pill each of them has built into its own DNA.

As long as a Christian holds on to the history centric Nicene Creed, he or she remains a Christian no matter how much he or she picks up from Hinduism and Buddhism to supplement his or her beliefs and practices. As long as a Muslim believes in the mandatory creed that

Mohammad was the final prophet and the Qur'an is literally the word of God containing his final and absolute commands, he will be a Muslim, regardless of what popular or fashionable ideas he might digest from others. Hindus cannot resort to history centrism in this way, as that would distort their open architecture.[7] Because most Hindus do not understand this, they naively get impressed when a Christian adopts some superficial Hindu symbolism or element in isolation.

There appear to be similarities between the concept of 'infidel' or 'non-believer' in the Abrahamic religions and my concept of nastika. Both refer to someone who is seen as an 'outsider'. But the criteria for being infidel and nastika differ dramatically. The Abrahamic religions define 'infidel' or 'non-believer' as someone who does not adhere to their exclusive, history centric dogma, whereas my definition of 'nastika' is based on opposition to the open architecture. In some sense, these notions are opposites: The person practising in the spirit of open architecture would be seen as an infidel in the Abrahamic religions (at least according to their conventional interpretation). Hence, the astika of my system is an infidel or non-believer in the history centric systems. Conversely, the 'true believer' in a literal view of Christianity or Islam would be nastika in my system, for all the reasons from history centrism to disembodied reliance on revelation that I have discussed above.

Another significant point of difference between these systems is that in the Abrahamic religions God gives a collective mandate that encourages group formation and mobilizations, putting the outsider at serious risk of persecution. In the open architecture of astika, there is no collective mobilization, and a nastika is merely to be left alone as long as he does not attack others; there is no injunction to go after him and convert him into astika.

This approach is a potential game changer in interfaith relations. The open architecture of astika is available to everyone to draw on; it can house and foster a wide variety of faiths and theologies. Yet it is a very Hindu paradigm that would allow us to engage with others on our own terms.

The criteria for nastika: Principles that must be rejected

In line with the project just laid out, let me articulate again the principles that would *disqualify* any religious or theological view from being included in the open architecture and characterized as astika. In other words, religions which adhere to some or all of the notions described below are considered nastika. Although many of these notions are characteristic of the Abrahamic religions, they are by no means confined to them.

History Centrism

A signature quality of nastika is insistence on history centrism, i.e., the mandated belief that God has revealed himself in history only in unique events and only to specific peoples or prophets, and in a way that is forever unavailable to others directly. This dogma demands that the exclusive path can be found only in the literal words of God as heard by specific prophets and mentioned in some particular text that comprises literal history.

One of the consequences of history centrism is that since religious practitioners are not privy to the direct revelation, they must fundamentally rely on others; thus, their connection to God can only be second-hand, separated by the church and/or the history of prophets available in canons. This weakens the quest for individual spiritual exploration.

Because the acts of God and his message are available to us solely through religious brokers, it is only through these sources that divinity can reliably be understood. The details of specific events, lives and texts become a crucial part of God's message. There is sharp and sometimes violent debate over minute historical trivia. Because the events in antiquity cannot ultimately be determined today, these debates can never fully be settled, and they remain an endless provocation to conflict.

Despite many attempts to revise and reinterpret such claims, they present serious barriers to the kind of universal respect and shared quest that define the astika. The barriers of history centrism are great and there is often a false pretense that they have gone away. For instance, in the Second Vatican Council (1962-65), official Roman Catholic doctrine espoused a weak form of what might be called pluralism in interfaith discussions, though the magisterium tends to be allergic to that word. But a closer look shows that this new doctrine has merely camouflaged the problem. The new doctrine holds that there are many truths in the various religions of the world, and that God operates through every spiritual tradition. *However, he does <u>not</u> do so with the fullness that is found exclusively in Jesus.*[8] So a Roman Catholic Christian can tolerate other faiths, even respect them to *some* extent, but eventually they serve merely as preparation for conversion into Catholicism.

Disembodied knowing and self-alienation

The second major quality that would cause a position to be classified as nastika has to do with the role of the body in spiritual development. 'Body' is here understood to mean not only the physical body but the subtler levels as well. According to many nastika views, the body and its experience are not reliable vehicles for spiritual insight. There is a pervasive sense of 'sin', or some innate failure built into human capacity, perhaps even a sense of doom or fate that prevents one from realizing his or her connection to the divine directly through sadhana.

This point was earlier explained in terms of the difference between the Christian Good News and the Hindu Good News. We have also discussed the term 'anubhava', which means precisely the embodied experience that the disembodied or self-alienated paths deny. In many cases it is even blocked as something sinister or devilish that is to be rejected out of fear.

This disqualifying attribute, which I have termed 'disembodiment' or alienation, can arise as a correlate of history centrism. History centrism invariably gets codified and turned into institutionally enforced canons. This in turn prevents the emergence of lineages of mystics who could freely develop advanced experiential technologies for the purpose of accessing higher states of consciousness. People become entirely dependent on third-person accounts of revelation by historical messiahs. Since revelation comes from high church authorities and from outside the meditation of a practitioner, nastika traditions are deficient in the techniques by which humans may realize direct experience (i.e., anubhava) of the divine.[9]

Another serious consequence of disembodiment is the failure to recognize the nature of mantras. The nastika view is that language consists entirely of arbitrary conventions for the purpose of communication. This view does not accommodate the nature of Sanskrit mantras which were discovered by rishis through inner sciences. These mantra sounds are not the product of arbitrary conventions, but were realized as direct experiences of the realities to which they correspond. The very vibrations of mantras carry effects that are universal and rooted in cosmic unity. Thus, they cannot be replaced by substitutes. Numerous meditation systems have been developed using these sounds, and these systems are part of the continually evolving inner sciences that enable a practitioner to return to a primordial state of unity consciousness.

Sanskrit thus provides an experiential path back to its source. Mantra is one of the important technologies for anubhava. This is why scholars who deny anubhava as a legitimate path also tend to ignore the vibrational power of mantras. There are many prominent scholars who promote Sanskrit but insist that mantras are 'secular' and conventional language.

Mantra may be further unpacked by observing that '*vac*' (speech) is at four levels, from gross to increasing subtlety. '*Vaikhari*' refers to the speech one hears, i.e., external sound. This is the grossest level. '*Madhyama*' refers to inner speech, as in what one is thinking. Mental chatter is subtler than the spoken word. Western ideas of language do not go beyond these two levels—what is spoken and what is thought. Reason lives in the domain of what can be thought of and said. But Hinduism gives elaborate treatment to '*pashyanti*' which is at a level subtler than any reason or mental idea. This is the stage when speech is unconscious only. It is not yet turned into a mental voice. Even deeper than this level is 'para', the transcendental realm where the vac lives as potential, i.e., unmanifest.

At this point, it is worth noting that 'darshana' is the term used for Indian approaches that are only approximately equivalent to what the West calls philosophy. The key distinction is that darshana includes embodied knowing, whereas philosophy is limited to reason. The embodied processes of darshana are natural for worldviews based on integral unity, as discussed in Chapter 11.

On the other hand, Western philosophy is based on disembodied 'reason', which is an alienation from the deeper levels of speech. There is no tradition of mantra-like use of language that goes beyond conceptual meaning. One of T.S. Eliot's contributions to Western thought was that he understood this limitation, being a serious Sanskrit student, and hence used Sanskrit mantras directly in his poetry, without trying to translate them.[10]

Replacing Sanskrit mantras with ordinary words removes the vibrational effects. A mantra carries not only meaning but the power and *tapas shakti* (ascetic power/spiritual energy) imbued into it by its rishis and chanters. Even where other religions and traditions have similar ideas, it will be essential to preserve the mantras for further explorations.[11]

Many nastikas elevate reason and/or revelation above the practitioner's embodied knowing. But in astika views, reason is driven by the intellectual part of the ego, which means it is inherently dualistic in nature. And historically transmitted revelation passes through a long series of egos in the process. As long as the practitioner has a separate sense of self, the ego's project is limited to analytical, intellectual reasoning. This, in turn, fortifies the ego and perpetuates it further. Reason bifurcates one's self and insulates this artificial selfhood. Such an ego, individual or collective, is prone to become aggressively extroverted as it seeks solutions to its anxieties.

Hinduism acknowledges the difference between parokshajnanam (which is indirect knowledge, the product of reasoning) and *aparokshajnanam* (which is direct, embodied knowledge). A practitioner must not only listen, reflect, analyse and understand a truth claim; he must experience it at a deep, embodied, internal level. Western concepts of reason and philosophy do not go so far.

Disembodiment may also be understood in terms of alienation at many levels: with one's higher self, with humanity, and with nature. Hinduism has specific teachings on one's inseparability from each of these.

Synthetic cosmology

The paths based on disembodiment lead to fragmentation. The Judeo-Christian faiths begin (with some qualifications) by viewing the divine as profoundly separated and infinitely far from the world and the human, each side of the divide entirely distinct from the other. Spiritual truth is seen as coming from a separate domain than nature and often working against it. The other source of Western civilization is the Greek or Hellenistic tradition. This is infused with extreme reliance on reason, atomistic metaphysics and Aristotelian binary logic, where the quest for unity has also been a troubled one. Like its Judeo-Christian counterpart, this dimension of Western culture lacks yoga or inner sciences. Hence, we find today's predilection for appropriating such techniques from India.

Historically speaking, there is an artificial unity that stems from the tension between the revelations of the Hebrew Bible (which are history centric) and the rational philosophy of the Greeks (which is based on reason, a form of disembodied knowing). But in both cases there is a sense of the need to impose unity, whether 'faith-based' or 'reason-based', on a fundamentally atomistic and fragmented universe. The West's religious and secular traditions are both disembodied, for they lack yoga or inner sciences. They begin with the premise that the cosmos is inherently an agglomeration of separate parts or separate essences. As argued at length in Chapter 11, the West's debates are not about how and why multiplicity emerges but about how unity can emerge out of the multiplicity. Furthermore, these two traditions were forced together in order to synthesize what is referred to as the 'West'. No amount of pursuit of some unity between the two can succeed in the true sense; any attempt to do so results only in a forced synthesis. So we find layers upon layers of synthetic unity comprising the very foundations of the West and an ongoing battle between religion and science going on which is unnecessary from a dharmic point of view.

Such unity is not innate; it must be sought and justified again and again, and the resulting synthesis is always unstable. Among the consequences are a sense of separation from nature, a need to force unity on a fundamentally divided world, and the alienation of 'private property' as a purely material asset that can be 'owned' and traded at will. All of these are characteristics of a nastika position. The frenzied attempts at harmonizing science and religion are attempts at forging a better synthetic unity. Indeed, the annals of Western culture are full of the evidence of this essentially artificial unity and its breakdown.

Fear of chaos

As we have begun to see, the principles and characteristics of nastika lead to great instability and anxiety. Dependence on others who lived a long time ago in a distant place and culture for revelation, distrust of the body, and the deep sense that the cosmos is essentially split between nature and spirit—all these are profoundly uncomfortable psychological states. They create what cultural historian David Loy has identified as a profound sense of *lack*, and a need to seek restlessly for ways to mediate this lack through material acquisition, dominance over others, and the imposition of order on what is taken to be a fundamentally chaotic world.

Fear of chaos is typical of nastika positions. It is a fear that can easily overwhelm the mind. Chaos is seen as a ceaseless threat, both psychologically and socially—something to be overcome by control or elimination. Psychologically, it drives the ego to become controlling. Because a cosmology based on synthetic unity is riddled with anxieties, order must be imposed so as to resolve differences relating to culture, race, gender, sexual orientation, and so on.

We see it played out in terms of a hegemonic impulse over those who are different. The result is tension between social groups, where some sort of uniformity must be imposed externally. This characteristic leads to a profound fear of the other and a desire to reduce all peoples to the same, whether it is the same race, the same 'look', the same values, the same consumer brands, or the same pastimes and desires.

According to this view, nature is in need of being 'tamed' and 'conquered' and made subordinate to centrally mandated structures. For this reason, the European conquerors of America saw a mutual tension between the lands they occupied ('civilization') and the lands inhabited by the Native Americans ('frontier'). The destruction of wetlands, which are seen as a site of 'chaos', is an outcome of this mental construct, as is the need to create manicured lawns, mutilated shrubs, and mono-cultures of same-species' plantings in suburbia.

Controversial implications of the Astika/ Nastika approach

The preceding discussion traces the somewhat fuzzy boundary between Hinduism's open architecture, or 'astika', and the signature characteristics of 'nastika'. The reader is reminded that I have redefined these terms in my own original way for my stated purpose. Through my exposition of nastika, I have sought to enable astika as the enormous space that remains when nastika is excluded.

The astika holds immense potential for the spiritual development of humanity and for the establishment of humane and sustainable conditions optimal for earthly life. It is clear that Hinduism and Buddhism have demonstrated this potential more vividly than other systems.

The two columns of the table below contrast some specific aspects of nastika and astika:

Nastika	Astika
History centric exclusive canons for authority	Living enlightened masters as discoverers and as authorities
Centralized, corporate institutions	Decentralized explorations
Disembodied processes (like doctrine, reason, history)	Embodied processes (like yoga, mantra)
Speech is only linguistic, mental	Mantra has vibrational levels beyond the mind
Key Sanskrit terms digested and replaced by substitutes, thereby losing rishis' discoveries	Key Sanskrit words protected and utilized as precious discoveries.
Only one life in this world	Karma-reincarnation
Christian Good News—Jesus has come to save us from original sin	*Hindu Good News*—there is no original sin; we are all originally divine.
Synthetic unity	Integral unity
Closed canons	Open architecture
Chaos is fearful, to be controlled by controlling nature and other humans	Uncertainty, ambiguity are inherent; they do not threaten the integral unity of Indra's Net

In drawing these comparisons, I simply wish to suggest that Hinduism and Buddhism are the best existing examples of what astika views look like in actual practice. It is possible to imagine many religions and faith traditions taking their places under the astika tent, including many Abrahamic faiths and paths as well as others that may exist in the future. The followers of all faiths are welcome, *provided* they are willing to make the fundamental revisions necessary to rid their worldviews and practices of nastika aspects mentioned above.

At the very least, it is necessary for individuals seeking astika to abandon history centric claims; Christians, for example, would need to repudiate the Nicene Creed to come under the astika tent. The centralized institutional authority of the church would need to be rejected, and the mantle of spiritual leadership passed on to living enlightened mystics who establish lineages based on their own anubhava (embodied knowing).

The idea of a separate otherworldly God, with its inherent implications of alienation from nature, would have to be challenged. In other words, respecting the immanent nature of God would open the door to worshipping God's immanence in the form of so-called 'idol worship'. Accepting God's immanence would also require Christian seekers of astika to respect the sacred geographies, rituals and symbols of others, and undertake never to insult or attempt the digestion of such things. In addition, precepts such as 'original sin' and 'need for salvation' would require profound revision.

A few pioneering Christian theologians have actually walked this path while seeking to appropriate aspects of Hinduism and help reformulate a better Christianity. Raimondo Panikkar was perhaps the one who went farthest in arguing against some of the Christian tenets that I have classified as nastika.[12] In his efforts to reinterpret Christianity in accordance with contemporary thinking, Panikkar borrowed so heavily from Hinduism that he became profoundly influenced by it; indeed, one might say that his Christian theology has 'Hinduism inside'. However, his main audience was Christian; to preserve their collective brand identity, he found himself searching endlessly for something specifically and uniquely 'Christian' in which to dress up his newly digested Hinduism. Like many others on the same path, he ended up offering some unconvincing arguments to claim that Jesus is necessary and ultimate in any 'universal' religion, using very complex writings to hide what I see as contradictions in his position.

Another prominent Christian thinker who walked the fine line separating Christianity and Hinduism was Jacques Dupuis, a Jesuit. He spent a long time in India studying Hinduism with great appreciation. In his book, *Toward a Christian Theology of Religious Pluralism*, he tried very hard to 'respect' others but his overall narrative is history centric with Christ's 'salvation' role seen as indispensable. Such theology ends up merely as interfaith diplomacy in a deceptive sense. Despite his overall tendency to slip 'Jesus inside' into all his pluralism, the Vatican condemned Dupuis after this book came out, because he was going too far from the official doctrine.

Others who have attempted similar approaches include the young Indian Christian theologian, Russill Paul, who has expanded on Panikkar's ideas with even deeper appropriations from Hinduism.[13] In fact, Paul promotes Sanskrit mantra, Hindu music, yoga and meditation—all as part of his new Christianity. Earlier, he used to learn at the feet of Westerners who were explicitly preaching Hinduism without hiding it. Another prominent and hugely influential Christian thinker of this genre was Father Bede Griffiths. Indeed, many such efforts to reinvent Christianity in ways that resemble astika begin with large-scale appropriations from Hinduism into Christianity. In making these appropriations, the thinker often acknowledges their Hindu sources, and may even praise Hinduism as being superior to Christianity in important ways. To date, however, all such new thought has ended with some argument where Jesus's central importance is eventually reinstated in an exclusive manner. This sleight of hand to 'sneak in Jesus' at some later stage in the thought process can take place in various ways and under different pretexts.

In contrast, the Jesuit priest Anthony de Mello is a prominent example of a Christian theologian who decided to go all the way to become astika in the genuine sense. While he did attempt to retain his personal Christian identity in the process, he did not compromise his teachings just for the purpose of impressing other Christians. Consequently, the Vatican authorities judged him harshly as having gone beyond the pale: they declared his positions incompatible with the Catholic faith, and ordered that his books be removed from their libraries. He had crossed the line into astika. Anand Nayak has written a detailed book on this saga, in which he explains the deep-rooted reasons for the Vatican's rejection of Hindu tenets.[14] It is a good analysis of what the Vatican regards as poison pills in Hinduism.

While encouraging the adoption of an astika approach, I caution that Jews and Christians who take it up must be well-educated in the subject, aware of the hurdles they will face, and committed to avoid the digestion that occurs under disguises. For Hindu leaders, my most important recommendations are to undertake a thorough purva paksha of other traditions, and to teach the core principles of Hinduism without compromise. These can then serve naturally as poison pills to protect the specificity of Hindu dharma.

I propose that Jews look for astika qualities in portions of the Kabbalah text; that Christians seek these out in some of the lesser taught texts in the Bible and the teachings of Jesus himself and some of their mystics, and the *Gospel of Thomas*; and that Muslims search for them in the writings of Sufi saints. Such explorations would merely be starting points; however, discovering the presence of a few astika ideas in their texts should not lead Abrahamic seekers to conclude that they have found the holy grail of astika within their traditions.

For this project to truly work, seekers would need the courage to 'delete' core elements and not just try to 'add' new ones. They must mobilize difficult, risky and controversial movements, challenging the nastika tenets that currently dominate the mainstream power structures of their traditions—a process akin to the eventual redefinition of Western cosmology following the discoveries of Galileo. Very few persons have been courageous enough to do this, and the example of de Mello provides a taste of the sort of repercussions that can result.

The Abrahamic movements seeking an astika status should first identify nastika elements within their main texts and authorities and attack them directly and forcefully. They must demonstrate, through argument, what is wrong with such tenets theologically, scientifically, and socially. They must not be afraid to cite Hindu and Buddhist sources that aid their arguments, and should give full credit to such sources. Nastika tenets would have to be taken to task and the following rejections made:

• Rejection of the explicit or implicit espousal of a hyper-masculine divinity that marginalizes the divine feminine principle as a subordinate entity.

- Rejection of the institutional power structure built on canons of history and dogma. Such structures typically profess and rely on claims of exclusivity, and on Western notions of 'order' and 'rationality' that in practice become mechanisms of control.

- Rejection of the digestion of astika from Hindu and Buddhist sources, especially without attribution or respect on par with the acknowledgement accorded to Greek and Roman sources of influence upon the West.

A proliferation of internal battles along the lines of astika vs. nastika would prompt debate, self-examination and healthy change within the Abrahamic religions. Hinduism and Buddhism would act as catalysts for this internally initiated process of improvement. Quite frankly, I am calling for nothing short of an 'Indian-inspired revolution' within each Abrahamic religion.

Many such movements using Indian ideas were attempted in the past. They have included the European Romanticism of the eighteenth and nineteenth centuries, numerous Vivekananda-inspired movements in the U.S. throughout the twentieth century, the New Age explorations guided by various Hindu gurus during the 1960s, Ken Wilber's Integral Theory which is galloping in the West today, several cognitive science revolutions which are currently under way, and many more.

Each such movement begins by severely criticizing nastika-type tenets within Abrahamic religions; yet, every such movement to date has failed to finish what it started in terms of categorically rejecting these tenets. In the end, the proponents of such movements invariably get hijacked by their own 'big brother' religious establishment. The mainstream power structures of the West have been aborting the astika explorations of lay Jews and Christians by inducing them to make 'U-Turns', by which I mean returning to their home religion just when the astika position forces them to truthfully confront difference and make changes. There are rewards for would-be revolutionaries to sell out rather than continue the fight. In this sense, the power of the West resides in its skill at digesting its opponents, including those individuals from within its own ranks who defy its nastika qualities.

Refuting the myth of sameness

Many Hindu leaders claim that all religions, while not exactly the *same*, are different paths leading to the same ultimate goal. This posture is premised on a superficial understanding of both Hinduism and the other religions involved in the comparison. Suffering from what is termed 'difference anxiety' in *Being Different*, they desperately try to tease out Vedanta from the Bible, even though no new insight gets added to what is already known in Hinduism.

The most common Sanskrit phrase quoted in this regard, often repeated at popular gatherings, is '*vasudhaiva kutumbakam*', which means, 'the world is one family'. This assertion is recited as a signature of Hindu benevolence towards others and is often used to promote a spirit of unconditional generosity towards others. The earliest occurrences of 'vasudhaiva kutumbakam' are found in the *Hitopadesa* and the Panchatantra, which are collections of fables discussing practical situations in life through talking animals. These stories are meant as an entertaining educational aid for children, and their popularity has carried them to distant places across Asia and Europe. It is important to note that these fables impart values that are pragmatic and contextual, as opposed to high philosophy.

In these stories the phrase is used in both ways—to advocate harmony towards others and also to advocate vigilance and suspicion towards those one does not fully understand. The moral of the story depends on the context. If one is operating from a position of power over others, and those others have good intentions, then the message is to include them with mutual respect. On the other hand, if one is ignorant of others' intentions, or one is operating out of weakness, then such behavior is seen as a mark of foolishness. It is by no means a blanket statement of an unconditional welcome as is often made out to be in popular usage.

In one story in the Hitopadesa, a cunning jackal, trying to create a place for himself in the home of a naive deer says 'vasudhaiva kutumbakam' in his appeal to the deer.[15] The deer ignores warnings from other animals, who caution that it is unwise to trust someone at face value without first ascertaining his history, nature and intent. Upon deceitfully acquiring the deer's trust and moving in his home, the opportunistic jackal later tries to get the deer killed. Indeed, the moral of this story is that one should watch out for cunning subversives. Blindly trusting those who preach 'universal brotherhood' can lead to self-destruction.

The Panchatantra encodes this same message in a different story. In this version, the man who utters 'vasudhaiva kutumbakam' is described as a *murkha* ('idiot'). He is determined to bring a dead lion back to life, and disregards a wise man's warning about the dangerous consequences of such an act. The idiot and his accomplices feel moved to resurrect the lion after citing this sentiment of universal brotherhood among all living things, and hence end up being eaten by the lion they help. The wise man lives to tell the tale.[16]

Clearly, the lesson taught in these stories is not one of blind adherence to a policy of unilateral disarmament. They ask us to examine the specific context of a given situation, and closely consider the characters of the persons involved. Neither of these stories uses the expression 'vasudhaiva kutumbakam' to illustrate the idea that all creatures are the same; in fact, the very point of each story is to show how persons of different character will act in ways that are profoundly distinct from one another.[17] It is a matter of great irony that the widespread misuse of this phrase today, by any number of ill-informed individuals, obviates the wisdom it conveyed in its original context.

Even the jackal and the idiot, who preach universal brotherhood in these stories, are not asserting that all creatures are the same; only that they are related to one another. Certainly, all living beings in the world can be considered relatives of one another. However, relatives can, and usually do, differ greatly among themselves. The two warring sides in the Mahabharata, the Kauravas and the Pandavas, are of the same family. Likewise, the *asuras* and the *devatas* in Hinduism are related in that they have the same father. People who misquote and misinterpret such phrases as 'vasudhaiva kutumbakam' by debasing them into politically correct slogans, are indeed like the murkha (idiot) in the Panchatantra.[18]

Returning to the broader subject of sameness, no well-informed thinker would ever equate moksha, the ultimate goal of Hinduism, with salvation, the ultimate goal of Christianity. These notions are premised on entirely different understandings of the human condition and the nature of ultimate reality. Moksha is based on the notion that the essential nature of humans is sat-chit-ananda (divinity, or more precisely, existence-knowledge-bliss), whereas salvation depends on the assumption that all humans carry the burden of original sin.

To ascertain what aspects of Christianity and Hinduism are similar to, or different from, each other, one would have to conduct a point-by-point comparison of all the assumptions and ideas on either side. I am unaware of any preacher of sameness having carried out such a rigorous analysis. Yet, many such preachers offer sweeping and essentially nonsensical statements with great aplomb.

Most certainly it is true that all religions share *some* commonalities with each other. The same can be said of all fruits and all medicines— but all fruits are not interchangeable with one another and nor are all medicines. Almost every religion makes a promise of some future human state that transcends the body's suffering. The various ideas posited by different religions about the human condition are very different (and often conflicting) theories of suffering, and the religions themselves offer diverse remedies. This is akin to the examination of a patient by several doctors, each of whom offers a distinct diagnosis and treatment plan. The fact that each doctor claims to be treating the same patient does not override the fact that the individual doctors' diagnoses and prescriptions are not the same. They are, indeed, competing (and often conflicting) approaches to solve a given problem, and they do not all produce the same outcome; some approaches might even harm the patient.

A close examination of most claims of sameness reveal that they advocate pluralism based on whatever specific system of metaphysics is most favoured by the person making the claim. In effect, all other religions are adjusted to fit the framework adopted by the particular advocate of such inclusiveness. This creates a hierarchy within which the advocate's own tradition occupies the highest rung; all others are force-fitted to the lower rungs of his scheme, through reinterpretation as lesser versions of his own tradition. Ironically, the advocates of sameness nonetheless go about in the foolish belief that they are doing other religions a favour.

Another variation of the sameness syndrome is the claim that all religions are simply expressions of one perfect and transcendent religion. This position does not address the problem of defining the attributes of this putatively perfect and transcendent religion (which is implicitly presumed to be the one followed by the advocate himself), nor does it provide any acceptable framework for ranking all religions against the supposedly perfect religion.

In fact, each religion is merely a set of truth-claims. Truth-claims ought never to be confused with truth itself. Our metaphorical patient clearly suffers from some sort of condition; the multiple diagnoses offered by different physicians represent divergent truth-claims regarding the nature of the patient's condition. Similarly, any world religion is simply a set of truth-claims, issuing from some tribe or culture that spread itself by successfully fighting a long series of battles over the ages. The current positioning of any world religion, therefore, is determined purely by the survival of the fittest. The socio-political success that popularizes and sustains a set of truth-claims over time has no bearing on truth itself.

One cannot assume, as the proponents of sameness routinely do, that all possible truth-claims are equally valid. This would imply that there is no such thing as a false proposition and make a mockery of all religiosity by dismissing it as the worst kind of relativism. When I press the proponents of sameness into serious debate on such issues, they often respond with: 'All genuine religions are true.' This argument, however, is a tautology; it is like saying all true statements are true. It does not define any framework for determining what qualities must be possessed by a 'genuine' religion. It is a mere semantic game, based on circular logic, that will invariably end up defining one unknown in terms of another unknown.

To the sameness proponents, I often ask whether the religious claims of Ravana, Hitler, Bin Laden and such others would meet their criteria of 'genuineness'. They often come back with even sillier responses; for example: 'Our definition includes only "good" religions.' One person responded by declaring he would affirm the validity of only those religions that produce benefits to humanity. I asked what constituted his definition of 'benefits', especially when a religion offers benefits that occur after one's death. How does a living person evaluate 'benefits' that await one after death? As usual, no logical answer was available.

Some experts have taken the position that each existing religion offers only pieces of a great jigsaw puzzle and that by combining all such pieces we can construct a whole and perfect religion applicable to all humanity. This position, too, lacks any sensible criterion for determining which pieces are to be selected from each of the various religions. The process of choosing would not be trivial since many pieces certainly contradict each other. Furthermore, the jigsaw thesis suggests that no religion thus far has been complete by itself. One scholar who recently made this claim was a Western nun of the Vedanta Society in America; she lacked any interest in discussing the alarming implication of her statement: that the Vedanta she had been teaching for decades was effectively incomplete and needed elements borrowed from other religions to become complete.

I hope the reader will take to task any 'experts' who say such foolish things. For far too long, Hindu teachers have got away with spouting this sort of nonsense, and the Hindu public has been seriously deceived and misled. Yet, large funds continue to pour into highbrow international gatherings where such 'experts' recite interfaith proclamations promoting the colossal stupidity of sameness.

All I am prepared to say regarding this issue is that each religion claims to address some of the same issues, questions, dilemmas and quandaries that face human beings. But they do not come up with the same diagnosis or prescription.

People who are already Hindus would benefit from learning how to articulate their faith more precisely, and from acquiring the knowledge to explain accurately how it *differs* from others. Perhaps more importantly, those who enter Hinduism from other faiths should be taught to identify which aspects of their religion of birth comprise nastika qualities; they must understand why the Hinduism they are learning cannot be digested by the faith into which they were born. Such a revision of curriculum is likely to generate some anxiety among the 'spiritual but not religious' window-shoppers and other new age groups. Moreover, it will require that Hindu gurus become better informed.

Poison pill versus digestion

Is the Christian appropriation of yoga from Hinduism a case of digestion that harms Hinduism or is it a poison pill that undermines Christianity and morphs it into Hinduism? In a digestion scenario, yoga will be disassembled and de-contextualized from its Hindu roots, and its parts reassembled into Christian theology under the name of Christian Yoga. In a poison pill scenario, yoga, on being ingested by Christianity, will transform Christianity from within; the old Christianity will die, to be replaced by some new entity that is no longer a predator but has an open architecture. In this case, yoga will have served as a poison pill to defeat a predator and transform it into what I would consider astika.

In theory, both scenarios are possible. Which outcome, then, will be the result of such an encounter? Which side will grow stronger, and, in so doing, compromise the other's existence? The answer will determine whether exporting yoga into Christianity turns out to be good or bad for Hinduism. Hence, it is critical for us to analyse this.

Under the present leadership of Hinduism, the result will be digestion, and indeed that is what is rapidly happening. Christianity today is protected robustly by its history centrism. In contrast, Hinduism, as explained by most current gurus, is an undefended open architecture, lacking any criteria for the identification and rejection of certain elements as nastika. Any healthy living organism possesses some sort of immune system: a mechanism to reject and fight against invading elements with the potential to cause harm. The poison pills I advocate are part of the immune system that Hinduism's open architecture must deploy in order to prevent nastika elements from entering and destroying it. The lack of such poison pills places us in danger of being digested.

To achieve a desirable outcome in the encounter between yoga and Christianity, the entire approach currently espoused by most Hindu gurus would need to change radically. People often tell me that Hinduism is being protected from digestion by some particular guru, who always insists on using non-translatable Sanskrit terms, who vehemently asserts the Hindu origin of his practices, and so forth. Such people miss the whole point. Using Sanskrit and acknowledging the Hindu origins of an idea are, by themselves, insufficient for preventing digestion. Most sophisticated digesters, in fact, are quite willing to accept that the historical origin of what they appropriate resides in Hinduism.

Some will even preface their books with historical summaries describing the Indian origins of their ideas. Acknowledging the history of a given element does not, in itself, preclude such digesters from appropriating that element; indeed, it only provides a veneer of legitimacy to the act of appropriation. Insidious digesters will claim that the content and substance they are appropriating are neutral to culture and religion. Therefore, even if some specific element historically arose from Hindu thought, it could just as readily be a part of Christianity today. The implicit assumption being made by them is that the element being appropriated can be decoupled from the metaphysics of the system whence it originated.

Positioning an element as metaphysically neutral makes it vulnerable to digestion, even if its historical origins in Hinduism are acknowledged. *It is not the links with history, but the links with philosophy that I wish to emphasize.* My prospective re-positioning of Hinduism calls for nothing short of the active deployment of poison pills as philosophical weapons. In other words, we must show that a given element being targeted for digestion is in metaphysical conflict with the core of Judeo-Christianity.

Most gurus with whom I have conversed proffer the confused rationale: 'Since our tradition is universal, it must be equally valid within any framework.' This assertion is logically unsound. The fact that the laws of mechanics are universal does not imply that every engineer who uses them will do so properly. The fact that human physiology has certain universal attributes does not mean that all research papers published on medical science are valid. The confusion here is between the validity of a principle and the validity of a specific application of that principle in some particular instance. The former can be universal, and yet the latter can be rendered fallible by human limitations.

Texts composed by humans are naturally subject to human fallibility. Hindu tradition refers to such texts as 'smritis'; in contrast, sruti texts are described as being 'a-paurusheya' (not of human construction). Any compilation of religious truth-claims made by human originators is, by definition, a smriti; in other words, the central text of every history centric religion is, at best, a smriti.

This issue is elucidated in *Being Different* (pages 276-280), which explains why the prophets of Abrahamic religions cannot be equated with the rishis of dharmic tradition. Moreover, pages 255-259 of that book explain that the Bible, being a smriti text, is not equivalent to the Vedas, which are sruti. Indeed, Abrahamic religions have no sruti texts at all for the simple reason that they lack such an entity as the rishi, even in principle. This deficiency, in turn, arose because such practices as yoga, adhyatma-vidya, and mysticism were never allowed to flourish in Abrahamic religions; consequently, these belief systems never developed long-term lineages of explorers who pursued anubhava (embodied experience) as a means of discovery.

The roots of the problem reside in the dogma of Christian Good News, according to which humans born through sex are considered the cursed progeny of Adam and Eve. The emergence of rishis can only occur in the framework of Hindu Good News, wherein we are all originally sat-chit-ananda and each one of us is endowed with the potential to 'see' like a rishi.

It is often heard that yoga will have the same effect regardless of whether a practitioner is Hindu, Christian or Muslim, because yoga is universal and applicable to everyone. The erroneous assumption here is that yoga can operate in the absence of a relevant context. The poison pill method works here by demonstrating definitively that certain dogmatic beliefs and lifestyles will interfere with yoga; this provides support that yoga must be considered inseparable from its metaphysics. It becomes inauthentic for a practitioner to de-couple yoga from its contextual background in Vedanta metaphysics or from its own inbuilt structure of *yama-niyama* (lifestyle norms).

How the poison pill strategy works

I will now summarize the strategic use of poison pills as a way to defeat digestion and related threats. First I will explain the asymmetric situation that presently exists in which Hinduism is positioned in a weak way, and then describe my alternative scenario to dramatically reposition things in its favour.

Figure 10 depicts the current one-sided nature of the relationship between Christianity and Hinduism. The top arrow going to the right shows what Christianity exports to Hindus as part of its strategic encounter. These export items might seem benign at first and even be positioned as doing Hindus a favour. But gradually they turn toxic once they are accepted into Hinduism. They are poison pills being sent by the nastika to undermine the astika.

A prominent example is the way Jesus gets brought into Hinduism in a range of ways from very subtle and respectful of Hindu deities all the way to blatant violence against Hinduism. For instance, to those who are interested in history Jesus might be introduced as a great yogi who had travelled to India, and hence the case is made that his teachings ought to be adopted as Indian teachings. For Hindus who practise bhakti, he might be presented as just another deity among many Hindu deities—i.e., another member of a kind of family of deities. To those who are philosophically inclined, Jesus might be presented as a teacher of what is being called 'non-dual Christianity' or even 'Advaita Christianity'. This is to confuse those who are bent on seeing the sameness of all faiths. Practitioners of yoga are told that Jesus was a great rishi and yogi, and that 'Christian Yoga' is a legitimate adaptation of yoga. Many parents send their kids to dance academies to learn Bharat Natyam in which the teachers introduce

Biblical stories enacted using Hindu dance vocabulary, clothes, music and symbolism.

Such inculturation strategies serve as clever entry points. Gradually, they lead to different kinds of stages in which the Christian history centrism begins to surface more explicitly. The exclusivity claims of Jesus begin to increasingly pop up. Hindu deities are declared deficient compared to Jesus and could even be demonized as evil. Once a person or community has been won over with charity, medical facilities, educational institutions, jobs and 'human rights empowerment' training, there is more blatant use of history centrism to deliver a knockout punch to defeat Hinduism.

There are also more subtle poison pills that do not seem 'Christian' to the uninformed. In fact, often what is seen as 'secular' is a way to 'de-Hinduize' Indians by disconnecting them from their own astika frameworks and categories. Secularism was Europe's response to aggressive Christianity and this response was expressed using many of the same categories and assumptions that are in Christianity. Hence, secularism is 'Christianity inside' to a large extent. It subverts dharma. (For a more detailed explanation of secularism and its relationship to dharma, see *Being Different*, section titled "Purva Paksha and Sapeksha Dharma", pages 338-41.) Unfortunately, Indians have assimilated the secularism poison pill as some sort of political statement of being broadminded and liberal. But broadmindedness is abundantly found in Hinduism already, as explained in the Indra's Net metaphor and further in Chapter 11. This secularism/dharma tension amounts to an issue about Western categories versus Indian ones. Often these ideas get implanted in the guise of 'sameness'.

Once the mask is removed from these ploys, there are further poison pills that explicitly try to demolish Hinduism as a fake, sinister religion. The earlier chapters of this book addressed a few of these attacks.

The arrow at the bottom that moves towards the left side depicts the frenzy of digestion that was summarized in Chapter 12. This is how the nastika depletes the astika by taking over those parts which the nastika considers worthy to appropriate and which it lacks within itself.

The left side and right side arrows feed off of each other—each trend supports the other. As digestion depletes Hinduism of its positive qualities, it becomes easier for the poison pills of predatory disciplines to infiltrate Hinduism because the immune systems of the prey are weakened. Over a period of time, these poison pills confuse Hindus and debilitate their cognitive dissonance even further, and they offer little resistance to being digested. In fact, many of them welcome digestion as a positive thing.

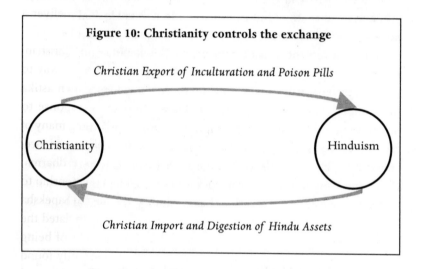

Figure 10: Christianity controls the exchange

Christian Export of Inculturation and Poison Pills

Christianity   Hinduism

Christian Import and Digestion of Hindu Assets

The mechanism depicted in Figure 11 has been used for many civilizational clashes and has become perfected along the way. For example, this is how pagans disappeared from Europe. It took many centuries to accomplish this in those days, but the processes are much faster and cleverer now. Many pagan symbols, festivals and ideas became digested into Christianized versions; today few people recognize them as being 'pagan' elements per se. They are seen as part and parcel of Christianity. At the same time, various means were adopted to infiltrate, confuse, distort and eventually undermine the pagans and their traditions. In the same manner, many Hindus today misinterpret the Christian inculturation projects as gifts, and even thank them for bringing such gifts. Some foolishly proclaim victory when in fact they are being digested.

It is important for leaders to become better informed of the game board, study the other side through purva paksha, to develop and test market strategies like the ones proposed below, in which I present a scenario that reverses the situation such that Hinduism is in control of its destiny.

The top arrow in Figure 11 shows the flow of Christian poison pills and inculturation; but in this scenario it gets blocked as part of my proposed policy to exclude elements that qualify as nastika. These elements subvert the astika for the reasons cited earlier and are to be rejected.

The bottom arrow moving towards the left now indicates elements that Hindus export into Christianity. These are positive astika ideas of openness, embodiment, integral unity, Sanskrit mantras, etc. But they are *not* digestible into orthodox Christianity because they include poison pills that violate the conventional Christian doctrine. Of course, Christianity might place its own blockade of these elements for its self-protection, which is what various bans against yoga, etc., amount to.

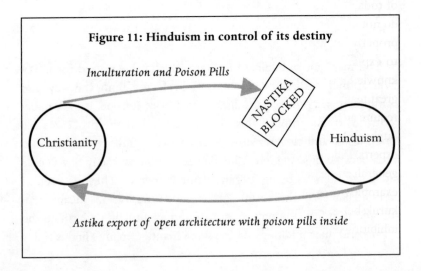

Figure 11: Hinduism in control of its destiny

Inculturation and Poison Pills

NASTIKA BLOCKED

Christianity

Hinduism

Astika export of open architecture with poison pills inside

This means there would now be parity between both sides wherein each is protecting itself by deflecting whatever it regards as dangerous, while exporting whatever it feels will give it an advantage by entering the other's space.

The strategy being proposed is that Hindus must shift from the dynamic shown in Figure 10 to that shown in Figure 11. This entails a radical re-training of its leaders. Hindu thinkers should research and test a variety of poison pills.

Digestion can only be deterred if today's Hindu gurus take a crash course in the deep purva paksha of Western religions, history and philosophy, and then undertake to protect Hinduism by insisting on its core principles and using poison pills in their teachings. They would have to research and discover an arsenal of devastatingly effective poison pills and then incorporate these philosophical weapons as intrinsic to their teachings (just as the sharp and forbidding quills of a porcupine are inseparable from the animal itself). They would have to educate their Western students about the effects of such poison pills on the digestive system of Judeo-Christianity, and inculcate changes in the mindsets and worldviews required to make their students astika-compliant.

This is unlikely to happen in the near future, simply because many of today's gurus do not think they need to learn anything that they do not already know, especially from a lay person like me who more properly ought to sit quietly and listen to their discourses. I have tried to explain to such individuals that there exist multiple domains of knowledge and expertise. In some of these domains, they are certainly great teachers and I remain a student; however, in other domains that require an incisive purva paksha of non-Hindu systems, they themselves ought to open their minds to the possibility of learning from various experts. I should clarify that I do not offer this description as a sweeping generalization applicable to all gurus. Indeed, I can cite many counter-examples of leaders who are interested in learning about the global kurukshetra, and are sincere about playing their part in forestalling and inhibiting digestion.

An attitude commonly found among the more recalcitrant gurus is overconfidence. Several gurus' movements are doing well if one measures performance in terms of the numbers of followers or the money they attract. This kind of success can be blinding; it is also dangerous because of the role many such gurus play as brokers of digestion. In the process of their teaching, they dissect Hinduism into small parts and feed these, piece by piece, into the mouth of Judeo-Christianity as convenient morsels for digestion. Some gurus have privately told me that they would lose a large number of Western followers (and much of their financial support) if they were to discontinue feeding the digestion process. Therefore, they come up with all sorts of justifications to defend digestion as something good.

Gurus who facilitate digestion have to be taken to task by their followers. Many of them have put Hinduism up for sale, as it were, and it is up to the lay Hindu public to mobilize opposition to this epidemic.

I conclude by offering the suggestion that the greatest of all poison pills lies in Hinduism's integral unity itself. For this philosophical *brahmastra* (formidable weapon) to be effective, it is critical that all practising Hindus remain constantly and acutely aware of this vital aspect of our dharma. With all our hearts, we must preserve and nurture a grand conception of Hinduism whose various aspects and components remain forever interwoven, each one of them reflecting all the others like jewels in Indra's Net.

Based on this foundation, we must constantly reiterate that karma and reincarnation can never be removed from Vedanta; yoga cannot be separated from Vedanta metaphysics; and yoga in turn must remain always inseparable from its own yama-niyama injunctions. At every turn, we must assert that the integral unity between all humanity, animals, plants and the environment is intrinsic to Hinduism and cannot be tampered with. All of which underscores a fundamental regard for nature that is built into the Hindu system. The Shakti principle, likewise, must be affirmed as inseparable from 'matter'.

Indra's Net is vast and its components must be understood as being inseparable from one another. This integral unity makes Hinduism too great for any predator to swallow. For this reason, we must never allow Hinduism to be divided into parts that can be selectively taken in isolation and digested.

My motive for using Indra's Net as the central metaphor of this book is to highlight the intricacy, the complexity and the delicate balances built into Hinduism, which becomes compromised the moment one dismantles its constituent parts and attempts to relocate them outside its framework.

The process of digestion, which thrives on exactly this type of separation, is thus best understood as a form of violence—even cultural genocide.

Dharma will remain secure as long as it is understood in the spirit of Indra's Net, as many inseparable parts that comprise an indivisible whole.

Notes

Preface

1   I was the chief protagonist of the book *Invading the Sacred*, and drafted much of its content; but it was edited by others.

Introduction

1   The mantra is: 'brihaddhi jaalam brihatah shakrasya vaajinivatah' (8.8.6). 'Ayam loko jaalamaasit shakrasya mahato mahaan' (8.8.8).

2   However, from the viewpoint within the provisional reality, all jewels are not the same. We must note the Buddhist (and Vedantin) notion of two truths, phenomenal and absolute. There is spiritual progress only from a phenomenal point of view.

3   Vatsyayan, 1997.

4   *Brhadaranyaka Upanishad* (2:5.17-18)

5   Aurobindo, *The Collected Works of Sri Aurobindo: The Renaissance of India.* 1997: 186.

6   Mahabharata, XII.72.20.

7   The same music may be performed in either temple or court settings, thereby enabling the Muslim courts to become patrons of Kathak, a Hindu spiritual dance form noted for its universal aesthetic appeal, without seeing it as a 'religious' performance per se, which would otherwise be condemned as idolatry.

8   Cook, 1977, p. 2.

9   In early Pali texts, there is the notion of 'paticca samuppada' (dependent, co-arising or interconnected origination). Nagarjuna established one of the central principles that there are no isolated entities bearing essential natures or existing as themselves. This is referred to as things being empty of their own separate distinct existence, i.e., not having any ultimate sva-bhava or self-nature. This developed into the Avatamsaka tradition's idea of sunyata along with interdependence comprised all reality. One of the famous chapters of the Avatamsaka Sutra includes the following explanation of interpenetration: 'All the lion's organs, the tip of every hair, being of gold, include the whole lion. Each of them permeates the whole lion; the eyes are the ears, the ears are the nose, the nose is the tongue and the tongue is the body. They come into being freely, without difficulty, without impediment.' Here the gold symbolizes the substance and the lion symbolizes the form.

10   Loy, 1993, p. 484.

11   Loy, 1993.

12   Odin, 1982.

13   Fahy, 2012.

14   See, for example, Mumford, 2002 and Debnath, 2006. The metaphor has also been applied to new ideas proposed in library science (Bair-Mundy, 1998).

15   Thiele, 2011.

16   Cook, 1977.

17   *Philosophy East and West*, vol. 37, no. 2, April 1987.

18   Park, 2010. Indra's Net has also been cited by activists who argue against climate change and other environmental concerns (Tam, 2008). There are also co-dependency arguments for helping salmon survive (Allendorf, 1998).

19   For example, see: Huffington Post - http://www.huffingtonpost.com/rajiv-malhotra/dharma-religion_b_875314.html and http://www.huffingtonpost.com/rajiv-malhotra/the-hindu-good-news-you-a_b_854904.html

20   The analogy should not be taken too far, because the same Hindu practices and traditions can manifest differently according to time, place and

context. This is not exactly the same thing as the linear progression of scientific 'progress'.

1: Eight Myths to be Challenged

1   While in theory Vivekananda accorded primacy to Advaita Vedanta, in practice he recommended a version that is closer to Bhedabheda Vedanta, which is consistent with Vijnanabhikshu (discussed at length in Chapter 8).

2   See, for example: Lorenzen, 1978.

3   For instance, the inspiration behind the Adnyapatra, a Marathi text of about 7,000 words outlining the state polity and policy of Shivaji (completed in 1715), may be traced back to Kautilya's Arthashastra and Panchatantra. Adnyapatra is a royal edict on the principles of policy written in Marathi by Ramchandra Pant Bavadekar, a diplomat (amatya) and warrior of the Maratha Empire, with the intention to guide Shivaji's grandson, Sambhaji II. It may be described as a formal documentation of Shivaji's ideals, principles and policies of state administration. It is presented in the traditional form wherein the ruling king orders his experienced prime minister to advise the prince on the history that was made and the state policy that was adopted by his forefathers for his guidance.

4   Early in the history of Christianity itself, the Orthodox churches opted out of this model of centralized control that was championed by the Rome-centric church.

5   'In recent years it has thus become an ironic, if not paradoxical, truism among many professional Western experts of Hinduism that the object of their expertise does not really exist. This misleading category of "Hinduism", it is argued, must be deconstructed in the interests of truth in advertising and atonement for the sins of our Orientalist forebears. The Indological authorities of the past created "Hinduism" and the Indological authorities of the present are now busy disestablishing its conceptual existence.' (Smith, 1998, p. 316). And: 'most Indologists of the nineteenth and twentieth centuries have declared Hinduism either too disorganized and exotically other or too complex and recondite to be subjected to the definitional strictures applicable to other religions and cultures'. (Smith, 1998, p. 321).

Chapter 2: The Mythmakers: A Brief History

1 Neither of them dealt with the substance of my book's arguments, which went well beyond this notion and offered several other interesting provocations for debate. When they did manage to touch on these other matters, they seriously misrepresented my position.

2 He simply bypassed all the philosophical arguments discussed in my book and turned it into a political piece which he saw as supportive of a repressive nationalistic identity. He found the 'identification of these two things—India the nation state and India the ancient civilization—troubling'. He said I was undertaking a project that is imbued with the identification of India with the Sanskritic and Hindu tradition, an identification that really disallows the association of any individual or community that does not identify itself in these terms. It seemed to me a strange way of vilifying my work, which had none of the implications that these quite reputable scholars insisted it had. Many scholars present in the audience rose to my defence in the question and answer period. These included Graham Schweig, a well-known scholar of Hinduism and Vaishnavism in particular, and Koenraad Elst, a Belgian scholar known for his candid critiques of the Western academy, who remarked that Pennington had been wrong to use India's minorities as a handle against Hinduism's unity. Sunthar Visvualingam, a prominent scholar of Kashmir Shaivism, also noted that *Being Different* had been praised by eminent scholars such as McKim Marriott whose work on India is prescribed reading throughout the academy.

3 Slater, 1902, p. v.

4 Slater, 1902, pp. 4-6.

5 Slater, 1902, pp. 4-6.

6 Halbfass 1995, p. 240.

7 Halbfass, 1995, p. 13.

8 Clooney wrote the following praise for Halbfass's volume of the translation of Hacker's writings: 'Hacker's work is indispensable for anyone who would understand Vedanta and related strands of Indian intellectual traditions both ancient and modern. The content of his essays is important, many of the articles are ground breaking, and Hacker's style of scholarship is paradigmatic: philologically expert, historically and critically attuned, capable

of handling the philosophical issues raised by the texts, sensitive to broader and deeper religious and theological issues.'

9 For an overview of the German role in the Aryan theory and its later links to Nazism, see: 'Breaking India', by Rajiv Malhotra and Aravindan Neelakandan.

10 W. Cantwell Smith, 'The Meaning and End of Religion', New York, 1962, p. 65.

11 Rambachan, 1984, p. 396.

12 Rambachan wrote: 'The thesis that there are four different paths to the attainment of moksha was employed by Vivekananda to demonstrate the superiority of Hinduism in its capacity to be able to cater for different spiritual needs and temperaments. Today, like so many of Vivekananda's interpretations, it has become a standard argument in Hindu apologetic writing and even in scholarly studies written by both Hindus and non-Hindus. When, however, Vivekananda's arguments are subjected to close scrutiny in relation to basic Advaita propositions about the nature of avidya and moksha, they are unconvincing. There is no attempt to carefully relate the nature of each method to the assumptions of avidya as the fundamental problem. At crucial points in his discussion, where it is necessary to clearly demonstrate the connection between a particular method and the attainment of moksha in the Advaita sense, he becomes vague and obscure in his terminology and concepts.' (Rambachan, 1984, p. 405.)

13 Thapar, 1985, p. 15.

14 Thapar, 1985, p. 22. She alleges that today's Hinduism is the work of politics and is 'being currently propagated by the Sanghs, Parishads and Samajs'.

15 Thapar, 1985, p. 22.

16 Thapar, 1985, p. 14.

17 Thapar, 1985, p. 15.

18 See: http://kelamuni.blogspot.com/2006/09/neo-vedanta-of-swami-vivekananda-part_11.html

19 *Frontline*, vol. 20, Issue 26, Jan. 20, 2003. See: http://www.frontlineonnet.com/fl2026/stories/20040102000607800.htm. Jyotirmaya Sharma's recent book adds to this rising tide. (Sharma, 2012)

20 Hawley, 1991.

21 van Buitenen, 1974, p. 519.

22 Staal, 1989, p. 397.

23 Frykenberg, 1989, p. 29.

24 Frykenberg, 1993, p. 526.

25 Kopf, 1980, p. 502.

26 Larson, 1995, p. 5.

27 This is a text called *Somasambhupaddhati,* a work on Saiva ritual compiled by the late eleventh-century author Somasambhu.

28 Lipner, Julius J., 1996, pp. 109-126.

29 Marshall, 1970, p. 43.

30 Lorenzen, 2006.

31 Mishra, 2004.

32 Mishra, 2002.

33 Mishra, 2002.

34 Mishra, 2002.

35 Mishra, 2002.

36 Indian Express, Feb. 13, 2013. See: http://www.indianexpress.com/news/why-india-must-allow-hyphens/1073206/

37 Gokhale, 1958, p. 186.

3: Paul Hacker's Construction of 'neo-Hinduism'

1 This chair was first held by A.W. von Schlegel.

2 Halbfass, 1995, 7.

3 Halbfass, 1995, 7.

4 Halbfass, 1995, p. 16.

5 Halbfass, 1995, p.16.

6 Halbfass, 1995. p. 240.

7 These Christian biases are pointed out in: Vishwa Adluri, Review of *Unifying Hinduism: Philosophy and Identity in Hindu Intellectual History,* by Andrew J. Nicholson, *Humanities and Social Sciences Online* (H-Net), 22 March 2012, http://www.hnet. org/reviews/showrev.php?id=32207. For a comprehensive bibliography of Hacker's writings on Hinduism and Christianity, see: Joydeep Bagchee, 'The Invention of Difference and the Assault on Ecumenism: Paul Hacker Becomes a Catholic', a paper presented at Rethinking Religion in India III, Pardubice, Czech Republic, Oct. 11-14. 'Inklusivismus', in Inklusivismus: Eine indische Denkform, ed. Gerhardt Oberhammer (Vienna: Akad., 1983), pp. 11-28.

8   Nicholson, 2010, p. 188.

9   Nicholson points out the huge borrowings made by Christianity: 'Does this apply equally to the Christian theology's illicit borrowing of the theological concepts of the immortal soul and the infinity of God from Greek philosophy? Such concepts are not found in Christianity in its pure, Semitic, pre-Hellenized form. The widespread tendency of "claiming for one's own what really belongs to another" is a primary means of change, growth, and innovation in all philosophical and theological traditions, not just in Hinduism.' (p. 188) The big difference worth noting is that in the case of Christian borrowings from Greek philosophy, it was an entirely different and alien system which did not have shared common origins, cosmological debates, cross-fertilization, categories or language. Hence it was synthetic as opposed to integral in the case of Indian cross borrowings internally.

10   Mohanty's article appears in: Franco, 2007, p. 164.

11   Franco, 2007, p. 164.

12   Halbfass's response appears in: Franco, p, 307.

13   *Kleine Schriften*, p. 802, as cited in Halbfass, 1995, p. 12.

14   Halbfass, 1995, p.231.

15   For example, Radhakrishnan describes the state of dejection he experienced as a student at Madras Christian College: 'I was strongly persuaded of the inferiority of the Hindu religion to which I attributed the political downfall of India ... I remember the cold sense of reality, the depressing feeling that crept over me, as a causal relation between the anaemic Hindu religion and our political failure forced itself on my mind.' (From 'The Spirit of Man' as cited in Halbfass, 1995, p 316.)

16   Halbfass, 1995, p. 324.

17   Halbfass, 1995, p. 324.

18   Halbfass, 1995, p. 324.

19   Hacker, 1995, p. 298.

20   Halbfass, 1995, pp. 307-308.

21   Halbfass, 1995, p. 322.

22   Halbfass, 1988, p. 220.

23   Halbfass, 1995, p. 327.

24   For example, Kelamuni claims that when Debendranath uses the compound 'svatahsiddha-atmapratyaya' it is clear that he means 'self-evident intuition'. Debendranath's notions concerning 'intuition' (atma-pratyaya) and the 'heart' (hrdaya) are said to sound much like the 'personal conviction' (atma-

tushthi) and 'inner voice' (hrdaya-koshana) referred to in the dharmashastra literature, and his use of the term 'svatahsiddha' is like the concept of 'svatahpramanya', the 'self-validating authority' of the Vedas referred to by the Mimamsakas. (See: http://kelamuni.blogspot.com/2006/09/neo-vedanta-of-swami-vivekananda-part_11.html)

25 Halbfass, 1995, p. 320.

26 Halbfass, 1995, p. 248.

27 Hacker further accuses Radhakrishnan of fabricating the notion that, according to the Hindu view, there is a goal in the world process of evolution. Hacker claims to the contrary, that 'there is no system in Indian philosophy at all that teaches that samsara has a purpose'.

28 Halbfass, 1995, p. 277.

29 Halbfass, 1995, pp. 242-3.

30 *Kleine Schriften*, pp. 561 and 563; and below, p. 305 ff.

31 Halbfass, 1995, pp. 298-299.

32 Halbfass, 1995, pp. 304-305.

33 Halbfass, 1995, p. 294.

34 Halbfass, 1995, pp. 303-304.

35 Halbfass, 1995, p. 240.

36 Halbfass, 1995, p. 238.

37 Halbfass, 1995, p. 270.

38 Halbfass, 1990, p. 56.

39 Halbfass, 1995, p. 12.

40 Halbfass, 1995, p. 16.

41 As summarized in Halbfass, 1990, p. 52.

42 Halbfas, 1995, pp. 245-6.

4: Agehananda Bharati on Neo-Hinduism as a 'Pizza Effect'

1 Bharati, 1970.

2 Bharati, 1970.

3 Bharati, 1970.

4 Bharati, 1970.

5 Bharati, 1970.

6 Bharati, 1970.

7   Bharati, 1970.
8   Bharati, 1970.
9   Bharati, 1970.
10 Bharati, 1970.
11 Bharati, 1970.
12 Bharati, 1970.
13 Bharati, 1970.
14 Bharati, 1970.
15 Bharati, 1970.
16 Bharati, 1970.
17 Bharati, 1970.
18 Bharati, 1970.

5: Ursula King's Bridge from Hacker to Rambachan

1   King, 1977, p. 127.
2   King, 1977, p. 138.
3   King, 1977, p. 142.
4   King, 1977, p. 145.
5   King, 1980, p. 48.
6   King, 1980, pp. 42-3.
7   King, 1980, pp. 44-5.
8   King, 1989, p. 87.
9   King, 1980, p. 46-7.
10 King, 1980, pp. 47-8.
11 King, 1980, p. 49.
12 King, 1980, p. 50.
13 King, 1980, p. 52-3
14 King, 1980, p. 53.
15 King, 1980, p. 55.
16 King, 1989, pp. 72-3.
17 King, 1989, pp. 75-6.
18 King, 1989, p. 80.
19 King, 1989, p. 82.

6: Rambachan's Argument to Fragment Hinduism

1   Rambachan, Anantanand. 'The *Attainment of Moksha According to Shankara and Vivekananda with special reference to the significance of scripture (Sruti) and Experience (Anubhava).'* Ph.D Dissertation, Department of Theology and Religious Studies, University of Leeds, 1984.

2   Rambachan, 1994, p. 7.

3   Vivekananda's admiration for Western culture does become clear in his first visit, based on his letters to Haridas Viharidas Desai, the dewan of Junagarh: 'America is a grand country. It is a paradise of the poor and women' (*Collected Works of Swami Vivekananda,* vol. 8, p. 325). Vivekananda hopes that future Indians will be 'combining some of the active and heroic elements of the West with calm virtues of the Hindus' in order to become 'a type of men superior to any that have ever been in this world'. (Ibid, vol. 8, p. 322). However, it is unfair to claim that it was only this factor or that it was the major factor shaping his thoughts, as if there were no internal influences and resources in Indian traditions.

4   Rambachan, 1984, p. 426.

5   Vidyasankar Sundaresan comments: 'My only objection to Swami Vivekananda is to his usage of the word "verify". What an aspirant for moksha needs to accomplish is to simply abide in Existence, with a capital E. The culminating moment of jnana serves not so much to verify the truth of the sruti, but as an accomplishment of personal certitude, amounting to, "I am indeed that Brahman". It is not a verification/refutation of sruti as if it were a scientific hypothesis to be empirically tested. This state of certitude is not achieved through more textual analysis, but through incorporating a yogic regimen. Indeed, the Upanishads teach that there is a stage where one has to give up the preoccupation with text and meditate on Om. Sankara quotes these references numerous times.'

6   Rambachan, 1994, pp. 3, 9.

7   Rambachan, 1994, p. 82.

8   Rambachan, 1984, p. 242.

9   Rambachan, 1984, p. 396.

10 Rambachan, 1984, p. 270.

11 Rambachan cites Swami Dayananda Saraswati as an authority to make

his case against Vivekananda's multiple paths of Hinduism, but he ignores the fact that Swami Dayananda Saraswati had devoted his life to promoting all the elements that Rambachan alleges are incompatible—jnana, bhakti, karma, meditation. Furthermore, Swami Dayananda Saraswati heads the Hindu Dharma Acharya Sabha whose very purpose is to promote the unity of Hindu lineages across the board.

12 Rambachan was one of the members on his dissertation committee.

13 Dalal, 2009, p. 1.

14 For example, Madhusudana Sarasvati wrote a textually rigorous Advaita Siddhi, as well as the Gudarthadipika, a text heavy on yoga and bhakti which is a commentary on the Gita.

15 The *Mundaka Upanishad* says—'tad vijnanartham sa gurum eva abhigacchet, srotriyam brahmanishtham'—(1.2.12). Trans.: 'To know that (Brahman), one should go to a guru who is a "srotriya" (one who has studied the sruti traditionally), and "brahmanishtha" (whose only pursuit is Brahman).'

16 Brahmasutra-bhasya 1.1.11. (sutra-srutatvacca) explanation of the verse on Chandogya 3-14-1 (Thibaut, 1890, vol. 1, p. 62).

17 Brahmasutra-bhasya 1.1.11. (sutra-srutatvacca) explanation of Sankarabhashya Aitareya Aranyaka- 1.3.2.1 (Thibaut, 1890, vol. 1, p. 63).

18 The same passage also states that smriti makes analogous, similar points—the implication being that sruti is not the exclusive means available.

19 In verse 1.52 of the great text, Naishkarmya Siddhi, by Sureshvaracharya.

20 Rambachan, 1984, p. 399.

21 Rambachan, 1984, pp. 400-401.

22 In Brahmasutra-Bhashya 1.3.33. Shankara quotes Brihadaranyaka 1-4-10, meaning: 'In the beginning this universe was only brahman, and it knew only itself (Atman), thinking: "I am brahman." As a result, it became the Whole. Among the gods, likewise, whosoever realized this, only they became the Whole. It was same also among the rishis and among humans. Upon seeing this very point, the seer Vamadeva proclaimed: "I was Manu, and I was the Sun." This is true even now. If a man knows "I am brahman" in this way, he becomes this whole world. Not even the gods are able to prevent it ...'.

23 Rambachan, 1984, pp. 426-7.

24 Collected Works of Swami Vivekananda, vol. 3, pp. 255.

25 Ibid., vol. 3, p. 283.

26 Rambachan, 1984, pp. 275-6.

27 Rambachan, 1984, p. 417. However, in the following passage,

Rambachan seems more accommodating and suggests a balanced approach between sruti and anubhava: 'While Sankara, as I believe, acknowledges the ultimacy of scriptural revelation for our knowledge of the absolute, his understanding of the relationship between scripture and personal experience (anubhava) is dynamic and creative. It offers scope for vigorous life of the intellect by preserving for it a necessary role in the spiritual quest.' (From: 'The nature and authority of scripture: Implication for Hindu-Christian Dialogue', by Anantanand Rambachan. Available at: http://www.wcc-coe.org/wcc/what/interreligious/cd32-02.html)

28 From: 'The nature and authority of scripture: Implication for Hindu-Christian Dialogue', by Anantanand Rambachan. Available at: http://www.wcc-coe.org/wcc/what/interreligious/cd32-02.html

29 For example, Vivekananda's influence on the famous physicist Nikola Tesla is narrated by the Tesla Memorial Society at the following web site: http://www.teslasociety.com/tesla_and_swami.htm

30 A first-person method is what I have called inner-sciences or adhyatma-vidya. All introverted practices such as meditation are of this kind. Third-person practices are those wherein an external deity or God is talked 'about' or 'referred to', such as a statement of the kind: 'God loves us.' All discourse about an entity is third-person. Second-person is intimate, direct interaction with someone immediately present before us. Hindu worship before an image is second-person whereas Abrahamic religions tend to emphasize God in heaven above and hence there is a third-person emphasis. Christianity does have second-person as well, such as when one speaks directly to God. But first-person practices in Abrahamic religions (referred to as mysticism) have been suppressed by their authorities for centuries. Only recently have these begun to be re-discovered using appropriations from Hinduism and Buddhism.

31 Rambachan, 1984, p. 287.

32 Along with other academics, Rambachan does not care to admit that *adhikara* (right/authority) to do anything has always been independent of gender, race or jati/caste from the rishi's perspective, and in this sense Vivekananda was not changing anything. To appreciate this, one must note that *varna* is based on one's personal *guna* and past karma, which is based on individual merit. Furthermore, Shankara also explicitly says that shudras and women are entitled to atman realization through means such as the smriti which are open to all humans. And the smriti most frequently cited by Shankara is the Gita. In other words, the academic criticism of Vivekananda

rests crucially on a misunderstanding and an almost wilful misrepresentation of Shankara's true position on this.

33 Quoted in Rambachan, 2007.

34 Coward, 1995.

35 Coward, 1995.

36 Based on Shankara's commentary on Brhadaranyaka Upanishad 1.4.7 (Bader, 1990, p. 91.) See also Madhavananda, 1950, pp. 111-140.

37 Bader, 1990, p. 97.

38 Sutra 1.4.1 and 4.1.2. Bader, 1990, p. 47.

39 Cited in Bader, 1990, p. 21, footnote 29.

40 See: http://lists.advaita-vedanta.org/archives/advaita-l/2007-May/018818.html

41 Skoog, 1989, pp. 69-71.

42 Skoog, 1989, p. 69.

43 Rukmani, 2006, p. 13.

44 Sharma writes: '[F]or assessing the use of the word pramana by Shankara in relation to anubhava, we need to know more unambiguously the senses in which Shankara uses the word pramana. In the course of this discussion itself we have seen him use it in relation to sruti but, more surprisingly in relation to jnana and anubhava as well. ... The fact that Professor Rambachan himself refers to Shankara's position variously—according to him the Vedas are "the only valid means" (p. 43), "the only vehicle" (p. 67), "the only source" (p. 46)—lends some support to this suggestion.' (Sharma, 1995, pp. 111-112.)

45 Sharma, 1993.

46 One should also add yoga texts that go by the name 'shastra'. In numerous places in the Brahmasutra, Upanishad and Gita commentaries, Shankara himself cites yoga-shastra texts, explicitly referring to them as such.

47 Sharma, 1993, p. 110.

48 For example: Chapple, 2003.

49 'The Yogadrstisamuccaya of Haribhadra', translated as the appendix in Chapple, 2003. Verse 129.

7: The Myth Goes Viral

1 King, 1999-B, p. 98.

2 King, 1999-B, p. 110.

3   King, 1999-A, p. 176.

4   King, 1999-B, p. 103.

5   King, 1999-B, p. 192.

6   King, 1999-B, p. 107.

7   King, 1999-B, p. 204.

8   King, 1999-B, p. 187.

9   King, 1999-B, p. 187.

10   King, 1999-A, p. 167. A good example is that of William Jones constructing the normative Dharmashastras as 'Hindu Laws', when in fact the book he compiled had never been imposed or used as the law anywhere in India prior to his time.

11   King, 1999-A, p. 146.

12   King, 1999-B, p. 123.

13   King, 1999-B, p. 123.

14   King, 1999-B, p. 93.

15   King, 1999-B, p. 256.

16   King, 1999-B, p. 106.

17   King, 1999-A, p. 159.

18   King, 1999-B, p. 178.

19   King, 1999-B, p. 127.

20   King, 1999-B, p. 23.

21   King, 1999-A, p. 146.

22   King, 1999-A, p. 147-8.

23   King, 1999-B, p. 103.

24   Halbfass, 1988, p. 333.

25   King, 1999-A, p. 181-2

26   King, 1999-A, p. 185.

27   Pennington, 2005, p. 87. Pennington mentions that the *Asiatik Researches* journal published by Asiatik Society from 1789 to 1839, totalled approximately 10,000 pages during this period, and that its overall attitude shifted in accordance with the East India Company's posture on India at any given moment. This journal exerted considerable influence upon Britons.

28   Pennington, 2005, p. 69.

29   Pennington, 2005, p. 59.

30   Pennington, 2005, p. 61.

31   Pennington, 2005, p. 170.

32 Pennington, 2005, p. 179.

33 Pennington, 2005, p. 100.

34 Pennington, 2005, p. 140.

35 Pennington, 2005, p. 170.

36 Pennington, 2005, p. 169.

37 Smith, 1998, p. 330.

38 van der Veer, 1993, p. 40.

39 van der Veer, 1993, p. 40.

40 van der Veer, 1993, pp. 25-26.

41 van der Veer, 2001, p. 11.

42 van der Veer, 1993, p. 41

43 van der Veer, 1993, pp. 42-43.

44 See the interview at: YouTube [https://www.youtube.com/watch?v=VXhInNUVZ6U, Minutes 9:44-21:24].

45 See the interview at: YouTube [https://www.youtube.com/watch?v=VXhInNUVZ6U, Minutes 9:44-21:24].

46 Lele, Jayant, 1993, p. 58.

47 Pirbhai, 2012.

48 Jaffrelot, 2007. Indian media give such voices considerable importance, as illustrated in his recent op-ed pontificating what India's policy ought to be on AfPak: http://www.indianexpress.com/news/on-kabul-take-a-wider-view/1160153/

49 Jaffrelot, 2007. He writes: 'This ideology [of Hindu Nationalism] assumed that India's national identity was summarized by Hinduism, the dominant creed which, according to the British census, represented about 70 per cent of the population. Indian culture was to be defined as Hindu culture, and the minorities were to be assimilated by their paying allegiance to the symbols and mainstays of the majority as those of the nation.'

50 Nanda, 2005.

51 Nanda, 2005.

52 http://www.firstpost.com/india/there-were-no-hindus-in-goa-before-portuguese-landed-church-thinker-953727.html

53 White, 2009. William Pinch of Wesleyan College and Frederick Smith of the University of Iowa are among the many scholars of Hinduism who have endorsed and promoted his works.

54 Basu, 2002, p. 172.

55 Basu, 2002, p. 69.

56 Morales (n.d.). He uses harsh language to denounce what he sees as neo-Hinduism: 'Seeing traditional Hinduism through the eyes of their British masters, a pandemic wave of 19th century Anglicized Hindu intellectuals saw it as their solemn duty to "Westernize" and "modernize" traditional Hinduism to make it more palatable to their new European overlords ... Neo-Hinduism was an artificial religious construct used as a paradigmatic juxtaposition to the legitimate traditional Hinduism that had been the religion and culture of the people for thousands of years. Neo-Hinduism was used as an effective weapon to replace authentic Hinduism with a British invented version designed to make a subjugated people easier to manage and control.' See his 'A devastating critique of Neo-Hinduism', Dharmacentral.com, Aug. 25, 2010. Posted at: http://www.dharmacentral.com/forum/content.php?126-Critique-of-Neo-Hinduism Also see his "The death of traditional Hinduism", posted at: http://Hinduism.about.com/od/history/a/neoHinduism.htm

57 Hatcher, 1999.

58 Sharma, 2000.

59 Sharma, 2000.

60 Hatcher, 1999

61 For example, Shankara's Brahmasutra 1.3.38 and 1.1.30.

62 Smith, 1998, p. 324.

63 Smith, 1998, p. 324.

64 Smith, 1998, pp. 325-6.

65 Smith, 1998, pp. 325-6.

66 Smith, 1998, pp. 325-6.

67 Smith, 1995, p. 330.

68 Smith, 1995, p. 331.

69 Smith 1995, p. 333.

70 Neusner 1983. p. 235.

71 Gupta, 1974, pp. 28-29.

72 Sweetman, 2003, p. 229.

8: Historical Continuity and Colonial Disruption

1 Nicholson, 2010, p. 179: '"Believer" and "infidel", though tempting, are also too fraught with Western connotations of right theological opinion (and

the latter too closely associated with medieval struggles between Christians and Muslims). The terms "affirmer" and "denier" are better, since these are neutral with regard to the question of right opinion versus right practice. An affirmer (astika)might be one who "affirms the value of ritual" (Medhatithi), one who "affirms the existence of virtue and vice" (Manibhadra), one who "affirms the existence of another world after death" (the grammarians), or one who "affirms the Vedas as the source of ultimate truth" (Vijnanabhikshu Madhava, etc.). The typical translations for the terms astika and nastika, "orthodox" and "heterodox", succeed to a certain extent in expressing the Sanskrit terms in question.'

2   Manusmriti 2.11.

3   Nicholson, 2010, p. 173: 'The words astika and nastika are derived from Panini's rule Astadhyayi 4.4.60. Panini simply provides the derivation of the two words (along with a third, daistika) without suggesting what exactly is being accepted by the astika or rejected by the nastika. The first substantive definition of the two words in the Paninian tradition comes in the Kasikavrtti, a commentary by the seventh-century authors Jayaditya and Vamana. They write, "The astika is the one who believes that 'there exists another world: The opposite of him is the nastika'".'

4   Estimates for the period when he lived vary from fifth to eighth century CE.

5   Nicholson, 2010, p. 175.

6   Nicholson, 2010, pp. 3, 5, 25.

7   Nicholson, 2010, writes that 'the sixteenth-century doxographer Madhusudana Sarasvati, argues that since all of the sages who founded the astika philosophical systems were omniscient, it follows that they all must have shared the same beliefs. The diversity of opinions expressed among these systems is only for the sake of its hearers, who are at different stages of understanding. ... According to Madhusudana, the sages taught these various systems in order to keep people from a false attraction to the views of nastikas such as the Buddhists and Jainas.' (p. 9)

8   Rukmani, 1981, argues that Vijnanabhikshu was influenced by the Navya-Naiyayika thinker, Raghunatha Siromani.

9   Nicholson, 2010, p. 179.

10 Another example of how astika got contested and redefined was the debate between Mrtyunjay Vidyalankar, a highly respected Calcutta based Hindu scholar of the early 1800s, and Ram Mohan Roy. The debate occurred

in 1817. Whereas Ram Mohan became famous as a result of his Western patronage, Vidyalankar has not been studied enough. He wrote pamphlets claiming that Hinduism was neither amorphous nor did it manifest in response to Westerners. His 'Vedanta Chandrika' (Moonlight of the Vedanta) was directly aimed at Ram Mohan's view of Vedanta. Many of these ideas were later adopted by Vivekananda. He defended the variety of Hindu institutions, ideas and practices over its long history. He referred to Ram Mohan's camp as 'intoxicated moderns' for recklessly transforming Hinduism into a 'marketplace theology'. He saw no contradiction between the Puranas and Vedanta, defended the worship of images, and emphasized the importance of Sanskrit. Initially, it was this approach to Vedanta that was translated as 'neo-Vedanta', but later on, the Christian missionaries appropriated that term, and gave it a whole new meaning, i.e., to signify a fabrication. (Kopf, 1969, pp. 204-6.)

11   One may ask why this consolidation into modern Hinduism took place in the medieval period. Some scholars have theorized that the arrival of Islam might have led to a coalescing of various Hindu streams into closer unities than before. It has been surmised that the attempts by Akbar and then Dara Shikoh to synthesize Hinduism and Islam into one hybrid might have been seen threatening Hindu digestion into a subset of Islam. This threat could have been a factor in this trend to bring many nastika outsiders into the tent as astika insiders. Regardless of the causes for this, there is ample evidence to suggest that multiple movements began to organize diverse Hindu schools into a common framework or organizing principle. Each of these rival approaches had its own idea of the metaphysical system in which it was at the highest point in the hierarchy, with the rest located in lower positions in terms of validity and importance, but the point here is that highly expansive unities were being constructed. Another scholar espousing this thesis of the development of an 'insider' sense of Hinduism as a response to Islam is David Lorenzen. He notes that between 1200 and 1500, the Hindu rivalry with Muslims created a new self-consciousness of a unified Hindu identity. Lorenzen draws his evidence from medieval literature, including the poetry of Eknath, Anantadas, Kabir and Vidyapati, and argues that the difference between Hinduism and Islam was emphasized in their writings. This emphasis showed the growth of an implicit notion of Hindu selfhood that differed from Islam. For instance, many bhakti poets contrasted Hindu ideas that God exists in all things, living and not living, with Islam's insistence on banning this as idolatry. Lorenzen concludes: 'The

evidence instead suggests that a Hindu religion theologically and devotionally grounded in texts such as the Bhagavad-Gita, the Puranas, and philosophical commentaries on the six darsanas, gradually acquired a much sharper self-conscious identity through the rivalry between Muslims and Hindus in the period between 1200 and 1500, and was firmly established long before 1800.' (Lorenzen, 2005, p. 53.)

12 This method of writing is common among historians of ancient civilizations, especially when they deal with works that have become extinct, and hence there is a need to fill in the blanks with some degree of invention.For example, Plato's book on Socrates gives the only information available today on an earlier philosopher called Anaxagoras. The same is true of the Charvakas in India: very little of their own work survives and it is only through third-party critiques that we can reconstruct what the Charvakas were thinking. In a sense, most of the known ancient history of the world is of this kind, because little is based on direct accounts written at the time.

13 Examples of Indian doxographies named by Nicholson include the following: 1) Cattanar's *Manimekalai* (sixth century): based on pramanas. Schools are Lokayata, Buddhism, Samkhya, Nyaya, Vaisesika, and Mimamsa. 2) Buddhist Bhaviveka's *Madhyamakahrdayakarika* (sixth century): covers Hinayana, Yogachara, Samkhya, Vaisesika, Vedanta and Mimamsa. 3) Jain philosopher Haribhadra's *Saddarsanasamuccaya* (eighth century): based on the deity each accepts and the means to moksha. Six schools are Buddhism, Nyaya, Samkhya, Jain, Vaisesika and Mimamsa. 4) Madhava's *Sarvadarsanasamgraha* (fourteenth century): most influential because of its depth. Treats sixteen schools with Advaita as the highest. Bhedabheda was omitted from this treatise. 5) Madhusudana Sarasvati *Prasthanabheda* (sixteenth century): organized around eighteen vidyas or prasthanas. Divides vidyas into four Vedas, six Vedangas, four upangas and four upavedas. Then fits Samkhya, Yoga, Vedanta and Mimamsa under these categories. Nastikas have their own six sources—four Buddhist sects, Carvakas and Digambar Jainas. Nyaya, Vaisesika, Mimamsa belong to *arambhavada* (atomistic theory) while Samkhya, Yoga and theistic schools belong to *parinamavada*. Vedanta espouses *vivartavada*. Note that Vijnanabhuksu did not write a doxography though he was motivated by similar concerns.

14 As suggested by BS 4.1.15 and *Ch. Up.* 6.14.2

15 Vishnu Purana, 6.7.35

16 Rukmani, 1981, p. 20.

17 Nicholson, 2010, p. 2.

18 Nicholson 2010, pp. 122-123.

19 Although Vivekananda was a passionate advocate of a Vedanta-Yoga philosophy and spirituality, he was not averse to drawing on elements of Western philosophy and metaphysics that were popular at his time. His predilection for Herbert Spencer and other Europeans of the time was to borrow English terminology in order to present his own philosophy more persuasively. He did so because his own philosophical tradition had been savaged by colonial and Orientalist polemics. (Nicholson 2010, pp. 65, 78)

20 Nicholson 2010, p. 65, 78.

21 The stakes were high, as the theories proposed resulted in assigning an internal hierarchy among Germans, English, French and other Europeans. Sanskrit and its civilization became a pawn in this game of identity politics among Europeans.

22 Herling, 2006, gives a good account of this debate as it related to the German understanding of the Bhagavad-Gita.

23 For various reasons, many modern commentators assume Samkhya was always atheistic. Some find that God is superfluous in the system. Others want Samkhya to function as an analogue to Darwin's theory of evolution, a rigorous school which was not other-worldly. Yet others such as Debiprasad Chattopadhyaya are Marxist historians who want to show a thriving atheistic tradition.

24 Larson, 1995, pp. 142-2, p. 58.

25 It is important to note that sruti is often trumped by smriti if the context so demands. For example, women's property rights and marriage age changed against the sruti, as per A.S. Altekar, 'The Position of Women in Hindu Civilization'. Delhi, Motilal Banarsidas, 1995, pp. 353-4.

26 Krishna 1991, p. 14.

27 Nicholson, 2010, p. 13.

28 Nicholson, 2010, p. 18.

29 Nicholson, 2010, p. 163.

30 Studies that avoid using the categories of 'dharma' or the 'West' (accusing them of being essentialist) invariably fall into this trap, crippling any further efforts to understand the intended objects of their gaze, and ultimately reinforcing the status quo of Western domination. My work steers clear of the infinitely regressive trap of pos-tmodern nihilism; it does not permit outlying exceptions to negate the overwhelming salience of characteristic features in either civilization, Indian or Western.

9: Traditional Foundations of Social Consciousness

1 Gupta, 1974, p. 27.

2 Gupta, 1974, p. 27.

3 Gupta, 1974, p. 27.

4 Gupta, 1974, p. 28.

5 Gupta, 1974, p. 44.

6 Gupta, 1974, p. 45.

7 Gupta, 1974, p. 47.

8 Gupta, 1974, p. 35.

9 Gupta, 1974, pp. 37-8.

10 This is elucidated in the *Chandogya Upanishad* (6.1.4) which explains that a clay pot is, in fact, name-and-form (namarupa) taken on by clay, so that the clay pot is not real, independent of the clay.

11 Mahabharata, XII.113.8.

12 The jati-varna system itself is a delicate balance of duties and responsibilities towards other sections of society: the Brahmin is required to share knowledge freely and without profiting from it; the Kshatriya is to protect the *rashtra* (nation/society); the Vaishya is to prosper in business and then share the riches with the rest of society through undertaking public works and through dana (philanthropic giving); the Shudra performs in what is nowadays called the 'service sector' of the economy.

13 Southworth, 2010, p. 4.

14 Beckerlegge 1998, p. 178. It is unfortunate that after publishing her work showing the pre-colonial origins of Hindu seva, she was subsequently influenced by identity politics to recant her stance. She was funded to infiltrate Vivekananda Kendra's yoga camp in order to write about them as a 'Hindutva-related organization' and thereby join the ranks of many Westerners engaged in denigrating Hindu traditions as being oppressive. On her web site she has posted the following statement, contradicting her earlier publications, presumably as a way to retain her status amongst her academic peers: 'Working on both seva and popular iconography led me in turn to iconographic allusions to Swami Vivekananda in the Rashtriya Swayamsevak Sangh (RSS) and its affiliates (the sangh parivar) and other sympathetic organisations. This has resulted in publications on iconographic representations of renunciation and activism in the sangh parivar and the

Ramakrishna Math and Mission; the appropriation of Swami Vivekananda by the RSS; and the development and understanding of seva within the RSS. As part of my ongoing research into seva in a range of contemporary Hindu movements, I have centred much of my recent work on Vivekananda Kendra, based at Kanyakumari. The outcome of my presence as a participant observer at its 2010 annual Yoga Shiksha Shibir (Yoga Training Camp), "Eknath Ranade, gurus and jivanvratis (life-workers): Vivekananda Kendra's promotion of the 'Yoga Way of Life'", will be published in Mark Singleton and Ellen Goldberg (eds.) "Gurus of Modern Yoga".'(Accessed 3 February 2013, from: http://www.open.ac.uk/Arts/religious-studies/beckerlegge.shtml)This book is now out (Oxford University Press, 2014). Singleton, mentioned above, is famous for his book claiming that yoga is not of traditional Hindu origin but that modern Hindus copied it from Westerners. See discussion on Singleton in Chapter 7.

15 Beckerlegge, 1998, p. 182.

16 Dharampal, 2003, Davis, 2002.

17 'So much is wrung from the peasants', wrote the chief of the Dutch Factory at Agra in 1616 CE that, 'even dry bread is scarcely left to them'. (Chopra et al. 1974, p. 144.) The gloom and doom were further compounded by three long famines in the Deccan towards the end of the fifteenth century, killing millions. (Deleury, 1960, p. 40) cited by Tilak, 2007.

18 This was one of the themes of Naoroji's speech delivered in the British House of Commons on 14 August 1894. He raised the issue again in a speech from the Pulpit of Free Church in Croydon, England on 30 April 1901. (See Suri and Zaidi 1985, pp. 124-148 and 232-245). Cited in Tilak, 2007.

19 Both Naoroji and Gokhale gave evidence before the Royal Commission on Indian Expenditure in 1897, which was presided over by Lord Welby. Gokhale drew particular attention to the disastrous famine affecting 97 million people in the Deccan. Cited in Tilak, 2007.

20 In a letter to Mary Hale of Chicago dated 30 October 1899, Vivekananda attributes the poverty of Indians and recurring famines in India to the foreign rule of the British and the Muslims. He quotes the Muslim historian Ferishta (ca. 1570-1611 CE) to the effect that in the twelfth-century Hindus numbered 600 million whereas their number now was less than two hundred million. (Jyotirmayananda, 1985, p. 592)

21 Bajaj, 1996.

22 An example of his pragmatism is as follows. There was a period when his followers were being abused and physically attacked because they stood out

in their dress and looks. So he initiated five hundred ascetics into the highest state of consciousness (known as *'paramhansa'*) and asked that they have no outward distinguishing marks that would identify them as targets for attack. The practice of appearing to be socially assimilated was pragmatic and was discontinued once the threats disappeared.

23 Lorenzen, 1978.

24 Majumdar, 1977, p. 716.

25 Williams, p. 23.

26 Thakur, Murli, no date, p. 209.

27 Williams, 1984, p. 24.

28 Beckerlegge, 1998, p. 188. Beckerlegge further cites the following: Joshi, 1981, ch. 33, p. 29; and Williams, 1984, p. 92f.

29 In medieval India the deity known as Vitthala (an incarnation of Vishnu that was popular in parts of Andhra Pradesh, Maharashtra, and Karnataka) was traditionally depicted as the advocate of the poor and the needy belonging to the weakest and most disadvantaged sections of society. Vitthala, then, should also be considered in this context. Vitthala was especially sympathetic to the poor and hence he was appropriated by the Hindu masses during that time of distress. There is no adequate evidence on the historical origin and development of this deity as a subaltern God. The word is non-Sanskritic and is probably of Kannada origin. The earliest epigraphic reference to Vitthala in this form dates from 1216 CE (Deleury, 1960, pp. 90-91). Vishnu manifested Himself as Vitthala (God of the poor), so described because the poor and the downtrodden were destined to be his primary audience and constituency. Over the centuries, Vishnu-Narayana, or Vitthala, evolved as advocate of the poor and destitute. This peculiar relationship obtaining between the poor and their advocate God constitutes the heart of the devotional literature created by the poet saints (men and women) of Maharashtra. The relationship with God is expressed in terms of identity and solidarity with the poor and the oppressed. Relating to God is not a purely intellectual affair; it means to love the poor through him. Vitthala was readily and directly accessible to the masses. Vitthala, God of the subaltern, became increasingly 'human'. Vitthala's devotees began to express their religiosity in utter material helplessness and with appeals for help. It was typically expressed as an urgent appeal of help with common references to Vitthala as: dinanatha (protector of the lowly), *dinabandhu* (friend of the poor), *dinavatsala* (compassionate to the needy), and dinadayala (merciful-to-the needy). Tukaram, perhaps the most famous of the

devotees of Vitthala, depicts himself in one of his devotional compositions in Marathi as a blind and crippled pilgrim on the road to the main temple of Vitthala. Dinkar, who was a medieval literary composer on miscellaneous subjects of philosophy, ethics, and social duties called Anubhavadinakara, appeals to Vitthala thus: *save the needy, provide a helper, protect in time of distress, O Brother-of-the-needy* (dinabandhu)(Abbott, 1929, p. 68). In the hymn of praise to Vitthala, Mahipati (eighteenth century) describes how Vitthala helped various female saints in their daily chores. The popular folklore and worship of Vitthala included his help to the poor, especially women.

30 Swami Shantatmananda explained this to me by private email, based on historical references.

31 Williams 1984, p. 17.

32 Williams, 1984, p. xi.

33 The four mahavakyas are as follows: 1) *prajnanam brahma* (Brahman is wisdom-consciousness), *Aitareya Upanishad* 3.3.13 of the Rig Veda; 2) *ayam atma brahma* (This Self [Atman] is Brahman), *Mandukya Upanishad* 1.2 of the *Atharva Veda*; 3) *tat tvam asi* (Thou art That), *Chandogya Upanishad* 6.8.7 of the Sama Veda; 4) *aham brahmasmi* (I am Brahman), *Brhadaranyaka Upanishad* 1.4.10 of the Yajur Veda.

34 The Complete Works of Swami Vivekananda, 1964, vol. 4: p. 368.

35 *The Complete Works of Swami Vivekananda, vol. 2*. Calcutta: Advaita Ashrama, 1995. p. 236.

36 Beckerlegge 1998, p. 192.

37 Tilak (2007, pp. 240-258).

38 Jyotirmayananda, 1986, p. 559.

39 *The Complete Works of Swami Vivekananda*, 1964, vol. 7, p. 245.

40 Bharati, 1980, p. 94.

41 For details, see Beckerlegge 1998, pp. 166-7.

42 Gupta gives further evidence that Vivekananda's formation of Practical Vedanta took shape prior to his travels to the West. Since 1890 Vivekananda had travelled across India by himself, and by 1893 he had already developed the elements of his programme. In fact, his first trip, in 1893, to deliver the famous lectures at the World Parliament of Religions in Chicago, was funded and sponsored by the Maharaja of Khetri, which shows that an embryonic support already existed in India before he visited the U.S. Furthermore, when during his U.S. trip he faced opposition by some American clergymen, he was able to demonstrate that he had support in India. His disciples in Madras

had organized big meetings with influential names and passed resolutions demonstrating their support, and these reports reached American journalists and other important Americans. Thus, Vivekananda already had credibility in India when he visited the U.S. Only later did he start to echo this in the reverse direction, i.e., by using his American success to create further support in India.

43 *The Complete Works of Swami Vivekananda*, vol. 5, pp. 12-13 (letter to Alasinga)

44 Gupta, 1974, p. 34.

10: Harmonizing Vedanta and Yoga

1 My objective here is not to defend Shankara per se. Rather, I am responding to Rambachan's broad charges which utilize Shankara explicitly.

2 *Brihadaranyaka Upanishad* says: 'atma va are drashtavyas srotavyo mantavyo nididhyasitavya'.

3 Brahmasutra is a text in four chapters (550 aphorisms) in which the famous thinker Badarayana reconciles the different doctrines prevalent at that time. He sought to unify the Upanishads into a set of coherent principles.

4 In a series of articles in 1992, 1993 and 1995, Arvind Sharma debated Rambachan very directly on the issue of whether Shankara claimed sruti to be the exclusive means for attaining moksha. I have utilized Sharma's position in some of my arguments. I have also seen other studies specifically devoted to Sankara's view of meditation, for example: Hajime Nakamura's article, 'Meditation in Sankara', and Barbara Doherty's unpublished Ph.D thesis, 'The Path to Liberation: Sankara, Metaphysician, Mystic, and Teacher'.

5 Shankara also debated many other schools of thought, such as Lokayatas, Jains, etc.

6 Ramakrishna expressed the idea of absolute and relative realities using his terms 'nitya' and 'lila', respectively.

7 These are called 'samvrti satya' and 'paramartha satya', respectively.

8 Bader, 1990, p. 55.

9 Bader, 1990, p. 92.

10 In his prefatory remarks to 3.38 (*Mandukya-Karika*), Shankara clearly equates brahma and samadhi. As regards 3.39 of the same text, the expression *durdarshah sarvayogibhih* may not necessarily mean that Patanjali's system and this yoga (i.e., Asparsha Yoga) differ. It may only refer to the difficulty of the concept for yogins in general (of his own time, perhaps). The fear referred to in

the verse may be due to the involvement of the dissolution of the mind which can make one apprehensive about the loss of one's own identity.

11 Nikhilananda, 1949, p. 213.

12 Furthermore, Brhadaranyaka 4.4.23 does use the term 'samahita', which is etymologically close to 'samadhi' and which Shankara himself interprets as '*citta-samadhana*'.

13 In sutra 6.14 and 6.38.

14 Shankara's commentary on Brahmasutra 2.1.9 (Thibaut, 1890, vol. 1, p. 312)

15 Eliade, 1973, p. 114.

16 For example, Shankara refers to yoga ideas in his commentaries on *Katha Upanishad* 1.3.13 and *Taittiriya Upanishad* 1.6.2.

17 Sutra 1.3.13 (Gambhirananda, 1972, p. 164.) *Katha* 2.3.11 and 2.3.18 are pertinent as well.

18 In his commentary on Brahmasutra 3.3.15 (Comans, 1993, p. 25)

19 Shankara explains this *Katha* sutra succinctly as follows: '"He should restrain speech in the mind" means that by giving up the operations of the external senses such as the organ of speech and so forth he should remain only as the mind. And since the mind is inclined towards conjecturing about things, he should, by way of seeing the defect involved in conjecturing, restrain it in the intellect whose characteristic consists in determining and which is said here by the word "cognizing self". Then bringing about an increase in subtlety, he. should restrain that intellect in the "great self", i.e., the experiencer, or the one-pointed intellect. And he should establish the "great self" in the peaceful Self, i.e., in that supreme Purusa who is the topic under consideration, who is the "highest goal".' (Brahmasutra-bhasya 1.4.1. See also: Comans, 1993, p. 25.)

20 Sutra 2.3.10-11 (Rukmani, 2006, p. 128.) See also: Gambhirananda, 1972, vol. 1, pp. 209-210.

21 *Chandogya Upanishad* 7.6.1. See: Jha, 1942, pp. 381-2; also Bader, 1990, pp. 81-2.

22 Bhagavad-Gita 6.20.

23 Sastry, 1985, p. 6. Sharma comments that the following footnote in Shankara's commentary is also relevant: 'It is considered incumbent on a commentator to state, before commenting on a work, the subject and the object, as well as the class of persons for whom it is intended, and the relation in which it stands to the three severally. Here the subject is the Para-Brahman; the object is Salvation, Moksha. It is intended for those who seek deliverance

from the turmoil of samsara. It is related to the subject as an exposition thereof, and to the object as a means of attaining it.' (Ibid.) Clearly, Shankara sees the Gita as a means to attaining moksha.

24 Bhagavad-Gita 2.46, trans. A. Mahadeva Sastri, 6th ed. (Madras: V. Ramaswamy Sastrulu & Sons, 1972), p. 62.

25 This also has enormous implications for one who has access to moksha. Shankara's Brahmasutra-bhashya 1.3.38 makes it clear that although the shudra is barred from the study of the sruti, moksha is not the monopoly of those who are twice-born men in this birth. There is no bar to anyone gaining *atmajnana* through the teaching of the Smriti and through the fruits of actions done in former births.

26 For example, Bhagavad-Gita 6.19, 2.39 and 2.53. See: Sastry, 1985, p. 177, pp. 49-50, p. 59, p. 135.

27 The term 'cognitive shift' here refers to a shift to superconsciousness, and not a shift within ordinary cognition.

28 Bader, 1990, p. 53.

29 Shankara adopts this from *Brhadaranyaka Upanishad* 2.4.11. See: Madhavananda, 1950, pp. 364-366.

30 In Shankara's commentary on *Brhadaranyaka Upanishad* 4.2.4. (Madhavananda, 1950, p 591.) Cited in Bader, 1990, p. 44.

31 Comans, 1993, p. 26.

32 Dalal, 2009, pp. 6-7

33 Shankara's commentary on the *Brhadaranyaka Upanishad* 3.3.1 See: Madhavananda, 1950, pp. 448-449.

34 Dalal, 2009, pp. 6-7.

35 Dalal, 2009, pp. 26-7.

36 Dalal, 2009, pp. 368-370.

37 Vidyasankar Sundaresan clarifies (via private communication to me) that this is not a rejection of *citta-vritti-nirodha* and that Shankara approves its usage in a specific manner. Shankara's discussion on *citta-vrtti-nirodha* involves a debate on the statement 'atma ity eva upasita' meaning 'contemplate upon Brahman only as the Self'. (In Brahmasutra-bhasya 1.4.7.) The debate is about whether this is an injunction (*vidhi*) to meditate upon the Self. Sankara rejects the position that this is a primary injunction to meditate upon Brahman as one's own Self. He also rejects the notion that this is an injunction to practise *citta-vrtti-nirodha*. His position has often been misunderstood. What Sankara rejects here is the notion that the Upanishad contains an injunction; he does

not reject citta-vrtti-nirodha itself. This is made clear when he says that in fact, the only way to achieve a cessation to various mental transformations is through the steady recollection of Self-knowledge. In other words, it is not as if practising yoga (separately from studying Vedanta) to achieve citta-vrtti-nirodha will lead to Self-knowledge and thereby to liberation. Rather, it is Self-knowledge, obtained through Vedanta, and its recollection that directly leads to what the yoga school describes as its goal, namely *citta-vrtti-nirodha*. Shankara's rejection of this as an injunction is extremely strong because *Self-knowledge is not an action that can be enjoined*. He explains that Self-knowledge itself leads to *citta-vrtti-nirodha*. If proper knowledge has already arisen, why is there any further discussion of steadily recollecting this knowledge and of *citta-vrtti-nirodha*? The answer given is that the tendency to maintain that knowledge may not be strong even after it arises. The tendency of speech, mind and body to keep indulging in action may be strong because of the prior momentum. To counter this, the Sruti teaches the recollection of Self-knowledge as a *niyama*, accompanied by other means such as renunciation and dispassion. Shankara makes clear that he views the Upanishad as teaching a restrictive injunction (*niyama vidhi*), but not a primary injunction (*apurva vidhi*). (In *Brhadaranyaka Upanishad bhasya* and *Chandogya Upanishad bhasya*.) Once known, the knowledge is to be consolidated and steadily recollected, and this is the only means to *citta-vrtti-nirodha*. It also counters the momentum of past karma. This discussion incorporates aspects of both yoga and purva mimamsa. The key message is that *atma-jnana* cannot be enjoined because it is the way out of action. Action leads to causation and cannot lead out of it. Nor can citta-vrtti-nirodha be enjoined because it is not by itself the means to liberation. The steady recollection of *atma-jnana* can be taken as being enjoined in an ancillary fashion (niyama vidhi) in order to check the tendency towards more action generated by the momentum of *prarabdha karma*.

38 Interestingly, the term 'nirvikalpa-samadhi' is not original to Patanjali's Yogasutras or the Vyasa bhashya on it. It is a term found predominantly in much later treatises on yoga, written during a period where the Advaita Vedanta influence was strong.

39 Skoog, 1989, p. 73.

40 Hiriyanna writes: 'The general term "pramana" and the special ones also like "pratyaksha", have three different, but closely connected meanings: They signify first, a source of knowledge, without reference to its being either true or false; secondly, a source of valid knowledge; and lastly, a means of scrutiny.

... Pramanas, in the second sense, are thought of as simply revealing truth. In the third sense also, their aim is taken to be the revelation of truth; but they are regarded as always presupposing doubt, and reaching truth after the discovery of the logical grounds for believing in one and not believing in the other of the two alternatives involved in doubt. If the emphasis in the one case is on the cognitive side, it is on the probative side in the other.' (Hiriyanna, 1957, p. 69.)

41 Sankara, Brahmasutra 11.2.29 as quoted in Sharma, 1992, p. 524.

42 Sankara's Introduction to the Brahmasutra.

43 Sankara, Brahmasutra 1.1.2.

44 Sharma, 1992.

45 This refers to Sankara's gloss on Brahmasutra 4.1.15 (Radhakrishnan, 1960, pp. 243-244). T.M.P. Mahadevan explains the same sutra as follows: 'How can one contest the heart-felt cognition of another as possessing *brahman*-knowledge, even though bearing a body?' (Mahadevan, 1992, p. 143)

46 Shankara writes in sutra 1.1.2: 'Scriptural text, etc., are not, in the enquiry into Brahman, the only means of knowledge, as they are in the enquiry into active duty (i.e., in the Purva Mimamsa), but scriptural texts on the one hand, and intuition, etc., on the other hand, are to be had recourse to according to the occasion: firstly, because intuition is the final result of the enquiry into Brahman; secondly, because the object of the enquiry is an existing (accomplished) substance. If the object of the knowledge of Brahman were something to be accomplished, there would be no reference to intuition, and text, etc., would be the only means of knowledge.' (Thibaut, 1962, pp. 17-18)

47 Brahmasutra-bhasya 1.1.4 (Thibaut, vol 1, 1890, p. 299).

48 Sharma, 1992, p. 522.

49 Bader, 1990, pp. 67-8.

50 Sutra 4.1.15. (Sharma, 1993, 741). See also: Hiriyanna, 1932, p. 381 n. 2; Mahadevan, 1971, p. 143. Furthermore, Sharma raises the following question: 'What evidence does Shankara adduce to establish the validity of jivanmukti? Does he appeal to sruti or to anubhava? He could have cited sruti (see *Brhadaranyaka Upanishad* 4.4.7 and *Katha Upanishad* 2.3.14) if sruti is the only valid means of knowledge about matters pertaining to Brahman. Why, then, the appeal to anubhava and not to sruti? One may note that Shankara uses the expression sva-hrdaya-pratyayam and not sruti-pratyayam. The role of anubhava is clearly acknowledged. ... In this case, one could even argue that Shankara accords priority to experience, for he first refers to direct experience and then says that passages from sruti and smrti also say the

same thing.' (Sharma, 1995, p. 111.) Then Sharma cites the following passage in Shankara's commentary: 'Moreover it is not a matter for dispute at all whether the body of him who knows brahman continues to exist for some time or not. For, how can one man contest the fact of another possessing the knowledge of Brahman—vouched for by his heart's conviction—and at the same time continuing to enjoy bodily existence? This same point is explained in scripture and smrti, where they describe him who stands firm in the highest knowledge. The final decision therefore is that knowledge effects the destruction of those works only whether—good or evil—whose effects have not yet begun to operate.' (Thibaut, 1896, p. 358. For another rendering, see Gambhirananda, 1977, pp. 840-841.) Sharma closes his discussion of this point with the remark: 'The matter is taken out of the realm of disputation by an appeal to experience—and personal experience at that—and not by an appeal to Vedic authority ...' (Sharma, 1995, p. 111)

51 Dalal, 2009, p. 371.

52 Dalal, 2009, pp. 371-2.

53 Private conversations with Vidyasankar Sundaresan, February 2013.

54 In Brahmasutra-bhasya 1.3.33, he quotes Yogasutra 2.44 and *Svetasvatara Upanishad* sutra 2.14.

55 In Brahmasutra-bhasya 1.3.33 and 2.4.12. (Bader, 1990, p. 5, 47.) See also: Gambhirananda, 1972, p. 164; Gambhirananda, 1972, vol. 1, pp. 209-210; Thibaut, 1890. Shankara's commentary actually cites Patanjali's Yogasutra 1.6 though it does not mention the name of the text.

56 Skoog, 1989, p. 69.

57 Brahmasutra-bhasya 1.1.2, trans. George Thibaut (Delhi: Motilal Banarsidass, 1973), pp. 17-18.

58 We can think of upasana as any second-person method of relating to a deity, in an 'I-You' relationship. This is different from first-person and third-person methods, though second-person methods can lead to the first-person experience.

59 In Brahmasutra-bhasya.

60 Shankara's Brahmasutra-bhasya 3.3.28, 4.1.7-10 (Thibaut, 1890, vol 2, p. 231, 350)

61 Shankara's commentary on Upanishads does not try to differentiate between dhyana and upasana. However, unlike upasana, dhyana does not necessarily involve a devotional attitude, and unlike dhyana upasana does not always refer to a specific method. Dhyana culminates in samadhi.

62 Bader, 1990, p. 44.

63 Bader elaborates on this point further as follows: 'While Sankara singles out the Samkhya component of the yogasmrti for criticism in his discussion of Brahmasutra 2.1.3, he takes the instructions regarding the disciplined activities of yoga practice to comprise the "portion" which is in accord with sruti. Sankara readily admits that the Upanisads themselves speak of yoga practice. He cites passages referring to yoga postures, control of the senses, and meditation. His illustration here of the injunction for meditation is most significant: srotavyo mantavyo nididhyasitavyah (BU 2.4.5). These instructions are certainly not characteristic of yoga texts. The discipline of hearing, reflecting, and constantly meditating upon the teachings concerning the Self is, of course, the method which is set out for students of Vedanta. That the phrase was probably singled out for special mention well before Sankara's time, is evident from the frequency with which it is cited by Sankara's opponents in the BUBh. Sankara himself attached great importance to the passage, though in adapting it to the Advaita viewpoint, he restructured the practice. Later Vedantins continued to assign a prominent place to the process of sravana-manana- nididhyasana. Sankara's acknowledgement that this sruti passage prescribes yoga shows that its practice is indeed an integral part of his Advaita Vedanta.' (Bader, 1990, p. 99) Bader also explains as follows: '[Shankara] maintains that yogis can acquire extraordinary powers such as the ability to become as small as an atom. Accomplished yogis may occupy several bodies at the same time. They may even have direct perception of the past and future. Sankara describes these powers as if they were an obvious fact of life. Yet rather than appealing to empirical evidence to support these claims, he is content to rely on the testimony of scripture. One cannot, he argues, simply deny the power of yoga, because it is supported by authoritative smrti and sruti texts.' (Bader, 1990, p. 101)

64 Shankara says that 'the teacher being friendly-minded says that there is no binding rule as to the particulars mentioned therein. The clause "favourable to the mind" moreover shows that meditation may be carried on wherever concentration of the mind may be attained'. Brahmasutra-bhasya 4.1.11 (Thibaut, 1890, vol 2, p. 351)

65 Bader, 1990, pp. 75-80.

66 Bader, 1990, p. 57.

67 A key thrust of Brahmasutra 2.1.3 is to refute the Samkhya positions. Shankara's commentary explains that the refutation of various Samkhya

positions automatically refutes the corresponding issues in yoga also, and there is a need to set apart Vedanta from yoga. This is because the Upanishads enjoin yoga practices only as a means (upaya) to the true vision of the Self.

68 In Patanjala Yoga, the seer (*drashta*) abides in its own nature (*svarupa*) in the state of *nirodha* (cessation), but this is not necessarily the same as non-duality per se. Yoga metaphysics allows for multiple drashta-s, whereas advaita Vedanta says there is only one drashta, that is Brahman.

69 Shankara's Brahmasutra-bhasya 2.1.3 (Thibaut, 1890, vol. 1, pp. 296-299)

70 Comans, 1993, p. 28.

71 Yogasutra 3.37, 4.29 and 3.51 warn against yogic powers becoming an obstacle to one's path, and for the highest samadhi to be achieved one must not get attached to samadhi. (Bader, 1990, p. 105.)

72 But Hacker was wrong in claiming that yoga and Advaita are mutually opposing philosophical systems, and in his theory that Shankara started out as a Yoga follower who later switched to Vedanta. Bader disagrees with Hacker that Shankara moved away from yoga in his later works. Hacker claims that Shankara had earlier suggested means for mental control that resemble Yogasutra 1.12, and reiterated Vyasa's comment that qualifies *abhyasa* as *viveka-darsana*, which he later rejected. But Bader points out in response to this that Shankara's later commentary on the Bhagavad-Gita refers indirectly to Yogasutra with approval, such as in 6.35. (I would also add Shankara's commentary to Gita 6.36 to this.) Shankara regards abhyasa and vairagya as necessary to control *viksepa-s*, even though viksepa is absent in this verse of Gita, and Shankara reflects Vyasa's statement that viksepa-s are obstacles to samadhi and should be controlled by practice and dispassion. (Bader, 1990, pp. 87-8)

73 Comans, 1993, p. 28.

74 Bhajanananda, 2010.

75 Shankara's explanation of the world as adhyasa or superimposition upon Brahman is original in Vedanta. (Bhajanananda, 2010)

76 These streams are: (a) the Vartika school, based on the views of Sureshvara; (b) the Vivarana school, based on the views of Padmapada and Prakashatman; and (c) the Bhamati school, based on the views of Vachaspati Mishra.

77 Ingalls, 1952, p. 8, as cited in Bader, 1990, p. 10.

78 Comans, 1993, pp. 31-32.

79 Rukmani disapproves of Sadananda's conflation of nididhyasana into something like samadhi in Yoga. She feels that 'Sadananda's efforts to equate *nididhyasana* to a two-fold *savikalpa-samadhi* and *nirvikalpaka-samadhi* does not do any justice to Sankara's Advaita Vedanta.' She disapproves of the way Sadananda blurs the boundaries thereby allowing the use of Brahman as an object of meditation when Shankara was adamant against this. (Rukmani, 2006, p. 130)

80 Singh, 2008.

81 I am relying on translation by Acharya Pranipata Chaitanya of the Chinmaya Mission, Tamil Nadu, India. See: http://www.advaitin.net/PranipataChaitanya/Vivekachudamani%20eBook%20FinalFinal1.pdf

82 Comans, 1996, p. xvi.

83 Bader, 1990, p. 11. But most important in this regard is the position held by Swami Dayananda Saraswati, arguably the pre-eminent interpreter of Shankara today who Rambachan has mentioned numerous times as his source of expertise on Shankara. Swami Dayananda Saraswati teaches courses on Vivekachudamani, calling it an important work that reflects Shankara's ideas, regardless of whether it might have been written later by one of the acharyas in his lineage. Swami Dayananda Saraswati said: 'I do not think we lose anything even if the authorship is attributed to any other Sankaracharya of one of the various *Sankara-mathas*.' Quoted on p. 4 at: http://www.advaitin.net/PranipataChaitanya/Vivekachudamani%20eBook%20FinalFinal1.pdf

84 Venkatesananda, p. 249.

85 Bader, 1990, p. 82.

86 Bader writes: 'Hacker claims that the text is genuinely Sankara's (Paul Hacker, "Sankara der Yogin und Sankara der Advaitin. Einige Beobachtungen", WZKSO, 12-13, 1968-69, p. 147). Vetter concurs with Hacker, but notes that aside from its theories on God, the work is not very original (Tilmann Vetter, Studien zur Lehre und Entwicklung Sankaras, Vienna, 1979, p. 21). Mayeda also agrees with Hacker, but holds slight reservations (A Thousand Teachings: The Upadesasahasri of Sankara, tr. Sengaku Mayeda, Tokyo, 1979: p. 6). Hajime Nakamura, who has written three articles in Japanese on this text, finds that there is "no bar to the authenticity of the text" (cited by Trevor Leggett, Sankara on the Yogasutra-s [Vol. I], Samadhi, London, 1981, p. xviii). Wezler does not believe that Sankara's authorship of the text has been established by Hacker's argument. However, Wezler accepts Hacker's assertion that

Sankara was initially a follower of yoga (Albrecht Wezler, "Philological Observations on the so-called patanjala-yogasutra-bhasya-vivarana", IIJ, 25, 1983, pp.35-36). Halbfass states that while the ascription of the text to Sankara is certainly questionable, "there is nothing in the form or contents of the Vivarana that would exclude the possibility that it is a work by the author of the Brahmasiitrabhasya" (Wilhelm Halbfass, Studies in Kumarila and Sankara, Reinbek, 1983, p. 108). All these scholars have pointed to various elements in Sankara's work which correspond to concepts found in the yogasutra-bhasya-vivaranam. Nevertheless no one has yet set out to specifically prove, or disprove, the authenticity of the text.' (Bader, 1990, p. 2, footnote 2)

87 Comans summarizes his analysis on the way Vedanta gradually digests yoga over a period of several centuries: 'Although the importance of concentration is evident from the early Upanisads, a form of yoga practice leading to the absorptive state of samadhi is only in evidence in the later texts. We have seen that Sankara does speak of a type of concentration upon the Self which is akin to yoga insofar as there is the withdrawal of the mind from sense objects, but he does not advocate more than that and he does not put forward the view that we find in classical Yoga about the necessity of total thought suppression. We have seen that he has used the word "samadhi" very sparingly, and when he has used it, it was not always in an unambiguously favourable context. It should be clear that Sankara does not set up nirvikalpa-samadhi as a spiritual goal. For if he had thought it to be an indispensable requirement for liberation, then he would have said so. But he has not said so. Contemplation on the Self is obviously a part of Sankara's teaching, but his contemplation is directed toward seeing the ever present Self as free from all conditionings rather than toward the attainment of nirvikalpa-samadhi. This is in significant contrast to many modern Advaitins for whom all of the Vedanta amounts to "theory" which has its experimental counterpart in yoga "practice". I suggest that their view of Vedanta is a departure from Sankara's own position. The modern Advaitins, however, are not without their forerunners, and I have tried to indicate that there has been a gradual increase in samadhi-oriented practice in the centuries after Sankara, as we can judge from the later Advaita texts.' (Comans, 1993, pp. 32-3)

88 Rambachan, 1994, pp. 117-118.

11: Mithya, Open Architecture and Cognitive Science

1   Original: *'Purnam adah, purnam idam purnat purnam udachyate; purnasya purnam adaya purnam evavasishyate.'* (Brihadaranyaka Upanishad, 5.1.1).

2   Difference and non-difference: Vijnanabhikshu argued that the terms difference (bheda) and non-difference (abheda) can each be understood in at least two ways. In Naiyayika, non-difference is understood as identity (tadatmya) while difference is the negation of identity, called 'mutual absence' (anyonyabhava). However, these two terms can also be understood to mean separation (vibhaga) and non-separation (avibhaga) of self from Brahman. By adopting this alternative interpretation, it is possible to explain both the statements of difference and the statements of non-difference that appear in the Vedas without arbitrarily subordinating one to the other. He argues this by appealing to the authority of the grammatical Dhatupatha, which sets down the meanings of Sanskrit verbal roots: And it is not the case that when there is the word 'non-difference' (abheda) in the sense of 'non-separation' (avibhaga) there is a figurative usage, due to the rule of the root 'bhid': 'bhid', in the sense of splitting (vidarana), meaning also in the sense of separation (vibhaga). Vijnanabhikshu takes pains to emphasize that 'separation' is a primary meaning of the word 'difference'; not a figurative meaning. Establishing this allows him to argue that understanding difference as 'separation' is just as legitimate as understanding it as mutual absence (anyonyabhava). (Nicholson 2010, 44). Wholes and Parts: To show that the doctrine of part and whole is logically coherent, Vijnanabhikshu makes a subtle distinction between two different Sanskrit words that are both typically translated as 'part': amsa and avayava. While the selves are the amsas of Brahman, they are not the avayavas of Brahman. Vijnanabhikshu wishes to make this distinction by saying that an avayava can be understood in the everyday sense of the word 'part'. However, an amsa has a specific technical meaning in the Brahmasutra and in his philosophical writings: to be a part (amsa), something must be of the same class (sajatiya) as the whole (amsin) and be the adjunct of non-separation (avibhagapratiyogin). The whole is the subjunct of non-separation (tadanuyogin). When referring to the part as being of the same class as the whole, one must be consistent with regard to the property under discussion. For instance, when discussing the part being a self, one should say it falls under the class of selfhood (jivatva). When discussing the part as existent, etc., one

Ramanuja declares emphatically that both are true. The apparent contradiction between them is resolved and harmonized by another category of sutras called 'ghataka-sruti', which explain that all sentient and non-sentient beings relate to Brahman in the same manner as the body relates to the indweller.

3   A similar point can be made using particulars and universals instead of parts and wholes.

4   Bhedabheda Vedanta provides an interesting and old interpretation of the relation between Brahman and the individual self (jivatman). This relation is commonly portrayed as a relation of cause and effect, or part and whole. But each Bhedabheda scholar has his interpretation of this. Bhaskara, for instance, takes the view that when the individual self (jiva)is termed a 'part' it is not a part in its normal sense; rather, it has a technical meaning: it is limited by the artificial conditions of mind. Vijnanabhikshu sees the relationship between Brahman and the individual self as non-separation obtained before God's creation of the world and after his destruction of it. However, during the world's existence, the individual self exists in a state of separation from Brahman, until it achieves the state of liberation when it exists in a state of non-separation. This allows Vijnanabhikshu to make sense of both statements of separation and non-separation. This appeal to differences of time is yet another strategy that Vijnanabhikshu employs to reconcile the apparent contradiction of difference and non-difference. If difference and non-difference occur at different times, and not simultaneously, then there is no problem: The difference and non-difference of the part and whole, in the form of separation and non-separation, is not a contradiction since it refers to differences at different times.

5   A more direct analogy is that Judaism, Christianity, and Islam share the reliance on historical prophets, without all the prophetic revelations being homogeneous. Their family resemblance is that prophetic revelations in history are the ultimate means for gaining access to religious truth, and yet there is discrepancy among the revelations.

6   See also Tilak, 2007.

7   *Aitareya Aranyaka* 3:2.3. See: Smith, 1994, pp. 209-210.

8   *Pamcavimsa Brahmana* 24:18.3. See: Smith, 1994, pp. 209-210.

9   Smith, 1994, pp. 209-210. Kaushitaki Brahmana Text: Herausgegeben und Uebersetzt von B. Lindner, Jena: Hermann Costenoble, 1887. See: http://ia700304.us.archive.org/BookReader/BookReaderImages.php?zip=/16/items/kaushitakibrahma00linduoft/kaushitakibrahma00linduoft_jp2.zip&fil

should refer to it as falling under the class of existence (sattva), etc. Following this procedure, there will be no confusion. In this passage, Vijnanabhikshu employs two relational terms from Navya-Nyaya: subjunct (anuyogin) and adjunct (pratiyogin). In the Naiyayikas' stock example, 'there is absence of the pot in the ground', the pot is the adjunct in the relation, while the ground is the subjunct. It is important to see that the relation of absence only goes one way: to say that there is absence of the pot in the ground is not the same as saying there is absence of the ground in the pot. Likewise, although it is possible to say the selves are parts of Brahman, it is something else to say that Brahman is the part of the selves. Therefore, to avoid the possibility that Brahman could also be called a 'part' and the selves called the 'whole', Vijnanabhikshu must argue that separation is a-one-way relation, not a two-way relation. In the relation of separation or non-separation, the anuyogin is the locus while the pratiyogin is that which separates from the locus. In the example of leaves falling from a tree, the leaf would be the pratiyogin of separation while the tree would be the anuyogin. In the case of the selves and Brahman, it is the selves that separate from Brahman at the time of creation and re-attach themselves to Brahman at the time of the world's dissolution. Throughout this entire process, Brahman, the whole, remains unchanged. This one-way relation of separation may be explained by paradoxical statements of difference and non-difference, such as one of Vijnanabhikshu's favourite passages from the Vishnupurana: 'There is nothing different from it, yet it is different from everything.' (1.16.78). Although all of the selves are its parts, Brahman is not dependent on, or affected by, the states of bondage and liberation of those same selves. (Nicholson, 2010, pp. 52-53) Western academics and their Indian followers typically translate Bhedabheda as 'Difference-in-Identity' philosophy, presumably to link it with Western thinkers such as Bonaventure, Spinoza, and Hegel. Although there are meaningful similarities with some Western thinkers, purely on the basis of Sanskrit grammar 'difference-in-identity' cannot be the translation of bhedabheda. According to Nicholson, a preferable translation would be the more literal 'difference and non-difference', because linguistically it leaves open the question of whether difference is ultimately subsumed under non-difference, or vice versa. (Nicholson, 2010, p. 39). The Upanishads contain two types of passages: statements of difference (bhedavakyas) and statements of non-difference (abhedavakyas). Since the Vedas must be unified, there are multiple interpretative strategies. Advaitins subordinate statements of difference to statements of non-difference, while Dvaitins do the opposite.

e=kaushitakibrahma00linduoft_jp2/kaushitakibrahma00linduoft_0007.jp2&
scale=6.353870458135861&rotate=0

For the Sanskrit text for sutra 2.7 dealing with rasa as essence pervading the universe, see:

http://ia700304.us.archive.org/BookReader/BookReaderImages.
php?zip=/16/items/kaushitakibrahma00linduoft/
kaushitakibrahma00linduoft_jp2.zip&file=kaushitakibrahma00linduoft_jp2/
kaushitakibrahma00linduoft_0022.jp2&scale=6.353870458135861&rotate=0

10 (Wallace 2002, pp. 13-14) Another Western scholar who has specialized in bringing dharmic principles and meditation to modern cognitive psychology is Eleanor Rosch Heider, professor of psychology at the University of California, Berkeley. For an overview by her, see: (Rosch, 1997). (Anantharaman, 2007) explains how adhyatma-vidya is described in classical Indian texts.

11 Rudolph Steiner was a German scholar who studied Hinduism in depth, and in the early twentieth century; he brought the idea to the modern West to cultivate both *Geistes-Wissenschaften* (science of spirituality) and *Natur-Wissenschaften* (science of nature). This has spread in the West ever since.

12 *The Complete Works of Swami Vivekananda*: Vol. 1, pp. 204-206.

13 Ibid., vol. 1, pp. 204-206.

14 See *Being Different*, p. 124-126.

15 For example, there has been intense debate over whether the individual self is intrinsically a doer of actions or whether the agency (doership) of the self is merely a consequence of adjunct conditions, such as being housed in a material body. Interestingly, Shankara himself did not shy away from parinamavada, but strongly held that the agency of the self is not intrinsic to it. A number of such interpretative issues arising from the Brahmasutra continue to be debated to this day, among Advaitins, Dvaitins, Visishtadvaitins and Bhedabhedins.

12: Digestion and Self-Destruction

1 Malhotra, Rajiv, '*Vivekananda's Ideas and the Two Revolutions in Western Thought*', in 'Vivekananda as the Turning Point: The Rise of a Tidal Wave'. Edited by Swami Shuddhidananda. Advaita Ashrama Press, Kolkata, pp. 559-583.

2 Some of the major Hindu gurus whose export-oriented teachings got digested include the following: Swami Muktananda, Yogi Amrit Desai, Swami Satchitananda, Swami Sivananda, Osho, J. Krishnamurti, Swami

Rama, Maharishi Mahesh Yogi, Paramhansa Yogananda (of an earlier era), to name a few. B.K.S. Iyengar survives, and the digestion of his teachings is expected to accelerate after he passes away. Haridas Chaudhuri, a follower of Sri Aurobindo, was specifically brought from India to introduce Americans to Sri Aurobindo's philosophy of the evolution of consciousness. But after his death, his work and the institution in California set up specifically for this purpose quickly passed into new hands beginning with Robert McDermott. Soon Choudhry and Sri Aurobindo were forgotten and replaced by Western thinkers as the sources. There have also been prominent Buddhist sources which are getting digested.

Conclusion: The 'Poison Pill' Defence of Hinduism

1   I am against attempts that try to digest Shiva into Satan and then try to promote Satanic worship by repositioning Satan as the true God. See for example: http://spiritualwarfare666.webs.com/Satanic_Symbols.htm

2   Some Hindu gurus do claim to remove or transfer karmic debts. But this is not the same kind of universal capability claimed by Jesus, and such Hindu claims tend to be limited to a given person and circumstances.

3   The Nicene Creed is the official doctrine in Catholicism, Eastern Orthodoxy, most Protestant Churches, as well as the Anglican Communion. It forms one of the bases of Christian unity, the other being the ritual of baptism. The Nicene Creed demands a pledge to the following beliefs, among others: (i) 'Lord Jesus Christ is the only-begotten Son of God.' (ii) Jesus had a virgin birth by the 'Holy Ghost of the Virgin Mary'. (iii) Jesus 'was crucified for us' and 'he suffered', died and was buried. (iv) 'He rose again on the third day and ascended into Heaven.' (v) Jesus sits in heaven on the right-hand side of God. (vi) Jesus will come again 'in glory' to judge the living and the dead. (vii)We look for the 'resurrection of the dead'. (viii) I accept baptism for the remission of sins. The full text of a 1975 ecumenical version reads as follows: *'We believe in one God, the Father, the Almighty maker of heaven and earth, of all that is, seen and unseen. We believe in one Lord, Jesus Christ, the only Son of God, eternally begotten of the Father, God from God, Light from Light, true God from true God, begotten, not made, of one Being with the Father. Through him all things were made. For us men and for our salvation he came down from heaven: by the power of the Holy Spirit he became incarnate from the Virgin Mary, and was made man. For our sake he was*

crucified under Pontius Pilate; he suffered death and was buried. On the third day he rose again in accordance with the Scriptures; he ascended into heaven and is seated at the right hand of the Father. He will come again in glory to judge the living and the dead, and his kingdom will have no end. We believe in the Holy Spirit, the Lord, the giver of Life, who proceeds from the Father and the Son. With the Father and the Son he is worshipped and glorified. He has spoken through the Prophets. We believe in one holy catholic and apostolic Church. We acknowledge one baptism for the forgiveness of sins. We look for the resurrection of the dead, and the life of the world to come. Amen'.

4 *Brhadaranyaka Upanishad* 1.4.10. Literally it means 'I am Brahman' as in saying 'I am God'.

5 Founded in 1946, ISO is an international standards organization composed of national standards bodies from over 75 countries. It has been highly successful in developing computer and telecom standards that virtually every vendor tries to comply with, or claims to do so.

6 The specific attributes that define nastika are inherently reductionist, and the nastika are natural reductionists. This frees the astika from the risk of a reductionist definition, and leaves room for the open architecture to function creatively. The reverse approach of precisely defining the astika first would make it vulnerable to reductionism.

7 This is why I disagree with attempts to semitize Hinduism. An example of semitizing Hinduism would be an interpretation of the Ramayana in which Ayodhya becomes like Jerusalem with Ram as Jesus. My concern is that such mappings are reductionist and damage the open architecture.

8 Consult the official conciliar document *Lumen Gentium*, Chapter II, Article 19, available online at www.vatican.va.

9 The notion of grace in Christianity is not the same thing for several reasons. It is initiated by God and not the result of one's yoga. It is not an innate human capacity similar to the Hindu claim of the self as being sat-chit-ananda. In other words, there is no claim equivalent to the mahavakyas, 'aham brahmasmi', or identity with Brahman.

10 He retained the actual Sanskrit mantra *shantih* as well as the Sanskrit terms '*datta*', '*damyata*' and '*dyadhvam*', in one of his most famous poems, *The Waste Land*.

11 Although the Judeo-Christian faiths also have their sacred languages—Hebrew and Latin—and although the claims made for them are sometimes similar to those that are made for Sanskrit, these languages have not served as the basis for embodied knowing in quite the same way. Furthermore,

Christianity, from the beginning, was not transmitted through a sacred language but through the vernacular—first the Aramaic that Jesus spoke, then the everyday koine Greek of the Mediterranean Basin. The New Testament, in its numerous translations, promulgates not a direct experience of the divine but a message or 'gospel' (meaning 'good news') about the divine. The emphasis here is on the meaning of the words and the historical deeds they recount and not on their sound or resonance or the embodied response they elicit. Christianity does not have a spiritual tradition similar to mantra; prayer is a petition, conversation or thanksgiving to an external deity, where the conceptual meaning is far more important than the sound or its empirical effects on the practitioner.

12 See for example, Raimon Panikkar: "The Intra-Religious Dialogue", Paulist Press, New York. 1999.

13 See for example, Russill Paul, "Jesus in the Lotus", New World Library, Novato, California. 2009.

14 Nayak, 2007.

15 The original verse is: 'Ayam nijahparo veti ganana laghucetasam udaracaritanamtu vasudhaiva kutumbakam'. (Kale, M.R., 1989. Hitopadesa of Narayana. Delhi. Motilal Banarsidas.) It may be translated as: 'The narrow-minded person asks, "Is this person one of us, or is he a stranger?" But persons of noble character see the whole world as one family.'

16 For a clear discussion on this point, see the 3-part article: http://bharatendu.com/2008/08/29/the-hoax-called-vasudhaiva-kutumbakam-1-hitopadesha/

17 Ramanuja's commentary on Mahopanishada (6.70–6.73) does use the phrase 'vasudhaiva kutumbakam' to make the point that the enlightened being sees all creatures as the forms of the One, a point we already know and appreciate as a core Vedanta teaching. However, this text is not meant as a practical prescription for the general public to organize their social lives. It is descriptive of the enlightened person, not prescriptive.

18 My position on sameness is further explained in the following Q&A, which is downloadable: http://beingdifferentbook.com/wp-content/uploads/2012/05/Sameness-Aug4.pdf

Bibliography

Abbott, Justin E.: Bahinabai: *A translation of her Autobiography and Verses.* (Poona: Scottish Mission Industries Co. Ltd, 1929.)

Allendorf, Fred W., and Bruce A. Byers: 'Salmon in the Net of Indra: a Buddhist View of Nature and Communities.' (*World Views: Global Religions, Culture, and Ecology.* ISSN 1363-5247, 1998, Vol. 2, Issue 1, pp. 37.)

Anantharaman, T.R.: *'Ancient Yoga and Modern Science.'* Project of History of Indian Science, Philosophy and Culture. (Delhi: South Asia Books, 2007.)

Araya, Victorio: *God of the Poor: The Mystery of God in Latin American Liberation Theology.* (New York: Orbis Books, 1983.)

Atmananda, Swami: *'Sankara's teachings in his own words.'* (Mumbai: Bharatiya Vidya Bhavan, 1989.)

Bader, Jonathan: *'Meditation in Shankara's Vedanta.'* (Delhi: AdityaPrakashan, 1990.)

Bair-Mundy, Donna G: *'From Neural Networks to Indra's Net: A Paradigm for Library Communication.'* (Collection Management. 1998, 23:1-2, pp. 139-150.)

Bajaj, Jitendra and Mandayam, Doddamane Srinivas: 'Annam Bahu Kurvita: Recollecting the Indian Discipline of growing and Sharing Food in Plenty.' (Madras: Centre for Policy Studies, 1996.)

Basu, Shamita: *Religious Revivalism as Nationalist Discourse: Swami Vivekananda and New Hinduism in Nineteenth-Century Bengal.* (London: Oxford University Press, 2002.)

Baumfield, V.M.: *Swami Vivekananda's Practical Vedanta.* (Newcastle: University of Newcastle Upon Tyne, 1992.)

Beckerlegge, Gwilym: 'SWAMI VIVEKANANDA AND *SEVA:* TAKING "SOCIAL SERVICE" SERIOUSLY.' Radice, William (ed.): *Swami Vivekananda and the Modernizaton of Hinduism.* (SOAS Studies on South Asia) (Delhi: Oxford University Press, 1998.)

Bhajanananda, Swami: '*Four Basic Principles of Advaita Vedanta.'* (*Prabuddha Bharata Calcutta:* Ramakrishna Mission (Advaita Ashrama), Jan-Feb, 2010.)

Bharati, Agehananda: 'The Hindu Renaissance and its Apologetic Patterns.' in the *Journal of Asian Studies.* (Vol. 29, No. 2 (Feb., 1970), pp. 267-287.)

Bharati, Agehananda: 'The Ochre Robe.' (Santa Barbara: 1980.)

Biardeau, Madeleine: 'Quelques Reflexions sur l'Apophatisme de Sankara.' (*Indo-Iranian Journal,* 3 (1959), pp. 81-101.)

Breckenridge, Carol Appadurai: *Orientalism and the Postcolonial Predicament: Perspectives on South Asia New Cultural Studies.* (Philadelphia: University of Pennsylvania Press, 1993.)

Chapple, Christopher Key: *Reconciling Yogas: Haribhadra's collection of views on yoga.* (Albany: SUNY Press, 2003.)

Chopra, P.N., B.N. Puri, and M.N. Das: *A Social, Cultural and Economic History of India.* (Delhi: Macmillan India, 1974.)

Comans, Michael: 'The Question of the Importance of Samadhi in Modern and Classical Advaita Vedanta.' (*Philosophy East and West,* Vol. 43, No. 1 (Jan., 1993), pp. 19-38)

Comans, Michael: *Extracting the Essence of the Sruti: The Srutisarasamuddharanam of Totakacarya.* (New Delhi: Motilal Banarsidas Publishers Private Ltd., 1996.)

Cook, Francis H.: *Hua-yen Buddhism: The Jewel Net of Indra.* (Philadelphia: Pennsylvania State University Press, University Park, 1977.)

Coward, Harold: Book Review: 'The Limits of Scripture: Vivekananda's Reinterpretation of the Vedas.' (*Journal of Hindu-Christian Studies,* Vol. 8, Article 11, 1995.) Available at: http://dx.doi.org/10.7825/2164-6279.1116

Dalal, Neil Akshay: '*Texts Beyond Words: Contemplation and practice in Shankara's Advaita Vedanta.'* (Austin: University of Texas, 2009.)

Davis, Mike: 'Late Victorian Holocausts: El Nino Famines and the Making of the Third World.' (Verso, 2002.)

De Michelis, Elizabeth: *A History of Modern Yoga: Patanjali and Western Esotericism.* (London: Continuum, 2004.)

Debnath, Lokenath: 'A brief historical introduction to fractals and fractal geometry.' (*International Journal of Mathematical Education in Science and Technology,* 2006. 37:1, pp. 29-50.)

Deleury, Guy A: 'The cult of Vithoba.' (Poona: Deccan College Postgraduate Research Institute, 1960.)

Dhal, Upendranath: *Goddess Laksmi: Origin and Development.* (New Delhi: Oriental Publishers & Distributors, 1978.)

Dharampal: 'Rediscovering India.' (Mussoorie, India: Society for Integrated Development of Himalayas, 2003.)

Doherty, Barbara: 'The Path to Liberation: Sankara, Metaphysician, Mystic, and Teacher.' Unpublished Ph.D thesis. (New York: Fordham University, 1979.)

Eliade, M: *Yoga: Immortality and Freedom.* (Bollingen Series, no. 56. New York: Princeton University Press, 1973.)

Fahy, Gregory M: HUAYAN BUDDHISM AND DEWEY: EMPTINESS, COMPASSION, AND THE PHILOSOPHICAL FALLACY. (*Journal of Chinese Philosophy,* 39:2 (June 2012), pp. 260-271.)

Farquhar, J.N.: *Modern Religious Movements in India.* (New York: The Macmillan Company, 1915.)

Forte, Antonino: *A Jewel in Indra's net: the letter sent by Fazang in China to Uisang in Korea.* (Kyoto: Italian School of East Asian Studies, 2000.)

Franco, Eli and Karin Preisendanz (eds.): 'Beyond Orientalism: The Work of Wilhelm Halbfass and its Impact on Indian and Cross-Cultural Studies.' (New Delhi: Motilal Banarsidass Publishers Private Limited, 2007.)

Frykenberg, Robert E.: 'The Emergence of Modern "Hinduism" as a Concept and as an Institution: A Reappraisal With Special Reference to South India.' In *Hinduism Reconsidered* (Heidelberg: 1989), 1-29, edited by Gunther Sontheimer and Hermann Kulke (reissued in New Delhi: Manohar Books, 1997), pp. 82-107.

Frykenberg, Robert E.: 'Constructions of Hinduism at the nexus of history and religion.' (*Journal of Interdisciplinary History,* 23, 3. 1993. pp. 523-50.)

Gambhirananda, Swami, trans.: *Eight Upanishads vols I & II.* Almora. (Advaita Ashrama, 1972.)

Gambhirananda, Swami, trans.: *Brahma-Sutra-Bhasya of Sri Sankaracarya.* (Calcutta: Advaita Ashrama, 1977.)

Ganeri, Jonardon: 'The Lost Age of Reason: Philosophy in Early Modern India 1450-1700.' (Oxford University Press, 2011.)

Gier, Nicholas F.: *Spiritual Titanism: Indian, Chinese, and Western perspectives.* (Albany: State University of New York Press, 2000.)

Gokhale, B.G.: 'The Making of the Indian Nation.' (Bombay: Asia Publishing House, 1958.)

Gupta, Krishna Prakash: 'Religious evolution and social change in India: a study of the Ramakrishna Mission movement.' In *Contributions to Indian Sociology.* 8:25. (Delhi: Sage Publishing, 1974.)

Hacker, Paul: *Kleine Schriften* (edited by L. Schmithausen, Wiesbaden, 1978). Published as a collection of his works on his 65th birthday.

Halbfass, Wilhelm: *'India and Europe: An essay in understanding.'* (Albany: State University of New York Press. 1988.)

Halbfass, Wilhelm: *'Tradition and Reflection: Explorations in Indian Thought.'* (Albany: SUNY Press, 1990.)

Halbfass, Wilhelm (ed.): *'Philology and Confrontation: Paul Hacker on Traditional and Modern Vedanta.'* (Albany: SUNY Press, 1995.)

Hatcher, Brian: 'Eclecticism and Modern Hindu Discourse.' (New York: Oxford University Press, 1999.)

Hatcher, Brian: *Bourgeois Hinduism, or the faith of the modern Vedantists: Rare discourses from early Colonial Bengal.* (Oxford: Oxford University Press, 2008.)

Hawley, John Stratton: 'Naming Hinduism.' (*The Wilson Quarterly,* Vol. 15, No. 3 (Summer, 1991), pp. 20-34.)

Herling, Bradley L.: *The German Gita? Hermeneutics and Discipline in the German Reception of Indian Thought, 1778-1831.* (New York: Routledge, 2006.)

Hiriyanna, M.: 'Indian Philosophical Studies.' (Mysore: Kavyalaya Publishers, 1957.)

Hiriyanna, M.: 'Outlines of Indian Philosophy.' (London: George Allen & Unwin, 1932.)

Ingalls, Daniel H.: 'The Study of Sankaracarya.' (Annals of the Bhandarkar Oriental Research Institute, 33 (1952), pp. 1-14.)

Jacobs, S.R.: *Hindu identity, nationalism and globalization.* (Lampeter: University of Wales, 1999.)

Jaffrelot, Christophe: 'Introduction: The Invention of an Ethnic Nationalism,' in Hindu Nationalism: A Reader. (Princeton: Princeton University Press, 2007, pp. 3-10.)

Jha, Ganganath, trans.: The Chandogyopanishad with The Commentary Of Sankara. (Poona, Oriental Book Agency, 1942) http://archive.org/details/Shankara.Bhashya-Chandogya.Upanishad-Ganganath.Jha.1942.English

Joshi, H.M.: 'Spiritual Humanism of Shri Swaminarayan,' in Anon., 'New dimensions in Vedanta Philosophy: Bhagwan Swaminarayan bicentenary commemoration volume, part 1.' (Ahmedabad, 1981.)

Jyotirmayananada, Swami, compiler and ed.: 1986. *Vivekananda: His Gospel of Man-Making with a Garland of Tributes and a Chronicle of His Life and Times with Pictures.* (Madras: Swami Jyotirmayananda.)

King, Richard: Orientalism and the Modern Myth of 'Hinduism', in *Numen.* (Vol. 46, No. 2 (1999-A), pp. 146-185.)

King, Richard: *Orientalism and Religion: Postcolonial Theory, India and the mystical East.* (Routledge, London. 1999-B.)

King, Ursula: 'True and perfect religion: Bankim Chandra Chatterjee's reinterpretation of Hinduism.' (Religion, 7:2, 1977, pp. 127-148.)

King, Ursula: Who is the ideal karmayogin? (Religion, 10:1, 1980, pp. 41-59.)

King, Ursula: 'Some Reflections on Sociological Approaches to the study of Modern Hinduism.' (Numen, Vol. XXXVI. Fasc. 1. June 1989. pp. 72-97.)

Kopf, David: *'British Orientalism and the Bengal Renaissance: The Dynamics of Indian Modernization, 1773-1835.'* (University of California Press, Los Angeles, 1969.)

Kopf, David: *'Hermeneutics versus History.'* (Journal of Asian Studies XXXIX, No. 3, May 1980.)

Krishna, Daya: *Indian Philosophy: A Counter-Perspective.* (New Delhi: Oxford University Press. 1991)

Larson, Gerald James: *India's agony over religion.* (Albany: State University of New York Press. 1995.)

Lele, Jayant: 'Orientalism and the Social Sciences', in Breckenridge, Carol Appadurai, *Orientalism and the Postcolonial Predicament: Perspectives on South Asia New Cultural Studies.* (University of Pennsylvania Press. 1993. pp. 45-75.)

Lipner, Julius J.: 'Ancient Banyan: An Inquiry in to the Meaning of "Hinduness".' (*Religious Studies,*1996, 32.)

356   Indra's Net

Lorenzen, David N.: 'Warrior Ascetics in Indian History.' (Journal of the American Oriental Society, Vol. 98, No. 1 (Jan. - Mar., 1978), pp. 61-70.)

Lorenzen, David N.: 'Who Invented Hinduism?' In Defining Hinduism: A Reader, edited by J. E. Llewellyn. 52-80. (New York: Routledge. 2005.)

Lorenzen, David: Who Invented Hinduism? In Essays on Religion in History. (Yoda Press. New Delhi, 2006.)

Loy, David: 'Indra's Postmodern Net.' (In Philosophy East and West, Vol. 43, No. 3 (July, 1993), pp. 481-510.)

Madhavananda, Swami, trans.: The Brihadaranyaka Upanisad with the commentary of Sankaracarya, 3rd edition. (Almora: Advaita Ashrama, 1950.) http://archive.org/details/BrahadaranyakaUpanishad-ShankaraBhashya-English-SwamiMadhavaananda

Mahadevan, T.M.P.: 'Outlines of Hinduism.' (Bombay: Chetana Limited, 1971.) Cited in Sharma 1992.

Majumdar, R.C.: 'The Maratha Supremacy.' (Bombay: Bharatiya Vidya Bhavan, Bombay, 1977.)

Malhotra, Rajiv and Aravindan, Neelakandan: Breaking India: Western Interventions in Dravidian and Dalit Faultlines. (Delhi: Amaryllis & Co., 2011.)

Malhotra, Rajiv: Being Different: Indian Challenges to Western Universalism. (Delhi: HarperCollins, 2011.)

Manninezhath, Thomas: Harmony of Religions: Vedanta Siddhanta Samarasam of Tayumanavar. (Delhi: Motilal Banarsidass, 1993.)

Marshall, P.J., ed.: The British Discovery of Hinduism in the Eighteenth Century. (Cambridge: Cambridge University Press, 1970.)

Morales, Frank: 'The Death of Traditional Hinduism.' http://Hinduism.about.com/od/history/a/neoHinduism.htm

Mishra, Pankaj: 'Holy Lies.' (The Guardian, April 6, 2002.) See: http://www.guardian.co.uk/theguardian/2002/apr/06/weekend7.weekend2

Mishra, Pankaj: 'The invention of the Hindus.' (Axess Magasin, 2004.) See: http://www.columbia.edu/itc/mealac/pritchett/00litlinks/pankajmishra/articles/txt_mishra_Hinduism_2004.html

Mumford, David, Caroline Series, and David Wright. 'Indra's Pearls: The Vision of Felix Klein. (Cambridge University Press, 2002.)

Murty, K. Satchidananda: Revelation and Reason in Advaita Vedanta. (New York: Columbia Univ. Press, 1959.)

Nakamura, Hajime: 'Meditation in Sankara' in *Journal of Religious Studies*. (Punjabi University, Patiala, 7 (1979), 1-18.)

Nanda, Meera: *Prophets facing backward postmodern critiques of science and Hindu nationalism in India*. (New Brunswick, N.J.: Rutgers University Press, 2003.)

Nanda, Meera: 'Making science sacred.' (January, 2005.) See at: http://www.india-seminar.com/2005/545/545%20meera%20nanda1.htm

Nayak, Anand: Anthony de Mello: His life and his spirituality. (The Columba Press, Dublin, 2007.)

Nehru, Jawaharlal: *The Discovery of India*. (New Delhi. Penguin Books India, 2004.)

Neusner, Jacob, ed.: *Alike and not alike: A grid for comparison and differentiation. Take Judaism, for example., 227-35.* (Chicago: University of Chicago Press, 1983.)

Nicholson, Andrew J.: *'Unifying Hinduism: Philosophy and Identity in Indian Intellectual History.'* (Columbia University Press, 2010.)

Nikhilananda, Swami, trans.: The Mandukyopanishad with Gaudapada's Karika and Sankara's Commentary. (Mysore, Sri Ramakrishna Asrama, 1949). http://archive.org/details/MandukyaUpanishadKarikaWithShankaraBhashya-SwamiNikhilananda

Niranjana, Tejaswini: 'Translation, Colonialism and Rise of English.' (*Economic and Political Weekly*, XXV, no. 15, 14 April 1990.)

Odin, Steve: 'Process Metaphysics and Hua-yen Buddhism.' (Albany: State University of New York Press, 1982.)

Park, Pori: 'New Visions for Engaged Buddhism: The Jung to Society and the Indra's Net Community Movement in Contemporary Korea.' (*Contemporary Buddhism: An Interdisciplinary Journal*, 2010. 11:1, pp. 27-46.)

Pennington, Brian K.: *Was Hinduism Invented?: Britons, Indians, and the Colonial Construction of Religion.* (Oxford University Press, 2005.)

Pirbhai, Reza: 'Demons in Hindutva. Writing a Theology for Hindu Nationalism.' (*Modern Intellectual History, Cambridge, UK*, vol.5.1, 2008, pp.27-53.) As quoted by Koenraad Elst in 'Reza Pirbhai and Voice of India', 10 May 2012. See: http://koenraadelst.blogspot.be/2012/05/reza-pirbhai-and-voice-of-india.html

Potter, Karl H. ed.: *Encyclopedia of Indian Philosophies*. (Delhi: Motilal Banarsidass, 1981, vol. 1.)

Radhakrishnan, S., trans.: *The Brahma Sutra: The Philosophy of Spiritual Life.* (London: George Allen and Unwin, 1960.)

Ramaswamy, Krishnan, Antonio de Nicolas and Aditi Banerjee, (eds.): *Invading the Sacred: An Analysis of Hinduism Studies in America.* (Delhi: Rupa & Co, 2007.)

Rambachan, Anantanand: *'The Attainment of Moksha According to Shankara and Vivekananda with special reference to the significance of scripture (Sruti) and Experience (Anubhava).'* Ph.D Dissertation. (Dept. of Theology and Religious Studies, University of Leeds, 1984.)

Rambachan, Anantanand: *Accomplishing the Accomplished: The Vedas as a Source of Valid Knowledge in Sankara.* (Honolulu: University of Hawaii Press, 1991.)

Rambachan, Anantanand: 'The Limits of Scriptures: Vivekananda's Reinterpretation of the Vedas.' (Honolulu: University of Hawaii Press, 1994.)

Rambachan, Anantanand: 'Response to Professor Arvind Sharma.' (*Philosophy East and West,* vol. 44, no. 4, Oct., 1994, pp. 721-724.)

Rambachan, Anantanand: 'Shankara's rationale for sruti as pramana.' (2007. Posted by Vedanta Shala, Center For Traditional Vedanta. Unpublished.)

Raychaudhuri, Tapan: 'Swami Vivekananda's construction of Hinduism' in Radice, William (ed.), *Swami Vivekananda and the Modernizaton of Hinduism.* SOAS Studies on South Asia. (Delhi: Oxford University Press, 1998. pp. 1-16.)

Rosch, Eleanor: Transformation of the Wolf Man. 1997. http://cogweb.ucla.edu/Abstracts/Rosch_97.html (accessed 8 September 2010).

Rukmani, T.S. ed., trans.: *Yogavarttika of Vijnanabhiksu* by Vijnanabhiksu [16th c. CE]. Vol. 1 (New Delhi: Munshiram Manoharlal, 1981.)

Rukmani, T.S.: *Yoga in Sankara's Advaita Vedanta.* (Annals of the Bhandarkar Oriental Research Institute, vol. 87, 2006.)

Sastri, Polakam, Sri Rama, and S.R. Krishnamurthi, eds.: *Patainjala-yogasutra-bhasya-vivaranam of Sankara-Bhagavatpada.* Madras Government Oriental Series, no. 94 (Madras, 1952.)

Sastry, Alladi Mahadeva, trans.: *The Bhagavadgita with the Commentary of Sri Sankaracharya* (Madras: Samata Books, 1985) http://archive.org/details/bhagavadgitawith00maharich

Shankara, Adi: Complete Works—Sanskrit PDFs

http://hinduebooks.blogspot.com/2010/08/works-of-sri-sankaracharya-sanskrit-20.html

Sharma, Arvind: 'Is Anubhava a Pramana According to Sankara?' (*Philosophy East and West*, vol. 42, no. 3 (July, 1992), pp. 517-526.)

Sharma, Arvind: Review of: 'Accomplishing the Accomplished: The Vedas as a Source of Valid Knowledge in Sankara by Anantanand Rambachan.' (*Philosophy East and West*, vol. 43, no. 4, Oct., 1993, pp. 737-744.)

Sharma, Arvind: 'A Reply to Anantanand Rambachan.' (*Philosophy East and West*, vol. 45, no. 1 January 1995, pp. 105-113.)

Sharma, Arvind: 'Eclecticism and Modern Hindu Discourse by Brian A. Hatcher: Review by Arvind Sharma.' (*Journal of the American Oriental Society*, vol. 120, no. 4, Oct.-Dec., 2000, pp. 633-634.)

Sharma, Jyotirmaya: *'Cosmic Love and Human Apathy: Swami Vivekananda's Restatement of Religion.'* (Delhi: HaperCollins, 2013).

Sil, Narasingha P.: *Swami Vivekananda: a reassessment.* (London: Cranbury, N.J.: Associated University Presses, 1997).

Singh, Kundan: 'Rambachan and the Limits of Social-constructivist Bias in the Analysis of the Thoughts of Swami Vivekananda.' (Unpublished paper presented at Waves Conference, Orlando, Fla., 2008.)

Skoog, Kim: 'Sankara on the Role of sruti and anubhava in Attaining brahmajnana.' (*Philosophy East and West*, vol. 39, no. 01 January 1989, pp. 67-74.)

Smith, Brian K.: *Classifying the Universe: The Ancient Indian Varna System and the Origins of Caste.* (New York: Oxford University Press, 1994.)

Smith, Brian K.: 'Questioning authority: Constructions and deconstructions of Hinduism.' (*International Journal of Hindu Studies*, 2, 3 (December 1998), pp. 313-39.)

Smith, W. Cantwell: *'The Meaning and End of Religion.'* (New York, 1962.)

Singleton, Mark: *Yoga Body.* (Oxford University Press, 2010.)

Slater, T.E.: *'The Higher Hinduism in Relation to Christianity: Certain aspects of Hindu thought from the Christian standpoint.'* (Elliott Stock, London, 1902.)

Southworth, Kristen L.: 'Hindu Worldview and Ecological Engagement.' http://www.breathofstatues.com/uploads/Hinduism_ and_Ecology.pdf, 2010

Staal, Frits: Rules Without Meaning: Ritual, Mantra, and the Human Sciences. (New York: Peter Lang, 1989.)

Stietencron, Heinrich von: 'Hinduism: On the proper use of a deceptive term' in Gunther D. Sontheimer and Hermann Kulke, eds., *Hinduism reconsidered,* I 1-27 (New Delhi: Manohar, 1989).

Stietencron, Heinrich von: 'Religious Configurations in Pre-Muslim India and the Modern Concept of Hinduism' in *Representing Hinduism: The Construction of Religious Traditions and National identity.* Eds.,Vasudha Dalmia and Heinrich von Stietencron. (New Delhi: Sage, 1995, pp. 51-81.)

Stietencron, Heinrich von: 'Hinduism' in *Secularization and the World Religions,* eds., Hans Joas and Klaus Wiegandt (Liverpool: Liverpool University Press, 2009, pp. 122-140.)

Tam, Angela: '*Saving Indra's Net: Buddhist Tools for Tackling Climate Change and Social Inequity*' in *HUMAN ARCHITECTURE: JOURNAL OF THE SOCIOLOGY OF SELF-KNOWLEDGE.* (Ahead Publishing House, 2008, vol. 3, pp. 129-132.)

Tambyah, Isaac: *Psalms of a Saiva Saint.* (London: Luzac & Co., 1925.)

Thakur, Debendra Lal: '*Namasudras: Religious Revolution of a Bengali Untouchable Community*' in *Dalit Voice* (May, 1991, pp. 1-15.)

Thakur, Murli: 'Gandhivani'. Sastu Sahitya Vardhaka Karyalaya (Ahmedabad (no date).)

Thapar, Romila: 'Syndicated Moksha?' in *The Hindus and their isms* (Delhi: Seminar Publications, 1985, pp. 14-22.)

Thibaut, George: trans.: *The Vedanta Sutras of Badarayana with the Commentary of Sankara* (New York: Dover Publications, 1962 (1890)) Pt. 1. http://books.google.com/books?id=uvYaAAAAYAAJ

Thibaut, George: trans.: *The Vedanta-Sutras with the Commentary of Sankaracarya* (Oxford: Clarendon Press, 1896). Pt. 2. http://books.google.com/books?id=0QowAAAAYAAJ

Thiele, Leslie Paul: '*Indra's net and the Midas touch: living sustainably in a connected world.*' (Cambridge: MIT Press, 2011.)

Tilak, Shrinivas: *Understanding Karma: In Light of Paul Ricoeur's Philosophical Anthropology and Hermeneutics.* (Charleston, S.C.: BookSurge, 2007.)

Van Buitenen, J.A.B.: Hinduism. (*The new encyclopaedia Britannica, macropaedia* 20. 1974, pp. 519-58.)

van der Veer, Peter: '*The Foreign Hand: Orientalist Discourse in Sociology and Communalism.*'

van der Veer, Peter: *Imperial Encounters: Religion and Modernity in India and Britain.* (Princeton: Princeton University Press, 2001.)

Vatsyayan, Kapila: *The Square and the Circle of Indian Arts* (New Delhi: Anibhav Publications, 1997.)

Venkatesananda, Swami: trans.: *'The Concise Yogavasistha.'* (Albany: SUNY Press, 1984.)

Vivekananda, Swami: *The Complete Works of Swami Vivekananda* (Calcutta: Advaita Ashrama, 1995.)

Wallace, Alan: *'Why the West Has No Science of Consciousness: A Buddhist View.'* (Infinity Foundation, July 2002.) http://www.infinityfoundation.com/indic_colloq/persons/person_wallace_alan.htm (accessed 30 March2011).

White, David Gordon: *Sinister Yogis* (University of Chicago Press, 2009.)

Williams, R.B.: *A New Face of Hinduism: the Swaminarayan religion* (Cambridge, 1984.)

Index

Acknowledgements

I wish to thank several persons for helping me complete this book. Kundan Singh was among the first persons who encouraged me to write it, and he provided some initial leads. I took the matter seriously after Rambachan essentialized my previous book, *Being Different*, seeing it as the same 'neo-Hinduism' thinking that was allegedly started by Vivekananda and various 'Hindu nationalists'. He failed to address my book's original thesis on its own merit, and simply applied his standard criticism of Vivekananda. This was the eye opener for me. Shrinivas Tilak read through the entire manuscript pointing out several areas of improvement which I have incorporated. Vidyasankar Sundaresan carefully examined the arguments concerning Shankara, and more broadly my statements concerning Advaita Vedanta and yoga; I have benefited immensely from his inputs. Krishna Kashyap helped me in the final stages by verifying many of the verses I cited from Vedanta texts. His expertise in this has been very useful. Prof. K.S. Kannan went through numerous Sanskrit citations used in the final stages and made important corrections to help me. In the early stages of my research, Sandeep Joshi spent tiring hours in the Princeton University library making copies of important reference materials that I asked for in order to help build my case. Jayant Kalawar made useful inputs at the final stages of the draft. Cleo Kearns (Princeton), Matagiri Perkins (Florida) and Thom Loree (Canada) each played important roles as editors of various portions of the manuscript at different stages, questioning my writing where it was unclear and suggesting many improved ways of presenting my case. Aditi Banerjee provided critical feedback and helped edit portions of the final draft. Kartik Mohan helped at the final stage and made an important impact in the Introduction and Conclusion chapters. Raghu Rao, Forum For Religious Freedom, Hari Kiran Vadlamani, Aditi Banerjee and Prashant Banerjee are among the many who provided funding in the final stages for hiring professional editors. I thank the management at HarperCollins for quickly appreciating the value in such a book when I first proposed it to them, Shuka Jain for yet another wonderful cover design for a book by me, and Usha Surampudi for her diligence in copy editing.